T0369471

THE COMPLETE HISTORY OF THE VIETNAM CONFLICT

(LE COMÉDIE VIETNAMIEN):

A "POPULAR" WAR
THAT WON'T GO AWAY

By **V. I. Brown**

Copyright © 2010

BLESSED BET PUBLICATIONS

www.blessedbetpubs.com

THE COMPLETE HISTORY OF THE VIETNAM CONFLICT

Other Books By The Author

Veterans Employment Preference Statutes: a state-by-state and Federal Government handbook, McFarland & Co., Jefferson, NC, 2001

The System Is The Key At Roulette: A Practical Guide To Interpreting Occult Patterns And Winning At Casino Gaming, Blessed Bet Publications/ iUniverse, St. Louis, MO /Bloomington, IN, 2009

THE COMPLETE HISTORY OF THE VIETNAM CONFLICT

(LE COMÉDIE VIETNAMIEN):

A "POPULAR" WAR THAT WON'T GO AWAY

By **V. I. Brown**

Blessed Bet Publications
St. Louis, MO

iUniverse, Inc.
Bloomington

Copyright © 2010 by V. I. Brown

All rights reserved. No part of this book may be used or reproduced by any means, graphic, electronic, or mechanical, including photocopying, recording, taping or by any information storage retrieval system without the written permission of the publisher except in the case of brief quotations embodied in critical articles and reviews.

Excerpts herein are from *THE BEST AND THE BRIGHTEST* by David Halberstam, copyright © 1969, 1971, 1972, 1992 by David Halberstam. Used by permission of Random House, Inc.

(Unless otherwise indicated, all of the excerpts from popular songs and from other previously published matter are duplicated herein in accordance with the provisions of Title 17, U. S. C.).

iUniverse books may be ordered through booksellers or by contacting:

iUniverse
1663 Liberty Drive
Bloomington, IN 47403
www.iuniverse.com
1-800-Authors (1-800-288-4677)

Because of the dynamic nature of the Internet, any web addresses or links contained in this book may have changed since publication and may no longer be valid. The views expressed in this work are solely those of the author and do not necessarily reflect the views of the publisher, and the publisher hereby disclaims any responsibility for them.

ISBN: 978-1-4502-6636-9 (sc)
ISBN: 978-1-4502-6638-3 (hc)
ISBN: 978-1-4502-6637-6 (ebook)

Printed in the United States of America

iUniverse rev. date: 03/10/2011

For *The Creator*, who timed my birth to witness great historical events, and whose imparted wisdom allowed me to complete the research necessary to write this book.

For "**M**" who desired to be a player in *Le Comédie Vietnamien* but because of Providence was not allowed to join the cast.

For **The Government Of The United States Of America** which allowed me to be a player and therefore to avail myself of the opportunity to gather the facts herein.

Lastly, for **D. H.**, a critic of the production who possessed an uncompromising devotion to his craft.

"Those who cannot remember the past are condemned to repeat it."
George Santayana, Spanish philosopher, poet and novelist (1863 – 1952)

"All the world's a stage, and all the men and women merely players; they have their exits and their entrances, and one man in his time plays many parts..."
As You Like It, Act II, Scene 7
William Shakespeare, English playwright, poet and actor (1564 – 1616)

"There is a time to kill and a time to heal ... a time of war and a time of peace."
The Gospel Of Jesus Christ, Ecclesiastes 4:3, 8

Preface

The Vietnam War of 1964 – 75 has been subjected to a number of appellations: a mistake, a tragedy, a joke, a fulfillment of treaty obligations. Economists would likely label it a confrontation between two opposing economic ideologies. The general consensus however is that the war should not have occurred. The most glaring attribute that one could place on that conflict however is that it did not accomplish anything positive for the United States. One thing is for sure, however. This nation was profoundly transformed by that conflict.

Another label which can be ascribed to the Vietnam Conflict is that it was a "popular" war. One could readily observe how the issues spawned by the war were reflected in the popular culture of motion pictures, phonograph recordings and the like. In this sense it was a continuation of the traditions of many nations which have been engaged in armed conflict with foreign adversaries. Popular composers have always been compelled to echo the sentiments of the citizenry of their respective nations in an effort to either instill patriotism to win the conflict or to express popular belief about some aspect of the war. The United States is of course no different. The tradition can be seen in at least two wars prior to the Vietnam/Indochina Conflict. During the First World War the popular composer George M. Cohan was a major voice in the government's effort to defeat Germany and its allies. His popular songs *Yankee Doodle Dandy* and *Over There* are still regarded as icons of that era. They indeed aroused patriotic sentiments and may have been a catalyst for the U. S.' eventual triumph in that conflict. The tradition continued in the Second World War when the popular crooner Perry Como made light of the saturation bombing of Japan by means of the Army Air Forces B-29 "Flying Fortress." As the 1945 song *Hubba Hubba (Dig You Later)* went:

> "*Hubba Hubba*, let's shoot some breeze.
> Say, whatever happened to the Japanese?
> I got it from a guy who was in the know,
> It was mighty smoky over Tokyo."
> Copyright © 1945, Robbins Music Corp.

One could thereby sense the amusement of the composer of the savagery of that war and the havoc to which the Japanese were subjected. Such levity was injected into the script of the 1945 film *Doll Face* in which Mr. Como introduced the song.

The lyric of another popular song of that war made light of another facet of the government's policies during that conflict, which policies continued to the conflict which will be detailed here. On 2 January 1941 the popular sister trio The Andrews Sisters recorded *Boogie Woogie Bugle Boy*. The song which is generally regarded as a musical icon of that conflict, appeared to make light of The Universal Military Training And Service Act of 1940. That law had just been enacted as the U. S. was gearing up for the Second World War. As the song went:

> "He was a famous trumpet man from out Chicago way.
> He had a boogie sound that no one else could play.
> He was the top man in his craft, but then his number
> came up, and he was gone with the draft."
> (Copyright © 1940, MCA Music, Inc.).

The song then details how the individual in question contributed to the nation's effort to win the war, however small. The song further was featured in the 1941 film *Buck Privates*. That motion picture which starred the popular comedy duo Bud Abbott and Lou Costello and featured The Andrew Sisters in mock army uniforms, made light of life in the Armed Forces. The film was in production as the first peacetime draft law was enacted. Such was the public's perception of conscription at the inception of the Second World War. It is worth noting that the song was resurrected during the Vietnam Conflict in 1973 by a contemporary artist at the conclusion of the second phase of the war. It was however resurrected apparently as a bit of camp nostalgia. The song remains a cherished part of the national cultural heritage.

As one will observe herein, public sentiment concerning the issue of conscription changed markedly from 1940 to 1975 when the instant conflict terminated. This will be one of the primary issues which the author will examine in detail. What sets The Vietnam Conflict apart from those preceding is that here popular composers used their skills to denigrate the government's efforts at waging war. Some songs which were popular during the instant conflict actually mocked the government's efforts to win the war. For this reason they deserve special merit. These will be detailed below.

On the subject of popular culture, the colonial society during the Revolution of course had such, as do all societies. Contemporary society might indeed be interested to know how the colonial culture was reflected in or was impacted by the Revolutionary War. A question which today's history fans might therefore have is: To what did colonial society "boogaloo" as the Minutemen retrieved their muskets as they headed off to do battle with the advancing Redcoats? For this reason the extent to which the popular culture was impacted by the Vietnam Conflict is hereby documented for the benefit of posterity.

In the one hundred ninety-ninth year of its existence, the U. S. lost a war for the first time. Even this distinction is cause for debate, however. The authors of one of the materials which this author used for research stated in their book that the U. S. did not lose in Vietnam. Using the criteria of every President since Truman however, the U. S. did *lose* Vietnam. Every one of the five presidents since Truman who served as Commander-In-Chief during the conflict stated that the policy of the U. S. is not to "lose" South Vietnam to the communist sphere of influence. There are certainly other schools of thought on this subject. The generally acknowledged view however is that in any military conflict which is ultimately settled, and one side thereto achieved its objective, then that side won and the other side lost. As of this writing, the government of The Socialist Republic Of Vietnam which represents all of that country and which is avowedly communistic, is a reality. It is a unified nation under a form of government of its choosing. They obviously won the war.

How did such occur? Given the various strengths of the United States, which of course include its military and its industrial capacity, the U. S. should have prevailed in the war in question. To help provide an answer, the author has gathered the facts herein. These will hopefully aid interested parties in drawing their own conclusions.

Further, the author hopes to provide an answer to a question which he and others have had since the end of the conflict: Was there a link between the war and a major political event which grew from a series of crimes, which crimes profoundly affected the political mood and therefore influenced the conduct of the war? Further, inasmuch as North Vietnam did eventually succeed in its military campaign to "conquer" South Vietnam, one burning question which interested parties have had since, is: Did Richard Nixon's anticipated departure from office on 8 August 1974 fuel the will of North Vietnam to embark on its eventually successful military campaign? Perhaps the question should be better phrased: Was the North Vietnamese successful military campaign in preparation even before Nixon left, because they knew that his position was untenable? The author asks these questions because both the war and the domestic political events in question have continued to reverberate through U. S. society ever since.

With respect to the depth and breadth of facts herein, the author of course hopes that he has written in sufficient detail. Some will doubtless decry an omission of a certain fact, or a lack of explanation in depth of a subject of the Vietnam War. If the author had chosen to describe the war in greater detail, he could have written at least twice as much. The audience should understand that it was the author's intention to provide information only in sufficient detail to allow his target audience to have a basic understanding of the subject in question. Where subjects are detailed in depth, then it was because the author believed that the subject justified such detail. Some facts were simply available and also pertinent. Further, the reader should keep in mind that though the author holds degrees in several fields, he is neither a professional historian nor a sociologist. Some of his avocations are history and popular culture.

The author concedes the omission of two pertinent facts concerning issues related to the war. First, the author omitted a reference to a member of the Federal Judiciary who had the courage to speak out against one of the burning issues of the war: the military draft. At least one Federal judge ruled in a case that the Universal Military Training And Service Act as it was administered during the war, was unconstitutional. He so ruled because the draft discriminated against males. The title of the law was of course a misnomer. The judge opined that men are entitled to equal protection under the law. That judge's argument failed to take hold. That is, the draft law was not subsequently modified because of his argument. When military conscription was suspended in 1973, the registration option was subsequently retained and it still only applied to males. However, the reader will surmise from the text that the controversy concerning the draft was so intense that such controversy likely hastened the end of the war. The author omitted reference to the judge in question because, despite that he distinctly recalls an obituary of the judge in *The Washington Post* in the 1980s, he could find no reference to the individual.

Second, the author omitted reference to an interview of the leader of North Vietnam during much of the war, Ho Chi Minh. The author distinctly recalls that the interview was published in *Playboy* Magazine shortly before Ho Chi Minh's death in 1969. Further, the author has a vivid recollection that he asserted therein that when he formed his government after the defeat of Japan in 1945, he sought aid from the U. S. He was aware of the history of the United States and that the U. S. was born of a fight for independence from a colonial master. Accordingly, he reasoned that the U. S. would support the efforts of the indigenous peoples of Vietnam to remain free of its colonial master. He knew that the French would return to assert its dominance over all of Indochina. The U. S. of course rebuffed his request because his Viet Minh party embraced communist ideology. The author omitted reference to the interview of Ho Chi Minh because, despite his best efforts he could find no record of the interview.

The reader should also be aware that this work was a learning experience for the author. Though much of this book was written from details of the war which the author recovered from memory, he also found many facts of which he was previously unaware. Indeed, the author is certain that many who examine these facts will concede that some had been all but forgotten. They are accordingly resurrected here and preserved for the benefit of posterity.

This work was originally conceived as a means by which the author would document for his own descendants his perception of and participation in the Vietnam War. Being a student of history, he perceived that his relations and his descendants would be interested, not only in what this major national undertaking was about, but also of how the ancestor viewed it, participated in it and then examined how the conflict had transformed his life. If for example, one had an ancestor who observed how the American Revolution evolved, and then that person had participated in that war and also observed its aftermath, then the descendant would likely be quite interested. Upon beginning this book however, the author realized that there might be a wider audience for this information. He accordingly started documenting the war with which he is intimately familiar, with an intent to publish such.

Comparison of this work with others on this subject should reveal that this is the most complete chronicle of the war available. The author's purpose was to provide a more detailed analysis of the war than has previously been published. An example of the need which historians may have for the information herein is to compare this war with the American Revolution. The general facts of that conflict are widely known. However, details of that war which are not now known and will likely never be revealed, but which should have been documented, might be of interest to succeeding generations. These generations might want to know for instance: What other motives the British Commander, Lord Cornwallis had for fighting for his king to quell the colonial rebellion? Did Cornwallis know that there were sizeable gold deposits in the colonies of Georgia and North Carolina which he may have stumbled upon on a search and destroy mission similar to those which U. S. forces used in Vietnam? Was his zeal in combat due to the fact that he desired to exploit these riches for The British Crown (and himself)? Was he however restricted in his desire to exploit said riches because he was otherwise preoccupied with his military duties?

Within that context, another subject which future generations might want to examine is the level of discord in the American colonies over the quest to free themselves from Britain. It has been documented that some colonists expressed their sentiments about the Revolution with their feet. They left what is now the United States. In this respect there was a link between the first war that the U. S. fought and the one examined herein. As did many men in the U. S. during the Vietnam War, those "Tories" left for Canada which was then firmly under British control. Further, concerning the few free blacks who lived in the colonies, one might be prompted to ask the question: Were there some who understood the issues of the war? Were they all of one accord? It has been documented that some black colonists fought against the British and were therefore instrumental in establishing this great experiment in democracy known as The United States Of America. If there was indeed discord among blacks in colonial society, then the Vietnam War accordingly can be labeled a case of "déjà vu." This book will describe the discord within the black/African-American community in the United States over the instant war. It could go without saying that if persons who lived in the late eighteenth century in the colonies had had the foresight and also a means to transcribe their sentiments, then contemporary society would have the benefit of their knowledge on this subject.

As the reader will surmise, there are several themes within these pages in addition to the vital facts of the Vietnam War. In addition to demonstrating the degree to which attitudes were transformed by the war and of how the lives of key persons were changed, the overriding aim however is to demonstrate how the conflict in question permeated the popular culture. For this purpose, the popular culture is defined primarily as phonograph recordings, television and motion pictures. Some of the issues of the Vietnam War have been firmly etched in the popular culture, to be enjoyed by succeeding generations. Indeed, some of these items of popular culture have been recognized by the government for their cultural value. The author has hopefully added to this national treasure by promoting a greater understanding of how the war in question has been portrayed in U. S. culture. It bears mention that a number of good films have been produced about the Vietnam Conflict, in addition to those mentioned in the text below, among them:

- *The Deer Hunter* (1978)
- *The Boys In Company C* (1978)
- *Go Tell The Spartans* (1978)
- *Coming Home* (1979)
- *Apocalypse Now* (1979)
- *Platoon* (1985)
- *Full Metal Jacket* (1987)
- *Gardens Of Stone* (1987)
- *Hamburger Hill* (1987)
- *Good Morning, Vietnam* (1988)
- *Born On The Fourth Of July* (1989)
- *Casualties Of War* (1989)
- *Heaven & Earth* (1993)
- *The War At Home* (1996)

These films will not be discussed herein because they were produced after the war ended. However, the author highly recommends them to all who are interested in how the war has been portrayed by Hollywood. Further, other films were produced about the war after its conclusion. Among these was *A Bright, Shining Lie* (1998). The above list only includes those films produced for commercial/theatrical release.

It could go without saying that the Vietnam War has had a most profound impact upon the lives of its participants, as well as upon society at large. This can be seen in output from the Hollywood motion picture industry in six of the films listed above. The director of three of these films, one Oliver Stone, saw ground action in that conflict. The U. S. is indeed blessed to have been provided with filmed versions of his experiences there in all of the films which bear his name. This is especially true in two of the above films which were recognized by the Academy Of Motion Picture Arts And Sciences. Another of Mr. Stone's films which was recognized by that body also provides insight into another facet of American society. That film entitled *JFK: The Story That Won't Go Away* (1991), bears relation to the subject of this book, but only peripherally. That excellent film details the controversy surrounding the assassination of President Kennedy in 1963. Questions surrounding that beloved President's death have never been fully resolved. Accordingly, questions about his death remain, even as of this writing. The subtitle of this book of course paraphrases the title of Mr. Stone's film. As of this writing the controversy over the Vietnam/Indochina Conflict has not gone away. Neither should it. This subject deserves to be examined in as much depth as is necessary to allow a complete understanding of how the war occurred, why it occurred and how the issues of the war have continued to reverberate within society. Societies which don't learn the lessons of history are indeed doomed to repeat them.

Lastly, there may be a greater power at work which compelled the author to document his observations of the Vietnam War. As examination of the government documents included herein will attest, the author may have simply been put in this place and at this time to write this book. His birth coincided precisely to the month that the Chinese Civil War (1911 – 1949) was settled in favor of the communist faction there. This in turn set off a chain of events in the U. S. which eventually led this nation to intervene in another Asian civil war. The advent of that war was what in turn caused the author to serve in the Armed Forces and to be a participant there. The rest is history. The author grew up with the Vietnam War. Just because something is gone does not mean that it has left one's consciousness. The author's older brother who desired to serve in the military at the advent of that conflict is now deceased. However, just because he is gone does not mean that he has departed the author's consciousness. As with the author's older brother, the Vietnam War is firmly etched therein. This complete "eye-witness" account of the Vietnam Conflict then, from the author's own hand, is *A "Popular" War That Won't Go Away*.

(In his research the author sometimes found disparity in the estimates of military forces fielded by any combatant. Accordingly, references herein to numbers of such forces are those which the author gave the greatest credence).

(All references herein to chart positions of recordings were obtained from either (1) Billboard's Top LP Charts and Top 100 Charts, courtesy Joel Whitburn's Record Research Publications or (2) The Guinness Encyclopedia Of Popular Music. Where no chart position for a song is provided, the song in question was either not released in a 45 RPM format or the chart data for a recording was not available).

Table of Contents

Introduction

This is a chronological account of the Vietnam War as observed by an individual who watched that conflict unfold, took part in those hostilities and also observed its aftermath. This account is being written in the immediate aftermath of the death on 23 April 2007 of a master journalist, David Halberstam, author of *The Best And The Brightest*. That book is a detailed account of the administrations of Presidents John F. Kennedy and Lyndon Baines Johnson. It gives a vivid picture of the decision-making process of these administrations and of how the U. S. arrived at its position on Vietnam which evolved into war. As the book states, "throughout the 1960s, the overriding question was Vietnam." Halberstam also distinguished himself as virtually the first reporter to uncover the deception that the government sought to perpetrate concerning U. S. involvement in Indochina. As a reporter for *The New York Times* in 1962, his reporting about what was actually occurring in Vietnam and environs, as opposed to the official version of events promulgated by the government, incurred the wrath of government officials. These included the President.

This account is also being written in the immediate aftermath of the resurrection of one of the ugliest incidents of the war: the Kent State killings of May, 1970. These will be detailed below. On 2 May 2007, on the approximate thirty-seventh anniversary of the killings, an article was published in numerous newspapers about new information having been uncovered concerning that incident. It seems that someone had made a recording of a person giving an order to shoot at unarmed student protesters. This news item and the obituaries written about Mr. Halberstam are another indication that the war had not, as of the beginning of the third millennium, departed the nation's consciousness. Further, the publication of those articles is also indicative of the fact that certain events of the war will likely be debated into perpetuity.

The author will do more than just detail the events of the war. In order to make this narrative more meaningful and also demonstrate how the war influenced the domestic situation as well as his personal situation, he will first provide a sketch of the events leading up to the war. Then he will detail how the events of the war were interwoven with political, societal and cultural events of the time. Particular emphasis will be placed on how the war's issues reverberated through the popular culture. Further, this document will detail how the author's life and those of other "players", both major and minor, were altered by the conflict.

In addition to David Halberstam's book and news reporting about Vietnam and how the U. S. became involved, a number of books have been written on these subjects. These are included in the bibliography. In addition to Mr. Halberstam's book, the author highly recommends them.

A final note is in order. With respect to the date of the beginning of the war, it bears mention that there is more than one school of thought. The Readers' Guide To Periodical Literature which aided the author in locating much of the information herein, refers to the conflict as the "Vietnamese War" and dates it from 1957. This was the year in which production began on one of the first films about U. S. involvement in Vietnam, *The Quiet American,* discussed below.

General Facts Of The Vietnam War

The basic facts of the Vietnam War are that:

- it was the longest war in U. S. history up to that time. The official dates of the inception and the termination of the war are 5 August 1964 to 7 May 1975, respectively, although hostilities in which the U. S. was directly involved terminated in January, 1973;

- the total cost in U. S. lives and money was estimated at 58,000 and $150,000,000,000, respectively;

- it was the first "living room war" in that much of the fighting was broadcast on television. One could watch it everyday on the evening news;

- it was the first guerilla war that the Armed Forces had to learn to fight;

- it was the first war that the U. S. lost, up to that time;

- it was the second effort by the U. S. in the same century to intervene in a foreign civil war and use military force to halt the spread of communism, the first having also failed;

- it was the third test of the government's sworn duty to fight the spread of communism by force of arms, one previous effort having succeeded;

- it was the first war to spawn protests which were also voiced in popular song;

- it was the most divisive conflict in U. S. history other than the Civil War, up to that time;

- it was an undeclared war, in that Congress never declared war against any foreign government;

- it was the only war which was fought in three distinct non-contiguous phases, the first phase being from 5 August 1964 to 28 January 1973, the second phase from that date to 15 August 1973 and the third and final phase from that date until 7 May 1975;

- it was the first war in which persons who were charged with fighting the war would organize to voice their objections to it while the war was still raging, some while still in uniform.

Documentation Of The Author's Involvement In The Vietnam War

In order to demonstrate the degree to which the author was involved in the Vietnam War, he has included two historical documents. The first document is provided as Figure 1, which is a Selective Service System (SSS) Form 252, Order To Report For Induction, dated 12 October 1971. Observe that the document is from the President Of The United States Richard M. Nixon. As Commander-In-Chief, Nixon had the authority to order individuals to military service. Note also on the Form 252 that the document neglects to inform the recipient of the statutory authority which the President invoked in order to conscript the individual. Neither did SSS Form 252 specify what penalties would befall the individual who willfully failed to comply with the President's Order.

The other document is provided as Figure 2, a Report Of Separation From Active Duty, Department Of Defense (DOD) Form DD 214N. This was the standard form which was used to document the basic conditions under which individuals served and were released from military service. Observe that the author served in "Indochina", which included Vietnam, sometime during the entire interval of the Vietnam War.

It bears mention that the term "Vietnam War" is a misnomer. The hostilities in Southeast Asia spread far beyond the boundaries of Vietnam. Indeed, the war engulfed all of the territory known as French Indo-China until 1954. As will be detailed later, major incursions by allied troops including those of the U. S. took place into Cambodia and Laos more than once.

Also as will be detailed later, these incursions had quite profound effects not only on the countries invaded, but also on the fabric of the discourse over the war in the U. S.

Lastly, note that the character of the author's service was Honorable, and that he was released from active duty with the rank of Lieutenant (j. g.) (O-2).

CHAPTER ONE:
THE FIRST COMMITMENTS, 1954

The Cold War was an international fact of life. Paranoia over the threat of communist subversion had reached a fever pitch. The rising crescendo of anti-communist fervor which had begun in 1946 compelled U. S. leaders to make firm decisions. Public sentiment accordingly demanded that the leader of the Free World act decisively to halt a perceived effort by the Communist Bloc to control the world.

The Geo-political Situation, 1954

The U. S. became involved in Vietnam in the immediate aftermath of the French defeat in May by the indigenous forces and the French departure soon after. The country was then divided between the North which favored unification under a communist form of government, and the South which supposedly favored a government modeled after that of the United States. The U. S. of course favored the South because of its avowed contempt of communism. Indeed, the U. S. provided significant aid, both military and otherwise to the French while that country engaged the indigenous forces who eventually prevailed.

The same year that the indigenous forces prevailed, all sides to the conflict convened at Geneva, Switzerland. There they ratified the Geneva Accords which formally settled the conflict and decided on the future of Vietnam. These Accords would be the standard used to judge the legitimacy of any subsequent government which would replace the French. The Accords would also be used to scrutinize the motives and activities of any other party which would intervene into Vietnamese affairs. The U. S. did not participate in the Geneva Conference. However, the U. S. did issue a declaration recognizing the Accords. In addition, the U. S. formally resolved not to inhibit their implementation.

However, the U. S. in the person of Secretary Of State John Foster Dulles conveyed its dismay at the French defeat. Despite his distress at the French defeat, in May he stated that the U. S. was successful in keeping the People's Republic Of China from entering the war on the side of the Viet Minh/Viet Cong. He believed that China had heeded the U. S.' warning to stay out of the conflict. This he opined was a U. S. foreign policy triumph. Indeed, it appeared that the U. S.' "warning" to China to refrain from interfering in Vietnamese affairs would characterize the entire coming conflict. During the entire war no nation engaged the U.S. and her allies other than the Vietnamese. Mr. Dulles further stated that the U. S. would use all of its resources to disrupt the efforts of the Northern part of Vietnam to impose a communist government on all of Vietnam. In addition, he pledged that the U. S. would fight the spread of communism in Asia.

Several years following the partition of Vietnam, it was agreed that elections would be held in order to determine what form of government a unified Vietnam would have. When it became apparent that the Northern part of Vietnam which embraced communism would prevail in the forthcoming elections, the U. S. was instrumental in having them cancelled.

Between the Japanese departure in 1945 and the truce of 1954, the situation in Vietnam was of such complexity that the author could not do it justice. The relationships between and among (1) the Vietnamese Nationalists, (2) their nemesis the Viet Minh, (3) the French, (4) the figurehead Emperor Bao Dai and (5) the U. S. were sensitive in the extreme. The Vietnamese regarded the U. S. as its only liberator. U. S. military personnel who arrived in 1945 were greeted with adulation because the people believed that the U. S. would help in attaining freedom from the French whom they despised. The leader of the Viet Minh Party, Ho Chi Minh, was successful in persuading many that he had established friendships with U. S. officials. Such friendship many believed would allow Vietnam to secure the independence which they craved. One individual who was a force in Vietnamese affairs during this interval and then to the end of U. S. involvement was one Bui Diem. His relative obscurity outside Vietnam belies his importance. However, he is likely the most eloquent and knowledgeable chronicler of the transition which Vietnam underwent from 1945 to 1975. In his memoirs he refers to his relationship with David Halberstam. He is discussed below.

The Author's Situation, 1954

The author began kindergarten in September.

CHAPTER TWO:
FINDING BASES FOR INTERVENTION;
THE U.S. ACTING AS "ADVISOR",
1955 – 61

The hostilities in Indochina had subsided. After watching from the sidelines and observing communist influence grow in Indochina, the Guardian Of Freedom could no longer allow communist ideology to further expand. National self-confidence in the validity of the capitalist system, its industry and technological innovation compelled the U. S. to impede opposing interests. The commitment to fight communism would have to increase.

U. S. Initial Intervention Into Vietnam

Immediately following the cancellation of the aforementioned elections, civil war erupted between North and South Vietnam. The U. S. intervened on the side of the South. The reason why the U. S. deemed itself justified in intervening was because of a treaty which the U. S. had ratified with the "Government" Of South Vietnam. The U. S. insisted that South Vietnam was a country distinct from the "Government" Of North Vietnam. According to The World Book Encyclopedia (2005), this Southeast Asia Treaty Organization (S. E. A. T. O.) treaty was an alliance among Australia, The United Kingdom, France, New Zealand, Pakistan, The Philippines, Thailand and the U. S. In the immediate aftermath of the aforementioned French defeat, the treaty was ratified on 8 September 1954. All of these nations allied to prevent the spread of communism in Asia. These nations further pledged to defend one another from military aggression from communist states. The U. S. feared that North Vietnam would use military force to conquer the South.

U. S. Initial Military Intervention In Vietnam

During the administration of President Dwight D. Eisenhower, from 1958 to 1961 the U. S. began sending military personnel to South Vietnam. In order to make their presence there palatable to the public, the government asserted that these personnel were there in a non-combat status. They were purportedly there to advise the "Government" Of South Vietnam on how to repel the "aggression" from the North. Subsequently however, the government could not ignore or deny that some of such "advisors" were being killed. Figures on the deaths of U. S. personnel grew steadily from the advent of the intervention until the war officially began in 1964. July 8, 1959 is the date which documented the death of the first U. S. "advisor." (Gottlieb, p. xix). Official casualty figures for the conflict to 1974 are provided in Figure 3.

U. S. Intervention In Indochina Placed In Historical Perspective

a. The U. S. Civil War

Precisely one hundred years before the U. S. formally committed to intervening in an Asian civil war, the United States itself was so embroiled. At the inception of the U. S. Civil War (1861 – 65) at least one foreign government, Britain, had a vested interest in one side to that war. The Commander-In-Chief and President Of The U. S. Abraham Lincoln warned that government and all others to stay out of U. S. affairs. They stayed out of them.

b. The Revolutionary War

Precisely one hundred eighty-eight years prior to U. S. official entry into an Asian civil war, the new United States was involved in a war of liberation. The aim of the new nation was to exorcise itself from domination by a colonial power. Much of this conflict of course was "conventional." That is, groups of soldiers formed into regiments, battalions, etc. and confronted one another on battlefields. However, it has been documented that a portion of the Revolutionary War was fought by the American colonists using guerilla tactics. These tactics entailed harassing the enemy without directly confronting them on the battlefield. This fact has been documented in the life of one Francis Marion, the "Swamp Fox" of the colony of North Carolina who gained fame from his exploits against the British. His attack style was guerilla-type, in that he would harass the enemy at will, and then depart before the enemy could find him. This tactic may indeed have been instrumental in the eventual victory of the colonists over the country which was then the preeminent military power on this planet. As such, he was a perpetual source of consternation for the British Commander, Lord Cornwallis. Quite coincidentally, and perhaps ironically, the new nation's principal ally against the British was France. That nation wanted the U. S. to return the favor in 1945. At the inception of the instant war France sought U. S. aid in retaining its Indochina colonies prior to U. S. involvement.

The lesson which the British apparently learned was clear: even a recognized military power such as Britain cannot succeed against an enemy while fighting against guerilla-style tactics on that enemy's home turf. In 1783 they lost the war and returned home. In 1964 the U. S. military had apparently not remembered this lesson of history. It would however recall or learn it soon.

c. The First World War

The U.S. was one of the Allies who opposed Germany. Among the British, the French, the Italians and others, one of the U. S.' allies was Russia. However, during that conflict in 1917 Russia had a change of government when the capitalist autocracy headed by a Czar was overthrown and replaced by a communist state. The new government immediately made a separate peace with Germany and then set about building the first communist society on this planet. This deprived the Allies of a principal ally and made the war against Germany harder to fight. Further, the U. S. was alarmed that an economic ideology opposed to its own had taken root. In 1918 Commander-In-Chief Woodrow Wilson then sent troops to northern Russia to aid the other allies in opposing the new communist Russian Government, thereby intervening in another nation's civil war. President Wilson was widely criticized for allowing U. S. troops to so intervene. The U. S. derived no benefit from the intervention. Further, the intervention into the Russian Civil War caused discord between the U. S. and the new Soviet Republic for many years in the future.

Prior Warnings Concerning Proposed U. S. Intervention In Indochina

The U. S. commitment to intervene in the civil war in Vietnam came despite a warning from a high ranking government official in 1950. Halberstam discusses such warning in his analysis of the policy making process within the State Department just prior to the beginning of the Korean War. Speaking of George Kennan, a close assistant to then Secretary Of State Dean Acheson, Halberstam states:

> "As American involvement in Indochina deepened, he (Kennan) had written a long memo to Acheson, saying that the French could not win in Indochina, nor could

the Americans replace them and win, and that we were now, whether we realized it or not, on our way to taking their place." (Halberstam, p. 414).

The U. S. and many nations were closely watching the situation in Indochina where the French had become hopelessly embroiled. Mr. Kennan knew, as did many knowledgeable observers, that the French had made a big mistake to have become so embroiled. The reasons for this were expressed by numerous State Department officials of whom Halberstam refers repeatedly. Besides the fact that the French may have had no right to be in Indochina in the first place, they opined, these officials knew that no military power could prevail against a guerilla force when fighting on that force's home turf.

CHAPTER THREE: SETTING THE STAGE FOR MILITARY INTERVENTION, 1961 – 63

*The rapidly deteriorating situation in Indochina required
a complete break with the past. It was obvious that the
Free World was losing ground. The new leadership was
expected to, and indeed had vowed to further commit
the vast resources of the U. S. to aid its allies in the fight
to impede the spread of the communist menace.*

The Domestic Political Situation, 1961 – 63

a. Initial government change in war policy

Upon his assumption of the Office Of President on 20 January 1961, John F. Kennedy pledged to continue the aid which his predecessor had committed to South Vietnam. However, the press reported that one of the things which Kennedy agonized over from 1961 to 1963 was the turmoil within South Vietnam. Especially egregious was the oppression and denial of human rights of the Buddhist majority by the "government" whose leaders were predominantly Catholic (as was Kennedy). As frequently reported in the media, Buddhist monks were committing suicide in the streets to protest the oppression. Such was accomplished by dousing themselves with fuel and immolating themselves. This was one of the biggest news stories of 1963.

As Halberstam superbly detailed in *The Best And The Brightest*, the Kennedy Administration represented a marked departure from the policies of his predecessor. In 1961 the U. S. began to send greatly increased numbers of combat "support" troops to aid South Vietnam. These numbered some 12,000 by the end of 1961. This increase marked a critical escalation in U. S. involvement.

b. Reaction to initial government change in war policy

There were no major U. S. protests in 1961 concerning the nation's deepening involvement in South Vietnam. However, some senior government leaders did question such commitment. Among these was the senior Senator of Tennessee, Albert Gore. His sentiments concerning U. S. intervention in Indochina were detailed in his book *The Eye Of The Storm*. He would remain one of the staunchest critics of the war for the rest of the decade.

c. Subsequent planned government change in war policy

Though it was not made public at the time, government leaders began to radically reassess Vietnam policies in 1963. Many years after the war would conclude, it would be revealed that Secretary Of Defense McNamara in consultation with President Kennedy had planned to retract the deepening involvement in Indochina. The documentary *The Fog Of War* which would be released in 2003 would reveal for the first time that the two principal architects of the war had discussed plans for the U. S. to extricate itself. They apparently realized that the nation had indeed made a mistake to have become so involved. The plan, of which McNamara makes specific reference in the film, was to remove all of the 16,000 U. S. forces in Vietnam at that time. The timeframe for the removal of the forces was to have been two years. The first group slated for removal was 1,000 personnel to be removed by the end of 1963. The remaining forces were to be gone by the end of 1965. Specific reference to this alleged plan was made in the 1991 film *JFK: The Story That Won't Go Away.*

However, *The Fog Of War* would also reveal that the aforementioned plans of President Kennedy and Secretary Of Defense McNamara would be aborted by unforeseen circumstances. The assassination of President Of South Vietnam Diem, discussed below, would cause the plan to be aborted. The subsequent assassination of President Kennedy, also discussed below, would also be instrumental in causing the plan to be scrapped.

The Political Situation In Vietnam, 1961 - 63

The President of South Vietnam in 1961 was one Ngo Dinh Diem. He initially welcomed increased U. S. aid in the form of greater numbers of troops that year. However, when the number of U. S. military personnel there rose above 10,000, Diem began to resent such. He perceived these increased numbers of personnel to be a threat to his authority. His resentment was widely reported in the press and was voiced to U. S. officials.

The "Government" Of South Vietnam at this time was notoriously corrupt. President Diem had a brother, one Ngo Dinh Nhu who was also an official in the "Government." The brother was married to a woman known in the press as "Madame Nhu", a.k.a. the "Dragon Lady." She was so-called because of her ability to influence her brother-in-law to oppress his political opponents. Inasmuch as President Diem was unmarried, Madame Nhu was compelled to act as the "First Lady." Indeed, she garnered as much press as did Diem in 1963. Further, her passion for ruthlessness was unparalleled. She was also reputed to have had formidable sexual prowess. This is perhaps the reason why she would be mentioned in the first U. S. popular song, detailed below, which would include in the lyric something related to Vietnam.

It bears mention that many years after the war would end, one of the most prominent leaders of South Vietnam during this decade would publish his account of the situation in South Vietnam at this time. Nguyen Cao Ky who would eventually become Air Marshal and then President, would label Madame Nhu "a venal and wicked woman." This despite that her name translated means "tears of spring." Ky further would reveal that Madame Nhu, upon being informed of the aforementioned mass suicides of Buddhist monks, was reputed to have stated that she would welcome more of the same. According to Bui Diem (no relation) Saigon had a daily English language newspaper called the *Times Of Vietnam*. It was considered the official government mouthpiece. However, that periodical often published anti-American propaganda which was supposed to have been inspired by the President's brother and his wife. (Diem, p. 110).

The South Vietnamese "government" was a family business. This is one factor which contributed to the contempt which many of the indigenous population held for their leaders. Diem's sister-in-law's father was the Ambassador To The United States. However, the family itself was wracked with discord. When Diem, his brother and Madame Nhu cracked down on the Buddhist majority, the ambassador, one Tran Van Chuong, resigned. According to Bui Diem she was widely disliked because of her shrill, abrasive manner. She was also apparently disliked by her own kin. When her uncle protested the brutalization of the Buddhists, she had him imprisoned. (Diem, p. 95). Perhaps this is why Bui Diem characterizes the Diem Regime as one of "arrogant authoritarianism." (Diem, p. 93). He further opined:

> "By 1961 it was clear beyond anyone's doubt that Diem had become a hopeless oligarch whose repressive methods had led to permanent discord in the society." (Bui Diem, p. 95).

On 3 November 1963 the U. S. awoke to the news that the President Diem had been assassinated. It has never been alleged that the U. S. instigated the coup and assassination of Diem. Indeed, the analysis of events there which were incredibly detailed in The Pentagon Papers, discussed below, indicates that the U. S. was in no way complicit in the internal affairs of South Vietnam. However, The Papers would also reveal that the Central Intelligence Agency (C. I. A.) encouraged the coup instigators with subtleties. The C. I. A. also provided valuable intelligence to them which enabled the plot against Diem to succeed. Upon the death of Diem, Duong Van Minh, a.k.a. "Big Minh" who was one of the coup plotters, became the leader of South Vietnam. The military junta ordered the *Times Of Vietnam* shut down. (Diem, p. 110).

Most revealing information about the above episode would come to light many years after the war would end. In an article entitled "Untold story of the road to war in Vietnam", published in the October 10, 1983 issue of *U. S. News & World Report* (pp. VN1 – VN 24), new, albeit inconsequential details of the circumstances of the above assassinations were revealed. The article detailed President Kennedy's reaction to the news of the deaths. He was reportedly quite stunned. This indicates that he did not advocate the assassinations, though he was aware of the planned coup against Diem long before it occurred. The article also stated that he welcomed the change.

In 1987 Bui Diem would publish his memoirs, *In The Jaws Of History*. He would state therein that he was of the same mind as Kennedy. He believed, as apparently did Kennedy that the U. S. should have informed President Diem in 1963 that his "government" should cease its repressive tactics and allow greater freedoms or the U. S. would depart. (Bui Diem, p. 97).

The Domestic Political Situation, 1963

Shortly after noon on 22 November (C.S.T.), the author and his high school classmates received news that President Kennedy had been assassinated. It has since been speculated that he was targeted for assassination because some government officials believed that he would pull U. S. forces out of Vietnam prematurely. This is what would be alleged in the 1991 film *JFK: The Story That Won't Go Away*. Such allegations have never had any basis in fact.

The Author's Situation, 1961 - 63

The author began the seventh grade in 1961, the first year of the Kennedy Administration. There he and his classmates were given copies of a magazine called *Junior Scholastic*. The magazine was laced with articles about young people similar to the author and his peers, descriptions of current movies, crossword puzzles and the like. The magazine also described how the government was helping South Vietnam to resist the "aggression" from the North. This was the author's first exposure to events in the exotic place called Vietnam. He concluded that the government was good and brave to help South Vietnam to have a democratic government such as that in the U. S. Basically he reasoned that if President Kennedy was behind it, then it must be O. K. Further, his teacher impressed upon him the possibility of his someday being compelled to provide military service to his government.

The national mood concerning military service among young persons was such that it was regarded as a means to elevate one's status or to find a career. The author's cousin, "A", was the first in his family to inform him that he desired to embrace military service. "A" graduated from college in June, 1961. He promptly stated his intention to join the Navy's aircraft carrier pilot program. He had accepted President Kennedy's inaugural challenge to do something constructive for his country. Because of his excessive height however, he was not accepted into the program.

In 1963 the author started high school.

The Popular Culture, 1957 – 64

a. Cinema
1. *The Ugly American*
In 1963 prior to the aforementioned assassinations, a film was released in which the actor Marlon Brando starred, *The Ugly American*. The film detailed the political situation in a fictitious Southeast Asian country called Sarkhan in which the U. S., coincidentally, was heavily involved.

The plot of *The Ugly American* specifically detailed Brando's role as the U. S. Ambassador and his interaction with said government. That nation was being threatened by its neighbor, North Sarkhan which was in turn supported by its powerful allies, The Soviet Union and The People's Republic Of China. The climax of the film was a crisis in which the country erupted into civil war and was also invaded by North Sarkhan. The President therefore invoked the treaty which his country had with the U. S. and other nations, which required military intervention in order to keep the President in authority. This was the only reference in the film to the actual S.E.A.T.O treaty which the U. S. had with several other nations.

The last scene of the film shows Brando on a television screen in the immediate aftermath of the aforementioned crisis. He was being observed by a citizen in his living room in the U. S., munching on what appeared to be a chicken drumstick and leafing through an edition of *T. V. Guide* Magazine. Brando, being interviewed by the press, then describes the crisis in Sarkhan and what, in his opinion, should be done to resolve the hostilities. Apparently uninterested in the events of the Asian nation, the citizen turns off the television.

The advertisement for *The Ugly American* labeled it "The Most Important Adventure Of Our Time!" Despite the apparent veracity of that advertisement, the public disagreed. When the film-going public substantially ignored it, this revealed the general indifference to events in Indochina.

The Ugly American was not the first portrayal of U. S. concern about or intervention into the affairs of Indochina. Several films had been produced prior to 1963 which concerned events there, among them (years refer to the year of release):

Saigon (1948)
China Gate (1957)
The Quiet American (1958)

With respect to *The Quiet American*, the activities surrounding its production gave an indication of what transpired during its filming and of the atmosphere in Vietnam at the time. Production began on location in Saigon in January, 1957. The film crew was aware that the communist Viet Minh, formally known as the Front For The Independence Of Vietnam, was in close proximity. Further, it was rumored that the Viet

Minh would try to disrupt the production. The rumor was eventually unfounded. However, the rumor was taken seriously by the star of the film, Audie Murphy, to the extent that he was reputed to have slept with a loaded pistol.

2. *Dr. Strangelove Or: How I Learned To Stop Worrying And Love The Bomb*

This was the first of two films which were released back-to-back, and which contain nothing related to Vietnam. Each film however pertains to the most fearsome aspect of the Cold War (1946 – 89): the rivalry between the U. S. and the "communist bloc" which included the Soviet Union. Many persons in and out of government feared that such rivalry would erupt into a "hot" war which would necessitate the use of nuclear weapons. Indeed, the two giants which both had sizeable nuclear arsenals, had already confronted one another over the nuclear weapons issue. Witness the face-off between President Kennedy and Premier of the Soviet Union Khrushchev when Kennedy acquired proof that his nemesis had placed nuclear missile sites on the island of Cuba in October, 1962. Both this film and that which follows were "what if" scenarios. Both posed the question: What if the safeguards which were supposedly put in place to ensure that the two most powerful nations with nuclear capability would not become engulfed in a nuclear conflagration, actually would fail? Nineteen sixty-four was indeed one of the years that the Cold War was still at its peak. This peak is of course evident in that the discourse reached into the popular culture this year. Further, this film and that below are glaring examples of the level of paranoia which existed both within and without the government concerning the aforementioned safeguards, and whether these safeguards were in fact viable.

The plot of *Dr. Strangelove*, a "black" comedy, concerns a scenario in which a senior military official, one U. S. Air Force Brigadier General Jack D. Ripper, apparently because of mental aberration, ordered the personnel under his command to strike military installations within the Soviet Union with nuclear weapons. This he did without authorization from The Pentagon. The general's rationale for initiating the confrontation was his avowed fear of what he believed was the world-wide communist threat of "communist infiltration, communist indoctrination, communist subversion, and the international communist conspiracy to sap and impurify all of our precious bodily fluids." The implication was that the "communist bloc" plotted to sterilize all of the citizens of the leader of the Free World. Communism would therefore prevail over the capitalist system, thereby causing the eventual extinction of the latter. Brig. Gen. Ripper sought to destroy "them" with nuclear ordnance before they destroyed the U. S. by sterilization.

The basic premise of the film was that the aforementioned safeguards to avert a nuclear catastrophe actually could fail because of the actions of a deranged individual. When it became apparent that the aforementioned safeguards which supposedly had been put in place had failed due to human error, steps were of course taken to remedy the situation. However, despite all of the best efforts of the President and his advisors to either shoot down the planes or recall them, which efforts included providing Top Secret military data to the Soviets, one plane got through. Accordingly, because of the actions of one deranged individual, the sophisticated infrastructure which everyone believed had been put in place to avert a nuclear disaster, had failed. The world ended.

It bears mention that forty years after *Dr. Strangelove* was released, an enhanced and augmented version of the film would be released in the DVD format. This celebration of the fortieth anniversary of the film's release would include a special feature documentary of an interview with the Secretary Of Defense at the time that the film was originally released. In a 2004 interview former Secretary Robert McNamara would analyze at length the complexities of the U. S.' relationship with the Soviet Union four decades previously. He would also state explicitly that there was real paranoia at that time that nuclear weapons might be used, either deliberately or otherwise, in a confrontation between the two nations.

3. *Fail Safe*

The second film got its title from a claim which the Department Of Defense had promulgated to the world. The claim was made in order to allay fears and ensure that the aforementioned system of safeguards to avert a nuclear catastrophe between the U. S. and the Soviet Union were indeed credible. The system was purportedly "fail safe." That is, it could not fail.

The basic plot of *Fail Safe* mirrored that of *Dr. Strangelove*. Because of human failure, a fighter wing of the Air Force was mistakenly ordered to attack the Soviet Union with a sizeable nuclear payload. The crews on the planes actually believed that total war had erupted. Also, as with the other film one senior official believed that the Soviets could not be trusted. They would therefore unleash the full fury of its nuclear arsenal against the U. S. when it became apparent to them that a catastrophe could not be averted. His rationale was that the U. S. should destroy "them" before they destroy "us." Again, despite the best efforts of the President (played by Henry Fonda) and his advisors to either recall the planes, shoot them down or provide ultra-sensitive military data to the Soviets, one plane got through. There was of course a sizeable loss of life on both sides. Both this film and that above of course included a caution from the producers that the Department Of Defense had assured the public that the events depicted in the films could not possibly occur.

Both of the above films deserve to be part of the history of the Vietnam War because they indicate the level of national paranoia then existing concerning a perceived world-wide communist threat. There were of course those who doubted that such paranoia existed. Some believed that national leaders were too rational to allow a confrontation with the nation's enemies with nuclear arms. It would be revealed during the height of the Vietnam War however that national leaders including the President had indeed become paranoid about what they perceived as an encroaching international communist threat. The sentiments of U. S. leaders would be examined in the Pentagon Papers which are discussed below.

It did not help to diffuse the aforementioned paranoia that in October, 1964 after the instant war had officially begun and after the above two films had been released, the world added another member to the nuclear club: The People's Republic Of China. That nation which was an ideological enemy of the United States detonated its first nuclear device.

Lastly on the subject of the degree of paranoia which existed over the issue of containment of communism, it bears mention that this issue would burn throughout most of the war. As will be revealed later, the individual who would be President during most of the war endeavored to soften the discord between the East and West. In 1972 as the first phase of the war would be concluding, President Nixon announced that he would, by invitation, go to The People's Republic Of China to meet with the leaders of that nation. Upon hearing this announcement, a member of Nixon's own political party and from his own state, one Congressman John Schmitz of California, stated that Nixon was "surrendering to international communism" when Nixon accepted the invitation. So stated Nixon in his memoirs. (*RN*, p. 554).

Further on the subject of government paranoia concerning the communist threat, even Nixon understood both the degree of this paranoia and also that it was becoming an anachronism when the war would be raging in 1971. He further seemed to understand that this paranoia would work against his efforts to end the war. Nixon conceded in his memoirs that in 1971 one of his chief law enforcement officers, F. B. I. Director J. Edgar Hoover was reputed to have been "trapped in outdated notions of the communist threat and was not moving with flexibility against the new violence-prone radicals." (*RN*, p. 596). The "radicals" were of course those citizens who would agitate against the war and also commit violent acts when it would be at its peak.

b. Phonograph recordings
1. *Lee Cross*
In 1964 the "soul" singer Walter Jackson recorded a song entitled *Lee Cross*. The releasing label was Okeh, a division of the entertainment conglomerate Columbia. The song was composed by Ted White, who would become the first husband of singer Aretha Franklin. The song described the powers which the song's namesake had over women. As the song went:

> "*Lee Cross*, he's a lady's boss.
> He's an ex-teacher from the school of life.
> They say that Madame Nhu wants to be his wife."
> (Copyright © 1964, Unichappell Music, Inc.).

Lee Cross holds the distinction of being the first U. S. popular song which referred to something related to Vietnam. In view of the song's entry onto the music charts in the early fall of 1964, it is likely that the song was written prior to 5 August. And the beat continued...

2. *So You See, We All Have Problems*

Also in 1964 the comedian, businessman, social activist and Presidential candidate Dick Gregory recorded an album, *So You See, We All Have Problems*. The releasing label was Colpix, a division of Columbia Motion Pictures. The album was recorded "live" prior to 5 August. One of the jokes therein made light of the alleged naiveté on world affairs of then Governor Of Alabama George C. Wallace. If asked by a reporter what he would do about Vietnam, Wallace would allegedly reply: "Viet *who*?" Mr. Gregory thereby opined that Governor Wallace was not qualified to be President. It bears mention that Governor Wallace would seek the Presidency as the war would peak in 1968 and also in 1972 as it would still be raging. This was Mr. Gregory's first release which referred to Vietnam. However, as will be revealed later it would not be his last.

In light of the above, it could therefore be said that Vietnam was on the minds of the public prior to 5 August 1964.

CHAPTER FOUR:
THE ADVENT OF
DE JURE MILITARY
INTERVENTION, 1964

The situation in Vietnam had reached crisis proportions. The U. S. had also convulsed in the wake of an assassination which some suggested had been instigated by the Soviet Union. Further, the leader who assumed power the previous year broke with his predecessor. The new Administration desired to demonstrate to the world that the U. S. was firm in its commitments to all of its ideological allies. A functional equivalent of declared war against its Indochina enemies ensued.

The Domestic Political Situation, 1964

a. Advice on the foreseen war

Early in the year Secretary Of Defense McNamara expressed his sentiments to President Johnson on the Vietnam question. Inasmuch as the North Vietnamese and the Viet Minh/Viet Cong were making significant progress towards their goal of unifying that nation, the situation had reached crisis proportions. However, Secretary McNamara expressed grave doubts about the wisdom of escalating U. S. involvement. He informed the President of the aforementioned plan to withdraw all U. S. forces from Vietnam by the end of 1965. However, the President was not of the same accord.

b. Congress acts

On 7 August Congress ratified the Gulf Of Tonkin Resolution. This Resolution was passed in response to a request from President Johnson on 5 August. Observe that this date coincides with the date indicated on the Form DD 214N in Figure 2.

The Resolution was passed in response to the alleged armed attack on Navy forces in international waters near the coast of Vietnam. The Gulf Of Tonkin is a narrow strait of water between the People's Republic Of China and the northern part of Vietnam. The U. S. claimed the right to operate in this area because these were international waters.

Here it must be clarified that the government's account of what occurred in the Gulf Of Tonkin has never been completely documented. The account which the government provided has been ever since murky at best. Indeed, Senator Gore stated such in *The Eye Of The Storm* (p. 8). Indeed, Secretary Of Defense McNamara conceded in the aforementioned documentary *The Fog Of War* that the account of what happened in the Gulf Of Tonkin was a confusing set of circumstances. Accordingly, there are indications that the event which the government claimed to have occurred, and which was used as justification to officially start the war, may never have occurred. However, in his address to Congress President Johnson asked that U. S. forces be accorded the right to respond with force to any aggression from forces opposed to the "Government" Of South Vietnam. Stated the President in his address to Congress:

"As I have repeatedly made clear, the U. S. intends no rashness, and seeks no wider war. We must make it clear to all that the U. S. is united in its determination to bring about the end of Communist subversion and aggression in the area. We seek the full and effective restoration of the international agreements signed in Geneva in 1954, with respect to South Vietnam."

Congress concurred with President Johnson's assessment of the situation in Vietnam by enacting the Resolution. The following is the complete text of the Joint Resolution of Congress, H. J. RES 1145, of 7 August:

Resolved by the Senate and House Of Representatives of The United States Of America in Congress assembled, That the Congress approves and supports the determination of The President, as Commander-In-Chief, to take all necessary measures to repel any armed attack against the forces of the United States and to prevent further aggression.

Section 2. The United States regards as vital to its national interest and to world peace the maintenance of international peace and security in Southeast Asia. Consonant with the Constitution Of The United States and the Charter of the United Nations and in accordance with its obligations under the Southeast Asia Collective Defense Treaty, the United States is, therefore, prepared, as the President determines, to take all necessary steps, including the use of armed force, to assist any member or protocol state of the Southeast Asia Collective Defense Treaty requesting assistance in defense of its freedom.

Section 3. This resolution shall expire when the President shall determine that the peace and security of the area is reasonably assured by international conditions created by action of the United Nations or otherwise, except that it may be terminated earlier by concurrent resolution of the Congress.

Thus the Vietnam War had *de jure* begun. The U. S. further committed itself to intervention in a foreign civil war. The government thereby echoed the sentiments of the aforementioned fictitious Brigadier General Ripper and began to put into place the infrastructure to halt the spread of communism.

To reiterate, the U. S. never declared war on any government. However, as stated by Senator Gore in *The Eye Of The Storm* (p. 9), the Department Of State interpreted the Resolution as the "functional equivalent" of a declaration of war. The Secretary Of State was one Dean Rusk who was one of the principal architects of the Vietnam War.

It bears mention that Vietnam was a minor consideration of Lyndon Johnson when he ascended to the Presidency in 1963. The subject of Vietnam was "placed on the back burner" by his Administration at its inception because other issues consumed its time. Halberstam was quite perceptive in his discussion of the dilemma with which Johnson was faced for approximately the first eight months of his Presidency when he stated:

"... It became harder and harder to convince the American public that the struggle there (Vietnam) was necessary. So 1964 became the year when Vietnam could no longer be kept on the back burner; events there would thrust the country in front of the American people ..."
(Halberstam, p. 303)

c. The citizenry responds to the Resolution
1. *The plebian response/Ron Kovic*
Though some were undoubtedly unaware of the magnitude of the urgency of the situation in Vietnam, some of the citizenry still desired to serve their country. These included one Ron Kovic who, fresh out of high school, joined the Marines at the approximate time that the Gulf Of Tonkin Resolution was passed. His rationale for doing so, in

addition to wanting to avoid mundane civilian employment, was pure, unvarnished patriotism. Mr. Kovic indeed heeded the invitation of his previous Commander-In-Chief not to ask what his country could do for him. Rather, he wanted to do something constructive for his country. Further, this may be another example in addition to that of the author, of a higher power compelling an individual to act. Mr. Kovic's birth coincided with the one hundred seventieth birthday of the United States. One might therefore say that his joining the military was something he was born to do. As will be revealed later, Mr. Kovic would eventually figure prominently in the national lore about the Vietnam Conflict.

2. *The patrician response/Senator Barry Goldwater*

President Johnson ran for election in 1964. On the campaign trail he stated that he "would not send American boys to fight in Asia." In retort, Halberstam states in his psychological profile of Johnson (p. 456) that what Johnson actually meant was that he would not send personnel to fight China. If Halberstam's assessment of Johnson was accurate, then history would prove the President to be a man of his word.

Johnson's opponent was one Barry Goldwater, Senator from Arizona and the leader of the Republican ticket. Goldwater's stance on the Vietnam question was more aggressive than that of Johnson. Goldwater was reputed to have favored the bombing of North Vietnam, possibly with nuclear weapons, in order to force their submission and cessation of "infiltration" into South Vietnam. In his autobiography however, aptly entitled *Goldwater*, he denies (p. 168) that he ever favored the use of nuclear weapons in Vietnam. He did however concede therein that in 1964 he discussed possibly using *tactical*, as opposed to *strategic* nuclear weapons. However, the Senator likely got much satisfaction from the fact that Johnson eventually adopted half of his recipe to win the war. Johnson would order the bombing of North Vietnam the next year, albeit with conventional ordnance.

The election of 1964 resulted in a "landslide" victory for President Johnson. His victory was widely believed to have resulted from the electorate's repudiation of Goldwater's "hawkish" rhetoric on the Vietnam question. Further, Johnson's victory was regarded by some as an endorsement of the government's position on Vietnam. Senator

Goldwater would state at the inception of the Vietnam buildup, that there was no way that the U. S. could win the war, the way that it was then being fought. These would prove to be prophetic words indeed. As Commander-In-Chief, he further stated in his autobiography:

> "...I would have warned the North Vietnamese by dropping thousands of leaflets on Hanoi and the rest of the country. My address and these messages would have said clearly that either they halt the conflict or we would wipe out all their installations - the City Of Hanoi, Haiphong Harbor, factories, dikes, everything. I would have given them a week to think about it. If they did not respond, we would literally make a swamp of North Vietnam." (*Goldwater*, p. 222).

Goldwater went on to state that he would have sent troops to invade North Vietnam. This statement brought up one of the most pertinent, albeit all-but-forgotten facts of the war: that no troops of any nation, including those of the U. S., Thailand, The Philippines, Australia or South Korea which all had troops "in country" during the war, ever crossed into North Vietnam. Further, this also appears to be the only lesson which the U. S. and its allies learned from a previous, similar conflict. During the Korean War of 1950 – 53, discussed below, the U. S. did indeed send troops to invade the enemy, North Korea. The allies led by the U. S. then achieved substantial victories against that nation's forces. However, a most unfortunate result of this initially successful campaign was of course that the People's Republic Of China entered the conflict on the side of North Korea. On the battlefield it proved that it was a match for the allied forces. As a result, the war was fought to a stalemate. The allies then realized that it could never prevail against the combined forces of North Korea and its ally. That war remained at a stalemate until it was resolved by treaty. All of the combatants then ceased hostilities, although the U. S. retained troops in South Korea, even to this writing. The two Koreas then reverted to the way that they were before the war. Nothing had been accomplished during the three years of hostilities.

The Pentagon Papers, discussed below, substantiates the government's wisdom of not invading North Vietnam. Those Papers (p. 332) would reveal upon their dissemination in 1971 that the government declined to invade North Vietnam because it feared the intervention of The People's Republic Of China on the enemy's side. The government understood that if it launched such an invasion, then the war would end up just like the Korean War: in a stalemate.

3. *The patrician response/Senator Wayne Morse*
Possibly the most prominent Senator who would consistently rail against further involvement in Indochina prior to and after the enactment of the above Resolution was Wayne Morse, senior Senator from Oregon. He would remain firmly opposed to the conflict for its duration.

4. *The semi-patrician response/"Ron Stone"*
One of Senator Morse's "cohorts" in the Senate was one "Ron Stone" who, according to Gottlieb stated that "I was on the floor of the Senate from the beginning of the American involvement in the war in Vietnam." ("Ron Stone" and all of the other individuals detailed by Gottlieb are known herein by pseudonyms). In 1964 "Mr. Stone" was appointed to be a Senate page boy by another Senator. As detailed in *Hell No, We Won't Go!* "Mr. Stone" was consistently subjected to the diatribes from Senator Morse concerning the folly of further escalation of the war. He had no choice. As Head Page, he was required to be on the floor of the Senate at all times. While he was initially supportive of President Johnson's Indochina policies, Senator Morse convinced him that U. S. commitment to greater involvement in Vietnam would be a costly mistake. However, as was the author and many others of his generation, the government would eventually require his participation in the conflict.

5. *The patrician response/Senator Albert Gore*
Also this year Senator Gore was apparently the first Senator to suggest the possibility of a negotiated settlement before the nation became more deeply involved in Vietnam.

The Political Situation In Vietnam, 1964 - 65

It is of course a basic tenet of warfare that when two opposing sides wage war, then the side which appears to prevail has superior resources. From August, 1964 to June, 1965 the forces of North Vietnam and its allies trounced the forces of the South by all accounts. Indeed, it was seldom reported during the entire interval of U. S. involvement in the war from 1964 to 1975 that the South triumphed militarily against the North.

The military victories of the North could have been due to a number of reasons, among them:

- the forces of the North outnumbered those of the South;
- the general populations of the respective "countries" were uneven;
- the triumphant side had a more worthy cause;
- the triumphant side had a greater will to win;
- the triumphant side could avail itself of greater resources, either domestically produced or from external sources;
- the triumphant side had greater popular support.

In 1960 the population of North Vietnam was approximately 18,000,000 according to the official census. That of South Vietnam was reported as 15,500,000 according to estimates. The military forces of the two "countries" were reported as 400,000 (army and militia), and 375,000, (225,000 army, 128,000 local guard and 22,000 U. S. Military Assistance Command), respectively. (Collier's Yearbook, 1965, Covering The Year 1964). The figures for both North and South Vietnam are of course misleading. The Pentagon could only use rough estimates to quantify the numbers of Viet Minh/Viet Cong forces in the South. Some of the South Vietnamese forces were known to be secretly fighting for the North. Bui Diem stated in his memoirs that a high-ranking officer in the South Vietnamese Army was eventually exposed as a double agent on the side of the North.

The above figure of 400,000 for North Vietnam deserves special scrutiny. Inasmuch as the North intensified its efforts to annex its rebellious southern provinces from 1960 to 1972, then the numbers of personnel under arms during this interval would likely have grown considerably. However, the individual who would assume the responsibility for conducting the war from afar by 1972 stated in his memoirs:

> "Almost the entire North Vietnamese Army – an estimated 120,000 troops that had poured across the DMZ during the spring invasion (of 1972) – was still in South Vietnam." (*RN*, p. 690).

The above figure quoted by Commander-In-Chief Nixon thereby indicates a glaring inconsistency. North Vietnam would likely have had considerably more than a mere 120,000 – strong regular army when waging war. Nixon quoted such figures when examining the peace terms which were then under negotiation with North Vietnam and the Viet Cong/Viet Minh. It is therefore apparent that in 1972 Nixon would be negotiating for peace with faulty intelligence.

Be that as it may, by mid-1965 it became apparent that personnel and war materiel were being funneled into South Vietnam from the North by means of a route which became popularly known as The Ho Chi Minh Trail, named after the leader of North Vietnam. These events were widely promulgated throughout the news media. The Trail was a lengthy and circuitous route which began in southern North Vietnam and wound indirectly into the South. Further, the Trail was quite off the beaten path. Indeed, the Trail veered through jungles, over mountains and through swamplands and into neighboring Cambodia and Laos (the other parts of the former French Colonial Empire). This was to the perpetual consternation of the Pentagon.

The Author's Situation, 1964 - 65

In September 1964 the author began his sophomore year in high school. During the entire interval of nine months until June, 1965 he observed that there was little reporting in the media of the events in Vietnam. There were of course events unfolding which would profoundly affect U. S. efforts there. However, these received little mention in the medium which the author most frequently visited: television.

Reports From The Print Media, 1964 - 65

There was frequent and detailed reporting of the activities in Vietnam through the printed media during the interval from August, 1964 to June, 1965. The following is a partial listing of topics of articles published during this interval:

1. *From Vietnam Battlefront: while U. S. hesitates, reds carry war south*
(U. S. News & World Report, 8/3/64)

2. *Misadventure In Vietnam*
(The Nation, 8/24/64)

3. *Negotiate Now!*
(The Nation, 9/7/64)

4. *Is It A Lost War For U. S. In Vietnam?*
(U. S. News & World Report, 9/7/64)

5. *Why U. S. Is Losing The War In Vietnam*
(U. S. News & World Report, 11/9/64)

6. *Along The Ho Chi Minh Trail*
(New York Times Magazine, 11/22/64)

7. *Brief Glimmer: Vietcong launch major assault on Binh Dinh Province*
(Newsweek, 12/21/64)

8. *American Special Forces in Action In Vietnam*
(National Geographic Magazine, 1/65)

9. *Can U. S. Win In Vietnam? – An Inside Report*
(U. S. News & World Report, 1/11/65)

10. *As Vietnam War Gets Bigger: what to look for next*
(U. S. News & World Report, 5/3/65)

The public could therefore avail itself of a detailed view via the print media during this interval of how events were unfolding in Vietnam.

CHAPTER FIVE:
THE YEAR OF THE EMERGENCY
&
THE POINT OF NO RETURN:
THE ADVENT OF *DE FACTO* MILITARY
INTERVENTION,
1965

The obvious Indochina crisis demanded that emergency measures be taken. U. S. leaders recognized that failure to act decisively this year would mean the loss of an ally to the communist sphere. U. S. prestige around the world would then diminish markedly. Combat troops would be the only means to save the cause. The line would be drawn in the sand in Vietnam.

The Domestic Political Situation, 1965

When the existence of the Ho Chi Minh Trail and the victories which the North had achieved made it appear that South Vietnam was about to be overrun, the U. S. began to act aggressively. It was widely reported in the press that emergency measures were needed and indeed were being taken in order to prop up the "Government" Of South Vietnam. Accordingly, this year could be labeled the year that the U. S. recognized the gravity of the situation.

Further, this is the year in which U. S. forces began to bear the brunt of the fighting. In this respect, this was a pivotal year. No longer was the U. S. in Vietnam to act as "advisors." Neither could the government continue to make this claim. To reiterate, the government had previously made U. S. presence there palatable by claiming that military personnel were only there to advise the forces of South Vietnam. To summarize, this can be labeled The Year Of The Emergency. In an emergency, one takes extreme measures to insure that the situation which one has been monitoring does not result in a disaster, i.e., one which is irrevocably lost.

Numerous elements compelled the government to act decisively and to commit combat troops to foreign soil. These were first of all the general public's attitude. Inasmuch as the nation had engaged in a similar conflict recent to the instant one, and had prevailed, then this factor certainly contributed. Then there was the ideological factor rooted in U. S. leaders' pathological fear of communism. Next there was the human factor, in that the President sought to have his name preserved as the leader who acted decisively to neutralize a threat to U. S. interests. An extension of that human factor was the President's desire to be perceived as he who prevailed in a game of "one-upsmanship" with the political party which opposed his own. A further extension of that human factor was that the President had previously acted decisively this same year. He was successful in neutralizing a threat in a nation in close proximity to the U. S. by having committed U. S. troops there. Lastly there was the nation's military capacity which was justly the envy of the rest of the world. These elements will all be detailed below.

a. The attitude of the general public

There was little reaction among the general public concerning the government's decision to increase military aid to South Vietnam. Most Americans either supported the war or regarded increased military intervention as a normal state of affairs. The rest appeared to be indifferent to the military buildup. There were no organized protests to U. S. activities in Vietnam. However, this year saw the advent of what would become a major issue during the war and also that which would symbolize reaction from those directly involved: draft card burning. A group of pacifists was photographed in New York City burning their draft cards. (Collier's Year Book For 1966, Covering The Year 1965, p. 583) These documents were a part of the Selective Service System discussed below. The individuals in question burned their draft cards specifically to voice disapproval of the burgeoning hostilities in Vietnam.

However, according to one source this year was not the first in which there was a documented instance of draft card burning. One source places the first instance and also the advent of a popular phrase which would become in common use as having occurred on 12 May 1964. Gottlieb states that on that date a group of students in New York burned their draft cards and also stated publicly that "We won't go!" (Gottlieb, p. xix).

Apparently in response to the draft card burning, this year Congress amended the current draft law to penalize any person who "forges, alters, knowingly destroys, knowingly mutilates, or in any manner changes any such certificate." As will be revealed later, one such individual named O'Brien who apparently prompted Congress to act in this regard would be a party to a celebrated Supreme Court case.

b The attitude of one senior government official

President Johnson of course had many allies within government who supported his cause. One of these was Senator Richard Russell of Georgia, Chairman of the Senate Armed Services Committee. Senator Russell was a notorious "hawk" concerning Indochina and he would so remain for the rest of his tenure in the Senate. However, Senator Russell was also notorious for his pragmatism. Before the decision was made to commit increased resources to Vietnam, he informed the President that to do so would not be practical. He further opposed the notion that a military victory in Vietnam was necessary to win the Cold War. Lastly, he was reputed by a noted historian to have informed the President that sending more troops to Vietnam would cost the U. S. 50,000 lives and then the U. S. would lose the war. (Michael Beschloss, Presidential Historian, *The Lehrer Report*, 11/24/09). His advice to the President which would prove to be quite prophetic, went unheeded.

c. Analogies with the Korean War

This is the year in which analogies were made between Vietnam and the Korean War of 1950 – 53. From the end of the Korean War in June, 1953 to the official start of the Vietnam War on 5 August 1964 was a period of merely eleven years. The prior war was still fresh in many people's minds. Accordingly, many government leaders and also many in the general public began to compare the two conflicts. It could go without saying that many Korean War veterans were still around. Further, because of the "success" of that war, one could safely say that the majority of such veterans harbored sentiments in favor of U. S. intervention in Indochina. Many of these individuals also likely believed that young persons should be required to perform their military duty as they themselves had been required to do.

Many citizens both within and without government believed that the U. S. had a right and a duty to intervene in order to prevent a communist takeover of South Vietnam. Such sentiments could regularly be observed in respected periodicals such as *Time* Magazine. Many in both circles also believed that the war could and would be won with military intervention. After all, that is what had been accomplished in Korea. That conflict had been fought to a stalemate. Then peace talks were begun which resulted in the two Koreas, North and South, reverting to their original status as two independent states. One government was communist as before and the other was supposedly modeled after that of the U. S. The end result was that U. S. military intervention saved South Korea's sovereignty. The general climate therefore this year concerning Vietnam was: "If we did it before, then we can do it again."

d. The Domino Theory

Another major cornerstone of U. S. rationale for increased involvement in Vietnam was the oft-mentioned "Domino Theory." This phrase was one of those most uttered by government leaders to justify greater military involvement. Simply put, the theory was that if one country (Vietnam, for example) was allowed to "fall" to communism, then all of the other countries in proximity were therefore vulnerable. Those which might lack the will to resist would also fall to communism like the proverbial stack of dominoes. The U. S. would then subsequently be surrounded and then overwhelmed by hostile communist states. The Bastion Of Democracy would therefore eventually succumb to communist subversion. It bears mention that Senator Gore invoked the Domino Theory in his initial support of U. S. escalation of military support for South Vietnam. He would however eventually modify his sentiments considerably.

Perhaps the most glaring peculiarity of the Domino Theory was the contention by some leaders that the U. S. itself would be ultimately and directly threatened by communism. To them the perceived communist threat was not just on foreign nations but also on the very existence of the U. S. as a free entity. This perception was stated explicitly by the President who was Commander-In-Chief when the war began in earnest. President Johnson stated that: "The U. S. must decide whether to help these (Indochina) countries or to throw in the towel and pull back our defenses to San Francisco." (*The Pentagon Papers*, p. 80). He therefore believed that if the U. S. failed to make a strong stand against communism in Asia, then the U. S. would eventually be directly threatened with invasion.

e. Presidential sentiments

The media reported that President Johnson did not desire to be the President who "lost" Vietnam to the communists. This indeed was a goal of each President after Harry Truman. Indeed, Senator Gore stated in *Eye Of The Storm*, (p. 34) that in conversation with President Johnson, the President informed him that after the commitments which Presidents Eisenhower and Kennedy had already made to the cause of freedom for South Vietnam, he (Johnson) "would not be the first President to run."

The Johnson Administration realized this year that its commitment to Vietnam was irrevocable. The nation was in too deep; miscalculations had been made which could not be reversed. Halberstam conveys this point quite clearly when he states, writing of Johnson's policy makers:

> "When they came to make the final, fateful decisions, there would be options, but the real ones would be long since lost; the options they would deal with in 1965 were artificial ones."
>
> and
>
> "...they would be driven to certain inevitable, highly predictable decisions, but they still had the illusion that they could control events." (Halberstam, p. 304).

As Dunnigan and Nofi opined in their book *Dirty Little Secrets Of The Vietnam War*, "the ARVN (Army Of The Republic Of Vietnam) lost the war about 1965. Then the U. S. took over." These incidentally are the individuals who assert that the U. S. did not lose this war.

f. The Political factor: Democrats vs. Republicans

Arguably one of the most significant factors in the decision to escalate U. S. involvement in Vietnam can be traced to the traditional rivalry between the two major political parties. It cannot be overestimated the degree to which politics influenced President Johnson's decision to increase support to South Vietnam. Immediately after the end of World War II when it became apparent that communist ideology was consuming much of the post-war world, this set off a competition between the two major political parties to demonstrate who could hate communism more. The aim was to earn political capital with the electorate. Halberstam often touches on this theme. He further mentions that shortly prior to his death in April, 1945 President Roosevelt conveyed his sentiments on continuing colonialism by Europeans including France and Britain. Roosevelt believed that European colonies such as Vietnam were entitled to be independent of foreign rule. He seemed to be oblivious to what form of government these independent states would eventually adopt. Such sentiments of course were conveyed before the "Red Menace", communist proliferation, became increasingly apparent to government leaders after the Second World War ended.

Often Halberstam refers to the fact that a previous President, Harry Truman, a Democrat, was viewed as the president who had "lost" China to the communists in 1949. This was the year in which the Chinese communists prevailed against the Nationalist forces who were the U. S.' ally. The implication was that if the U. S. had intervened militarily on the side of its friend, then China may not have become communist. Prominent Republicans explicitly made this assertion at that time and for many years after. When the communists prevailed in China and 700,000,000 people then became "enslaved" by communism, this was regarded in some circles as a major failure of U. S. foreign policy. Much of the public accordingly viewed the Democrats as being "soft on communism." This perception in turn was used as a major political weapon by the Republican Party to regain political ground which it had recently lost. Indeed, this is one of the likely reasons why the Republicans regained control of the White House in 1952 and also of both houses of Congress, albeit with a slim majority. In 1954 the composition of Congress would be reversed with the Democrats regaining control of both houses, albeit with a slim majority. Such was the sensitive mood of the electorate. It should be noted that this reversal was in the immediate aftermath of the French defeat in Indochina. It further demands mention that because of the 1954 reversal, the Senate Majority Leader would be one Lyndon Baines Johnson. The individual who would be President during most of the war, Richard Nixon, conceded as much in his memoirs (*RN*, p. 118).

One should further understand that this traditional rivalry between the two major political parties over U. S. war policies would be a major factor for most of the Vietnam War. Indeed, during the height of the war in 1968 the issue of which party could demonstrate greater hatred of communism would resurface. The discourse would cause discord, not only between the two parties but also within one party. On the campaign trail Vice Presidential candidate Spiro Agnew would hurl one of his most vicious attacks on his rivals. He charged that the Democratic candidate for President, Hubert Humphrey, was "squishy soft on communism." This in turn prompted a stalwart Republican, Senator Everett Dirksen, to denounce Agnew's assertion. Senator Dirksen stated that there was no evidence to back up Agnew's claim. Agnew was thereby obliged to retract the mud which he had slung. Such would be the character of the Presidential campaign that year, which would go down in history as the "mud-slingingest" in U. S. history, up to that time.

Further, the issue of rivalry between the two political parties would extend far beyond U. S. borders during the war. Indeed, Nixon who would assume responsibility for the war in 1969, would be compelled to examine this subject in his memoirs. The passage which Nixon would devote in his memoirs to this subject is both stark and startling in its detail of how even the nation's adversaries comprehended how U. S. politics affected the conduct of the war. When the hostilities would be close to concluding, Nixon would travel to the People's Republic Of China in 1972. Notwithstanding the purpose of his visit, he would be compelled to reveal in his memoirs how well the leaders of that nation understood the complexity of the relationship between the Republicans and the Democrats. Describing the exchange between himself and Chou En Lai, a senior member of the Chinese leadership, Nixon examined the situation thusly (quoting Chou En Lai):

> "'The most pressing question now is Indochina, where the whole world is watching', he said. The Democratic Party tried to put you on the spot by alleging that you came to China to settle Vietnam. Of course this is not possible. We are not in a position to settle it in talks.'"
> (*RN*, p. 568).

To reiterate, it cannot be overestimated the degree to which the aforementioned rivalry permeated both U. S. foreign policy and also the conduct of the war. As will be revealed later, the assertion by some government leaders that the U. S. could have intervened militarily in 1949 and therefore stopped China from being "lost" to communism, would return to haunt these proponents when the hostilities would be close to concluding.

Accordingly, the fact that China had apparently been "lost" to the communist sphere in 1949 profoundly affected the political sentiments of every Democratic president after Truman, until the war would eventually end. Therefore, when the U. S. decided to assume the greatest responsibility for the war this year, this was an obvious effort on the part of President Johnson, a Democrat, to prove that his party was not "soft on communism." He was determined not to let another 17,000,000 people suffer having to live under that form of government. This was the estimated population of South Vietnam. (Collier's Yearbook, 1966, Covering The Year 1965).

Lastly, the subject of the rivalry between the Democrats and the Republicans over U. S. war policies would be an issue which would reverberate and cause debate long after the conflict would conclude. In an article in the December 5, 2008 edition of *The New York Times* it would be revealed that during the 1968 presidential election, President Johnson had accused his successor of "treason." This he opined because he had received credible intelligence that Nixon's associates had tried to sabotage Johnson's efforts to end the war in order for Nixon to win the election. These allegations had indeed been revealed at the time that they allegedly occurred. However, inasmuch as these phenomena would be resurrected forty years after they had allegedly occurred, then this is another glaring example of how Vietnam is a war that won't go away. This issue will be discussed in greater detail below.

g. The Dominican Republic factor

U. S. intervention in Indochina was not the only U. S. military intervention into the civil war of another country this year. Just before the Vietnam incursion, in April President Johnson sent 22,000 combat troops to the Dominican Republic. The stated reason for intervening was ostensibly to restore order. That country was in the throes of civil unrest which stemmed from a dispute between communist forces and those opposed to them. Of course the U. S. favored the latter. U. S. State Department officials believed that the communist faction was about to take over that government. The State Department's rationale was therefore that the intervention was justified. When impartial observers accused the U. S. of aiding the anti-communists, U. S. officials denied this claim. However, this accusation then proved to be fact.

U. S. intervention in the Dominican Republic would ordinarily have little bearing on the affairs of Vietnam. Halberstam asserts (p. 574) that there was however a link between the two interventions which were 8,000 miles apart. He details President Johnson's flagrant optimism that the U. S. could prevail militarily in Vietnam because it prevailed in the Dominican Republic intervention. Also, as with U. S. intervention in Korea fifteen years previously, the prevailing mentality in the government was "We did it before. We can do it again." Accordingly, as Halberstam suggests, the Dominican Republic intervention set the stage for the intervention in Vietnam. President Johnson apparently made an analogy between what the U. S. had accomplished in the Dominican Republic with what the U. S. hoped and expected to achieve in Vietnam: the denial of a country to the communist sphere of influence.

The intervention in the Dominican Republic was short-lived, however. By the end of June U. S. troops had been withdrawn. As of this writing the Dominican Republic embraces democracy.

h. Military capacity

Lastly, the U. S. obviously believed that it could prevail in Vietnam because of its military hardware, expenditures on the military and also the infrastructure which these expenditures purchased. World War II had reaffirmed the U. S. as the preeminent military power on this planet. In addition to the hardware which included sizeable numbers of ships, tanks and airplanes, the U. S. also had (and still has) a formidable nuclear capability in its arsenal.

Military hardware and the will to use it are of course no good unless a nation has trained personnel. The other element which the U. S. had at the inception of the Vietnam War was, in addition to a highly trained and well equipped professional military, the Selective Service System.

The Selective Service System, 1965

a. How the System was supposed to be administered

The means which the U. S. had to fuel its military with personnel, apart from the normal screening and recruitment process, was formally known as the Selective Service System (SSS), popularly known as the "draft." The system had originally been put in place by Congress in 1940 when it became apparent that the nation could become involved in the Second World War (WW II). The law by which the government invoked its right to conscript men into the military during the Vietnam War was formally known as The Universal Military Training and Service Act Of 1948 (as amended, 1951).

Since the end of WW II and with the advent of the Vietnam War the Selective Service System went through profound changes. By this year when vast numbers of personnel were needed to meet the "emergency" in Vietnam, the System had evolved into one in which all males were required to register therein within thirty days after their eighteenth birthday. After registration, each individual was assigned to one of the various classifications which would determine the order in which the individual would be liable for military service. Some major provisions of the Selective Service System were that:

- it only applied to males between the ages of 18 and 26;

- it was administered by a national network of draft boards staffed by civilians from the communities in which they lived, which board had jurisdiction over all persons eligible in such community;

- a cornerstone of the SSS was *registration* of all those included in the aforementioned age group;

- certain persons were exempted from military service under the law which created the SSS (ordained priests, those studying for the ministry or towards a college degree, habitual users of illegal narcotics, homosexuals), but even these had to register with their local boards;

- the SSS exempted individuals by the means of deferments. If one believed that he merited an exemption from immediate induction, then he could apply for a deferment on one of the grounds specified in the law;

- certain persons who objected to participation in war were designated *conscientious objectors* and were not required to request a deferment, but only if they could convince their local board of the validity of their sentiments. However, the law allowed for even these persons to be conscripted. It was also specified in the law however that conscripted conscientious objectors were to be assigned to noncombatant military service.

Further, individual states could also tailor their own laws on how veterans who had conscientiously objected to war could be treated. As indicated in the author's first published work, *Veterans Employment Preference Statutes: a state-by-state and Federal Government handbook*, one state bars veteran conscientious objectors from receiving employment preference based on prior military service;

- any person who sought to avoid or evade the applicable law would be subjected to penalties up to and including imprisonment for a period not exceeding five years and a fine not exceeding $10,000;

- all persons registered with the System were required to have a card which indicated the classification to which the individual had been assigned. The individual was required to carry the card on his person;

- The various draft classifications began at I-A which was the highest, and then descended to minor classifications depending on the needs of the government. Depending on the severity of hostilities in which the U. S. was involved, the government would enter the next lowest classification until the level of manpower needed to staff the military was reached. It was never documented during the war that the government reached lower than the I-Y classification;

- The draft did not apply uniquely to the Army.

As will be revealed later, the law and the SSS would go through profound changes during the course of the war. This is because of the controversy which the System would generate, and because the System was such an integral part of the war. Indeed, the System would have quite profound and lasting effects on the fabric of American society and in the lives of many men, including the author.

As will further be revealed later after the war had concluded, in 1977 it would be uncovered that there had been a small hole in the law in question. To reiterate, the cornerstone of the law was *registration*.

All individuals who might have come under the System's jurisdiction were supposed to register therein. However, the government would become aware during the Administration of President Jimmy Carter two years after the war would conclude, that many individuals had not so registered when the law had been in effect. Further, cognizant officials would understand in 1977 that there was no way the government could determine who these non-registrants were in order for them to be located and properly disciplined for having so failed to act.

The Selective Service System classifications in effect for the duration of the war were:

I-A: registrant available for military service

I-A-O: conscientious objector available for non-combatant military service

I-C: member of the Armed Forces, the Coast And Geodetic Survey or the Public Health Service

I-D: qualified member of a reserve component, or a student taking military training including the Reserve Officer Training Corps (R. O. T. C.) or accepted for aviation cadet training

I-O: conscientious objector available for civilian work contributing to the maintenance of the national health, safety or interest

I-S: student deferred by law until graduation from high school or attainment of the age of twenty, or until the end of his academic year at a college or university

I-W: conscientious objector performing civilian work contributing to the maintenance of the national health, safety or interest, or who has completed such work

I-Y: qualified for military service only in time of war or national emergency

II-A: occupational deferment other than agricultural or student

II-C: agricultural deferment

II-S: student deferment

III-A: extreme hardship deferment or registrant with a child or children

IV-A: registrant with sufficient prior active military service or who is a sole surviving son

IV-B: official deferred by law

IV-C: alien not currently liable for military service
IV-D: minister of religion or divinity student
IV-F: not qualified for any military service
V-A: over the age of liability for military service

Persons who embraced provision I-D became commonplace during the conflict. An individual could avoid active military service by joining the National Guard. Such affiliation would likely preclude the individual from active service. It has been documented that many individuals who might have otherwise been liable for such service, avoided such by service in the National Guard. As will be revealed later, this category would include some prominent members of U. S. society.

b. How the System was actually administered
1. *Preston King*

The Selective Service System as a Federal law was of course supposed to be administered on a non-discriminatory basis. All classes and all ethnicities were to be treated the same in being evaluated and called for military service. Whether the case of Preston King occurred during the instant war is a subject of debate. To reiterate, the official start *de jure* of the Vietnam War was 5 August 1964. However, according to the U. S. Department Of Commerce, the advent of the war occurred several years earlier. Refer to Figure 3. The figures therein which declare the advent of the war to be 1961, were taken from the Statistical Abstract Of The U. S. Accordingly, the circumstances in which Preston King found himself actually occurred during the Vietnam Conflict. During the war the SSS was not administered equitably among all ethnicities. It was accordingly in violation of Federal law.

Mr. King, a native of Georgia and an African-American, was treated differently than the European – Americans who were under the jurisdiction of his draft board. In 1958 members of the latter group were addressed by that board as "Mr. _____." Mr. King was addressed by that draft board as "Preston." Believing that he was a victim of racial discrimination, he protested by refusing to be examined for military service. He was subsequently indicted, prosecuted and convicted in 1961 of violation of the applicable law by an all European-American jury. He was then sentenced to eighteen months in a Federal prison. Mr. King had stated that he was willing to report for a physical examination and also serve in the military if his draft board would address him in the same manner as it did the European-Americans. His draft board had refused.

All of the above occurred after Mr. King had graduated *magna cum laude* from Fisk University (TN). Before his refusal to be examined for military service, he had requested an additional deferment to pursue graduate studies at the London (England) School Of Economics. His draft board refused to grant the additional deferment. It bears mention that when the war would peak in 1968, manpower needs for the military would be so great that the Selective Service System would end graduate school deferments. Prior to 1968, requests for such deferments were routinely approved. In the matter of Mr. King, the situation was further complicated by the fact that when he was released on bail after his refusal, he then fled the country to pursue his studies. As will be revealed later, the plight of Mr. King would eventually merit a footnote in the annals of the Vietnam War.

2. *George Hamilton*

In his book *Confronting The War Machine: draft resistance during the Vietnam War,* Michael Foley confirms what many knew during the war: that the Selective Service System was not administered equitably among all classes. Indeed, the lack of uniformity in the administration of the System incurred the wrath of a Congressman. In June, 1966 when the war would be rapidly escalating, and as a consequence many men were being drafted, one Alvin O'Konski lamented the unfairness of the System. He represented a Wisconsin district in the House Of Representatives. He complained publicly that many of the men drafted from his district came from homes of quite modest means. He then compared the plight of these men with that of one George Hamilton. Mr. Hamilton was a popular movie star with a six figure income. However, he had a III-A Extreme Hardship deferment because he was supporting his mother. His mother also had had four husbands. In addition, Mr. Hamilton was frequently seen in public with one Lynda Johnson, daughter of the President. This was prior to her marriage to one Charles Robb, a Marine Corps officer the next year. Mr. Robb would eventually figure prominently in U. S. society.

The point of the above is that the provisions of the Selective Service System were not administered equally across the board at that time. Further, it has never been documented that, in the case of Preston King, the government took steps at that time or at anytime during the war to correct the above inequities in the way that the System was administered.

3. *Richard Cheney*

One of those whose life was not affected by the draft was one Richard Cheney. This year he graduated from college and was then classified 1-A, eligible for immediate call-up by the President. He was however married, but with no children. His marriage status protected him from immediate call-up. Accordingly, he was not one of the 230,991 men who President Johnson ordered into military service this year. However, this year would see Cheney further deferred from military service when he entered graduate school in November, receiving a requested II-S student deferment. Accordingly, the fact that the SSS had already removed its ban on drafting married men with no children was immaterial to Cheney. However, despite that he would never serve in the military, as will be revealed later Cheney would eventually figure prominently in U. S. society.

It is ironic that this major component of the military infrastructure which was deemed so vital to the war would eventually also prove to be one critical element in the war effort's undoing. Further, as will be revealed later it is also likely that the public's perception of the SSS hastened the end of the war.

The Federal Judicial Perspective On The Draft Law, 1965

Possibly the greatest point of contention between the government concerning the draft law and those subjected to it was the question of who was fit to serve. An individual named Seeger had challenged the law concerning his claim of conscientious objection. His draft board denied his claim. A major question was whether an individual was bound to embrace a *bona fide* religious faith in order to claim and then be granted exemption from service based on his conscientious objection. Seeger was an admitted pacifist, but he did not embrace any religious faith. The Supreme Court thereupon ruled this year that confirmed pacifists are indeed conscientious objectors, irrespective of their religious background. (*U. S.* v *Seeger*, 380 U. S. 163).

The U. S. Military Presence In Vietnam, 1965

It is noteworthy that the U. S. mission in Vietnam was never clearly delineated. Also, the number of troops which the Pentagon believed was needed was never accurately quantified. On this point Halberstam dwells at length. He revealed for example (p. 597) that this year in a policy meeting among all of the principals, the designated Commander of U. S. forces, General Westmoreland, stated that the number of troops necessary would depend on any number of variables. However, the number of such troops should be capped at 175,000, he stated. He opined that this was the maximum number which should be allocated before the South Vietnamese would give up and then let the U. S. do most of the fighting. As will be revealed later, this expected reluctance by the South Vietnamese to fight their war is indeed what eventually would come to pass.

By the end of the year the number of U. S. military personnel in Vietnam was approximately 200,000. Most of the personnel who were there in the first part of the year were still not actively engaged in combat, however. Rather, they were primarily engaged in the "support" activities of the Army component known as the Green Berets, discussed below. The only U. S. combat units then in Vietnam were a few tactical squadrons of the Air Force. (Collier's Year Book For The Year 1966 Covering The Year 1965).

The individual who would soon become South Vietnam's Ambassador to the U. S. would utter quite profound sentiments on the dual issues of the numbers of U. S. troops there and also the manner in which the U. S. waged the war. Bui Diem stated in his memoirs that the introduction of large numbers of U. S. troops this year was substantially done unilaterally. The Vietnamese were not consulted. He further stated that the U. S. seldom, during the entire course of U. S. involvement, consulted with the ally concerning the deployment of U. S. troops or about the bombing of targets within South Vietnam. In his summation of the "Americanization" of the war this year he stated:

"...the Americans took full responsibility for waging war. Gen. Westmoreland ... formulated a three-pronged strategy that consisted of 'search and destroy operations', then 'clear and hold' or mopping up, operations, and finally 'securing operations', in which Saigon troops would establish authority over pacified villages." (Bui Diem, p. 155).

The Domestic Political Situation Of A U. S. Ideological Ally, 1965

U. S. intervention in Indochina was borne of an avowed contempt of communist ideology. In this respect the U. S. had many allies around the world. One of the most prominent of these was the vast Southeast Asian archipelago known as Indonesia. This nation was prominent because of its population of 106,000,000 and also because of its oil wealth. That nation however is separated by a considerable distance from Indochina, and also in most other respects. Accordingly, a geo-politicist would be hard pressed to make analogies between the two. However, some senior U. S. politicians attempted to do just that. The most prominent of these was President Johnson. Another person who echoed his sentiments was one of his principal cohorts in escalating U. S. involvement in Vietnam: Secretary Of Defense Robert S. McNamara.

The sentiments of the above two persons concerning the containment of communism in Southeast Asia can be observed in The Pentagon Papers, discussed below. Both of these individuals attempted to make comparisons between the two countries in question in order to justify U. S. intervention in Vietnam. The statements which they made on this issue, which were recorded in the Pentagon Papers, clearly demonstrate that the two men based their reasoning on fallacial assumptions.

A memorandum from Secretary McNamara to President Kennedy dated November 8, 1961 which was detailed in the Pentagon Papers (p. 148, document # 29) deserves special mention. In the memo, he informed the President:

"... the fall of South Vietnam to Communism would lead to the fairly rapid extension of communist control, or complete accommodation to Communism in the rest of mainland Southeast Asia and in Indonesia."

That statement by Secretary McNamara is possibly the most glaring example of how flawed U. S. reasoning was in assessing the threat of communism. Accordingly, this assessment by senior government leaders is evidence that their fear of communism which instigated the military buildup in Vietnam was not only based on false assumptions, but that it had also reached the level of hysteria.

In light of the above, it should be noted that what occurred this year in Southeast Asia can be labeled another "quirk" of history. Two seemingly unrelated events occurred virtually simultaneously and in close proximity. They were linked by the fact that both stemmed from the same ideology. In October, simultaneous with the U. S. military buildup in Vietnam, Indonesia experienced a most profound upheaval. Such an event had never occurred before or since the Russian Revolution in 1917. That year the Russian Government which was headed by an autocratic, capitalist Czar was overthrown by communist ideologues. The Czar and his family were among those murdered in a bloody upheaval.

It must be noted that Indonesia was not a member of the aforementioned Southeast Asia Treaty Organization (S. E. A. T. O.). The U. S. could therefore not count Indonesia as its ally, by treaty, in its effort to halt the spread of communism. However, the events which unfolded at this time is proof conclusive that nations other than the U. S. had a pathological fear of communism.

The events in Indonesia which stunned the world were detailed in the October 18 issue of *U. S. News & World Report* in an article entitled "One place communists met a setback" (pp. 46 – 48). Indonesia at this time was wracked with strife, primarily between the communist and anti-communist factions. The President definitely leaned towards the former. Many government leaders however opposed his efforts to institute communist-style reforms in every area of that society. It also bears mention that many of them were fiercely loyal to their faith, Islam. The ideals of that faith and those of communism are diametrically opposed, hence the apparent reason why the Indonesian Communist Party (P. K. I.) was annihilated during September – October.

In keeping with the vow which the founders of the first communist state on this planet had made in 1917, that communism will only prevail through bloody revolution, the P. K. I. initiated an armed coup against the government on 30 September. The ploy didn't work. The reaction to the attempted coup was not what the P. K. I. expected. There then ensued a popular uprising led by the army which was staunchly anti-communist. President Sukarno tried to prevent the bloodletting, but he failed.

The most profound aspect of the reaction to the attempted coup was that the annihilation of the communists reached beyond the army. The slaughter was primarily carried out by mobs of bloodthirsty demonstrators who roamed the streets at will, especially in the capital, Jakarta, to hunt down and kill any known communist. They further demanded that the P. K. I. be outlawed. Another most profound repercussion of the massacre was that the mobs were reputed to have been heard shouting "Long Live America." It is also noteworthy that the P. K. I. has never resurfaced in Indonesia. The message conveyed by the Army and by the mobs was therefore clear: that the majority of the people of Indonesia does not like communists.

One should understand that the above events were the worst nightmare which the U. S. had envisioned: a large, powerful communist party within a government ideologically friendly to the U. S., attempting to seize control by force of arms. Further, it was known that the elements which began the coup were openly backed by the People's Republic Of China, an arch-nemesis of the U. S.

The lesson of the above events were clear, or they should have been: that if a nation is truly opposed to communism, and it has the will to resist the elements of their society which advocate that ideology, then it will act decisively to neutralize the threat. It therefore needs no help from the United States. Again, these events occurred at the precise time that the U. S. was providing generous military and economic aid to the "government" of South Vietnam to aid it in fighting a communist threat. This of course raises the question: Did the majority of South Vietnamese at this time actually oppose the communist threat within their "country's" borders?

It is further worth noting that the aforementioned memorandum from Secretary Of Defense McNamara to President Kennedy was approximately four years previously to the date that the massacre occurred. Further, in a memorandum dated January 13, 1962 from the Joint Chiefs (the government's most senior military advisory board to civilian authority) to Secretary McNamara entitled "Possible Eventualities' if South Vietnam should be 'lost' to communism" (p. 153, Document #31, The Pentagon Papers), the Joint Chiefs echoed the sentiments of their civilian leaders.

Evidence of how profound the aforementioned bloodbath was can be seen in its dramatization in a motion picture to which the Academy Of Motion Picture Arts And Sciences awarded an "Oscar": *The Year Of Living Dangerously* (1983).

The Diplomatic Arena, 1965

a. U. S. Overtures To North Vietnam

Of course there were efforts to resolve the hostilities via diplomacy. U. S. officials made overtures to opponents of U. S. interests in Vietnam. Possibly the most prominent of these were the overtures to North Vietnam and its leader, Ho Chi Minh. In the midst of massive bombing raids over North Vietnam, coupled with large numbers of combat troops, President Johnson offered to participate in unconditional peace talks. Ho Chi Minh rejected this offer and instead detailed specific points which he proposed to be discussed at any subsequent talks. Among these points were that the U. S. (1) withdraw all of its forces from Vietnam, (2) end its military alliance with the South and (3) halt the bombing of the North.

b. Overtures From European Allies To North Vietnam

Further, it was reported that other countries such as Britain and Italy sent peace feelers to North Vietnam. Both of these countries were of course allied with the U. S. economically as well as militarily. These efforts by them were not fruitful, however. Ho Chi Minh stated in response to the peace feelers that his "country" would fight for at least another twenty years to achieve its goal of a unified Vietnam under a communist government. This estimate of the time needed to prevail in the conflict would prove to be extravagant.

c. U. S. Overtures To European Allies To Enlist Support For The War

Inasmuch as the U. S. was allied with many European nations, both ideologically and militarily through the North Atlantic Treaty Organization (N.A.T.O.), the U. S. of course expected that some of these nations would support the war. Throughout this year the U. S. pressured its European allies to contribute military support. These diplomatic efforts to gather support for the war were ignored.

The Author's Situation, 1965

The author began his junior year in high school in September. Here was his first exposure in an academic setting to a discussion of the merits of the nation's deepening involvement in Vietnam. His history teacher was a staunch proponent of the war. She freely expressed her sentiments which advocated increased U. S. support of South Vietnam to remain free. The author also was a supporter of the war, in that he saw nothing wrong with the U. S. coming to the aid of its allies. His general attitude was that if President Johnson was behind it, then it must be O. K.

One of the most important phenomena which the author observed during this interval was that many of his peers had no objections to military service. Indeed, his cousin "G" had been drafted into the U. S. Air Force immediately upon his graduation from high school in January. "G" had no objections to serving in the military, and indeed he seemed to welcome the opportunity to improve his life. He believed that serving in the Armed Forces would enable him to "find himself." Also, the author's older brother "M" desired to join the U. S. Navy upon his scheduled graduation from high school in June. "M" was not "Gung Ho" on the war. Rather, he had heard of the military lifestyle from his acquaintances who had joined the military. He believed that he could "groove" on the military lifestyle. However, he was not allowed to join the Navy because of personal circumstances. In addition, the author met an individual shortly after the Indochina buildup began who was the son of a friend of his family. All this individual could talk about was enlisting in the U. S. Air Force upon his scheduled graduation from high school in 1968.

In addition to his family, the author also observed that many of his high school classmates were embracing military service. None of these individuals appeared to be "Gung Ho" on the war. Rather, they seemed to regard military service as a normal means to improve their lives. Some dropped out of high school because they could not handle the rigors of high school academics. They then voluntarily joined the military. Still more graduated and then joined the military as planned. An astute observer at the time might wonder why the government needed a draft when so many young persons were joining the military.

Lastly, it bears mention that military service was such an accepted part of life for young persons at this time that when some of such persons began to question the rationale for the war, and consequently questioned military service in general, there is one documented instance of a pro-draft rally. Such occurred at The University Of Pittsburgh. (Collier's Year Book For The Year 1966, Covering The year 1965, p. 582). This event was likely the first and last of such rallies during the war.

The Popular Culture, 1965

No sentiments concerning the war were voiced in popular song this year. There was however a song released which expressed anger and cynicism concerning the atmosphere in the U. S., and war in general. Indeed, the song appeared out of place because it was out of time. The song appears to have been released three years too early because the national mood would not become angry and cynical over the war until 1968, as will be revealed later. However, the song would eventually become known as a prophetic song. It also holds the distinction of being the angriest U. S. song ever recorded, up to that time. There would however be more and angrier popular songs recorded and released in the U. S. during the war, apparently in reaction to the conflict.

The song which was to become known as the first antiwar song of the Vietnam Era was *Eve Of Destruction*, recorded by the folk singer Barry McGuire. As the song went:

> "You're old enough to kill, but not for votin'
> You don't believe in war, so what's that gun you're totin'?
> And even the Jordan River has bodies floatin'
> And you don't believe we're on the *Eve Of Destruction*."
> (Copyright © 1965, Universal Music Corp.).

Further, the song was recorded and released at the approximate time that the U. S. recognized the emergency in Vietnam. The releasing label was the independent Dunhill. To reiterate, there were no large scale organized protests concerning U. S. intervention in Vietnam this year. However, the song-buying public propelled *Eve Of Destruction* to the #1 spot on the national music charts the week of August 28. Record collectors are still debating whether the song was written and recorded as a reaction to the military buildup in Vietnam, or if the two events merely coincided.

And the beat continued ...

CHAPTER SIX:
THE YEAR OF THE NATIONAL MISSION: ESCALATION OF THE WAR; THE ADVENT OF THE ANTI-WAR MOVEMENT, 1966

Ever self-confident, the U. S. fulfilled its treaty commitment to its friend. Mobilization of the vast resources it had at its command would mean that the U. S. would prevail in its effort to oppose alien philosophies. It was a part of the national psyche that no earthly power could impede the most efficient war machine the world had ever seen. This armor would however start to disintegrate from within.

The National Mood Over The War, 1966

Nineteen sixty-six began with much patriotic fervor. As such, this year can be regarded as the Year Of The National Mission. Most Americans still either supported the war, or were indifferent to such, or regarded it as a normal course of events. In the first half of the year there were no large scale protests concerning the war. This would soon change.

One popular song which appeared to foretell the controversy which would eventually characterize the national mood, was recorded by the folk singing duo Simon & Garfunkel. The song entitled *Silent Night/The 7:00 News* was the traditional Christmas song superimposed over a recitation of prominent news events during the year. In addition to reporting the death of comedian Lenny Bruce, the "newscaster" also reported former Vice President Richard Nixon's opinion of the unfolding conflict. Nixon was reputed to have stated that unless there was an immediate substantial increase in U. S. aid to South Vietnam, then the U. S. could look forward to five more years of war. That is, the former Vice President apparently expected that the war would last at least until January, 1971. The former Vice President further was alleged to have opined that the greatest opposition to the war would likely come from within the U. S., rather than from without. These alleged sentiments would indeed prove to be prophetic.

In addition, apparently because of the stature which he previously enjoyed in government, Nixon apparently traveled to South Vietnam as a private citizen in order to observe U. S. efforts there. The circumstances of his apparent visit would be resurrected in the 1988 film *Good Morning, Vietnam*. The star of that film, the comedian Robin Williams made light of Nixon's visit in 1966. Stated Mr. Williams as the character Adrian Cronauer (paraphrased): "Former Vice President Richard Nixon is in town. That's right, 'The Big Dick' is here. Get ready!"

However, the national mood concerning the war was mostly upbeat in 1966. Perhaps the most glaring example of the national mood was reflected in popular song. A member of the military, one Army Staff Sergeant (SSgt) Barry Sadler, co-wrote with one Robin Moore and recorded a song entitled *The Ballad Of The Green Berets*. This component of the Army was considered the elite, of which SSgt Sadler was a member.

Moreover, he seemed to believe in what he was doing in support of his Commander-In Chief. As the song went:

> "Fighting soldiers from the sky,
> Fearless men who jump and die.
> One hundred men they'll test today.
> But only three win the green beret."
> (Copyright © 1965, Barry Sadler & Robin Moore).

As indicated in the lyric, many applied to be among this elite component of the Army. However, few were chosen because of the rigorous training and high standards required of its members. According to Hans Halberstadt in his book *Green Berets: Unconventional Warriors*, the principal skill and mission of these Special Forces is "to lead novice warriors to defeat larger conventional forces." Their mission was not to confront the enemy directly on the battlefield. Rather, they operated clandestinely to disrupt the enemy's operations. As such, they were the counterpart to the enemy's guerilla tactics. Indeed, the Green Berets were a primary component of the government's effort to secure the "hearts and minds" of the Vietnamese. This phrase "hearts and minds" would become one of the most enduring of the jargon which came into common use during the war. The Green Berets were used quite extensively in Vietnam. Of the 20,000 military personnel in that "country" in the first part of 1965, 13,000 of these were Army Special Forces working directly with units of The Army Of The Republic Of Vietnam (ARVN). (Collier's Year Book For The Year 1966, For The Year 1965).

What is most pertinent about the aforementioned recording is that it was released by a major record label, The Radio Corporation Of America (RCA). SSgt Sadler had no prior exposure as a recording artist. He was virtually unknown outside of the military. Accordingly, because such a major label would record SSgt Sadler and then release his recordings, in itself is testimony to the degree to which the popular culture embraced the government's war effort. The record-buying public embraced the song to the #1 spot on the national music charts the week of February 19. It was to remain there for five weeks. An album of a slightly modified title would also reach #1 the week of March 12. The album *Ballads Of The Green Berets* also contained the songs *Letter From Vietnam, Badge Of Courage, Saigon, Salute To The Nurses, The Soldier Has Come Home* and lastly, *Trooper's Lament*. With the exception of *The Ballad Of The Green Berets*, SSgt Sadler had composed all of the songs after he had been wounded in Vietnam while leading a combat patrol. The wound resulted from his being caught in a booby trap. He was then evacuated to CONUS and then given light duty.

The Ballad Of The Green Berets also holds the distinction of being the first and only U. S. popular song which expressed sentiments in favor of the war, or a component thereof. Only one other popular song, discussed below, was released this year concerning some aspect of the conflict. Also, as will be revealed later no popular song was subsequently released during the course of the war which echoed patriotism. The release of *The Ballad Of The Green Berets* and its LP counterpart accordingly represent the high point of patriotic sentiments expressed in popular song. The national mood concerning the war reached a plateau during 1966 and a portion of the following year. However, as will be revealed later a number of forces would come into play to cause the national mood over the war to deteriorate markedly.

Perception Of U. S. Efforts In Indochina By The International Community, 1966

The United States was of course a member of the United Nations (U. N.), having signed on as a charter member in 1945. Anytime a conflict began between or among nations, then the U. N. would as a matter of course initiate efforts to resolve the cause of the dispute. *Great Debates At The U. N.: an encyclopedia of fifty key issues, 1945 – 2000* described the question concerning Vietnam, thusly:

> "The civil war in Vietnam was a multifaceted situation involving the disposition of French colonial rule, the independence of Vietnam, the interplay of communist and Western democratic ideologies, foreign intervention, superpower relations, and Cold War ideology."

It is an all-but-forgotten fact that the United States brought the matter of Vietnam to the attention of the U. N. Security Council (which debated the most prominent issues brought before that body) this year. However, the debate over the issue of Vietnam was muted, primarily because of the veto power held by both the U. S. and by the Soviet Union, two members of the Security Council. The matter was further complicated by the fact that neither North nor South Vietnam were members of the U. N. At least one member of the Security Council however, the Netherlands, raised the issue that the Council was permitted by the U. N. Charter to entertain any issue involving threats to peace and security anywhere, regardless of whether the nations in question were members of the U. N. Accordingly, because of the discord among the members, especially within the Security Council, no formal debate on the issue of Vietnam was ever held. Therefore, the U. S. suffered no sanctions from the U. N. because of its war policies.

The Advent Of The Anti-war Movement, 1966

a. The case of Muhammad Ali, a.k.a. Cassius Clay

Possibly the first crack in the positive national mood over the war, in addition to the aforementioned documented draft card burning, occurred early in the year. After it was promulgated that the military buildup in Vietnam was occurring, one of the first indications of dissent or disinterest in the war came from an unlikely source. On 7 January when questioned about his opinion of the war, the heavyweight boxing champion Muhammad Ali stated during a press conference that: "I got no quarrel with no Viet Congs."

When Mr. Ali uttered his disinterest in the war, he did several things. First of all he was guilty of a misnomer, though probably not intentionally. The term "Viet Cong" was not the term by which that indigenous guerilla force was first known. According to the Encyclopedia Britannica Micropedia Ready Reference, 15th Ed. (2005), the term "Viet Cong" is an abbreviation of the phrase "Viet Nam Cong San." The term "Viet Cong" was reputed to have been coined by the President Of South Vietnam Ngo Dinh Diem. It was apparently meant as a derogatory term to denigrate the cause of the indigenous force which opposed him. The term "Viet Minh" on the other hand is an abbreviation of the phrase "Viet Nam Doc Lap Dong Minh Hoi", or League For The Independence Of Vietnam. The Viet Minh was the first to fight against an invader, the Japanese. After that invader was driven out in 1945, and before the French returned, the Viet Minh was the first political organization to assert that it was the legitimate government of all of Vietnam. Perhaps this is why, during the instant war when an enemy was captured on the battlefield after the U. S. arrived, and the captive was interrogated about his affiliation with the Viet Cong, he would sometimes state: "I not Viet Cong. I Viet Minh."

It is also a pertinent fact that the term "Viet Minh" was the term which the U. S. initially used to describe the indigenous communist forces in Vietnam. The appellation "Viet Minh" can be seen in much of the first part of The Pentagon Papers, discussed below. For some reason however which has never been explained, the Papers began to use the term "Viet Cong." This last term was used throughout the rest of the Papers. It is also the phrase by which the indigenous forces which opposed the U. S. will forever be remembered.

Second, when Mr. Ali uttered his disinterest in the war he made an irrelevant statement. Previously, when he initially registered with the Selective Service System in 1960 he was examined and subsequently found to be unfit for military service on mental grounds. Upon taking the written exam he scored in the lowest mental category, I-Y. When questioned about this in an interview in *Playboy* Magazine in October, 1964 Mr. Ali stated: "I have said I am The Greatest. Ain't nobody ever heard me say I was the smartest." These facts he also detailed in his autobiography, *The Greatest: My Own Story*. When he failed the mental aptitude test he was given a classification below that which would have made him eligible for immediate call-up for military service. By some accounts, the government had an abundance of individuals designated I-A, the highest draft classification. The number of persons above Mr. Ali on the register would likely have precluded him from ever being inducted because of the unique circumstances of the war at that time. To reiterate, the Vietnam War was a limited, undeclared conflict. It was not a declared war on the scale of World War II. Accordingly, Mr. Ali therefore would likely not have been inducted unless Congress declared a national emergency such as had been recognized on December 7, 1941.

The advent of that war, incidentally, occurred at the approximate time of Mr. Ali's birth in January, 1942. Only such an emergency would likely have required persons below the primary draft classification, I-A, to be conscripted.

Third, in addition to mis-speaking on the issue, Mr. Ali also apparently incurred the wrath of government officials. Shortly after he uttered his disinterest in the war, his draft classification was changed to I-A. He was subsequently notified that he would be inducted into the Army. However, when he reported to an Armed Forces Examining and Entrance Station as ordered, he refused to step forward to be inducted. This effort to induct him occurred despite his prior claim of and application for the aforementioned conscientious objector status. The same year he refused to be inducted, he was indicted for violation of the Universal Military Training And Service Act. As will be revealed later, this entire affair would receive much media attention throughout much of the war.

Fourth, Mr. Ali's stated disinterest in the war compounded the wrath directed against him by much of the public two years earlier. On 25 February 1964 in an upset he won the heavyweight boxing title from the then-reigning champion, Charles "Sonny" Liston. Shortly thereafter he announced that he was a member of an organization then known as the "Black Muslims." This religious sect was greatly feared and despised by much of white America, and also scorned by much of black America. However, as will be revealed later, another large component of the American public of all hues would eventually gravitate to his side or at least became sympathetic to his sentiments. Lastly, though likely not by choice Mr. Ali would eventually become during the first part of the conflict, arguably the most visible and powerful symbol of the national division over the war.

Further, the controversy which Mr. Ali generated offers a glaring example of the discord over the war which existed within certain segments of society, including the black community. A most glaring example of such discord could be observed during a filmed interview with the baseball player Jackie Robinson shortly after the conflict began. He was questioned about his views on Mr. Ali's objection to military service. He stated that he believed Mr. Ali was wrong. Mr. Robinson, an Army veteran of WWII, having served as a commissioned officer, stated that the pugilist should want to enter the military to set an example to other young "Negroes" (as blacks were commonly described then). Mr. Robinson opined that Mr. Ali should want to be a symbol of the black community's support for the war. Apparently in response to the opinion of Mr. Robinson and others of the same mind, Mr. Ali stated at that time (paraphrased):

> "Why should me and other so-called Negroes go 10,000 miles from America to drop bombs and bullets against other brown people?"

Mr. Ali's views on the war were documented in a Public Broadcasting System (P.B.S.) documentary about him which would be produced in 2007. The program entitled *Made In Miami* chronicled the career of the pugilist which substantially began in that Florida city. Much of the program also was devoted to Mr. Ali's battles outside of the ring, especially his conflict with the government concerning his disinterest in the war. Many of Mr. Ali's biographers and sports writers were interviewed in the aforementioned documentary. Stated one of these, a European-American sports writer: "He didn't want to be a black man sent by white men to kill brown men."

It also bears mention that Mr. Ali was known at the time as "The Louisville Lip." He earned this appellation because of his penchant for uttering colorful prose on a variety of subjects. He is an African-American and also a native of Kentucky. The following passage from the statutes of that state which were in effect this year is indicative of the state of U. S. race relations at that time:

> **Sec. 2097, Marriage – between what persons prohibited and void**. Marriage is prohibited and declared void: 2. Between a white person and a negro or mulatto.

> **Sec. 2114. Parties contracting in void marriage – punishment of**. Any party to a marriage between a white person and a negro or mulatto, shall be fined not less than five hundred nor more than five thousand

dollars, and if, after conviction, the parties continue to cohabit as man and wife, they, or either of them, shall be imprisoned not less than three nor more than twelve months in the penitentiary.

Many states including that of which the author is a native, and also the state in which Mr. Ali's draft board was located, had similar laws. Accordingly, the government sought to compel him to bear arms to support a system which relegated him to second class citizenship because of his ethnicity. Further, it bears mention that at the approximate height of the war, the series of laws in question would be declared unconstitutional in 1967 by the Supreme Court in the case of *Loving Et Ux* v. *Virginia* (388 U. S. 1). Such unanimous declaration by the Court would occur, ironically, at the approximate time that Mr. Ali would face justice for his refusal to serve in the military.

It also bears mention that the most prominent civil rights leader of this period, the Rev. Dr. Martin Luther King, Jr., also an African-American, began to voice his objections to the burgeoning war. Because of his vocal opposition to the conflict, he incurred the wrath of government leaders, including the President. As will be revealed later, Dr. King's opposition to the war may have cost him his life.

b. The case of the expatriates

Although this year can be labeled one of much patriotic fervor, in some circles this year can also be labeled the year when a lack of patriotic fervor became apparent. This year the public became aware of an alarming phenomenon. Men who were subject to conscription to fight the war began to voice their sentiments with their feet. They left. The number of men who departed for other countries apparently in order to avoid military service was initially small. As the war grew however, so did the numbers of men who departed. These likely included the fictitious "Curt", described below. The numbers of these men rose to such an alarming level that the government began tracking statistics on this phenomenon this year.

Gottlieb pegs the number of "draft émigrés" at between 30,000 and 150,000. She concedes however that the number of such persons varies widely, depending on the sources of the figures. Further, Gottlieb states that irrespective of the number of those who left the U. S. to avoid military service, one quarter of these never returned.

The primary destination of such men was of course the U. S.' "friendly" neighbor to the north, Canada. The climate for absorption of U. S. war protesters was favorable for a number of reasons. However, as will be revealed later this would change when the first phase of the war would be close to concluding.

c. The case of "Howard Kaylan"

"Howard Kaylan", one of the individuals detailed by Gottlieb, was a member of a popular rock band, The Turtles. That group had numerous successes on the popular music charts beginning in the mid-1960s. This year "Mr. Kaylan" graduated from high school just in time to be subjected to the Universal Military Training And Service Act. He was quite reluctant to be so subjected. Upon being notified of his impending induction into the Armed Forces, which first entailed a physical examination, he thereupon began an elaborate ruse to cause his draft board to reject him.

By mid-year it became common knowledge among those subject to the draft that certain ruses could be used to cause one to be rejected for military service. Among these were (1) faking homosexuality, (2) securing documents from doctors which supposedly would attest to mental deficiency, or (3) ingesting various substances, both legal and otherwise, which would cause the ingestee to appear to have physical/mental abnormalities. The ruse which "Mr. Kaylan" chose worked. After convincing the examining physician that he was mentally unstable, he was rejected and assigned to the category IV-F, Not Qualified For Any Military Service. However, "Mr. Kaylan's" association with the aforementioned rock band would merit him and his band members a footnote in the history of the war, as will be revealed later.

State Legislative Reaction To The Advent Of The Anti-war Movement, 1966

On 10 January the Georgia Legislature refused to seat one who had been elected to that body. Previously, Julian Bond who was a member of an organization known as the Student Non-violent Coordinating

Committee (S.N.C.C.), an advocate of civil rights, was elected to the Georgia House Of Representatives from a district in Atlanta. The S.N.C.C. had already stated its opposition to the war the previous year. Mr. Bond of course echoed this opposition. He sued in order to secure the seat to which he was elected.

Subsequently the matter went to a U. S. District Court. The court upheld the Georgia Legislature's position that Mr. Bond could be excluded from that body. The matter wound up in the Supreme Court. The nation's highest Court ruled in the case of *Bond v. Floyd* (385 U. S. 116) that the Georgia House Of Representatives had denied Mr. Bond his freedom of speech when it excluded him from the legislative seat to which he had been elected. That Court further ruled that he should be seated.

The Political Atmosphere In South Vietnam, 1966

There were little known and eventually all-but-forgotten events occurring in South Vietnam this year. Among these were that the "country" was wracked with internal strife, over and above the guerilla insurgency pursued by the Viet Minh/Viet Cong. These events were revisited in an obituary published in *The New York Times* on 26 June 2007. A little known figure in the South Vietnamese hierarchy, former General Nguyen Chanh Thi, died the previous Saturday in the U. S.

General Nguyen was perceived by some as a war lord because of his control over one of the four distinct regions of South Vietnam. He ruled over the portion of South Vietnam closest to the North, known as the I Corps. Further, the general did more than just command the military there. He also essentially governed this region, to the consternation of Premier Nguyen Cao Ky. As stated in the *Times*, South Vietnam was at this time four separate "governments", with General Nguyen in charge of one of them.

In Gen. Nguyen's obituary, the *Times* detailed his firing early in the year by Premier Ky. The general's removal set off additional civil warfare because the general was a popular figure, especially with the Buddhist majority. The rebellion which resulted from General Nguyen's removal would become known as The Struggle Movement. By summer the Movement had been quelled by forces loyal to Premier Ky with the aid of U. S. troops. Accordingly, the U. S. was briefly charged with fighting two separate insurrections.

This year the aforementioned Bui Diem was elevated from Deputy Foreign Minister in South Vietnam to Ambassador To The U. S. In his memoirs he was at his most eloquent in detailing the strife which characterized all of Vietnam after the Japanese departure in 1945. He stated that such strife was never-ending. Even after the partition of Vietnam in 1955, he stated that South Vietnam was perpetually wracked with strife. The above insurrection was merely the most profound manifestation of such. Indeed, Diem was at his most brutally honest when he opined that South Vietnam was deserving of its eventual fate of "annexation" with the North. It never learned to settle the petty squabbles which kept it from uniting against a common enemy.

Congressional Action On The War, 1966

Despite the lack of large scale dissent from or protest of the war, certain members of Congress did act to alter war policy. Senator Gore stated in *The Eye Of The Storm* (p. 40) that by this year the Senate, after voicing its objections to the deepening involvement in Vietnam, and also acknowledging its failure to reach the President on the issue, then began steps to influence public opinion. He claimed that the Congress did this with great success.

Possibly the strongest voice in opposition to the war during the entire conflict was that of the Senior Senator from Arkansas, J. William Fulbright, Chairman of the Senate Foreign Relations Committee. The means by which the Committee promulgated information concerning U. S. activities in Vietnam was via television. Those government officials primarily responsible for the buildup in Vietnam, including the Secretary Of State Dean Rusk, were interrogated by the Committee during televised hearings. The Committee under the leadership of Senator Fulbright thereby challenged the Administration's war policies and also its honesty on the issues.

In a major break with the Administration concerning war policies, Senator Fulbright suggested that the war was illegal because it appeared to his Committee to be a civil war. Also, he questioned the wisdom of U. S. intervention because some on the Committee believed that such intervention might draw in Vietnam's neighbors, mainly The People's Republic Of China. Here it must be reiterated that U. S. ground forces never crossed into North Vietnam at any time during the war, though the North was subjected to almost continuous bombing. Further to reiterate, the reason for this is the lesson learned from the prior war in Korea that sending forces into a "country" neighboring China would only draw in the Chinese. To reiterate, when the U. S. crossed into North Korea, this incursion resulted in U. S., Chinese and North Korean troops engaging one another in ground combat. This resulted in a stalemate.

Another voice which emerged from the Senate concerning the war was from Robert F. Kennedy, the brother of the slain President. Senator Kennedy went further than did his colleague, Senator Fulbright, by asserting that the Viet Cong/Viet Minh be given full representation in any subsequent peace negotiations. As will be revealed later, when all of the parties eventually submitted to negotiations, the U. S. was forced to adopt Senator Kennedy's recommendation.

Military Operations In Vietnam, 1966

a. The Allied Roster

It must be noted that the U. S. was not alone in pursing military action in Vietnam. Significant aid came from most of the other signators to the aforementioned S.E.A.T.O. treaty, including the Philippines, Australia and Thailand. An additional U. S. ally, South Korea, was the most actively engaged in ground operations.

b. U. S. and Allied military action

The level of fighting reached staggering proportions this year. For the first time U. S. troop levels began to exceed those of the Korean War. At the beginning of the year troop strength was about 200,000. By the end of the year this figure had doubled. These numbers only included troops stationed "in country." Another 70,000 personnel were stationed in neighboring Thailand (30,000) and the rest aboard ships along the coast of South Vietnam and in the Gulf Of Tonkin. The proximity of Thailand to North Vietnam made it quite useful for bombing raids over the North. In addition, U. S. air raids against Vietnam were launched from Mactan Air Base on the island of Cebu, Republic Of The Philippines.

The other source of bombing raids over North Vietnam came from U. S. aircraft carriers which patrolled the Gulf Of Tonkin and adjoining waters. This type of ship, upon which the author would eventually serve, is one of the most important in the U. S. arsenal. The ship is essentially a floating air force base. It can carry upwards of seventy-five jet aircraft which could be launched on short notice. A major feature of the aircraft carrier is also that it is quite mobile and it can be placed in a myriad of locations, depending on where it is needed.

The level of air actions which were concentrated mostly against North Vietnam resulted in a dramatic rise in losses of U. S. planes and pilots. It was widely reported in the media that the escalation of air actions against the North failed to achieve the desired results, however. North Vietnam still retained a significant capability to sustain its military with personnel and war materiel.

On the ground, the allies mostly engaged in search and destroy missions which were meant to kill as many of the enemy as possible. This was done at the expense of concentrating on efforts to conquer or retain territory.

This year the U. S military was still establishing the infrastructure necessary to efficiently pursue the war. Military bases were being constructed and modified. It was from these that the U. S. would pursue the search and destroy missions which came to represent the bulk of U. S. operations. One of those who participated in building this infrastructure was the author's cousin "G." He arrived in South Vietnam at the village of Tuy Hoa near the central coast of South Vietnam in October as a member of a battalion of Air Force Combat Engineers. His regular duties were to help construct and modify the aforementioned military bases. As will be revealed later, his tenure there would affect his life in ways which he could not have surmised.

The expanding ranks of military personnel also included one Army Col. Harry G. Summers, Jr. He was sent to Vietnam as an Assistant Operations Officer (Infantry) in February. Subsequently he occupied a variety of responsible posts there. During his seventeen month tenure he was wounded twice. For his heroism he was decorated with the Silver

Star and the Bronze Star with accompanying "V" for valor. A star was awarded to augment the Combat Infantryman Badge which he already wore. Col. Summers would eventually figure prominently in the annals of the war.

1. *Weapons*

Special mention must be made of the types of weapons used. The U. S. of course had impressive numbers of sophisticated airplanes, tanks and personal firearms. However, these would not be the weapons which would generate controversy during the conflict. One should understand that weapons other than those mentioned are also used to further a military campaign. The use of chemical weapons by the military is an idea as old as war itself. However, the U. S. would take the use of these types of weapons to a new level of sophistication in Vietnam. The war would introduce two words into the American lexicon: napalm and Agent Orange.

a. Napalm

Napalm was not developed specifically for use in Vietnam but it was used extensively by U. S. forces there for the first time. It was used mainly as a defoliant to clear the dense brush in order to deny the enemy cover. The chemical is a kind of jelly which is an incendiary. It not only sets things on fire but it also clings to whatever it touches for a significant period. This in turn causes the object to which it clings to burn severely.

The other properties of napalm are that it takes oxygen from the air which can cause death by asphyxiation. It also generates lethal poison gas. Because it clings to whatever it touches, it will cause severe pain to human skin. As will be revealed later, it was documented that Vietnamese civilians were sometimes subjected to it, inadvertently the U. S. claimed.

The domestic repercussions would be quite profound when the public was made aware of the extent to which civilians were being killed and maimed by napalm. This news resulted in U. S. defense plants which manufactured the chemical being picketed by protesters. A most ugly demonstration occurred at the manufacturing facility of the Olin-Matheson Company in East Alton, IL which had a government contract to make the chemical. The disturbance was widely reported in the St. Louis area news media.

b. Agent Orange

The other chemical weapon which U. S. forces used extensively and which generated controversy was Agent Orange. Like its cousin napalm, it was also used as a defoliant/herbicide which was likewise deemed necessary in order to clear the dense jungle and thereby deny cover to the enemy.

The use of Agent Orange by U. S. forces deserves special mention because it was eventually proven to have caused grave harm to military personnel who came in contact with it. Significant numbers of such personnel eventually developed exotic ailments peculiar to those who had served "in country." As will be revealed later, the subject of military personnel who served in Vietnam and who eventually would suffer serious health problems many years after the conflict would end, would hit close to home for the author.

Much of the controversy which Agent Orange would generate centers around the lack of disclosure of its potential dangers to personnel subjected to it in Vietnam. This is possibly due to the fact that when it was first used, it was not known what the effects would be on humans. This revelation would reverberate through the media for many years after the war would end. The level of controversy concerning the chemical would eventually become so great that the chemical's manufacturer, Dow Chemical Company, would establish a $180 million fund to compensate persons who had been unwittingly exposed to it in Vietnam.

2. *Activities of the two principal combatants*

In addition to directly engaging enemy troops, the Pentagon became more aware of two major phenomena: (1) infiltration of personnel into South Vietnam via the so-called Demilitarized Zone (DMZ) and (2) lack of effort on the part of the South Vietnamese.

The number of troops fielded by the insurgency was estimated at nearly 300,000 by year's end. It was further estimated that enemy casualties were 1,000 dead weekly. However, it was known that these losses were being more than replaced by personnel from North Vietnam and from the indigenous population. Intelligence reported a dramatic rise in the numbers of personnel which North Vietnam and the Viet Minh/Viet Cong were able to field.

Intelligence further confirmed that the enemy was being well supplied with arms from other sources, especially from The People's Republic Of China and The Soviet Union. This aid from the enemy's "friends" primarily took the form of surface-to-air missile (SAM) defenses. These proved to be quite effective in shielding the North from raids from U. S. planes. Further, these SAM installations were known to be manned by Soviet technicians. The effective use of the SAMs resulted in a dramatic rise in losses of U. S. planes and pilots. Further, this fact contributed to a rise in tensions between the U. S. and the Soviet Union. A by-product of the effectiveness of the SAMs was that the numbers of U. S. pilots shot down by the North and then incarcerated would eventually become a major bargaining chip used by the North in subsequent negotiations to end the war.

In addition to the SAMs, the insurgency was being well supplied with Chinese-made small arms which turned up among enemy dead and captured.

a. Infiltration from the North

A major cause of consternation by the allies was that personnel were coming into the South from North Vietnam across an area designated the Demilitarized Zone (DMZ). This narrow strip of land was along the 17th parallel which divided the two "countries." It was supposed to be devoid of military operations. All sides traded charges that the DMZ was being used for military operations, in violation of a prior agreement.

b. The Army Of The Republic Of Vietnam (ARVN)

One major cause of frustration by the allies was that the South Vietnamese Army, or ARVN, was apparently not shouldering its share of the war. The greatest impediment to the South's full participation appeared to be low morale. This was one of the most significant factors which caused U. S. policy and the perception of the war by the public to be altered during the entire course of the war. The South Vietnamese did not appear to be fighting for their own "country." This could be seen in the level of desertions which plagued the ARVN. It was reported that there were about 110,000 desertions throughout 1965. This figure was reported to have risen dramatically during the first half of 1966. Further, this was the apparent reason why the U. S. and South Vietnam agreed that the ARVN would mostly devote its activities to "pacification." That is, they were designated not to be directly involved in the fighting. This in turn is the obvious reason why the level of fighting between the allies on one side, and the North Vietnamese and the Viet Minh/Viet Cong on the other side caused the level of casualties on both sides to rise dramatically.

The Domestic Atmosphere Concerning The Military, 1966

Protests concerning the war, or matters related thereto, began in earnest. Especially on college campuses, large scale demonstrations occurred, apparently because draft quotas were at their highest level since the Korean War. These averaged about 30,000 per month. Men with and without deferments were threatened with conscription, depending on the needs of the war. On the campuses also, as elsewhere, fierce debates began about U. S. war policies. As a result, the public began to criticize the Selective Service System because of its requirement that students be tested to determine their draft eligibility, and also because the government required that student grades be reported to the System. Males who were registered with the System but who had previously received a II-S Student Deferment, had to keep their grades up in order to continue to retain the deferment.

There were a number of proposals to modify the law which governed the draft. The Universal Military Training And Service Act was by law scheduled for review the next year. One of the proposals for modification of the law was a lottery. This incidentally was the means by which the government had selected men for military service in 1940 with the advent of World War II. This was the advent of the modern draft.

Still, the government continued to induce greater numbers of men into uniform this year because of the growing needs of the war. According to Collier's Year Book For 1967, Covering The Year 1966, 900,000 new personnel entered the rapidly expanding Armed Forces in 1966. Of these, about 520,000 volunteered. The rest were conscripts.

The official number of men drafted this year was 382,010. Further, according to the same source, out of about 10,000,000 men registered with the Selective Service System, only about 700,000 were needed to maintain troop strength.

The aforementioned Richard Cheney was not one of those drafted. On January 19, apparently because of his wife's recently discovered pregnancy, Cheney applied for and received a III-A Hardship Deferment.

The Author's Situation, 1966

In September the author began his senior year in high school. This year he also took the Scholastic Aptitude Test (S.A.T.), required of all high school seniors. Based on his examination scores he would be offered a scholarship to the University Of Missouri the following year. He would be accepted. This would delay his entry into the war until the first phase of the conflict would be close to concluding.

The Popular Culture, 1966

To reiterate, no popular songs protested the war this year. However, one song did mention something related to Vietnam. The soul singer Aretha Franklin recorded a cover version of her husband's composition, *Lee Cross.*

a. *Coming Home Soldier*

One popular song appeared to reflect the mood within a certain segment of society, those veterans returning from the war. The popular singer Bobby Vinton recorded *Coming Home Soldier.* The song appeared to reflect the relief which a soldier felt at having completed the most arduous task of participating in combat. He finally was allowed to return to a normal life. As the song went:

> "I am a <u>soldier</u>, a coming home soldier.
> No Purple Heart do I wear on my chest.
> I know that I have done my best."
> (Copyright © 1966, Feather Music)

The public embraced the song to the extent that it reached #11 on the national music charts the week of 19 November. The releasing label was one of the largest, Epic (Columbia).

b. *The Cheater*

The popular culture further experienced repercussions from the war, both in the U. S. and in one its allies. The rock band Bob Kuban & The In-Men, based in the author's home town of St. Louis, scored on the popular music charts early in the year with the song *The Cheater*. The song which was released by the independent label Musicland U. S. A. neglected to refer to anything related to the war. However, one could dance to it. The public embraced the song to the extent that it rose to #12 on the national charts the week of 19 February. This success of course happened to coincide with the military buildup by both the U. S. and Australia in Indochina. The song was also quite popular in Australia, to the extent that *The Cheater* rose to #1 there. The result was that the artist was offered a series of concert dates in Australia.

The group in question declined to accept the offer of concert dates in Australia, however. The reason was that one of the members of the group had been deferred from military service with a II-A occupational deferment because he was a teacher. This is one of the occupations which the government deemed critical and therefore worthy of a draft deferment.

The leader of the group provides a detailed discourse on the band's activities as the war was heating up early in the year. In *My Side Of The Bandstand* he states (p. 143) that besides Australia, the band was precluded from traveling to any foreign shore to perform, despite being asked to do so. The band was also precluded from traveling to Canada where *The Cheater* made the top ten on that nation's popular music charts. Mr. Kuban stated that his draft board informed him that if he left the U. S., then he would lose his teaching deferment. He would further have been drafted forthwith.

And the beat continued...

Reports From The Print Media, 1966

Meanwhile this year the printed media continued to report on the war effort. As in the year immediately preceding, there was frequent and detailed reporting of the growing U. S. involvement in Vietnam. The following is a partial listing of topics of articles which were published during this interval:

1. *Vietnam: Reality Of War, Talk Of Peace*
   (U. S. News & World Report, 1/3/66, p. 6)

2. *Terror In The Streets: Vietcong Attacks In Saigon*
   (Newsweek, 1/3/66, p. 30)

3. *Budget Escalates: $12 Billion Added To Vietnamese War*
   (Business Week, 1/8/66, pp. 27 – 28)

4. *Truce Or Bigger War: showdown ahead in Vietnam*
   (U. S. News & World Report, 1/10/66, pp. 27 – 28)

5. *First Major U. S. North Viet Battle*
   (Aviation Week & Space Technology, 1/10/66, pp. 30 – 31)

6. *People Beneath The War: The Vietnamese*
   (The Nation, 1/17/66, p. 61 – 63)

7. *Bombing Reds' Lifeline In Laos: Eyewitness Report, Ho Chi Minh Trail*
   (U. S. News & World Report, 1/24/66, pp. 37 – 39)

8. *Untold Story Of Vietnam War*
   (U. S. News & World Report, 1/24/66, pp. 29 – 32)

9. *Vietnam: The Problem Of Candor*
   (Newsweek, 1/24/66, pp. 61 – 63)

The broadcast media provided limited visual coverage of the war at this time.

CHAPTER SEVEN:
INTENSIFICATION OF HOSTILITIES AND ANTI-WAR SENTIMENT, 1967

The message was becoming increasingly clear that the U. S. had miscalculated its ability to prevail in a guerilla war. Even though vastly greater resources were being committed, no progress was being made in Vietnam. Public opposition to the war accordingly rose dramatically. National leaders demanded that the U. S. radically reassess the situation.

The National Mood Over The War, 1967

This year the war can be characterized as a continuation of the preceding year, only on a grander scale. This year a term which would describe U. S. efforts in Vietnam for much of the conflict came into common use: escalate. The war and everything associated with it seemed to escalate at this time: personnel directly engaged in combat operations, battle casualties, coverage of the war by the media, numbers of men conscripted, controversy over the war and related issues and also war protests, to name a few.

During most of the year however, the national mood was substantially the same as in the previous year. President Johnson still had the support of most Americans for at least the first six months. An example of the public's support of the war effort came from an unlikely source. The African-American concert pianist turned war correspondent Philippa Duke Schuyler was known to be a vehement supporter of the war. Here, as with Muhammad Ali and Jackie Robinson, one could also observe the discord within the black community over the conflict. As her biographer Kathryn M. Talalay detailed in her biography of Ms. Schuyler, <u>Composition In Black And White,</u> she was firmly anti-communist. Further, she believed that if African-Americans would support the war against communism, then this would promote greater acceptance of blacks in U. S. society. It bears mention that the struggle by African-Americans for full equality had become quite intense within the preceding ten years. Witness the March On Washington in August, 1963 where hundreds of thousands of all hues led by Dr. Martin Luther King demonstrated for racial equality. Further, this struggle seemed to have reached a climax by 1967. Witness the violent clash which Dr. King and his supporters encountered the previous year when he led a march in Cicero, IL for equal housing. Such was the mood of the times.

Another glaring example of the discord within the black community over the war could be seen in the activities of two individuals at opposite ends of the spectrum. As reported in *Time* magazine, the African-American son-in-law of the Secretary Of State, an Army officer, volunteered for helicopter duty in Vietnam this year. At the opposite end of the spectrum was one Stokely Carmichael, an avowed "militant" who urged other blacks not to participate in what he labeled a "white man's war." He further labeled blacks who participated in the conflict "black mercenaries." When called by his draft board to be examined for military service, he informed the board that he would rather go to prison. Lastly, his sentiments on the war will likely be forever remembered in the chant for which he is still famous: "Hell no, we won't go!" (apparently into the military to participate in the war). Mr. Carmichael of course did not speak for all black Americans.

Ms. Schuyler's coverage of and support for the war effort cost her her life. In May she was killed in a helicopter accident off the coast of Vietnam while covering the war as a correspondent. She was not the only celebrity whose observations of the war and physical presence in Vietnam would result in tragedy, however. It also bears mention that this year the only known son of the late actor Errol Flynn disappeared while covering the war as a correspondent. No trace of him has ever been found.

During the last half of the year the support which President Johnson had earlier in the year began to dwindle markedly. At the end of the year only about 28% of the public supported his Vietnam policy. His overall job approval rating was also at a record low. The obvious reason for this loss of support was that no real progress had been made in winning the war, which was at a stalemate by the end of the year. A collateral reason for public dismay over the war was that resources were being diverted from social programs to fund the military. Controversy over the issue of "guns vs. butter" was becoming quite heated.

With the war at a stalemate and a presidential election looming the next year, the end of 1967 saw the rise of potential opponents to President Johnson in the upcoming election. Among the first and most visible of these was the senior Senator from Minnesota, Eugene ("Clean Gene") McCarthy who advocated an end to the hostilities. For a period he would prove to be the most visible embodiment in Congress over the public's dissatisfaction over the war.

The aforementioned Richard Cheney's apparent disinterest in the war became immaterial this year. In January he turned twenty-six years of age. He accordingly became too old to be conscripted.

Military Operations In Vietnam, 1967

a. The Allied Roster
The U. S.' allies increased their contributions to the war. The South Koreans principally aided the U. S. in ground operations. News reports promulgated the zeal of the South Korean Army in combat. That country provided the greatest number of personnel to ground efforts, at 45,000. In addition The Philippines sent a number of personnel, some of whom were engaged in combat. The Filipinos were however primarily engaged in support activities. New Zealand and Australia also greatly increased their contributions to combat operations. Although Thailand provided some combat personnel, the contribution from that country was still primarily in the form of bases from which the U. S. launched air raids.

b. U. S. ground operations
As in 1966, U. S. forces bore the brunt of the fighting. Moreover, this year saw what would come to characterize U. S. combat strategy. Upon receipt of intelligence, forces under the command of General Of The Army William C. Westmoreland, would first target an area where the enemy was known to be strong. Forces would then mount an offensive to "pacify" the area which was usually a village, kill as many of the enemy as possible, take prisoner those suspected of being Viet Minh/Viet Cong and then destroy the village. This was of course done after the villagers and all portable possessions had been removed from their homes.

Indeed, this "pacification strategy" was to characterize much of U. S. strategy in the war. When it had been determined beforehand the number of troops needed to hold a rural area such as a village, and the number of troops needed could not be mustered, military authorities would then decide to destroy the area. The numbers of the enemy which U. S. forces killed and captured was the standard by which combat operations were deemed a success. More often than not however, forces would encounter light resistance upon entering a village. Eventually the Pentagon came to understand that enemy forces were either not where they were thought to be, or that they had managed to elude detection when they became aware that an offensive was imminent. Further, most of enemy personnel who were found after U. S. forces had entered an area were support personnel such as medical technicians. Such is the character of a guerilla war.

During the "search and destroy" missions, U. S. forces of course sustained many fewer casualties than did the enemy. However, military authorities eventually came to understand the hazards of fighting a guerilla war on another nation's turf. Simply put, the indigenous population was more familiar with the place than U. S. troops were. Most of the casualties which U. S. forces sustained were not from direct confrontation with the enemy, but rather from "booby traps." Many personnel were either seriously or permanently wounded from these. The aforementioned SSgt Barry Sadler was one of those who experienced such injury. His activities after having suffered such war wounds are detailed below.

This year also saw the most intense fighting in one of the most famous battles of the war at a place called Quang Tri near the DMZ. For the first time U. S. personnel engaged in heated confrontation with the regular forces of North Vietnam. This hard fought battle in turn made U. S. forces more aware of the logistical problems involved in moving and stationing its troops and materiel.

c. U. S. air operations

The year was characterized by a steadily increasing barrage of air strikes from U. S. planes. These were directed primarily upon North Vietnamese munitions works, bridges and air fields. This in turn resulted in North Vietnam stationing more of its planes within The People's Republic Of China along their common border, where they would be safe from U. S. raids. The damage inflicted upon the North was of course devastating. However, these efforts did not "bring them to their knees", as the Pentagon had hoped.

There were limits to U. S. efforts in the air. Population centers in North Vietnam from which non-essential persons had been mostly evacuated, were avoided. Likewise the system of dikes which the North used for crop irrigation was declared off-limits by The Pentagon. This decision was made because of concern that striking these places would adversely affect world opinion of the war effort because it would hinder the North from growing food.

Further, the harbor of Haiphong which was deemed vital to the

North was not raided because U. S. authorities feared that such air raids might result in destroying ships of other nations. These included those from the Soviet Union which routinely visited that port. These vessels of course carried materiel and personnel to aid the North Vietnamese. This of course was one of the major frustrations with which U. S. authorities had to deal in pursuing the war. Damaging Soviet vessels or the killing of its personnel would of course exacerbate tensions between the U. S. and the Soviets, which tension was already quite high.

This year also saw a dramatic increase in U. S. losses of planes, which rose to a total of eight hundred since the air war began. Deaths and captures of pilots also rose dramatically. The capture of a U. S. pilot was referred to by the military as a "kill." In October one Lieutenant Commander (LCDR) John McCain was "killed" while on a bombing mission over North Vietnam. His mission was to unload one of the newest types of ordnance devised by the U. S. munitions industry, the Walleye "smart bomb." This type of ordnance was deemed "smart" because it was designed to destroy armaments and buildings while minimizing civilian casualties. LCDR McCain did indeed release his ordnance. However, it was not documented that the bombs reached their target. Instead, he was forced to eject from his plane over the target because his plane had been hit by enemy fire. He was then "killed" shortly after parachuting into enemy territory.

U. S. pilots came to understand what they were up against and what to expect whenever they embarked on a bombing mission over the North. In his autobiography *Faith Of My Fathers: a family memoir,* then LCDR McCain conceded that he was indeed up against a worthy adversary. His respect for the North Vietnamese missile defense system was conveyed thusly:

> "Hanoi, with its extensive network of Russian-manufactured SAM sites, had the distinction of possessing the most formidable air defenses in the history of modern warfare." (*Faith Of My Fathers: A Family Memoir,* p. 187).

In his memoirs LCDR McCain detailed graphically his experiences on board the *U.S.S. Forrestal* (CVA-59) from which he was catapulted on his final mission over North Vietnam. He succinctly describes life on the flight deck of an aircraft carrier. Such can be as dangerous as on a bombing mission, as will be detailed below.

d. Progress (?)In Pursuing The War, 1967

Despite the numbers of the enemy which U. S. forces killed and captured, by the end of the year the Pentagon could not report that significant progress had been made in defeating the enemy. The only thing that had really changed from the year preceding was the greatly increased body count on both sides. U. S. deaths during the year amounted to approximately one hundred eighty weekly. This was a forty percent increase over the previous year. Personnel losses which the enemy sustained also rose in the same proportion. Further, this lack of success on the battlefield was in spite of the fact that the number of U. S. ground forces approached 500,000. South Vietnamese (ARVN) forces were approximately fifty percent greater. These numbers were in addition to the forces of the other allies and the numbers of Navy personnel stationed in waters adjacent and in Thailand. Accordingly, this year ended with the war in a stalemate. However, as will be revealed later bigger things were soon forthcoming.

In summary, this year can be labeled The Year Of The Mistake. The U. S. mistook the enemy's resolve, the enemy's strength, the enemy's capacity to re-supply its troops, the ability of the government to rally public support for the conflict, the mistaken assessment of the numbers of personnel needed to win the war, and nearly every other component of the hostilities. Lastly, what is also noteworthy is that the U. S.' primary ally recognized the "mistake" which the U. S. had made in providing large numbers of ground troops. The new President of South Vietnam, Nguyen Cao Ky, expressed misgivings about the number of U. S. troops now stationed there. He made public his opposition to the nearly 500,000 U. S. troops which were "in country" by the end of this year. His sentiments echoed those of President Diem in 1962, shortly before he was assassinated. This issue of South Vietnam's objections to the rising U. S. troop levels was raised by Senator Gore (p. 31) when he seemed to ridicule President Ky for raising such objections. According to Senator Gore, President Ky was reputed to have stated that:

"American policy was wrong in the past when the U. S. wanted to pour in troops to win the guerilla war."

President Ky's Ambassador To The U. S. echoed the same sentiments about U. S. troop levels. He understood that the massive U. S. presence would only work against South Vietnam. He opined that "... outsiders (the U. S.) would give the communists the most powerful propaganda weapon they could hope for." (Bui Diem, p. 131). He also described the growing resentment of many South Vietnamese because of their increasing dependence on the U. S.

Domestic Dissent Within The Military, 1967

The still-escalating war produced a rare phenomenon: dissent within the military because of the war. On 10 May the General Court-martial of one Army Captain Howard Levy began. He was charged with "promoting disloyalty and disaffection" within the Army and also with disobeying a lawful order. This is likely the first documented instance of dissent within the military because of the war since its official start.

CAPT Levy had been drafted at the advent of the war in 1965 immediately after completing medical school. Although a conscript, because of his medical training he received a direct commission. It is a regular military practice to directly commission persons who have professional degrees. He began his military career as an O-3. However, once in uniform he became a vocal critic of the war. He was reputed to have advised an African-American associate that if he were black, he would not fight in Vietnam. CAPT Levy was white. After labeling the war "a diabolical evil", he refused to train others in his specialty of dermatology, pursuant to his official duties. He had been ordered to train medics in the Special Forces who were headed for Vietnam. On 2 June, less than thirty days prior to the end of his two year tour of duty, he was convicted. He was then sentenced to three years of hard labor and then dishonorably discharged.

The Galvanizing Of The U. S. Christian Clergy Against The War, 1967

a. Enter the Protestant faction

This year would see the Christian clergy become galvanized against the war. A group of such clergy and its supporters would organize in its opposition to the ongoing hostilities. These would become known as The Clergy And Laymen Concerned About Vietnam. On 4 April the group was addressed by arguably the most widely known member of the Protestant community in the U. S. In New York City at the Riverside Church the Rev. Dr. Martin Luther King spoke before the aforementioned group. He was in usual top form in his analysis of the issues concerning U. S. involvement in Vietnam. His analysis crystallized certain issues which U. S. Christians faced in their perception of their role in the debate over the war. The fundamental question which faced the U. S. Christian community was of course the dilemma of patriotism vs. adherence to Christian doctrine. The burning question was: How could one be true to one's faith and also support a war which they believed was illegal and also contrary to any notion of The Gospel? Further, Dr. King grasped the historical significance of the clergy's organizing to oppose the war. Stated Dr. King:

> "This is the first time in our nation's history that a significant number of its religious leaders have chosen to move beyond the prophesying of smooth patriotism to the high grounds of a firm dissent based upon the mandates of conscience."

Further, one of the most startling yet spiritual statements which Dr. King uttered was the obvious link between his faith and that of the majority of Vietnamese. South Vietnam was primarily Buddhist. In his diatribe against further U. S. intervention in Vietnam he stated that:

> "We (the U. S.) have cooperated in the crushing of the (Vietnamese) nation's only noncommunist revolutionary political force, the unified Buddhist Church."

Dr. King was widely vilified for his opposition to the war, reportedly even by the President Of The U. S. Many persons within and without of government suggested that he was (1) a dupe of the communists, (2) that he was sympathetic towards communism or (3) that he was a "closet" communist. He had stated that he was none of these. Such perception of his character would follow him long after his eventual death. As will be revealed later, Dr. King's outrage and eloquence may have returned to haunt him precisely one year later.

b. Enter the Catholic faction

Dr. King and his cohorts in opposition to the war received support from the individual who was arguably the most prominent U. S. representative of the Catholic Church. This same year Bishop Fulton J. Sheen of the Diocese Of New York came out as a staunch opponent of the war. No one would dare question Bishop Sheen's anti-communist credentials, as some had with Dr. King. Indeed, he had written his doctoral dissertation as a diatribe against Marxism, of which communism is its successor. Further, Bishop Sheen had established his reputation during the preceding ten years as probably the primary force in the U. S. to make Catholicism more acceptable. Catholicism had been, ever since the inception of the U. S., denigrated by many non-Catholics. Accordingly it is safe to say that his opposition to the war likely caused his Catholic followers and also other Christians to follow him in his opposition to the war.

It should further be noted that a counterpart to this galvanization of the U. S. clergy to oppose the war never materialized. It has never been documented that any faction of the clergy in the U. S. ever opposed the efforts of the aforementioned Christian factions to dissent from or actively oppose the war.

The Federal Judicial Perspective, 1967

In the midst of the general rancor which the war had generated, a segment of U. S. society which seemed to be above the controversy began to weigh in on the issues concerning the war. The Federal judiciary began to regularly assert its Constitutional duty to render judgment on persons or institutions involved in the controversy.

In June Muhammad Ali, who had the previous year refused to be inducted into the Army, was convicted in the U. S. District Court For The Eastern District Of Texas of violation of the Universal Military Training And Service Act. He was then ordered to serve a prison term of five years coupled with a fine of $10,000, the maximum penalty under the law. He immediately appealed and was released on bail pending appeal. Subsequently Mr. Ali's conviction was affirmed by the U. S. Court Of Appeals For The Fifth Circuit (New Orleans). His attorneys then petitioned the Supreme Court for a *Writ of Certiorari* to overturn his conviction.

The legal controversy concerning Mr. Ali's conviction for draft resistance would ordinarily have gone unnoticed. However, he was such a visible symbol of resistance to the war effort, even though he never actively opposed the war, that his case would prove to be one of the most profound examples of the national division over the conflict. Indeed, his case would prove to be <u>the</u> most profound example of the Federal Judiciary's perception of the war and related issues. As will be revealed later, the Supreme Court would soon set the pace of the mood within "The Establishment" concerning the war.

Change In Civil Structure In South Vietnam, 1967

The "Government" Of South Vietnam appeared to be making improvements in its civil structure. This year the military junta which had seized control in 1963 upon the assassination of President Diem, was abolished. With the elimination of that junta, South Vietnam ratified a new constitution and then elected a "government" to replace it.

The Communist Perspective, 1967

One of the peculiarities of the Vietnam War was that it was rooted in ideology. Indeed, all military conflicts stem from ideological disputes between or among the parties. The ideological dispute which spawned the instant war deserves special attention however, because both sides in the dispute suffered from dissention within their respective ranks. The U.S. and its allies were not in complete accord on the subject of the means with which they should or could contain communism.

Neither were they in complete accord on how to pursue military action.

What is most unusual about the Vietnam War is that there was also much discord within the side which opposed U. S. interests. Anyone who observed the war unfold would logically have assumed that when the U. S. sent troops to fight the communist insurgency in Vietnam, one or both of North Vietnam's powerful ideological allies, The Soviet Union and The People's Republic Of China, would also send their troops to aid their ideological partner. This was not to be the case, however.

It had been reported the same year that the U. S. officially sanctioned the war, 1964, that there were border skirmishes between The Soviet Union and The People's Republic Of China. The individual who would eventually assume responsibility for the war, Richard Nixon, expressed his knowledge of the discord between the two nations in his memoirs. Stated Nixon: "The Chinese regarded the Soviet Union with a mixture of utter contempt and healthy fear." (*RN*, p. 567). Accordingly, anyone who observed the situation at the time and who would logically have assumed that these two communist giants would send troops to aid their ideological allies, would have been quite wrong. This type of aid would never come from either of the two nations. This was because the tensions between the U. S. and the Soviets, and also between the Soviets and the Chinese, were quite exacerbated because of U. S. intervention in Vietnam. The "bottom line" was that no side wanted to widen the war.

However, what is unique about the instant war was that there was great mistrust also between The People's Republic Of China and Vietnam. Indeed, there had always been such mistrust. It is a historical fact that for at least the prior two millennia the Chinese had tried to control its neighbor to the south. The apparent reason was that Vietnam has always been known to have quite fertile land which is primarily used for the growing of rice. The Chinese knew that the Vietnamese could feed themselves and China also with such fertile land. The Vietnamese in turn had always resisted such domination. As will be revealed later, shortly after the war would conclude this historical strife between the two would again flare.

It was opined by the experts at the time that the Vietnamese did not want or solicit aid from China in the form of troops because if China arrived with its military, then it would never leave. Vietnam would therefore come under permanent domination from China, which it had always resisted. These facts are the best indication of the complexity of issues surrounding the war.

Halberstam in particular understood the complexity of the issues within this context. When comparing both sides to the conflict he seemed to suggest that the North Vietnamese and the Viet Minh/Viet Cong had a more worthy cause than did South Vietnam under Diem before his death. Stated Halberstam:

> "Diem turned to white foreigners for help, for more aid, for air power, for a new treaty with the Americans. The idea of Ho Chi Minh needing help or reassurance from the Russians or the Chinese is inconceivable; the idea of Diem being able to understand the needs of the peasants and respond to them in kind is equally inconceivable." (Halberstam, p. 150).

The North Vietnamese and the Viet Minh/Viet Cong continued to pursue its overriding goal: a unified Vietnam under a communist government. What is most interesting is that U. S. intervention only served to aid its enemies. Halberstam again is quite astute in his perception of the likely reason why this occurred when he states:

> "The very presence of Caucasian (U. S.) troops (in Vietnam) was likely to turn quickly into a political disadvantage, more than canceling out any military benefits." (Halberstam, p. 172)

Sending U. S. troops to Vietnam was thereby akin to throwing gasoline on a fire. The U. S. failed to remember the lesson of its own Civil War. During that conflict, when Confederate troops were captured and interrogated as to why they were fighting, they would sometimes state: "Because you're down here." The presence of Union troops in the states of the Confederacy thereby caused more southerners to want to fight to drive persons who they regarded as invaders from their "country." So it appeared to be the case in Vietnam. When the Vietnamese observed

U. S. troops in their "nation", this likely caused more of the indigenous population to fight to repel the persons who they perceived had invaded their homeland.

Perception Of The International Community, 1967

There was little formal debate in the U. N. on the subject of Vietnam. However, Secretary General U Thant pressed his program to address the issue of the intensifying hostilities in Vietnam. His program advocated (1) negotiations among all parties involved, (2) cessation of hostilities and (3) an unconditional halt to all U. S. bombing. His program was not immediately considered.

The Popular Culture, 1967

a. Phonograph recordings
1. *I Feel Like I'm Fixin' To Die Rag*
To reiterate, no popular songs protesting the war were released this year. However, one song was released which made light of the war. The conflict was indeed becoming a joke within some circles. The country/rock band Country Joe And The Fish recorded a song which became one of the most memorable of the war. *I Feel Like I'm Fixin' To Die Rag* will always be remembered as the only song which made light of the Vietnam Conflict. The releasing label was the independent but highly respected Vanguard Recording Society. As the song went:

> "Come on, all of you big, strong men,
> Uncle Sam needs your help again.
> He's got himself in a terrible jam,
> Way over yonder in Vietnam.
> Now it's 1-2-3 what are we fighting for?
> Don't ask me, I don't give a damn!
> Next stop, it's Vietnam.
> (Copyright © 1967, Alkatraz Korner Music Co.)

The song which was released in the LP (album) format, was covered by other artists.

2. *For What It's Worth*

Another popular song was recorded and released in 1967 which seemed to suggest the confusion which the war had generated. The rock band Buffalo Springfield recorded on the major label Atco (Atlantic) *For What It's Worth*. The song holds the distinction as being the "coyest" protest song released in apparent reaction to the war. It did not mention the war, however. It merely seemed to reflect the national mood over the amount of societal discord in general, which of course mostly emanated from the controversy over the war. As the song went:

> "Battle lines being drawn.
> Nobody's right when everybody's wrong.
> Young people speaking their minds,
> Getting so much resistance from behind.
> It's time to <u>stop</u>! Hey, what's that sound?
> Everybody look what's going down."
> (Copyright © 1967, Cotillion Music, Inc.)

The public embraced the song's message to the extent that it rose to #7 on the national music charts during the week of 18 February.

3. *Tighten Up*

Another example of how the war began to affect the popular culture could be seen in a popular song which had nothing to do with Vietnam. However, the war had a profound effect on the artist who recorded it. This year the rhythm & blues group Archie Bell & The Drells, of Houston, Texas, recorded on the Atlantic label the song *Tighten Up*. Shortly after the song was recorded, the leader of the group was drafted into the Army and then was sent to Vietnam where he was wounded. The song was then released and it began to sell. As Mr. Bell was recovering in a Veterans Administration (V. A.) hospital, he heard his song frequently on the radio. By the week of 13 April 1968 the song was #1 on the national music charts. It is not likely that the huge sales of the recording were due to the public's sympathy over the artist's plight.

One could dance to it. The song remains a popular icon of the era and also an excellent example of the early disco sound which would capture the public's fancy as the war would conclude.

And the beat continued...

b. Television
1. *The Final War Of Ollie Winter*

This year the broadcast media showed the first made-for-television movie about Vietnam and related issues. Others were to follow during the course of the war. However, it is noteworthy that at the height of the conflict when domestic controversy over the war was growing exponentially, the first T. V. movie about the war concerned the plight of an African-American who served "in country" during the conflict.

The Final War Of Ollie Winter, broadcast by the CBS Playhouse, concerned the experiences of a combat soldier, portrayed with sensitivity by the character actor Ivan Dixon. The film concerns the observances of Master Sgt. Winter in combat against the communist forces in Vietnam. The character was the head of an infantry platoon and acting as an "advisor" to the Army Of The Republic Of Vietnam (ARVN). His platoon was ambushed by the Viet Minh/Viet Cong and he then found himself the only survivor. In his search to return to his unit, he of course comes in contact with several of the indigenous population. They then become quite human to him.

MSgt. Winter, a veteran of WWII and The Korean Conflict found himself engaged in a war which he did not completely understand. He was understandably weary of war. He was accordingly in the company of many of his fellow citizens. However, as he was sworn to do, he did his duty. Because of his fatigue from this and previous conflicts, he decides that this would be his final war.

For his efforts Mr. Dixon was nominated by the Academy Of Television Arts And Sciences for an "Emmy" Award for Best Single Performance By An Actor. The teleplay was also nominated for Best Dramatic Program, Best Director For A Drama for Paul Bogart and Best Performance By An Actress In A Supporting Role for Tina Chen.

The Literary Community Input, 1967

This year would see the publication of the first book which examined the growing involvement in Vietnam. The book entitled *Why Are We In Vietnam?* was authored by the well-known journalist Norman Mailer. The book also holds the distinction of being the first novel using the war as its subject. It is not a discourse on the pros and cons of the U. S. presence there. Rather, the book is about the "mindset" of the American public and why this national mood allowed or encouraged the war. The book was generally well received.

The Author's Situation, 1967

a. Registration with the Selective Service System

The author graduated from high school and then began college in September. Upon entering the institution of higher learning he was, at 17, too young for military service. However, within sixty days of beginning a college curriculum he turned eighteen. In accordance with the Universal Military Training And Service Act, he registered with his local draft board, #111. Upon registering, inasmuch as he had already embarked upon a college curriculum he requested and was granted a II-S Student deferment. This deferment would enable the author to complete his studies before possibly being required to serve in the Armed Forces. He anticipated that the war would end by the time he was scheduled to complete college in June, 1971.

b. Embarking on a college course of study

One of the courses required of the author in college was an elementary course in political science. Here was his first exposure to a person in authority voicing opposition to the war. Shortly after the course began, his professor stated flatly that the war was illegal. One reason for his opposition to the war was that it had not been declared by Congress. In this respect he was in accord with a member of the U. S. Senate. Even before the conflict had begun in earnest in 1964, the senior Senator from Oregon, Wayne Morse, had railed against further U. S. involvement in Vietnam. Senator Morse specifically objected to the official commitment to the war that year because such commitment was in violation of Article I, Section 8 of the Constitution. That Article explicitly prescribes the power of declaring war only to the Congress. No one in the classroom composed primarily of freshmen voiced any objections to the professor's statements, however. Some did question him why he came to his conclusion.

Upon hearing his professor voice his personal opinion of U. S. efforts in Vietnam, the author was stunned and incredulous that a professor in a state university would oppose official government policy. He envisioned that agents of the Federal Bureau Of Investigation (F. B. I.) would storm the classroom to arrest his professor. This did not come to pass. However, because a person in authority and also a government employee had voiced opposition to the war, the author then understood for the first time the level of discord which the war had generated.

In addition, the author became educated in the economic repercussions of wars on an economy in general, and of the effect that the Vietnam War was having on the U. S. economy in particular. He minored in economics. While pursuing economic coursework he was made aware of the classic dichotomy of "guns vs. butter." Simply put, when an economy devotes more of its resources to purchasing guns, then the other side of the economy which desires more "butter", will have to lose. In other words, a wartime economy is a Zero Sum Game. The individual who would lead the nation during the greatest period of U. S. involvement in Vietnam, Richard M. Nixon, would state in his memoirs:

> "(President) Johnson had tried to satisfy everyone; he had encouraged the American people to believe that even in time of war they could have butter as well as guns." (*RN*, pp. 516, 754).

The situation was complicated by the fact that the purchase of guns, as in military hardware, is an inefficient way for a nation to use resources. The author came to understand that the war was taking a toll on the economy because resources were being drained by military expenditures. In addition, a most profound result of the then-escalating war was that the conflict was placing severe inflationary pressures on the economy. The level of inflation rose to alarming levels after years of having been negligible. It is worth noting that Richard Nixon stated in his memoirs his perception of how the war had negatively impacted the economy. Stated Nixon:

> "The economy that (President) Eisenhower had bequeathed to (President) Kennedy in January 1961 was remarkably stable, with a rate of inflation of about 1.5 percent. By 1968, largely because of the effects of the Vietnam War, inflation had soared to 4.7 percent." (*RN*, p. 515).

Because so much money was being spent on the war, which put more money in peoples' pockets, this resulted in "too many dollars chasing too few goods", as the author's economics professor repeatedly emphasized. Hence the reason for the escalating rate of inflation.

Reports From The Print Media, 1967

Meanwhile, this year the printed media continued to report on the war effort. As in the year immediately preceding, there was frequent and detailed reporting of U. S. involvement in Vietnam. The following is a partial listing of topics of articles which were published during this year:

1. *Civilians weren't the target, but: U. S. air raids in North Vietnam*
   (Newsweek, 1/9/67, pp. 17 – 18)

2. *Facts In A Propaganda War Over U. S. Bombing; civilian casualties*
   (U. S. News & World Report, 1/9/67, p. 6)

3. *Pentagon Answer To Critics Of Bombing: controversy of civilian casualties*
   (P. G. Goulding, U. S. News & World Report, 1/16/67, p. 16)

4. *Rusk Tells Student Leaders: why America is in the Vietnam War*
   (U. S. News & World Report, 1/16/67, p. 16)

5. *Pull Out Of Vietnam? What key Senators say about next moves in the war*
   (U. S. News & World Report, 1/23/67, pp. 40 - 45)

6. *New Turn In The Ground War In Vietnam: attack on Iron Triangle of Viet Cong*
   (U. S. News & World Report, 1/23/67, p. 8)

7. *Stand By To Launch Aircraft; operation in USS Independence; excerpt from Vietnam: the confusing war*
   (Readers Digest, Jan. 1967)

8. *Brighter Side Of The Vietnam War: communists badly shaken*
   (U. S. News & World Report, 4/10/67, pp. 40 – 41)

9. *Dark Portents; war nearing point of no return*
   (E. J. Hughes, Newsweek, 5/29/67, p. 19)

Reports From The Broadcast Media, 1967

One of the most enduring memories of the Vietnam War is the images which began to be promulgated in the media of the havoc being leveled against the indigenous population there. Moving images and still photographs of old men, women and children fleeing from their burning homes and carrying their belongings were permanently seared into the minds and consciousness of the public this year. The promulgation of these images was instrumental in causing the American public perception, and indeed the world perception of military efforts and the rationale for pursuing the war, to deteriorate.

Further, one of the most enduring images broadcast on television this year concerned a criminal act. To reiterate, the boxer Muhammad Ali refused to be inducted into the military at the Armed Force Examining And Entrance Station (AFEES) in Houston, TX. It was quite a rare event for an individual's induction, or refusal to be so inducted, to be filmed and televised. However, Mr. Ali's refusal to take the traditional step forward when his name was called, was broadcast and seen by a large audience. This filmed account of his defiance of the law was used as evidence against him in a court of law. As a result, he was convicted of violation of the law in question and was appropriately sentenced.

CHAPTER EIGHT:
WAR'S CLIMAX:
THE ADVENT OF WAR CRIMES;
THE TURNING POINT IN PUBLIC
SENTIMENT, 1968

The foretold moment of truth had arrived. The U. S. was in a squeeze because it finally comprehended that it could never prevail in a guerilla war. The public also comprehended the gravity of the situation and became firmly entrenched against the conflict. New solutions and also new leadership were demanded to extricate the U. S. from the quagmire.

Military Operations In Vietnam, 1968

For the first month of this year, the situation in Vietnam continued as in the prior year. Indeed, the atmosphere seemed to improve because for a few weeks the situation had calmed considerably. A brief truce had been declared because of an upcoming holiday. However, the aforementioned Ron Kovic of the U. S. Marine Corps was seriously wounded during combat operations in Vietnam. He was left a quadriplegic and was sent back to CONUS (see Glossary) to recover from his war wounds and then be Honorably Discharged on full disability. His war medals included a Bronze Star for heroism and a Purple Heart for his wounds received in battle.

In spite of this relative calm in Vietnam, Mr. Kovic's situation notwithstanding, the world would soon be aware that this period was the calm before the storm. What occurred on January 31 was an event which would be named after a traditional holiday in Southeast Asia. This is the celebration of the advent of the Lunar New Year known as Tet. The South Vietnamese in particular were so unsuspecting of any emergency, and apparently so preoccupied with the impending holiday that about half of their military personnel were granted leave.

Allied intelligence sources had suspected that something profound would occur because of known movements of enemy personnel and materiel in several sectors of the region, including neighboring Laos. Then, on the night of January 31 forces of North Vietnam and the Viet Minh/Viet Cong unleashed a fury which would stun the world. Indeed, given the level of fighting which followed for the next several weeks, the enemy appeared to unleash the full force of its military against the Allies. During the next several weeks the tension which had been building since U. S. intervention began, then exploded in an orgy of violence which would be known as the Tet Offensive. This would go on record as the biggest offensive of the war by the forces of North Vietnam and the Viet Minh/Viet Cong.

For the first time, cities were being targeted by the enemy. The names Da Nang, Khe Sahn and Hue would be firmly etched in the annals and nomenclature of the war. Eventually, every major city in South Vietnam including Saigon would succumb to major violence. Accordingly, the prevailing mentality within The Pentagon that the cities were safe, would be forever destroyed. What is most noteworthy is the fact that the U. S. had recently built a new compound surrounding its embassy in Saigon. Of course security within this area was strong, with significant numbers of U. S. Marines on guard. The enemy managed to penetrate even this area. The fighting within the compound was quite intense and resulted in significant carnage on both sides. The enemy apparently had used suicide squads to mount the offensive. The embassy compound was overrun but was eventually retaken by the Marine Security Detachment, but not without heavy U. S. casualties. When the carnage had subsided, the whole affair was deemed a massive failure of intelligence. Morale within the military and in the U. S. plummeted.

The figures of casualties reported during the Offensive give an indication of the level of fighting. U. S. dead were approximately 1,000. The numbers of ARVN killed were placed at double those of the U. S. Official figures of enemy dead were thirty times those of the U. S. For the rest of the year the level of fighting remained high. Deaths of U. S. personnel averaged 300 weekly.

The Tet Offensive also provided the world with possibly the most disturbing image of the war. The Saigon Chief Of Police, one Brig. Gen. Nguyen Ngoc Loan, pistol in hand, summarily executed one of the insurgents. The incident, which was captured on film and promulgated worldwide, showed the bullet being fired into the head of one of those who had instigated the Offensive. The collapse of the shooting victim in the street with the blood rushing from his head is an image which was permanently seared into the minds and consciousness of the U. S. public, and possibly of the world. It was subsequently revealed that the shooting victim had murdered the police chief's family.

Military Repercussions Of The Tet Offensive, The U. S. Side, 1968

U. S. forces reeled from the shock of the offensive from North Vietnam and the Viet Minh/Viet Cong. The optimistic predictions which the U. S. commander, General Westmoreland had recently given were shattered. He was accordingly compelled to radically reassess the situation with respect to the deployment of his troops. In response to the offensive he requested that U. S. forces which were already "in country" be augmented by forty percent, to just over 700,000.

The fury of the Tet Offensive is also the apparent reason why U. S. forces began to engage in war crimes. Passions ran high among the forces, to the extent that these passions apparently caused U. S. soldiers to murder unarmed civilians. The place where some of these crimes occurred, My Lai, is another name which is firmly etched in the annals of the war and of military history.

The incident at My Lai occurred on March 16 in the immediate aftermath of the Tet Offensive. On a "search and destroy mission" to root out the enemy, some troops with the designation Charlie Company engaged in an orgy of violence in which the most egregious atrocities by troops during the war were likely committed. The platoon of soldiers which numbered just over 100, slaughtered over 500 old and young men, women and infants. Some were beaten and tortured without provocation. Women were violated. Some of the villagers who had greeted the U. S. forces or who later surrendered were gunned down.

Charlie Company was under the command of one 1st Lieutenant William Calley. It has been documented that when he gave orders to his subordinates to kill unarmed civilians and they refused, he then murdered them himself. His immediate senior, Captain Ernest Medina was in the immediate vicinity and became aware of the killing spree. He apparently chose to do nothing, however. Further, he failed to report the crimes to his seniors as he was required to do under military law. The crimes were covered up by all in the chain of command and were not promulgated in the media at the time. As will be revealed later however, the crimes would come to light more than a year later.

It would further subsequently be revealed after the war's end that the enemy had been badly mauled. The aforementioned Col. Harry Summers would emerge as the foremost chronicler of the war. He would state that the Viet Cong/Viet Minh had been virtually annihilated during the Tet Offensive. Accordingly, the pursuit of the goal to unify Vietnam would after 1968 fall to other communist factions, he opined.

Military Repercussions Of The Tet Offensive, The South Vietnamese Side, 1968

South Vietnam was compelled to reassess the numbers of troops required to fight the insurgency and also the manner in which troops would be deployed. The military authorities decided that a large buildup of troops was needed. The ARVN which also used conscripts, widened the age limits of men required in uniform from those aged 20 to 33, to men aged 18 to 35. This was done in order to induce another 200,000 men to arms by the end of the year. This would bring the total number of personnel under arms by South Vietnam to 775,000 in a "country" with a population of approximately 16.7 million (1967 est.). In addition, men in other age groups were required to serve in civilian defense units. This was done in spite of the fact that morale within the ranks plummeted to a new low and desertions rose accordingly.

Domestic Repercussions Of The Tet Offensive, 1968

The Tet Offensive would prove to be one of the pivotal events of the war. Public support after the Tet Offensive did not just fall to a new level. This was a turning point which caused most of the public's support for the war to evaporate. Prominent news reporters including the man who many regarded as the "Dean" of U. S. broadcast news reporters, Walter Cronkite, voiced their pessimism on television. Demonstrations and public protests against the war increased commensurately. Debates over U. S. war policy, which had been quite intense before the Offensive, increased to astounding levels. One Senator stated at a press conference that the U. S. should simply declare itself the winner and then depart. The Senator foretold the future, five years before the "future" would be realized.

Possibly the most enduring effect of the Tet Offensive was the advent of another term which would characterize domestic perception of the government's war efforts. The term "credibility gap" was coined and came into common usage. The public seemed to perceive that there was a significant gap between what national leaders were uttering about progress on the war, as opposed to what was actually occurring. Indeed, this perceived lack of government honesty seemed to spawn a general mistrust of government which has endured even unto this writing.

The decreasing public support for the war could be seen in a number of places, most prominent of these being in the Congress. Legislators in record numbers were jumping on the bandwagon to urge an end to the hostilities. Congress refused to grant a request for more troops to be sent to Vietnam. Instead, legislators advocated negotiations to end the war. Senator Al Gore was among those at the forefront of Senate opposition to increased troop strength, in addition to Senator Mansfield of Montana, Senator Fulbright of Arkansas and the man who would be President Johnson's most visible opponent initially, Senator McCarthy of Minnesota.

However, the Commander-In-Chief was the politician to suffer the most profound repercussions of declining fortunes in Vietnam. As in the Congress, President Johnson also embraced a radical reassessment of the situation. First of all, he ordered a halt to the bombing in most of North Vietnam. He further authorized a slightly increased troop strength, to 550,000. However, he also announced that General Westmoreland would be replaced.

What President Johnson did next would stun the public as much as did the level of fighting during the Offensive. In a televised address he uttered the words which would be permanently etched in the annals of American politics. On 31 March he stated: "I shall not seek, and I will not accept, the nomination of my party for another term as your president." The progress of the war, or lack thereof, was then regarded as the reason for Johnson's decision to leave the political arena. It could therefore be said that the war was instrumental in bringing down a President.

However, facts have been revealed which substantiate that Johnson's decision not to run again for office was incidental to the Tet Offensive or the apparent lack of progress on the war. He would die on 22 January 1973. On 11 July 2007 his widow, "Lady Bird" Johnson would also die. In the midst of all the accolades which she received, it was revealed that she was the pivotal influence in her husband's decision to forsake The White House. It seems that in the immediate aftermath of the Tet Offensive, Ms. Johnson, and indeed many around the President, could see that the war was taking a heavy toll on the President. He had suffered a near fatal heart attack thirteen years previously. Fearing that her husband would not likely survive a second term in office, in light of the toll that the "normal" pressures which the office of President entailed, in addition to the added burden of pursuing the war, she urged him not to run for reelection.

When Ms. Johnson died in 2007 the public was again reminded of one of the most disturbing episodes of the war. Before Ms. Johnson died, upon having been interviewed about her tenure in The White House, she recalled the voices of the war protesters outside her residence, which voices taunted her and the President. They often retired nightly, she said, to the taunts of "Hey, hey, L.B.J., how many kids did you kill today?" These voices did not help the President's physical or mental well being.

However, before he was "brought down" President Johnson began to reassess the U. S.' role in the war. He and his second Secretary Of Defense, Clark Clifford, suggested a program whereby the South Vietnamese would play a greater role in the defense of their own "country." Shortly before Johnson left office, the phrase "Vietnamization" began to be uttered in political circles. Stated Secretary Clifford:

> "We will continue to seek ways to effect a reduction of hostilities, to lower the level of violence in South Vietnam, and to turn over more and more defense responsibilities to the South Vietnamese themselves."

Accordingly, though the term "Vietnamization" is usually associated with the advent of the Nixon Administration, the concept was actually the brainchild of his predecessor.

Domestic Repercussions Of The War, 1968

Public opposition to the war reached astounding levels this year. The rancor over the war would then reach into the home of the President and his wife, albeit inadvertently. This year "Lady Bird" Johnson gave a luncheon in the White House for selected guests. Included on the guest list was an individual who had established herself as the consummate entertainer, the African-American singer and actress Eartha Kitt. Ms.

Kitt had been quite active in the entertainment world for more than a twenty year period. She had distinguished herself on the stage, in motion pictures, on phonograph recordings and lastly, on television both in the U. S. and abroad. Since 1966 she had been a regular performer on one of the most popular shows of the era in that medium, *Batman*. After this year however, she would be effectively banished from performing in the U. S. She would not reestablish her career in the U. S. for another ten years.

The reason why Ms. Kitt fell out of favor in her native land was because at the aforementioned luncheon, she voiced her opposition to the war directly to the President's wife. The apparent cause of Ms. Kitt's distress over the war was that African-Americans were shouldering an unfair portion of the burden for fighting the war, she believed. Further, she told Ms. Johnson that the war appeared to her to be the cause of growing civil unrest in the U. S., including greater use of illegal narcotics.

Ms. Kitt's frank opinions about the war directly to the President's family cost her her career. Contracts for performances for which she had already signed, evaporated. She was effectively blacklisted in the U. S. After the Central Intelligence Agency (C. I. A.) investigated her and then began to spread rumors about her personal life, she fled to Europe where she was still widely known and admired. She pursued her usual occupation there.

A corollary to the above affair was that this year the C. I. A. was found to be in violation of the law. The charter which formed the agency in 1947 from the Office Of Strategic Services (O. S. S.), specifically prescribed that the agency limit its activities to foreign operations. It was expressly prohibited from conducting domestic surveillance. One could safely speculate that the cause of such illegal activities was the rancor over the war. The resultant disclosure that the organization had violated the terms of its charter caused a public uproar.

Possible Domestic Repercussions Of The War, 1968

On 4 April the Rev. Dr. Martin Luther King, Jr., regarded by many as the preeminent civil rights leader of the era, was shot and killed in Memphis, TN. Ever since that tragic event, numerous circles have pondered the assassin's reason for taking the life of the individual who had been awarded the Nobel Prize for Peace in 1964. Theories have abounded since then, many of which have speculated that the government was complicit in Dr. King's murder. One circle of U. S. society has theorized that Dr. King was killed because he opposed the war. It has never been confirmed that these allegations have any basis in fact. However, Dr. King's assassination had a profound impact on the anti-war movement. Such impact is detailed below.

The Political Arena, 1968

President Johnson's decision not to run for reelection also caused others in the political arena to begin "jockeying" for the Office of President. These of course included Senator McCarthy who had come on strong against Johnson in the first political primary of the season in New Hampshire. He nearly won that contest. Senator George Romney of Michigan also joined the fray. His presence in the race for President was short lived, however. He was the target of considerable ridicule in several circles, not the least of these was in the press. When he announced that he had been a supporter of the war because of the reports that he had seen from military authorities in Vietnam, but that he had been "brainwashed" by them, his political fortunes in the Presidential race evaporated quickly. Senator Robert Kennedy of New York also saw an opportunity in Johnson's decision not to run. These were of course just a part of the roster. Others would soon join in the Presidential race, not just from the two traditional political parties, but also from third parties. One could then see the turmoil in the oven of U. S. politics which resulted from the war.

With respect to Senator Kennedy, he had originally supported most of U. S. policies in Vietnam. However, the events of early 1968 would cause him to reassess his position on the war considerably. It is noteworthy that after he announced his quest for the Presidency, he would usurp Senator McCarthy as the most audible voice in the Senate among the Presidential contenders who advocated an end to the war. Many began to view him as the best hope to end the hostilities. He managed to rally so many to his cause that he would achieve a stunning political victory. On June 5 he won the Democratic Primary in California, beating formidable rivals. This virtually guaranteed him the nomination at the convention to be held in Chicago in August. His ambitions and the hope which many saw in him to end the war were to be short-lived, however. On the night of his primary victory he was shot and killed at the Ambassador Hotel in Los Angeles, his headquarters. It is interesting to note that the individual who would be convicted of the murder gave no indication that the ongoing war was the reason for his having so acted. Lastly, it was subsequently suggested by some that had Kennedy lived, he would have been elected President and he would have then ended the war much sooner than the date of its eventual conclusion.

In conjunction with the above, it should be noted that Senator Kennedy's brother, President Kennedy had laid plans to end U. S. involvement in Vietnam some five years prior. In view of the close relationship which the two had, it could be speculated that President Kennedy had confided in the Senator what his plans were. One could therefore safely speculate that Senator Kennedy's election to the Presidency this year would have furthered his brother's plans and also would have been the catalyst for U. S. withdrawal from Vietnam five years prior to the actual departure.

a. The Final Roster
1. *The Democratic side*
On the Democratic side, the person who would eventually be chosen to succeed President Johnson was Hubert H. Humphrey, the Vice President. His running mate was the Senator from Maine, Edmund Muskie. Their stance on the war substantially echoed that of President Johnson. They believed in pursuing the war as it had been, albeit with negotiations with North Vietnam and the Viet Minh/Viet Cong. As such, their nomination was opposed by a large segment of the public.

2. *The Republican side*
On the Republican side, the former Vice President Richard M. Nixon, was nominated on the first ballot for the office of President at the Republican National Convention in Miami Beach. His running mate was then-Governor of Maryland, Spiro T. Agnew. Nixon never clearly asserted his position on Vietnam during the campaign. In lieu of a firm

policy on this issue, he stated that he had a plan to end the war. When asked what such a plan entailed, he stated that he could not reveal such, because such revelation might disrupt peace initiatives or might aid the enemy.

3. *The "Law And Order" candidates*

A third party aspirant to the Office Of President was the former Governor of Alabama George C. Wallace. He chose for his running mate former General Of The Air Force Curtis LeMay. These were the "law and order" candidates who assigned no name to their political banner. U. S. policy on Vietnam was apparently secondary to them. However, in addition to their stated policy of neutralizing the influence of persons who they regarded as unworthy to participate in U. S. society, the two candidates were distressed about certain aspects of the war. Wallace's and LeMay's primary aim was to "Put the Negroes and the beard-growing, draft card-burning student demonstrators back in their places." (Collier's Year Book For 1969, Covering The Year 1968). Their position on Vietnam was basically to continue the present Administration's policies. The two were not in complete agreement on how to pursue the war, however. General LeMay stated publicly that he would not rule out the use of nuclear weapons on North Vietnam. Governor Wallace did not agree.

4. *The Freedom And Peace candidate*

The comedian and human rights activist Dick Gregory contributed to the debate over the war by running for President on a fourth party ticket, the Freedom and Peace Party. A major part of his platform was to end the war.

5. *The Peace And Freedom candidate*

Another figure of note who ran for President was the civil rights activist Eldridge Cleaver. A major part of his platform on the fifth party ticket, the Peace and Freedom Party, was also to end the war.

6. *The final judgment of the electorate*

The result of the hotly contested campaign for President was that Richard Nixon was elected the thirty-seventh President Of The United States.

b. the organized opposition to the war
1. *Boston, Massachusetts*

This year Boston would regain its stature in the eyes of many as the cradle of a revolutionary movement. The city which had hosted the Boston Tea Party in 1773 had indeed been the cradle of American democracy during the Revolution which drove the British out of the fledgling United States. Now the city endeavored to compel the U. S. to withdraw from Indochina. During the instant war the city again expressed its opposition to an alien cause which it believed was morally wrong. No other city can claim to have had more activity to resist the military draft, and therefore to impact national efforts to end the war, than did Boston.

In *Confronting The War Machine*, Michael Foley thoroughly and eloquently argues the case of Boston's preeminent role in the anti-war movement. The three primary organizations which Foley examines which organized to oppose the war are (1) The Cambridge (MA) Committee To End The War In Vietnam (CCEWV), (2) The New England Resistance (NER), and (3) The Boston Draft Resistance Group (BDRG). These organizations began shortly after the war had begun in earnest in 1965. Their efforts culminated in a mass rally which occurred in Boston in October, 1967. The BDRG appeared to have had the most impact on the Boston draft resistance scene, and possibly on the anti-war movement nationwide. Its efforts centered around organizing to oppose the draft, as opposed to directly agitating to end the war. The BDRG's rationale in directly opposing the draft, as opposed to directly opposing the war, was that forming a radical constituency through draft resistance was the tactic which they believed most likely to mobilize opposition to the war where it would have the most impact. The decision of the BDRG to oppose the draft was borne of the fact that the draft law as it was then being administered, was quite inequitable. One can observe below under the heading *The Draft, 1969*, that this sentiment was echoed by many, including by at least one senior member of the military.

In light of the events which would occur this year, it indeed appears that the BDRG's efforts to impede the government's war-making capability were at least minimally successful. The government was apparently so alarmed at the efforts of the anti-war movement that it decided to use a group of certain individuals as an example in its efforts to punish draft resisters. On 29 January the Boston Five, a group of individuals including the noted pediatrician Dr. Benjamin Spock, was indicted in the U. S. District Court For The District Of Massachusetts in Boston. The group was prosecuted primarily for allegedly conspiring to counsel others to violate draft laws.

The indictment of the Boston Five seemed to backfire on the government however, because the outrage which then ensued after the government's case was announced, set off a firestorm of even more anti-war activity in the form of greater draft resistance. The nationally organized effort to impede the government's ability to conscript men to further the war effort, had finally come to a climax.

During this interval another of the war's "quirks" came to pass. Two separate events occurred virtually simultaneously which were not directly related. However, these two events appear to have been linked because they stemmed from the same issue: the war. Shortly after the war officially began in 1964, officials of the Johnson Administration, having been informed of the budding efforts to oppose the war, had tried to establish a link between this anti-war movement and the progress that the enemy was making on the battlefield. That is, prominent officials including F. B. I. Director J. Edgar Hoover and the Selective Service System Director Gen. Lewis Hershey stated publicly that the anti-war movement fueled the enemy's resolve. The movement, they publicly opined, was communist-inspired. In other words, they believed that citizens who opposed the war were not just aiding and abetting the enemy. Such individuals were also suspected of being communist agents encouraged and/or funded by foreign governments.

The "quirk" was that the indictment of the Boston Five on 29 January which fueled the anti-war movement was virtually simultaneous with the previously discussed Tet Offensive on 31 January. The two events occurred approximately forty-eight hours apart. Accordingly it indeed appeared that the anti-war activists had fueled the enemy's resolve. However, in light of the fact that the Tet Offensive was of such magnitude that it must have been in the planning stages long before it materialized, it does not appear that the enemy considered the actions of the anti-war protesters when it launched its military action. Accordingly, it appears that the government was mistaken in its efforts to blame citizens for encouraging the enemy. However, inasmuch as the anti-war movement had been going on for at least two years before the Tet Offensive began, the purported link between the two phenomena is another facet of the war which will likely be debated into perpetuity.

It is further worth noting that the draft resistance movement was apparently energized this year by an event which, to reiterate, may have been caused by the war. Foley clearly makes the point (pp. 267 – 68) that the anti-war/anti-draft movement nationwide, in addition to the indictment of the Boston Five, was likely further fueled by the murder on 4 April of the Rev. Dr. Martin Luther King. The previous year Dr. King had begun efforts to forge a link between the anti-war movement and the issue of civil rights for non-whites. When Dr. King was killed, the members of this movement, who were coincidentally nearly all white, understood that both of the movements were linked. Many in the anti-war/anti-draft movement finally believed what Dr. King had been asserting: that the war and the racism which is so pervasive in U. S. society were both part of the government's efforts to silence those who held opposing views. Foley further makes the point that upon receipt of the news of Dr. King's murder, this in turn fueled the civil rights movement. The mostly white groups involved in opposing both the draft and the war also began to make racism their enemy.

However powerful the government was in silencing its critics concerning the war and the draft, the anti-war/anti-draft movement in question received a great deal of satisfaction on 31 March. Recall that on this date President Johnson announced that he would not seek reelection. In the same televised speech he further stated that (1) he had called a halt to the bombing of North Vietnam and (2) his administration would start efforts to secure a negotiated peace. Upon hearing the news, on the night of 31 March the members of the BDRG, the NER and the CCEWV, among others, were literally dancing in the streets of Boston (in the rain). They believed that their efforts to end the war had indeed impacted the government's position on the subject.

Accordingly, in view of the likely impact that the anti-war/anti-draft movement had on the conduct of the war, it appears that the purported statement of Richard Nixon which had been recorded in 1966, that the greatest threat to the war effort would come from within the U. S., rather than from without, was indeed prophetic.

2. *Catonsville, Maryland*

Another facet to the organized opposition to the war occurred on 17 May in Catonsville, MD. In an effort to express their outrage over the burgeoning war, nine persons invaded a Selective Service office there, poured a flammable liquid on draft records which the group had ripped from file cabinets, and then set the records on fire. This act may have been another reaction to the Tet Offensive. The reason why they so acted, they stated, was to protest soldiers being sent to Vietnam. Whatever other motives they may have had, their actions did convey their outrage over the war.

Two of the individuals in question were ordained priests: The Rev. Daniel Berrigan (Jesuit), and his brother, The Rev. Philip Berrigan (Josephite). The seven others were: (1) Brother David Darst, (2) John Hogan, (3) Tom Lewis, (4) Marjorie Melville, (5) her husband Thomas Melville, (6) George Mische, and (7) Mary Moylan. There were nine in all.

Prosecution of the Catonsville Nine immediately began for violation of the Selective Service Act Of 1967, destroying U. S. Government property and destruction of draft files. The trial of the group commenced in the U. S. District Court For The District Of Maryland on 5 October, with noted attorney William Kunstler representing the defendants. Every member of the group was convicted. All appealed the verdict to the U. S. Court Of Appeals For The Fourth Circuit (Richmond).

3. *Chicago, Illinois*

By the time of the Democratic convention in Chicago, various groups who opposed the war would descend on that city to make known their sentiments to those responsible for the raging conflict. Having been made aware of the expected appearance of these organizations, law enforcement personnel also made their presence known in force. The major groups which law enforcement officers confronted were: (1) The Students For A Democratic Society (SDS), an organization devoted to social justice, (2) The National Mobilization Against the Vietnam War, (3) The Youth International ("Yippie") Party, which had no firm agenda, and (4) The Black Panther Party which included Eldridge Cleaver and which advocated a program of self-defense for the African-American community. These groups were united only in that they wanted an end to the war. As one can see below, the leaders of three of these groups would become collectively known as The Chicago Seven. This group would face serious retribution from government authorities for their anti-war activities.

What occurred in Chicago on the night of August 29 is another event which would shock the public and also galvanize domestic dissent over the war. Violence erupted in several areas near the convention hall where the balloting was to occur to choose the Democratic nominee. What is odd was that the violence was instigated by an institution regarded as a bulwark against disorder. The Chicago police rioted. The images of billy club swinging police, tear-gassing people who had gathered in a public park at dusk and pushing people through shattered windows in front of the Hilton Hotel will be forever seared into the public consciousness.

It has never been documented that the police were provoked by the demonstrators, or by anyone else. What is known is that the police indiscriminately assaulted anyone who they could find. Groups of police officers beat and clubbed innocent bystanders. These even included elderly persons, women and children who were attending the convention. A report published in *The New York Times* on the date in question stated that a group of bystanders standing in front of a hotel was charged by the police and pushed through a hotel window. In the midst of the broken glass, some of the victims already injured, they were then beaten by the police. As the disturbance was occurring, news of such reached the delegates and the news reporters inside the convention hall. Walter Cronkite of CBS News voiced his outrage at the brutality of the police. The next day the CBS Evening News broadcast a segment in which a gentleman who appeared to be European-American, was interviewed on his front lawn, blood rushing down his face. When asked what had happened, he stated that a police officer approached him as he was standing on his lawn, which was near the sight of the convention. When the officer asked the gentleman what he was doing, he stated that he was "just standing here." He claimed that the officer then clubbed him without provocation.

The riot primarily resulted from confrontations between the Chicago police and the groups in question. The police were joined however by other law enforcement organizations including the National Guard and also a contingent of the U. S. Army. The protesters who were estimated at approximately 5,000, were outnumbered by about 4:1.

The Chicago police force thereby apparently expressed its sentiments concerning those who opposed the war. It must be noted that reporters on the convention floor were also assaulted by persons who appeared to be law enforcement officers. The Chicago riot represents the degree to which the public was polarized over Vietnam. Also, during the melee Mayor Richard Daley, generally regarded as the "boss of all political bosses" uttered what would be remembered as one of the greatest "misspeaks" of that era. Stated the Mayor when he was questioned at a news conference about the disturbance: "The policeman isn't there to create disorder. The policeman is there to *preserve* disorder." A joke making the rounds after the disturbance was that the convention was a segment of the show *"Beat The Press* and *Mace The Nation."* The entire episode was immortalized shortly thereafter in popular song. The folk/rock group Harvard Lampoon recorded the song *Welcome To The Club* which made light of the disorder at the convention. The releasing label was Epic (Columbia). As the song went:

> If you're down, come up to Chicago!
> It's a rock 'em, sock 'em kick in the head.
> A swingin' town, oh, yes, sir, that's what Chicago is.
> A welcoming committee set on knocking you dead.
> For excitement that's built in, come on down to the Hilton.
> When we do it there, we do it with class!
> So long peace and quiet, a regular riot.
> Yeah, the folks who know Chicago say it's really a gas!
> (Copyright © 1968, The Harvard Lampoon).

Immediately after the police riot, Vice President Humphrey was nominated on the first ballot for the Office Of President Of The United States.

The Draft, 1968

a. Points of controversy
Meanwhile, the efforts of organizations opposed to the draft notwithstanding, men continued to be drafted into the Armed Forces in greater numbers, especially into the Army. The abolishment of

deferments to attend graduate school helped to fuel the numbers of men in the available pool of potential conscripts. Controversy over the draft intensified this year when the government also abolished many occupational deferments. Previously, to reiterate, if an individual held a certain occupation in which there was a shortage, or which was deemed vital by the government, one could request and be granted a deferment from military service on those grounds.

Also this year the international community began to assert its viewpoint on conscription in general, not just in the U. S. The World Council Of Churches which met in Uppsala, Sweden issued a document which supported each individual's right of conscientious objection to *specific* wars. This was in conflict with the existing U. S. draft law which allowed for conscientious objection, but only to war in general. This would of course add fuel to the debate over the issue.

The aforementioned body of churches was therefore in moral accord with the individual who served as Commander-In-Chief during the U. S. Civil War. While serving in the House Of Representatives in 1847 Abraham Lincoln strongly opposed the Mexican War (1846 – 48). Though Congressman Lincoln was not subject to conscription, he alleged during that conflict that the current Commander-In- Chief had trumped up charges that the war had been instigated by Mexico.

b. The case of Perry Watkins

Among those conscripted this year was one Perry Watkins, an avowed (open) homosexual. To reiterate, homosexuals were barred by law from serving in the Armed Forces. However, Watkins had previously informed his local draft board of his sexual orientation before he was inducted. Ordinarily his induction into the Army would have gone forever unnoticed. However, it would eventually come to pass that his very presence in the Armed Forces would be an issue which would receive much notoriety long after the war would conclude.

c. The case of William Jefferson Clinton

One of those subject to immediate conscription this year was one William Jefferson Clinton. He had registered for the draft in August, 1964 as required by law. He did however apply for and receive a II-S Student Deferment which guaranteed his being deferred from military service until his undergraduate studies were completed. Upon his scheduled graduation from college in mid-1968, he was reclassified I-A, liable for immediate call-up to military service. Clinton then applied for but was denied a deferment to enter graduate school. Such deferments had been abolished by the SSS this year. This individual then wrote letters to persons who were in a position to alter his draft status. He was eventually allowed to enter graduate study at Oxford University in England as a Rhodes Scholar. There he participated in demonstrations against the war.

It must be noted that when Clinton completed his graduate studies the first phase of the war was still on. Accordingly, when he completed such studies he was still liable to the government for military service. It has never been revealed why he was not conscripted at this time. He was never inducted. However, his apparent efforts to elude the draft would return to haunt him many years in the future.

The Judicial Perspective, 1968

a. *Holmes v. United States*

This year the judiciary further weighed in on issues related to the war. Several cases which pertained to the draft reached the Supreme Court. The first of these was *Holmes* v. *United States* (391 U. S. 145). The individual Holmes petitioned the Court because he did not believe that the government had the right to conscript men when no war had been declared by Congress. Holmes had been prosecuted and convicted for violation of the Universal Military Training And Service Act when he failed to report for induction as ordered by his draft board. His petition to the Court to overturn his conviction by grant of *Writ Of Certiorari* was refused. His conviction was allowed to stand.

b. *O'Brien v. United States*

The second of the three draft-related cases which reached the Supreme Court this year was *O'Brien* v. *United States* (391 U. S. 367). In March, 1966 the aforementioned individual O'Brien, in collusion with several others, publicly burned their draft cards. Inasmuch as Congress had outlawed draft card burning in 1965 when it amended the applicable law, O'Brien was prosecuted and then convicted for violating that statute.

What is noteworthy about this case is that the U. S. Court Of Appeals For The First Circuit (Boston) to which O'Brien had appealed to have his conviction overturned, did not overturn his conviction. That court did however hold the 1965 amendment to the law unconstitutional under the First Amendment. That Amendment of course guarantees freedom of expression. The Supreme Court responded in turn by holding that the 1965 amendment to the law which outlawed draft card burning was indeed constitutional.

c. *Hart v. United States*

The third Supreme Court case, *Hart* v. *United States* (391 U. S. 956), merely echoed the sentiments of the *Holmes* case. The individual Hart also claimed that the government had no right to conscript men when no war had been declared by Congress. As with the individual in *Holmes*, his conviction for refusing to be inducted when ordered to do so by his draft board was upheld.

d. The initial adjudication of *Benjamin Spock, et. al.*, a.k.a. "The Boston Five"

Lastly, on 14 June each of the aforementioned Boston Five was convicted in the U. S. District Court For The District Of Massachusetts. Their convictions were immediately appealed to the U. S. Court Of Appeals For The First Circuit (Boston).

Diplomatic Initiatives To End The Hostilities, 1968

On May 13 talks began in Paris to end the hostilities. It was a major effort to coax all interested parties to the negotiating table. Possibly the greatest impediment was deciding who were entitled to sit at such a table. The U. S. initially agreed to meet only with representatives from North Vietnam. Much of the controversy centered around the status of the National Front For The Independence Of Vietnam, now known as the National Liberation Front, or NLF. This was the new name for the Viet Minh/Viet Cong.

The South Vietnamese were reluctant to have the NLF present, however. The U. S. was finally forced to adopt Senator Kennedy's advice that the NLF be present. The NLF was eventually afforded a seat at the negotiating table as an agent independent from North Vietnam. Accordingly, the South Vietnamese were reluctantly compelled to acquiesce.

Perception Of The Hostilities From The International Community, 1968

The two most prominent branches of the United Nations, the Security Council and the General Assembly, still failed to make the war a part of its agenda this year. However, when President Johnson ordered a complete halt to the bombing of North Vietnam on 31 March, Secretary General U Thant expressed his pleasure at such.

The Televised Broadcast Media Weighs In, 1968

a. The advent of the promulgating of The Credibility Gap
Recall that during the Kennedy Administration David Halberstam was among those reporters who were courageous enough to report the difference between actual events in Vietnam as opposed to what the government claimed. This year the deception which the government had sought to perpetrate would finally register in the collective public's mind. Prior to this year, U. S. television declined to allocate extensive coverage to the war. With the burgeoning hostilities however, as evidenced by the aforementioned Tet Offensive, this began to change. It became apparent to the public that there was a marked gap between what government leaders were telling the public, and what in fact was going on in Vietnam. The U. S. broadcast establishment apparently sought to close this gap. This in turn spawned the aforementioned term "Credibility Gap" which term is firmly etched into the nomenclature of the war.

b. The chief proponent of The Credibility Gap
To reiterate, Walter Cronkite, the dean of broadcast journalists at the time, was the leading proponent in the effort to bring truth to the public

about the war. In March, in the immediate wake of the Tet Offensive, Mr. Cronkite stated on the CBS Evening News where he was anchor, that the government was wrong to continue the war as it had been. Several of his nightly news broadcasts ended with this criticism.

Though there were some who questioned Mr. Cronkite's qualifications to criticize the government's Vietnam policies, he had indeed visited Vietnam. For a two week period during the Tet Offensive he examined the war first-hand. He returned convinced that the war was a lesson in futility. It should be noted that Mr. Cronkite had such credibility with the public that one could conclude that his broadcast opinion was the pivotal point in swaying public sentiment against the war.

In a subsequent interview in *Playboy* magazine in January, 1973 Mr. Cronkite stated:

> "I think the effect (of his broadcast editorials) was to finally solidify doubts in a lot of people's minds – to swing some people over to the side of opposition to our continued policy in Vietnam. I must be careful not to be immodest here, but I happen to think it may have had an effect on the (Johnson) Administration itself."

Mr. Cronkite further stated during that interview that in conversation with President Johnson several times including ten days before Johnson's death in January, 1973, the former President never stated that he regretted any of the policies he had pursued in Vietnam.

The Literary Community Input, 1968

This year Norman Mailer followed up on his triumph of the previous year with another work, a non-fiction novel entitled *The Armies Of The Night*. This Pulitzer Prize and National Book Award-winning work is a "historicized" and "novelized" account of the October, 1967 march on the Pentagon which protested the war. That historical event was the first large-scale organized protest during the conflict.

Armies Of The Night was universally lauded as a masterpiece of journalism. However, it was an important literary work for another reason. The book articulated the sentiments of a segment of U. S. society which would have a profound impact upon the nation's consciousness, especially concerning the war: the New Left. This appellation distinguished it from the Old Left, that is, those who had embraced the politics of President Franklin Roosevelt. The New Left would include the Chicago Seven, discussed below. This group would be the driving force behind the organized movement to end the war.

The Popular Culture, 1968

a. Phonograph recordings
1. *Herbert Harper's Free Press*
No popular songs were released this year which protested the war. However, in addition to the aforementioned *Welcome To The Club*, the blues singer Muddy Waters recorded *Herbert Harper's Free Press*. The song indeed reflected the mood of the times by echoing the general level of turmoil in society, especially as it pertained to the war and the military draft. The releasing label was the major independent Chess Recording Corporation. The title of the song stems from the proliferation of underground/counter-culture newspapers which gained popularity because of profound changes in U. S. society. The root cause of such changes was of course the war. As the song went:

> "Headline news!
> There's a war going on.
> The hippies sing a flower song,
> While draft card burning is going on."
> (Copyright © 1968, Chevis Publishing Corp.)

Herbert Harper's Free Press was included on the album *Electric Mud* which was released on 11/9/68. It rose to # 127 on Billboard's album chart.

And the beat continued…

2. *Pat Paulsen For President*
The "dry wit" comedian Pat Paulsen recorded before a "live" audience *Pat Paulsen For President*. The album's subtitle was *Politics is a dirty business. This is a dirty record*. The releasing label was the conglomerate

Mercury Record Corporation. On the recording Mr. Paulsen addressed a variety of subjects. All of these centered around the political turmoil because of the burgeoning war. Concerning the military for instance, Mr. Paulsen was in top form in offering a stinging commentary with his contribution to the debate over the issue of conscription. Stated Mr. Paulsen in his *Soldier's Lament*:

> "A good many people today feel our present draft laws are unjust. These people are called soldiers. Let us take this step-by-step. When we talk about the draft, we are talking about a law duly enacted by Congress, in which men should be drafted first, women second and Congressmen last. And what are the arguments against the draft? We hear that it is unfair, immoral, discourages young men from studying, and ruins their careers and their lives. Picky, picky, picky." (Copyright © 1968, KSF Music & Big Drum Music).

Pat Paulsen For President was released on 10/19/68 and it rose to # 71 on Billboard's album chart.

b. Television
1. *Rowan & Martin's Laugh-In*
The war also became the butt of televised humor. Two of the most memorable broadcasts this year were seen on the show *Rowan & Martin's Laugh-In*. According to Tim Brooks and Earle Marsh in their book *The Complete Directory To Prime Time Network And Cable T.V. Shows, 1946 – Present*, the show:

> "... was one of T. V.'s classics, one of those rare programs which was not only an overnight sensation, but was highly innovative, created a raft of new stars and started trends in comedy which other programs would follow. It crystallized a kind of contemporary, fast-paced, unstructured comedy 'happening' that was exactly what an agitated America wanted in 1968."

America was certainly agitated this year for a number of reasons, the most likely of which was the turmoil over the war. This is possibly what prompted the show's co-host Dan Rowan to utter the comment: "According to an official statement from the Department Of Defense, U. S. military personnel are only in Vietnam in an advisory capacity. Now it looks like we've got over half-a-million advisors in Vietnam." Also, a broadcast from October showed then-Presidential candidate Richard Nixon in a "cameo" role, uttering one of the show's standard gags, "Sock it to me?"

As a result of pandering to "agitated" America's concerns, *Rowan & Martin's Laugh-In* quickly rose to the #1 spot of nationally televised shows. It would remain at that spot for much of the war.

b. The cinema
1. *The Green Berets*
Hollywood capitalized on what was left of the patriotic fervor concerning the war by releasing a motion picture directed by and starring a national hero, John Wayne. He was the driving force behind the film *The Green Berets*. The film was unabashedly pro-Vietnam War. Though the film was released to nearly universal unfavorable reviews, it did well at the box office.

2. *Patton*
Further on the subject of the cinema this year, filming began on *Patton*. This was to be a cinematic biography of one of the heroes of the Second World War, Gen. George S. Patton, Jr. The reason why the production of this film bears mention here is that there was opposition to the film at the studio which produced it. Some studio executives opposed the production of the film because of the turmoil with which the nation was gripped because of the instant conflict. They believed that the film was too pro-war. Some of these executives further believed that the film would not be well received because of increasing anti-war sentiment. Such sentiment had increased markedly from the previous year. Indeed, the actor who was selected to star in the film, George. C. Scott, personally objected to the film. It bears mention that Mr. Scott was an Army veteran of the Second World War who had volunteered to participate in that conflict out of pure, unvarnished patriotism. He would subsequently discuss his military experiences and his rationale

for appearing in *Patton* during an interview after the Vietnam War would conclude.

It bears mention that the motion picture director Oliver Stone would, many years in the future, opine that upon viewing *Patton*, President Nixon was energized to expand the Indochina War into Cambodia. Mr. Stone would state in his analysis of the film *Nixon* which he would write, produce and direct in 1995, that Nixon was motivated after having viewed *Patton*, to begin a massive bombing of Cambodia. This he would state in the documentary which would be included with *Nixon* in the DVD format release of the film in 2008. The U. S. experience over Cambodia will be discussed below.

3. *Head*

This year would see the release of the first "counterculture" film which included actual images of troops engaged in hostile action in Vietnam. The term "counterculture" is apropos because prior to the instant conflict, it would have been unthinkable for the producer of a movie to alternate images of the horrors of war with images of humor/popular culture. Here is another indication of the cultural revolution which the U. S. was experiencing because of the turmoil over the war. Now the war would be for the first time firmly entwined with the popular culture. The film *Head* was not about Vietnam or any issue related thereto. Rather, it might best be labeled a "screwball" comedy which happened to include graphic images of U. S. troops in combat "in country." The film also included the aforementioned images of a Viet Cong/ Viet Minh saboteur being summarily executed by virtue of a bullet fired into his brain. Additional sequences include Vietnamese peasants cowering amidst the carnage occurring around them. It must be noted that the film declined to make light of the burgeoning war. The film is difficult to characterize. Even the world-renowned movie critic Leonard Maltin had difficulty characterizing the film which included actor Jack Nicholson (who co-produced). However, because of its imagery which at times interspersed elements of the U. S. "pop" culture with the aforementioned combat sequences, he stated in his assessment of the film that it is "Well worth seeing."

c. Broadway
1. *Hair*

Also this year the issues of the war finally made it to The Great White Way. The biggest hit on Broadway this year was the wildly successful, controversial and irreverent musical show *Hair*. The show examined a multitude of issues in U. S. society, among them sexual practices previously considered taboo, narcotics use, miscegenation between blacks and whites, and of course the burning issue of the time, the war.

Hair opened on Broadway on 29 April after having been staged successfully off-Broadway for several months. Because of its unique nature, it is hard to characterize. Suffice it to say that it is a love-tribal-rock-musical. Oddly, one of the three persons who conceptualized the show was one who had reversed the stream of U. S. citizens who fled to Canada in order to avoid military service. Galt McDermott was a Canadian national who immigrated to the U. S. to produce the musical, among other things. The central character was Claude who was about to be drafted into the Army. Though his anticipated entry into the Armed Forces was not the central theme of the musical, it did address issues concerning military service and the war. One of the songs therein was explicit in addressing both the communiqués about the war's "progress" to which the public was being constantly subjected, and also how the war was being pursued. The song *Three-Five-Zero-Zero*, characterized as a "surrealistic anti-war song", summarized the war thusly:

> "*Two hundred fifty-six Viet Cong captured. It's a dirty little war.*"
> (Copyright © 1968, EMI Music Publishing Inc.).

Among the lyrics in another song in the musical was one which would become one of the catch phrases of the war: "Hell no, we won't go!"

As with *Rowan & Martin's Laugh-In*, the aforementioned television show which debuted at approximately the same time, to paraphrase Brooks & Marsh, *Hair*:

> … was one of Broadway's' classics, one of those rare musical productions which was not only an overnight

sensation, but was highly innovative, created a raft of new stars and started trends in the theater which other musicals would follow. It crystallized a kind of contemporary, fast-paced, unstructured musical 'happening' that was exactly what an agitated America wanted in 1968.

The war had indeed ignited a domestic cultural revolution.

d. The college lecture circuit

The pugilist and convicted draft-resister Muhammad Ali also made his presence known this year. Having been stripped of his heavyweight title, then denied a boxing license in every state, and also denied the right to fight abroad, he embarked on a new means of livelihood. This year saw him on a tour of college campuses, preaching his message of draft resistance and his philosophy of life in general. His audience of mostly white college students greeted him warmly wherever he spoke.

The Author's Situation, 1968

The author began his sophomore year in college. During the year he would hear his second political science professor mock then-Presidential candidate Richard Nixon's secret "plan" to end the war. On the campaign trail, Nixon insisted that he had such a plan to end the hostilities. However, he would not divulge the plan. Hence the mocking from the author's professor. Subsequent to Nixon's electoral victory, it was revealed that his "plan" to end the war was a campaign marketing gimmick.

Reports From The Print Media, 1968

Meanwhile, the U. S. print media cranked out its assessment of the situation in Vietnam. The following is a partial listing of journalists' findings published this year:

1. *Stand Firm In Vietnam! interview ed., by D. Reed*
   (Reader's Digest, 1/68, pp. 102 – 106)

2. *U. S. misadventure in Vietnam,* H. J. Morgenthau
(Current History, 1/68, pp. 29 – 34)

3. *End the war talks?: what General Wheeler thinks*
(U. S. News & World Report, 1/1/68, E. G. Wheeler, p. 10)

4. *Hearts and minds in Vietnam*
(The Nation, 1/1/68, p. 4)

5. *Guilty minority: first U. S. war crimes trial to come out of Vietnam*
(Time, 1/5/68, pp. 31 – 32)

6. *Vietcong cadre of terror: operations of F-100 unit,* D. Moser
(Life, 1/12/68, pp. 19 – 29)

7. *Talks with G. I.s on their way to combat in Vietnam,* J. N. Wallace
(U. S. News & World Report, 1/15/68, pp. 56 – 57)

8. *Vietnam's daily toll: twenty-six U. S. dead*
(U. S. News & World Report, 1/15/68, p. 12)

9. *Fighting with the Vietcong: photographs*
(Look, 1/23/68, pp. 62 – 63)

CHAPTER NINE:
THE ADVENT OF "VIETNAMIZATION";
THE BEGINNING OF DISINVOLVEMENT,
1969

The new leadership recognized the new reality that dictated the U. S. must extricate itself from Indochina. This new leadership fulfilled its promise to disassociate the U. S. from a war which had proven to be a costly mistake. National passions cooled commensurately.

The National Mood Over The War, 1969

This year began on a note of hope to find a way out of the quagmire known as Vietnam. The inauguration of Richard M. Nixon on 20 January as the thirty seventh President helped soothe the sentiments of many. This despite the fact that Nixon's assumption of power was the realization of an effort to halt what is arguably the second most fearsome aspect of the Cold War. Nixon repeatedly emphasized in his memoirs (*RN,* pp. 71, 281) his perception that the Soviet Union desired to dominate the world. Frequently he stated therein his belief that the instant war was a manifestation of the Soviets' effort to dictate its policy of worldwide domination to every other communist state. The instant war was therefore the government's effort to halt not only the spread of communism but also to impede the Soviet Union's desire to dominate the world. Since Nixon's elevation to Congress in 1947 he had made his reputation as a rabid anti-communist. Upon his assumption of the Presidency however, he still did not put forth a definite plan to end the hostilities. His previously asserted secret "plan" to end the war was still unknown. This caused dismay among certain circles.

The first major protests over the war occurred in coordinated demonstrations nationwide. On April 5 and 6, these took place in Atlanta, Chicago, Los Angeles, New York, San Francisco and Seattle.

After a short while in office however, the Nixon Administration finally crystallized its position on the war. The major characteristic of this Administration was to expand on the concept of "Vietnamization" of the war effort. To reiterate, South Vietnam's military, the ARVN, had always fought poorly against the Viet Minh/Viet Cong and the North Vietnamese. Morale therein continued to be appallingly low. U. S. leaders and of course the public had become increasingly impatient with South Vietnam because it seemed to be uninterested in defending its own "country." Accordingly, machinery began to be put in place to require, or allow, the South Vietnamese to shoulder most of the burden of fighting.

In June the Nixon Administration officially adopted its policy of Vietnamization. Indeed, this was the cornerstone of Nixon's Vietnam policy for the rest of the first phase of the war. It was announced that as the burden of fighting the war by the South Vietnamese rose, then this would dictate the degree to which U. S. forces would be withdrawn from Vietnam. However, one of the paradoxes of this policy was that, as stated before, the South Vietnamese had consistently demonstrated that it could not fight the war on its own. Therefore, to shift more of the burden on the ARVN would mean that the war would eventually be lost, some suggested. The opinion of these pundits would indeed prove prophetic.

Another of the areas in which one could see a marked departure from the policies of his predecessor was in Nixon's declaration that the war could not be won militarily. Accordingly, most observers knew that the U. S. would have to pursue a negotiated peace. Nixon would continue to stress that the U. S. would only accept a "peace with honor." This was because he was concerned that anything less than such a peace would irreparably damage U. S. prestige in the eyes of the rest of the world. Further, Nixon knew that a premature withdrawal of U. S. forces from Indochina would result in a bloodbath of U. S. supporters in South Vietnam. He did recognize however that it was politically necessary to end the war because the electorate was simply tired of the ongoing hostilities.

The Nixon Doctrine on the war was marked by a certain amount of rigidity. This stemmed from his Administration's insistence that South Vietnam was still a "country" separate and apart from North Vietnam. That "country" therefore had the right of self-determination. Nixon therefore pledged continued support of South Vietnam as a separate entity. He stressed this message to the troops who he visited there. Congress also still supported the Administration on the war by giving a vote of confidence to the Administration's efforts to negotiate a just peace.

Vice President Agnew also contributed to the debate over the war. He was generally regarded as the Administration's "hatchet man" concerning those who opposed the government's war policies. Beginning in October, Agnew began maligning and insulting nearly everyone and any organization that voiced opposition to the President's war policies. His increasingly vicious rhetoric further polarized the public and only served to energize the war's critics.

However, the nation was still quite distressed over the war. In the latter part of the year the Administration was much criticized because opponents believed that the U. S. was not moving rapidly enough to end the war. Much of the nation's attention and indeed that of the world was focused on the Moratorium Day, 15 October. Antiwar activists had designated this day to demonstrate for the hostilities to cease. All over the country millions were involved in demonstrations, marches and rallies.

The national opposition to the war culminated in what was arguably the largest organized protest of the entire conflict. Although most Americans supported the President on the war, on 15 November a quarter million people marched on Washington to demonstrate against the ongoing conflict.

Further, this was a pivotal year in another important aspect. Particularly since the end of WWII, most Americans had held the military in high esteem. It was previously regarded as blasphemous to denigrate the Armed Forces. However, this was the year in which many citizens, particularly young persons who had no recollection of previous conflicts, began to look upon the military with disfavor. The reason for this change in attitude was of course because of the war. As is discussed below, the My Lai Massacre finally came to the world's attention this year.

However, there was another likely reason why the military began to be scorned in some circles. The U. S. has always had a problem with the subject of race. During this decade race became the subject of quite heated debate, with the result that various forms of discrimination, including that based on race, were outlawed. This outlawing occurred incidentally at the approximate time that the war officially began. Witness the passage of the 1964 Civil Rights Act on 2 July, approximately one month before the enactment of the Gulf Of Tonkin Resolution of 5 August 1964. The law allowed individuals who had suffered discrimination in certain areas, including in employment, to sue and to recover damages therefor. As will be discussed below, the law would have profound repercussions for the author after the war would conclude.

Without dwelling on the subject of race in the U. S., one phenomenon which became more prevalent in U. S. society during this period was that many white Americans were moved to speak out on the issue. This is one apparent reason why some white Americans had become less reluctant to label the Vietnam War racist. U. S. military personnel who were fighting the war, and who were of course mostly white and were fighting against an Asian enemy, were accordingly perceived as racist by many. Some questioned if U. S. troops would have engaged in crimes and savagery such as those exposed at My Lai if the civilian population had been the same color as themselves.

Further, one of the most profound references to a subject related to race as it pertained to the war was uttered by a senior military official. A most glaring example of the degree to which the country was divided on the war could be seen in the labeling by one Brigadier General Hugh Hester that the war was genocidal. This he opined because of the types of weapons used in Vietnam. He would further eventually side with a group of veterans, the Vietnam Veterans Against The War (VVAW), discussed below. These would soon organize to voice their opposition to the war.

Military Operations In Vietnam, 1969

The level of fighting continued intensely. However, the hostilities were noticeably reduced from the level of the previous year. The fighting can best be characterized as sporadic. The enemy would frequently assault allied forces for a short while, then the level of fighting would subside. This pattern was observed for almost the entire year. There were virtually no major confrontations among the various groups of combatants: the allies, the Viet Minh/Viet Cong, the South Vietnamese or the forces of North Vietnam.

Observers contributed the aforementioned pattern by the enemy to the fact that its forces had been depleted greatly the previous year during the Tet Offensive. The opposing forces had apparently thrown all that it had against the allies during that Offensive. However, to reiterate, the Offensive did not succeed. The enemy had lost a great deal of resources which apparently could not be immediately replenished.

a. Bien Hoa

One name is firmly etched into the annals of the war: Bien Hoa, which was the site of a major U. S. air base near Saigon. Here the enemy launched a major assault which resulted in significant allied casualties. It was however obvious during the assault that the enemy did not demonstrate the will which it had shown during the previous year's Tet Offensive. The overall result from the decreased level of fighting from the previous year was that U. S. fatalities dropped to approximately 900 per month. This was a decrease of 500 monthly.

b. Tranh Phong

The South Vietnamese village of Tranh Phong is one which would likely have been forgotten had it not been the site of an alleged atrocity by U. S. forces, which in turn generated much controversy. In this village on 25 February a group of six Navy S.E.A.L.S., the Navy's elite Sea, Air And Land Division, led by one LT Joseph Robert Kerrey, assaulted the village during a night search-and-destroy mission. They were seeking to assassinate an official of the Viet Minh/Viet Cong. Instead they wound up killing over a dozen old men, women and children. To kill innocents in wartime is a violation of the Uniform Code Of Military Justice. It is also a violation of the internationally accepted rules of war, The Geneva Convention accords. However, the officer in charge of the mission was awarded the Bronze Star, a medal for bravery, and also a Purple Heart for having been wounded. A photograph of him also being awarded the Congressional Medal Of Honor, the nation's highest military honor by President Nixon was widely promulgated in the media. The Viet Minh/Viet Cong official who they had sought was not found. As will be detailed later, in testimony to the lingering societal effects of the war, this incident at Tranh Phong would resurface many years in the future.

As promised, President Nixon began the withdrawal of combat troops from Vietnam. When Nixon took office there were approximately 530,000 U. S. troops "in country." By the end of the year the number of such troops would be significantly below the authorized strength of 480,000. The Administration also announced that it planned for a major cut in authorized troop strength the next year. Another indication of U. S. disengagement in Indochina is that one of the U. S. air bases in the Philippines, Mactan Air Base on the island of Cebu in the Central Philippines was deactivated this year. Air raids had been launched from this base since the war had begun in earnest. The author would be informed of this by the natives when he would visit Cebu as a civilian the year that the war would end.

It bears mention that one individual among U. S. military personnel in Vietnam this year was one Albert Gore, Jr., son of the Senator from Tennessee. Although he opposed the war as did his father, upholding the ideals of The Society Of The Cincinnati he joined the Army this year.

Congressional Perspective On The War, 1969

Senator Albert Gore, Sr. continued to voice his opposition to the war. Of the "government" of South Vietnam, he opined:

> "...the Saigon Junta makes a mockery of the right to free speech and freedom of the press, jails political and religious leaders who advocate either neutrality or a coalition of all of the people of South Vietnam, and, lastly, subverts the very principles of self-determination and democratic freedom for which the U. S. professes to be fighting." (Senator Gore, *The Eye Of The Storm*, p. 14).

Senator Gore further stated in his book (p. 27) that in response to President Nixon's request for funds to widen the war into Laos and Thailand, Congress limited the use of such funds. For some reason Cambodia was spared from this legislation. No mention was made of the use of funds to widen the war into Cambodia. However, Congress still supported the Administration on the war by giving a vote of confidence on the Administration's efforts to negotiate a just and "honorable" peace.

Diplomatic Initiatives To End The Hostilities, 1969

The Paris peace talks continued amid much controversy. It was finally decided that there would be four parties at the bargaining table: (1) South Vietnam, (2) the NLF, (3) North Vietnam and (4) the United States. These talks occurred after one of the major points of contention was settled: the shape of the negotiating table.

The talks were hampered however by the rigidity of all sides on certain points of the negotiations. All of the parties wanted a de-escalation of the hostilities. However, North Vietnam and the NLF insisted that a political settlement would have to occur before troops would be withdrawn. Elections would have to take place first, they insisted. In response to that point of contention the South Vietnamese insisted that no communist could take part in any proposed elections and certainly not in any postwar government. Add to the points of contention that the U. S. still considered South Vietnam a "country" separate and apart from North Vietnam. The negotiations were therefore at a stalemate.

The Atmosphere In North Vietnam, 1969

The leader of North Vietnam, Ho Chi Minh, died on 3 September. His passing merited his portrait being placed on the cover of *Time* Magazine. The caption accompanying his portrait read: "What Next In Asia?" It bears mention that Ho's passing did not appear to have any appreciable effect on either the level of fighting or on the efforts to resolve the ongoing dispute diplomatically. Further, this year will also be remembered as that in which U. S. war protesters would chant "Ho, Ho, Ho Chi Minh!" in their protests.

The Military Judicial Perspective, 1969

This year the public was made *more* aware of the seamier side of the war, in that some military persons were suspected of having engaged in corruption and in war crimes. "More" is emphasized because even though this year would always be remembered as that in which war crimes by U. S. troops would receive notoriety, the issue had been promulgated before. Refer to the prior section entitled Reports From The Print Media, 1968. The January 5 issue of *Time* magazine that year detailed the first documented instance of war crimes by U. S. troops. The crimes therefore obviously had been committed in 1967.

This year a group of eight persons who were members of the aforementioned Special Forces/Green Berets were charged with the murder of a Vietnamese national who was suspected of being a double agent. The group included the commander of Special Forces in Vietnam, one Col. Robert Rheault. The prosecution of the group ended however when Army prosecutors realized that to put these persons on trial would entail testimony from the U. S. Central Intelligence Agency (C.I.A.). Revelation of such testimony during the resulting trial would therefore compromise national security.

a. First revelations of the My Lai Massacre

This year will be forever remembered as the year in which the aforementioned My Lai Massacre would be exposed to the world. To reiterate, on 16 March 1968 about five hundred Vietnamese old and young men, women and children and infants were murdered. Other atrocities also had occurred, it was reported. The world was stunned by the level of carnage. However, no action was taken on the allegations of war crimes and atrocities at that time. These were apparently covered up by those responsible. However, one soldier in Vietnam at the time had heard of the crimes and then informed the President, members of Congress and Army officials by personal correspondence.

The individual who had become aware of the carnage at My Lai was one Ronald Ridenhour, a veteran of the war who by this time was out of the military. Several months before the government and military officials acted to determine what had happened at My Lai, he had written to them to make them aware of what he had heard about the alleged atrocities. He had received his information from other soldiers in Vietnam, and had not participated in the alleged crimes. In response to Ridenhour's letters, the government compelled the Army to investigate the allegations.

b. Initial inquiries into the My Lai massacre

Upon reviewing Ridenhour's letters, government and Army officials immediately ordered a formal inquiry into allegations that crimes had occurred at My Lai in March, 1968. The evidence having been gathered, a criminal investigation was then begun by the Army Criminal Investigations Division (CID). Hundreds of military personnel were questioned and thousands of pages of testimony taken before a final report was completed.

c. The criminal investigation

In September numerous Army personnel were charged with crimes under the Uniform Code of Military Justice. However, the Army decided not to charge most of those who had been suspected of war crimes. There was considerable evidence against some of the accused. Many had left the Army however, and therefore could not be prosecuted. Most of the others who were tried were found not guilty. In the end, only one individual was convicted: the commander of Charlie Company, 1ˢᵗ Lt. William Calley (O-2). At trial, Calley testified that his immediate senior, Captain Ernest Medina (O-3) had ordered him to kill all of the civilians who he encountered in the village. Medina was one of the few others who were tried for the crimes. At trial and from then on, Calley insisted that Medina ordered him to "take out" the village of My Lai.

However, some soldiers took action to mitigate the crimes which they witnessed. Three persons were responsible for keeping the aforementioned carnage from being worse than it was. As they witnessed Charlie Company murdering unarmed peasants, a helicopter came over the scene manned by pilot Hugh Thompson, his door gunner Lawrence Colburn and the craft's crew chief, Glenn Andreotta. The team ordered the rampaging soldiers to cease fire, or they warned that the craft would open fire on them. Thompson then landed his craft between Charlie Company and the remaining civilians. The helicopter crew then evacuated those civilians who required medical attention. Their names would eventually figure prominently in the annals of the war long after it would end.

d. The conviction

Upon conviction Calley was sentenced to life imprisonment at hard labor. He was however released pending appeal upon the personal order of President Nixon. This was after the President stated publicly that any U. S. military personnel who had perpetrated the alleged crimes would be punished. For the next three years Calley remained under house arrest at a domestic Army base. His sentence was subsequently cut to ten years. He was released after having served one-third of that sentence. His Army career ended with his being dishonorably discharged.

e. Calley's background/quality of Army leadership

An investigation of Calley's background was also begun by the media. It found that Calley had been an unemployed college dropout before he entered the Army, and that he had flunked out of college. However, he applied and was accepted for Army officer training. He graduated from the Army's Officer Candidate School where he was commissioned a 1st Lieutenant in 1964, the first official year of the war. The media then opined that the quality of Army leadership was substandard because of the type of persons who were leading our troops in Vietnam. Media commentators suggested that if officers of better quality had been leading our troops there, then atrocities such as what occurred at My Lai would likely not have happened. Indeed, a study by military authorities subsequently found that there was widespread failure of the Army's leadership, morale and discipline in Vietnam. Also, at about this time a term came into common use in the debate over the war. The term "fragging" was used to describe the practice of junior soldiers harassing or even sometimes killing seniors, often with fragmentation grenades. This type of ordnance was simply thrown into the tents of the seniors while the unit was in the field.

f. The Peers Inquiry
Simultaneous with the investigation of allegations of war crimes at My Lai, the government also began to collect information about the alleged cover-up of the atrocities. This Peers Inquiry was separate from the aforementioned criminal investigation. The Inquiry would be completed and its findings promulgated the next year.

The Civilian Judicial Perspective, 1969

This year the Federal Judiciary would again figure prominently in the debate over the war and of related events. Prosecution of those blamed for the aforementioned riot near the Democratic National Convention in August, 1968 would be further etched into the public's consciousness. The term "The Chicago Seven" would be forever synonymous with the turmoil over the war. In March the government indicted these persons on various charges. Prosecutions soon followed.

a. The U. S. District Court For The Northern District Of Illinois
It is a violation of the Civil Rights Act Of 1968 to cross state lines for the purpose of causing civil disorder, or to conspire to do so. The Chicago Seven were indicted in the U. S. District Court For The Northern

District Of Illinois for doing just that. These individuals were: (1) David Dellinger, a pacifist and also Chairman of the National Mobilization Against The Vietnam War, (2) and (3) Rennie Davis and Tom Hayden, the leaders of the Students For A Democratic Society (S.D.S), (4) and (5) Abbie Hoffman and Jerry Rubin, leaders of the Youth International Party, or "YIPPIES", and (6) and (7) John Froines and Lee Weiner, organizers of the protest. To reiterate, the war was not the only matter on the agendas of these groups. However, the war was at the top of their agendas. The public including the Chicago Police Force perceived them as primarily war protesters.

The trial of the aforementioned seven persons began on 24 September with U. S. District Judge Julius J. Hoffman presiding. His name will always likely be remembered as a primary representative of "The Establishment" which sought to stifle dissent over the war. The group's primary defense was that their rights of free speech and of assembly under the First Amendment were violated.

b. The U. S. Court Of Appeals For The First Circuit

This year would see the Federal Judiciary begin to reverse itself on issues related to the war. On 11 July the U. S. Court Of Appeals For The First Circuit (Boston) reversed the convictions of Dr. Benjamin Spock and others in 1968 for allegedly counseling persons to evade military service. The ground for the court's reversal was insufficient evidence to convict in the lower court. In this respect, the reversal of the charges against Dr. Spock and the others can be regarded as a pivotal point in the Federal Judiciary's perspective on issues related to the war. The Federal Judiciary would soon further act even more decisively on such issues.

The Draft, 1969

a. The law is rewritten to accommodate the changing needs of the government

The draft which was administered by the Selective Service System (SSS) had been reviewed the previous year as required by law. This year would see major changes in the way the law would be administered.

Although the SSS had ended graduate school deferments the previous year, this year would see the greatest overhaul of the Universal Military

Training And Service Act since the law was amended in 1951. On 1 December the SSS reverted to the means originally used to conscript men in 1940: a lottery. Only men between the ages of 18 and 26 were still subject to the system. However, at this time men were chosen by randomly picking from a glass bowl the dates of the year, from 1 to 366. The dates chosen first would dictate the order in which individuals would be called. Such a lottery was scheduled to be held each year. The year in which the lottery was held would only affect those nineteen years old in the year in which the lottery occurred.

The officials who administered the system announced that individuals whose birthdays fell in the first one-third, that is, from 1 – 122 would likely be called. However, eventually the public would come to know that no draft board was reaching beyond 125. Accordingly, if one had drawn a number above 125, then he knew that he would never be called.

Lastly, controversy over the draft would climax this year when a Presidential commission headed by former Defense Secretary Thomas Gates would release the results of the commission's study. The results were that an all-volunteer military was not only feasible but also that such a force should be established. The estimated annual cost was to be an additional $2-$4 billion.

b. Issues concerning the law which generated controversy

To reiterate, the draft had generated a tremendous amount of controversy since the official beginning of the war in 1964. A major reason for such controversy was the common belief that the law was simply inequitable. It favored the affluent, which meant that the law was biased against the disadvantaged. The law definitely discriminated against men. Some continued to speak of the war as a "rich man's war being fought by poor men's sons." Many in both the white and non-white communities believed that minorities unfairly bore more responsibility for fighting the war than they should. It was promulgated in the media this year that the percentage of blacks in the Army, which service branch of course shouldered most of the burden for fighting the war, was approaching twenty percent. According to the Statistical Abstract Of The U. S., in 1960 African-Americans represented approximately eleven percent of the general population. Further, Latinos (Hispanics) were at that time represented in the military in greater numbers than their percentage of the general population.

c. Informed opinion on the issue of conscription

Even senior military persons believed that the draft law was unfair. They further opined that the law therefore needed revision over and above the changes enacted this year. According to the aforementioned Col. Harry G. Summers, Jr. in his *The Vietnam War Almanac*:

> "During the Vietnam Era slightly over 53 million Americans were of draft age. Half were women and not liable for the draft. Of the 26,600,000 men of draft age, 8,720,000 enlisted voluntarily, 2,215,000 were drafted and 15,980,000 never served. Of those who did not serve, some 15,410,000 were deferred, exempted or disqualified."

Col. Summers then opines that:

> "These statistics obscure the fact that the Vietnam-era draft was a national disgrace. Those who benefited the most from American society – the affluent, the well-educated – were the least likely to serve. College deferment, which did not end until Dec. 1971, was a major loophole."

d. The Commander-In-Chief's take on the issue of conscription

The person who assumed authority to order men into military service this year, President Nixon, subsequently would offer his take on the issue of conscription after he left office. It has never been documented that Nixon ever voiced his opinion of the draft while he was in elective office, or before he became President this year. However, he did convey his sentiments on this subject long after the war had ended, and long after he had left office. Stated Nixon in his memoirs:

> "…when I came into office, one of the severest and most unfair restraints on the free market was the

military draft, which is a way of compelling military
service from everyone rather than hiring service from
those who supply it voluntarily. Thus the elimination
of the draft and the introduction of a volunteer Army
in January, 1973 were also major steps to meaningful
economic freedom." (Nixon, *RN*, p. 522).

Thus did Nixon offer an economic perspective on the issue of
conscription. However, Nixon was likely not the driving force behind
Congress' eventual unilateral suspension of the draft. Abolishment of the
Universal Military Training And Service Act occurred in 1973 because
the draft was no longer necessary. It would however be reinstated in
1980 on a contingency basis. Only males eighteen years of age would
still be required to register with the System.

However, the Commander-In-Chief continued to draw upon
available resources. Despite the provisions of the aforementioned I-D
draft classification which exempted members of reserve components
from active service, some reserves were called to active duty this year.
The government needed persons from certain reserve components who
had a specialty in which the military was deficient.

e. The situation of a patrician who found himself subjected to the law

One person who fell under the jurisdiction of the law found himself
in an awkward position this year. One James Danforth (Dan) Quayle,
the scion of a wealthy and prominent Indiana family, graduated from
college in June at age twenty-two. His II-S student deferment thereby
ended. He had planned to attend law school even though he had already
passed his pre-induction physical. As with many men in this position at
this time, he may have had some apprehension about being conscripted.
Accordingly, he did what many men did at that time when faced with
such a situation: he joined the National Guard. He thereupon received
a I-D deferment which barred him from active military service.

However, Mr. Quayle faced a peculiar situation. Though he
could not have been aware of it at the time of his June graduation,
the applicable law would soon face revision. To reiterate, the law was
revised on 1 December. In the aforementioned lottery on that date, he

unwittingly was awarded a lottery number of 210 out of the possible 366. Accordingly, upon the change in the law on 1 December, Mr. Quayle became aware that he had no chance of being conscripted. Accordingly, the gap between Mr. Quayle's June graduation and the change in the law on 1 December possibly caused him to join the National Guard for nothing. He joined The Guard for nothing if indeed he joined to avoid active military service. However, as would subsequently be revealed, his decision to join the National Guard would return to haunt him many years in the future.

f. The situation of a plebian who found himself subjected to the law

The aforementioned "Ron Stone" found himself between a rock and a hard place this year. Having begun college in 1965, inasmuch as he enjoyed a II-S student deferment, he was required to satisfy his draft board that he was progressing satisfactorily towards his academic goal. This year he fell short. According to Gottlieb, "Ron" had, by this year become quite active and outspoken about the war. He admitted to knowing Richard Nixon personally and also to being a close confidant to Senator Kennedy. Among the parties he attended at the Senator's house and his travel to anti-war rallies around the country, he found that he had neglected his studies. This was of course uncovered by his draft board. Inasmuch as "Ron" had not made academic progress sufficient to satisfy his draft board, he requested extra time to make up college credits. His draft board refused. He was immediately reclassified I-A, subject to immediate induction into the Armed Forces.

After Nixon's election, "Ron" vowed to never serve in uniform under that Commander-In-Chief. "Ron" then began to dodge the draft. Having encountered many in his circumstance who loathed military service, he became aware of the various ploys used to avoid conscription. When he suggested to his fiancé that they both relocate to Canada, that ended that relationship.

"Ron" then created an elaborate scam to outwit the authorities. He went to Canada alone. The first persons who helped him to perpetuate his scam were, coincidentally, Americans living there. However, in accordance with the rumors he had heard, he eventually found the Canadian branch of the Unitarian Church. This Church had created an underground railway system to help "Ron" and his cohorts in crime to outwit U. S. authorities.

Gottlieb is quite detailed in her examination of "Ron's" escapades in escaping the law. She is also quite adept at detailing the resourcefulness and dedication of the Federal Bureau Of Investigation to foil the plans of those such as "Ron." Fifteen individuals who had tried to dodge the draft along with "Ron" were apprehended and then sent back to the U. S. Gottlieb is further adept at detailing the procedures which the Canadian Government had prescribed to scrutinize those persons who arrived there from the U. S., seeking permanent landed immigrant status.

"Ron's" scam worked, but not without his family in the U. S. paying a price. His family was subjected to harassment from the F.B.I. for years after "Ron" left the U. S.

g. The reaction to the change in the law by some who had been subjected to it

An apparent side effect of the change in the law was that it only seemed to fuel the level of dissent concerning the war. Thousands of men with high draft lottery numbers were free to protest the war if they so chose. Men with lottery numbers above one hundred twenty-five would no longer fear retribution from their draft boards if they engaged in anti-war activities. Some no longer feared that the government would "get even" with those who protested the war by drafting them. This is what was alleged to have happened to Muhammad Ali when he uttered his statement in 1966 that "I got no quarrel with no Viet Congs." The same year he made that statement, his draft classification was changed to 1-A from I-Y. He was therefore eligible for immediate call-up into the military. He appealed the reclassification. His involvement in this issue would eventually become the subject of much notoriety.

The Popular Culture, 1969

This year would see more and angrier songs released concerning the war. Albums would also be released which concentrated on the issues of the conflict. The recordings which attained the greatest notoriety were:

1. Phonograph recordings
a. *Give Peace A Chance*

The first of the songs released concerning the war or some aspect thereof, was *Give Peace a Chance,* recorded by the rock group Plastic Ono Band. The song was released by a major label, Apple Records. It seemed to beg the Establishment to pursue a peaceful end to the hostilities. As the song went:

"All we are saying, is *Give Peace A Chance!*"
(Copyright © 1969, Sony/ATV Tunes LLC).

The public embraced the song to the extent that it rose to # 14 on the national music charts the week of 26 July.

b. *Fortunate Son*

The rock band Credence Clearwater Revival recorded one of the angriest songs of the entire conflict. The song lamented the fact that, to reiterate, the war was being fought mostly by the most disadvantaged. The composer may have had the aforementioned James Danforth Quayle in mind. The song *Fortunate Son* seemed to echo the sentiments of the aforementioned Col. Summers when the song appeared to decry military service and participation in the war. As the song went:

It ain't me, it ain't me,
I ain't no Senator's son, naw!
It ain't me, it ain't me,
I ain't no fortunate one, naw!"
(Copyright © 1969, Jondora Music).

The implication of the song's lyric is that if one is "connected", or privileged, as with the aforementioned Mr. Quayle, then one could avoid military service. Because of his family's wealth and his connections, he indeed appeared to be a most fortunate son. However, the composer was apparently oblivious to the fact that a son of a Senator joined the Army this year as an enlisted man. By the time the song became popular he was serving in Vietnam, albeit in a non-combat role. The song was released on the independent label Fantasy, based in the hotbed of protest against the war, Berkeley CA. The record-buying public propelled the song to #14 on the national music charts the week of 8 November.

c. *Ruby, Don't Take Your Love To Town*

The country-rock band Kenny Rogers And The First Edition recorded *Ruby, Don't Take Your Love To Town*. This song reflected what was becoming increasingly apparent to the public: that veterans of the war were returning with severe wounds. The song tells the story of one such individual who expresses his opinion of the conflict and who also is living in a rural area and married. He is dying from his war wounds. His wife desires attention which the veteran cannot provide because of his infirmity. As a result, the couple's sex life is apparently non-existent. The wife then decides to go where she will get the attention which she craves. This of course causes strains in the relationship. As the song went:

> "It wasn't me who started that old crazy Asian war.
> But I was proud to go and do my patriotic chore.
> It won't be long they say until I'm not around.
> Oh, *Ruby, don't take your love to town.*"
> (Copyright © 1967, Universal Cedarwood Publishing).

The song was released by the major label Reprise (Warner Brothers) on 7 June. The public embraced the song to the #6 spot on the national music charts during the week of 2 August. And the beat continued…

d. *The Light Side, The Dark Side*

This year would also see Dick Gregory, defeated for the Office Of President Of The United States, go on a national tour of college campuses to motivate young persons to oppose the war. Portions of these lectures were recorded and released on the major label Poppy (United Artists) as *The Light Side, The Dark Side*. Mr. Gregory would demonstrate various means to get his point across to his audiences. For instance, he conveyed to his audiences that, at age eighteen they were old enough to be conscripted to fight in Vietnam. However they were also not old enough to vote for the officials who had the authority to conscript them. This may indeed have been a factor in the change the next year in the election laws in most states. These would allow persons from eighteen to twenty-one years of age to vote for the first time. During this year however, only Kentucky allowed those eighteen years of age to vote.

Though *The Light Side, The Dark Side* decried numerous inequities in U. S. society, the overriding theme was issues related to the war. For instance, on the subject of using combat troops to ensure freedom and democracy for South Vietnam, Mr. Gregory opined that if a U. S.-styled democratic government is such a valuable commodity, then why do we try to "ram it down peoples' throats?" If a people places such a great value on something, Mr. Gregory opined, then they will steal it.

The Light Side, The Dark Side was released 8/16/69 and it rose to # 182 on the Billboard album chart.

e. *David's Album*

This year would also see the release of possibly the only album dedicated to an individual who was part of the anti-war movement. The folk singer Joan Baez recorded *David's Album* and dedicated it to her incarcerated husband David Harris. Mr. Harris was incarcerated for having violated the Universal Military Training And Service Act. In 1967 he had returned his draft card to his draft board. He then organized with others to persuade persons to resist induction into the military. Prior to Mr. Harris' incarceration, he and Ms. Baez (Harris) were married in 1968. He was then sentenced to three years in a Federal correctional facility.

David's Album contained no songs which protested the war. Neither did any of the songs therein mention its namesake. The album did however contain several songs of faith. Perhaps the selection of the songs therein was in keeping with the widely held belief that the war was immoral. *David's Album* was released 7/26/69 and it rose to # 36 on the Billboard album chart.

f. *The Incredible Year*

The citadel of responsible journalism CBS News recorded and released *The Incredible Year*. The album, narrated by one of its most respected broadcast journalists, Charles Kuralt, was similar in format with the aforementioned 1968 recording by Pat Paulsen, but not in tone. No humor could be detected therein. As with Mr. Paulsen's recording, this album centered around the general level of domestic turmoil which resulted from the war. The year in question was of course 1968.

The Author's Situation, 1969

The author began his junior year in college. When the aforementioned draft lottery occurred he was assigned the number seventy-nine which corresponded with the date of his birth, 31 October. Accordingly, the author understood that if the hostilities did not end prior to June, 1971 and his anticipated graduation, or if conscription did not end, then he would be liable for military service. The author then embraced the ideals of The Society Of The Cincinnati. On the aforementioned Moratorium Day, 15 October, the author participated by wearing a black arm band to signify a commonly held belief that there should be a moratorium on the war.

Reports From The Print Media, 1969

Meanwhile, the print media continued to assess the war and related issues. The following is a truncated list of such articles published this year:

1. *"Since the bombing halt, more G.I.s are dying".*
   (U. S. News & World Report, 2/17/69, p. 10)

2. *"Grim reminder that the war goes on".*
   (Time, 2/28/69, p. 28)

3. *"Nixon's war in Vietnam: continued escalation".*
   (The Nation, 3/3/69, pp. 262 – 264)

4. *"Time of testing in Vietnam: North Vietnamese and Viet Cong attacks".*
   (Time, 3/7/69, pp. 29 – 30)

5. *"Mini- offensive: North Vietnamese attacks".*
   (Newsweek, 3/10/69, p. 48)

6. *"Nixon's hard choice in Vietnam".*
   (Time, 3/14/69, pp. 20 – 21)

7. *"Progress in Vietnam?"*
   (Newsweek, 4/14/69, p. 37)

8. *"Those sanctuaries: Laos and Cambodia".*
   (Time, 4/25/69, p. 34)

9. *"Now a new kind of war: report from Vietnam".*
   (U. S. News & World Report, 5/26/69, pp. 28 – 30)

CHAPTER TEN: "VIETNAMIZATION" CONTINUES; ANTI-WAR PROTESTS REACH THEIR ZENITH, 1970

The Commander-In-Chief continued to fulfill his campaign promise to extricate the U. S. from Indochina by withdrawing troops. However, his decision to widen the war into other countries enraged certain constituencies. The resulting domestic turmoil drove a wedge into society from which the U. S. would not fully recover until the war would end.

The National Mood Over The War, 1970

a. Revelations of The Peers Inquiry Report

The first part of this year can be characterized as on a plateau from the previous year. In March the government released the findings of the Peers Inquiry which had begun the previous year to examine allegations of war crimes by U. S. military personnel in Vietnam. The public was accordingly becoming more aware of the details of the behavior of our troops. The Report substantiated that some of our personnel indeed had engaged in the atrocities which had been alleged. Moreover, the Report found that senior military persons had substantial knowledge of the crimes in question, but that they failed to take disciplinary action as required by military law.

b. Persistent domestic rancor over the continuing hostilities

There continued to be considerable rancor over the war even though U. S. forces were becoming less involved in ground combat operations. The government promulgated that the numbers of our troops in Vietnam were, by April, more than 110,000 fewer than had been "in country" when President Nixon took office. His policy of "Vietnamization" seemed to be paying off. The South Vietnamese were indeed shouldering a greater burden of fighting their war. This helped to soothe the domestic rancor, at least for the first four months of the year. There then ensued a "bombshell" which energized the anti-war movement.

c. The expansion of the war into Cambodia

This year will forever be remembered as that in which the war escalated into neighboring areas. To reiterate, fighting had for several years spilled over into some of the countries adjacent to Vietnam. These included Laos and Cambodia where the Ho Chi Minh Trail veered. The enemy continued to use these neighboring countries to traffic in personnel and materiel to fuel their military operations.

President Nixon had in 1968 campaigned on a platform of ending the war. This year he widened the war into Cambodia. The reason for this incursion was that the enemy had been using Cambodia as a staging ground and sanctuary to launch raids against allied personnel. After harassing allied troops and disrupting their operations, enemy troops would then return to their sanctuaries in Cambodia where they were safe from retribution.

Apparently frustrated with harassment by the enemy, on 30 April President Nixon ordered U. S. troops into Cambodia for the first time to "clean out" the areas where the enemy was known to be hiding. This was a major operation involving thousands of U. S. troops. The government tried to make the incursion into Cambodia palatable to the public by stating that the incursion was only temporary, and that this incursion would hasten the end of the war.

d. Reaction to the Cambodian military incursion

However, the Cambodian incursion set off a firestorm of demonstrations and protest all over the country. The incursion was promulgated because the public watched some of the military operations on television. As the public had been used for the last several years, the war had become the first "living room war" which could be seen every day on the news.

One of those outraged by the aforementioned massacre at Kent State, discussed below, was the aforementioned Ron Kovic. This was in addition to the outrage which he already felt that the government was not providing the proper consideration to its disabled veterans, of which group he was a part. On the day of the violence at Kent State, he attended his first anti-war protest. It would be revealed that this would be the first of many of Mr. Kovic's protests against the government, for both of the above reasons. Indeed, he would join efforts with those of one Bobby Muller, who would be one of the founders of a group known as Vietnam Veterans Of America.

1. Kent State University, Ohio

The adverse reaction to the Cambodian incursion was most prevalent on college campuses, many of which were closed because of the disruptions thereon. The most prominent of these disruptions was on the campus of Kent State University in Ohio. Here occurred the ugliest and deadliest domestic event concerning the war. On 4 May the campus was disrupted to the extent that the National Guard was called to restore order. What then occurred will likely be debated in perpetuity. The student demonstrators threw rocks at the Guardsmen. The Guardsmen responded by firing into a crowd of students, killing four of them. The photograph of one individual who was not a student at the school, kneeling over one of the slain students, is another image which will forever be etched into the memory of those who will recall the war. In 2007 the press would reveal that an audiotape had been made of an individual ordering the Guardsmen to fire upon the unarmed protesters. In 2010 on the approximate fortieth anniversary of the massacre, the iconic photograph of the aforementioned individual would be resurrected. The May 11, 2010 edition of *The St. Louis Post-Dispatch* again published the infamous photograph of one Mary Ann Vecchio screaming as she knelt over the body of one of the slain. The photograph won a Pulitzer Prize.

2. The University Of Wisconsin-Madison

Passions over the Cambodian incursion also flared elsewhere. The violence which occurred at The University Of Wisconsin-Madison was a direct result of that which had occurred at Kent State. The institution which was the place of the earliest protests against the war was the site of a bombing that resulted in death.

On 24 August a building on the campus which housed a research center funded by the Army was blown apart by a bomb. This was the most violent of the protests which had occurred at the building since the research center began in the 1950s. One person was killed and several injured. The person killed was a physics researcher who was known to be against the war. The Army Mathematics Research Center which was the target, sustained little damage.

The stated motive of the perpetrators was to protest the war. It would be revealed that they acted out of their distress over the Kent State Massacre. The four persons who perpetrated the bombing of the building which they believed to be empty were: (1) Dwight Armstrong, (2) his brother Karleton, (3) David Fine and (4) Leo Burt. None were associated with the university. All were immediately placed on the F. B. I. Most Wanted List. Three of these would be apprehended, though not at the same time. Karleton Armstrong was the first to be caught, in Toronto, Canada in 1972. In 1973 he pleaded guilty to several state and Federal charges for which he received a sentence of twenty-three years.

As will be revealed below, Dwight who drove the getaway vehicle and David Fine would elude capture until after the war would end.

The whereabouts of Leo Burt remain a mystery. The efforts of law enforcement authorities to apprehend him would continue into the first decade of the twenty-first century. Such efforts would be detailed in the July 10, 2010 broadcast of the television show *America's Most Wanted*.

A plaque was placed on the bombed building to honor the person who died.

e. Congressional reaction to the Cambodian incursion
The Senate in particular reacted predictably and sternly to the Cambodian incursion. Two amendments were introduced therein, one to halt funding for the Cambodia incursion after 30 June, and the other to stop appropriations for the war after 31 December 1971. Both of these bills eventually died, however. President Nixon vowed to terminate the Cambodian incursion by 30 June.

f. The general public's reaction to the Cambodian incursion
The reaction of the general public was more subdued than the violence and class disruptions which had occurred on the college campuses, but still quite vocal. Indeed, much of the public still supported the President on the issue. This support could be seen in New York City where 100,000 construction workers demonstrated in support of the President's decision to send troops into Cambodia. This demonstration occurred shortly after war protesters had been assaulted by construction workers. According to polls, most of the public believed that the students had invited the violence which had occurred at Kent State University.

The Reaction Of A "Typical" American Family To The Ongoing Hostilities, 1970

a. The general national attitude towards royalty
The American Revolution abolished the last remnant of royalty in the United States. No individual in this country is known by a royal title. Indeed, it is a violation of the Constitution (Art. I, Sec. 9) for any government official to accept a title of nobility from a foreign government, without the consent of Congress. The Constitution further bars the government from granting titles of nobility.

b. The general national attitude towards "American-style" royalty

In spite of U. S. distaste for royal personages, there is one group of citizens which is perceived as being on the same level as royalty: film celebrities. It cannot be overstated the degree to which citizens who achieve notoriety through film have been adored and examined by the public. The status which they achieve through acting on film has elevated them to a status which is indeed akin to that which the foreign nobility have achieved within their respective societies. A glaring example of the adulation which the American public heaps upon film celebrities could have been observed in "The Flying Fondas and how they grew", an article with interview of the three members of this American acting dynasty: Henry, Jane and Peter. This dynasty made the cover of *Time* Magazine and was examined in the aforementioned article published in the February 16 issue. This family will be used herein to demonstrate the degree to which the Vietnam War affected a "typical" American family. Further, the Fonda clan will be used as an example of how the war permeated the popular culture.

c. The American concept of proper "royal" behavior

Film actors who pursue activities contrary to what the public expects of them have traditionally been examined and sometimes scorned. Before the Vietnam War, it was axiomatic that the degree to which a film celebrity would stray from the societal norm would determine the degree to which they would fail to find favor with the public. Before the instant war, these would usually go up and down in direct inverse proportion. Further, it has been documented that some of such celebrities have been subjected to scorn or ridicule by society if the celebrity engaged in any activity outside of their craft, which would call attention to themselves. Such activity would often be labeled a "publicity stunt." That is, the celebrity would be accused of engaging in the activity in question in order to gain publicity to further their career. Accordingly, before the instant war any celebrity would be loath to do or say anything which might jeopardize their career. Such behavior was labeled "box office poison." Witness the absence from motion picture screens by the famed actor Edward G. Robinson. In the late 1940s after an illustrious career on stage and in film he was "blacklisted." He was then prohibited from pursuing his craft for allegedly having communist sympathies. As a result, he was conspicuously absent from motion picture screens from 1950-55.

The government of course recognized the power that the film industry has to influence public sentiment on any issue. This is why Hollywood came under intense scrutiny by Congress before Mr. Robinson was "blacklisted." When communism began consuming much of the post-war world and the U. S. began to feel threatened, the House Un-American Activities Committee (HUAC), and arm of Congress, was convened to examine the influence of Hollywood. The "Hollywood Ten" was a group associated with the film industry including producers and screenwriters as well as actors. In 1947 these were subpoenaed to testify before Congress about their allegedly disloyal activities. Many had their careers halted or suspended because of government scrutiny and accusations of disloyalty to U. S. interests. This perception of disloyalty and communist influence in the film industry would not subside for many years. Animosity between Hollywood and the government concerning various issues is firmly entrenched even unto the twenty-first century. During the instant war however, Hollywood would begin to assert its power.

The American penchant for judging the moral fiber of those in the film community by the degree to which the celebrity would conform to a societal norm, indeed continued into the Vietnam War era. However, the image of the film celebrity would, like so many other facets of American society, be radically altered during the instant war. Indeed, the war would spawn what could be labeled the era of the advent of the "counter-culture celebrity." During this era celebrities would be more open to embracing controversial causes. Witness the pro-civil rights activities of Marlon Brando, star of the aforementioned film *The Ugly American*. The year he made that film he would also become embroiled in the civil rights issue. His passionate advocacy for racial equality in Birmingham, AL was televised. He was criticized in some circles for such because his televised appearance was deemed by some a publicity stunt. However, his advocacy for civil rights did not hurt his persona in the eyes of the public. As with the movie studio star system which had been an integral part of Hollywood ever since that town was invented, the notion of what was proper behavior for movie stars during the instant war would begin to crumble.

Specifically with respect to official government policies, prior to the era of the Vietnam War, it would have been unthinkable for a film celebrity to engage in behavior which is viewed as unpatriotic by the public and especially by the government. Indeed, prior to the Vietnam War there is no documentation that any film star engaged in behavior regarded as detrimental to official government policy, especially a war. However, one film celebrity would emerge during this war a notorious spokesperson against U. S. involvement in Vietnam. This person can further be regarded as the first "counter-culture" film celebrity. One might therefore be prompted to ask: To what degree, if any, was this individual's career affected by their opposition to the war? An answer to that question follows.

d. The change in behavior of some of America's "royals"

Jane Fonda stated in her autobiography *My Life So Far* that she was, like so many of her countrymen, initially supportive of the government's efforts in Vietnam. She believed, like so many of her fellow Americans, that the war was a normal state of affairs and that she should support her President. This sentiment she concedes may indeed have been instilled by her father, the late actor Henry Fonda who was notoriously patriotic and also a *bona fide* member of American-style "royalty." During World War II he temporarily abandoned his lucrative film and stage career to join the military despite the fact that he was too old to be conscripted and he also had a wife and two children. Because he helped to win that conflict he was accordingly hailed as a "true, red-blooded American" in addition to being the consummate professional actor.

e. The gap in the generations of a "royal" clan

A societal phenomenon which evolved or was magnified because of the Vietnam War was the "generation gap." This gap often manifested itself in the way that different generations within families perceived the war. Simply put, the younger members of families tended to be opposed to the war; the older members tended to support it. Within the Fonda family however, there appeared to only be discord over the degree to which the older and younger generations perceived the war. Jane was vehemently opposed to the conflict, to the consternation of her father. Mr. Fonda stated in an interview many years after the war would end that "Vietnam was a 'crock'." His assessment of U. S. efforts there however did not preclude him from embarking on a "handshaking tour" in Vietnam, albeit reluctantly, on behalf of the United Servicemen's Organization (U.S.O.) during the early part of the conflict (*Playboy* interview, Dec. 1981). He was therefore apparently not as vehemently opposed to the war as was his daughter. He did however state that he was quite distressed over Jane's visit to Hanoi which will be discussed later.

f. The catalyst for behavioral change in a member of an American "royal" family

Jane Fonda stated in her autobiography that like so many of her fellow Americans, she underwent a "transformation" when she became aware of the details of U. S. efforts in Vietnam. Such transformation was spawned by news reports of "free-fire zones" which was a tactic commonly used in air assaults in Vietnam. These zones were areas in which planes were allowed to unload their ordnance in any area deemed appropriate, without regard to what was underneath. Examining Ms. Fonda's autobiography, one can feel her outrage at this activity which she regarded as barbaric, inhumane and contrary to any civilized notion of warfare. She stated that she observed innocent civilians, hospitals and churches being obliterated. One can therefore observe within the Fonda clan a glaring example of the "generation gap" which plagued many American families because of the war. Ms. Fonda stated in her autobiography that her father was quite outraged at her opposition to the war. Further, as discussed below the issue of the aforementioned "free fire zones" would reverberate in 1972 as the first phase of the war would be close to concluding.

At the time that Ms. Fonda became aware of how the war was being fought, she resided in France. There she observed that sentiments against the war were not confined to the United States. Heated discussions and anti-war rallies were held there also by the people who had previously fought, and lost, in Vietnam. French intellectuals and celebrities warned her what would likely become of U. S. intervention in an Asian civil war. During this year when her anti-war activism became widely known, she also became aware of similar sentiments by members of the U. S. military.

g. The induction of an American "royal" into the ranks of organized opposition to the war

Resisters Within The Army (RITA) was the formal name of those U. S. military personnel who opposed the war. They were determined to let their sentiments be known. Their stated goal was to spread anti-war information within the military. Ms. Fonda decided to support them. Another anti-war organization which Ms. Fonda joined was the Mobilization To End The War (MOBE). She stated in *My Life So Far* (p. 237) that her first protest against the war occurred this year at a MOBE rally in Denver, CO.

h. Government reaction to the anti-war efforts of an American "royal"

Ms. Fonda's anti-war activities were soon recognized by the U. S. Government. To reiterate, the government is aware of the degree to which film celebrities can influence public sentiment. Apparently for this reason she became the subject of harassment by government authorities, she stated. These were the Federal Bureau Of Investigation (F.B.I.) and the Central Intelligence Agency (C.I.A.). In one incident she described in her memoirs how she was arrested at an airport and her luggage subjected to an illegal search. Ms. Fonda described in vivid detail how the arresting officer confiscated what was thought to be narcotics. The substances were found to be vitamins.

In addition, Ms. Fonda asserted that the government began a smear campaign against her, apparently because of her anti-war activities. She described how government authorities supplied an influential gossip columnist with false and damaging information about her (*My Life So Far*, p. 256). She further asserted that this information was supplied directly to President Nixon. The columnist however, knowing Ms. Fonda declined to discredit her. Below will be revealed what would become of the government's apparent efforts to destroy her character in the mind of the public.

i. The "blacklisting" of an American "royal"

Lastly on the subject of Ms. Fonda for this year, she was listed in a prominent publication, Collier's Year Book For The Year 1971, Covering The Year 1970. Though her notoriety would rise both in her usual profession and also in her anti-war activities, she would not again be listed among Personalities In The News in that publication for the duration of the war.

j. Summation of the different perceptions of the war within one "royal" family

One last word is in order concerning this "typical" American family's stance on the war and related issues. To reiterate, here one can truly observe a phenomenon which permeated many U. S. families: that there was a marked difference of opinion within them. Within the Fonda clan one can see three extremes. To summarize, the patriarch Henry was not in favor of the war, but he supported his government. No one has ever questioned that he did so out of anything but pure, unvarnished patriotism. Jane acted decisively to oppose the war, even at the risk of her lucrative film career. The junior member of the family Peter appeared to be quite indifferent to the conflict. He could afford to be. Having been born on 23 February 1940, on the same date in 1966 when the Indochina buildup was accelerating rapidly, he became too old to be conscripted. It has never been documented that he ever uttered any sentiments on the war, either pro or con.

Ongoing Military Operations In Southeast Asia, 1970

a. Ground operations

To reiterate, on April 30 the U. S. sent troops into Cambodia primarily to destroy enemy arms caches and to flush out enemy troops who were known to be hiding there. However, this incursion followed the South Vietnamese incursion into the same area on 29 April. The reason for both incursions was that the equation in Indochina had recently changed considerably. Cambodia had acquired a new military government when the previous leader, Prince Sihanouk, was deposed. Sihanouk had always maintained a position of neutrality towards the hostilities in Vietnam. The new Cambodian Government however was now allied with the U. S. and with South Vietnam. Accordingly, the U. S./South Vietnamese offensive was permitted by Cambodia to flush out the enemy from Cambodian soil. The result of this concerted effort was that significant amounts of enemy supplies were found and then destroyed. The Pentagon reported that this destruction of enemy supply centers in Cambodia would severely disrupt the enemy's efforts.

This year there were no major confrontations between U. S. and enemy forces. The major clashes were among the South Vietnamese, the North Vietnamese and Viet Minh/Viet Cong. Pentagon communiqués stated that the South Vietnamese were indeed giving a better account of themselves. This was the best indication that the Administration's policy of Vietnamization was working. The enemy however seemed to concentrate on political rather than military efforts. There were more assassinations of South Vietnamese officials and also greater efforts to indoctrinate the rural population on the virtues of communism.

Another significant development was that some U. S. allies were scaling back their operations in Vietnam. Australia and Thailand both announced that their troop strengths would be reduced significantly by the end of the year.

b. Air operations

Meanwhile, the U. S. escalated air raids on North Vietnam. Since 1968 when President Johnson had halted the bombing of the North, the U. S. had concentrated on reconnaissance flights in order to observe enemy troops. When the reconnaissance planes began to be shot down however, air raids were again launched against supply depots.

c. Prisoners of war in South Vietnam

A major revelation this year was that the South Vietnamese were found to be torturing prisoners of war. U. S. Congressmen who visited combat areas found that prisoners of war were being held in animal-like cages, and in quite inhumane conditions. The reporting of this fact in the U. S. media helped to fuel domestic rancor over the war.

d. Prisoners of war in North Vietnam

This year the public was made aware of one of the most disturbing facets of the war: hundreds of our military personnel were being held as prisoners-of-war (POWs) in North Vietnamese camps. Most of these were pilots who had been shot down. One of these was the aforementioned Lieutenant Commander John McCain who had been shot down in October, 1967. The Administration had up until this time not widely promulgated the plight of the POWs, although they were not being ignored. These persons were of course being used as a bargaining chip by the enemy in order to gain concessions in the ongoing peace talks in Paris. Concern over the number of our personnel and the reportedly abominable conditions under which they were being held, prompted military officials to take drastic steps to free them. Accordingly, in November a helicopter task force was sent into North Vietnam, commando-style, in order to rescue our personnel from one of the camps. When the force arrived they found the camp empty.

Reaction Of The Electorate To The War, 1970

This was of course an election year. As in 1968, the elections were viewed as a referendum on the war. The results of the off-year elections can best be characterized as negligible. The President's party gained a few Senate seats including the seat of one who opposed the President's war policies. However, the Republican Party lost a few seats in the House.

One noticeable casualty in these elections was the defeat for reelection of Senator Albert Gore, Sr. of Tennessee. His defeat was attributed in some part to his persistent opposition to the war. Senator Gore called the aforementioned invasion of Cambodia:

> "…perhaps the most bizarre of the mistakes we made in Southeast Asia in 1970. The result of this invasion of a sovereign state was a visible increase in our casualties merely to destroy a few arms caches which, no one can doubt, will be replaced readily enough by the Viet Cong and its allies." (*The Eye Of The Storm*, p. 22).

Senator Gore further recommended while running for reelection that "we cut the umbilical cord which binds us to the amoral junta in Saigon." (*The Eye Of The Storm*, p. 35).

Diplomatic Efforts To End The War, 1970

The talks in Paris which started in 1968 were at a stalemate. These talks continued to take the form of one side offering a solution, then the other side rejecting it. On October 7 for example, President Nixon went on television to propose a settlement in the form of a five point program including a cease fire. The North Vietnamese rejected it. In addition the South Vietnamese were rigid in their assertion that it would never agree to a coalition government with the North Vietnamese.

The Civilian Judicial Perspective, 1970

a. The U. S. District Court For The Northern District Of Illinois
The trial of the Chicago Seven ended with the conviction of five of the members on February 20, of violation of the Civil Rights Act Of 1968. They were found guilty of crossing state lines to incite persons to riot. These sentences were immediately appealed to the Seventh U. S. Circuit Court Of Appeals (Chicago).

b. The Supreme Court
The Supreme Court ruled on two cases involving draft issues. In *Welsh v. United States*, (90 S. Ct. 1792), the Court ruled that draft-age men are entitled to be afforded conscientious objector status if their refusal to serve in the military results from deeply held moral or ethical grounds.

Also, in the case of *Gutknecht v. United States* (90 S. Ct. 506), the Court ruled that the Selective Service System (SSS) could not accelerate a person's induction into the military, apparently in retaliation because the person had previously returned his draft card to his draft board.

The Perspective Of The International Community, 1970

The United Nations (U. N.) was still peculiarly silent on the ongoing hostilities. There was little debate on the issue. However, the U. S. did bring to the attention of that body the plight of prisoners of war (POWs) held in North Vietnam. In December when the U. S. asked the U. N. for protection for the POWs, the U. N. supported the issue and called for regular inspections of POW camps and also humane treatment of those incarcerated.

The Popular Culture, 1970

a. Boxing

The issues concerning the war also spilled into areas of popular culture/ sports, including the world of boxing. Recall that the boxer Muhammad Ali had his career in the ring disrupted because of his indifference to the war and because of his attitude on serving in the military. Despite the aforementioned turmoil over the war this year, one could observe in the government's treatment of Mr. Ali a "thaw" in the national discourse over the war.

Recall also that Mr. Ali had been denied a license to fight in every state because the New York State Athletic Commission suspended his boxing license in 1967 after his conviction on draft evasion. The suspension continued while his conviction was under appeal. The State Of Georgia however granted Mr. Ali a boxing license this year. The reason why he was allowed to return to the ring was because of the ruling on 14 September by Judge Walter Mansfield of the U. S. District Court For The Southern District Of New York. The judge ruled that the suspension of Mr. Ali's boxing license was arbitrary and unreasonable. Accordingly, the Commission was compelled to reinstate the boxing license. This reinstatement in turn prompted the Georgia Boxing Commission to allow Mr. Ali to fight again. On 26 October he had his first licensed bout since March, 1967 in Atlanta against one Jerry Quarry. Mr. Ali scored a third round knockout.

Mr. Ali's second fight this year was against one Oscar Bonavena, the South American champion. The bout was scheduled for December 7. Prior to the bout there was a televised broadcast of the pre-fight weigh-in. What occurred during the weigh-in is another glaring example of how the war had permeated popular culture. At the weigh-in his opponent taunted Mr. Ali. Talking directly to him, Bonavena teased: "Why you no go into Army? Cheep, cheep." Bonavena thereby implied that Mr. Ali was a "chicken" because he opposed military service and refused to be inducted into the Army in 1967. Mr. Ali did not retort directly to Bonavena. However, instead of being his usual jovial self, one could see that he was visibly angered at Bonavena's suggestion that he was a "chicken." Uttered Mr. Ali: "I'm going to punish him!" Punish Bonavena, he did. He knocked Bonavena down more than once during the bout and he prevailed with a fifteenth round T.K.O (technical knockout). This ended Bonavena's previously unblemished record.

b. Phonograph recordings
1. *War*

This year would see the release of possibly the angriest song of the entire war. The soul singer Edwin Starr recorded *War* which uttered explicit lyrics which decried war in general, while not referring to the Vietnam War in particular. The releasing label was the large independent Motown. As the song went:

> "*War!* What is it good for? Absolutely nothing!"
> (Copyright © 1970, Stone Agate Music)

This song would also prove to be one of the most popular of the protest songs released during the war. As such it is a glaring example of the public's outrage at that time over the hostilities in Vietnam. The public embraced the song to the extent that by 25 July the song was #1 on the national music charts. This would not however be Mr. Starr's last entry onto the music charts with a song on the same subject.

2. *Ball Of Confusion*

Also this year one other recording lamented continued U. S. presence in Vietnam. The soul group the Temptations recorded *Ball Of Confusion*. The releasing label was the same as the song preceding. The song did not explicitly criticize the war. Rather, it seemed to lament the state of society in general with respect to the fatigue which many nations felt over the ongoing hostilities. As the song went:

> "People all over the world are shouting: 'End the war!'"
> (Copyright © 1970, Stone Agate Music)

Again one can see that opposition to the war was a popular theme embraced by many. The public liked the song to the extent that by May 23 the song was #3 on the national music charts.

3. *American Woman*

This year the international rancor over the war also permeated U. S. culture. Though there had been demonstrations abroad which protested continuing U. S. involvement in Vietnam, such rancor had not previously been echoed in phonograph recordings, at least not by a foreign artist in the U. S. This year however the Canadian rock band Guess Who? recorded on the major U. S. label RCA the song *American Woman*. Ironically, this was the label which had released the aforementioned patriotic song *Ballad Of The Green Berets*. The song did not mention the war specifically. The song's message was however angry and unmistakable. Further, the song mirrored the mood of the times in the U. S. as well as those in Canada. As the song went:

> *American Woman*, mama let me be!
> Don't come-a-knockin' around my door,
> Don't want to see your face no more!
> I don't need your war machines …
> (Copyright © 1970, Shillelagh America Music)

The song seemed to express the revulsion felt by the U. S.' neighbor to the north at some elements of U. S. society in general, not just concerning U. S. war policies. *American Woman* was released on 28 March. The U. S. public embraced the song to the #1 spot on the national music charts during the week of 9 May. This date incidentally coincided precisely with the aforementioned killings at Kent State University.

4. *Dick Gregory At Kent State*

This year the humorist and activist Dick Gregory again weighed in on the debate concerning the war in an album entitled *Dick Gregory At Kent State*. The releasing label was Poppy, a division of the conglomerate United Artists. Portions of the album were obviously recorded "live" in front of an audience on a college campus. The album is a diatribe against the injustices which Mr. Gregory perceived in U. S. society in general, especially the pursuit of the war. Moreover, *Dick Gregory At Kent State* is another glaring example of the divisiveness within U. S. society over the war and related issues. Near the beginning of the recording, as Mr. Gregory starts to offer his opinion of what is wrong with U. S. society, one individual can be heard loudly protesting his diatribe. However, as that individual starts to loudly condemn Mr. Gregory's denigration of U. S. society, one can hear a physical altercation between his supporters and his detractors. Such was the degree of national discord over the war.

The basic theme of *Dick Gregory At Kent* State is that the tragedy of the aforementioned massacre at Kent State University was indicative of a profound shift in the societal equation in the U. S. The narrative suggests that the American "Establishment" had found a new ethnic enemy upon which to direct its scorn: itself. As is apparent on the record, the "Establishment" no longer directed its scorn towards traditional "minorities" such as Jews, blacks, Native Americans, Irish and Italians. White Americans seemed to be turning against other white Americans who opposed traditional American values such as contempt of communism. Such contempt is of course what the war was about. All of those killed at Kent State were white college students.

5. *Why I Oppose The War In Vietnam*

The estate of the Rev. Dr. Martin Luther King Jr. released on the major independent label Motown an album entitled *Why I Oppose The War In Vietnam*. The recording had been made in 1967 and was released posthumously. On the recording Dr. King was in top form in his analysis of the conflict and in his utilization of Christian principles to justify his opposition to the war. His speech dissected the negative aspects of the war from every possible perspective. These aspects included the degree to which the war degraded both the blacks who were required to serve there, and also the Vietnamese whose lives were shattered by the hostilities.

On the recording Dr. King was true to his faith, in that he stated he had a duty to speak out against a war which he labeled "unjust, futile and evil." Dr. King was of course an admitted pacifist. He also stated that, had he been subjected to military service in World War II, he may indeed have put aside these pacifist sentiments and participated in the conduct of that war. However, the conduct of the Vietnam War, he believed, was diametrically opposed to the Christian Gospel. Hence his opposition thereto. *Why I Oppose The War In Vietnam* was awarded the National Academy Of Recording Arts & Sciences "Grammy" Award for Best Spoken Word Recording Of 1970.

6. *The Begatting Of The President*

This year would also see the release of the only "concept" album concerning the issues surrounding the war. The world-renowned stage and screen actor Orson Welles recorded *The Begatting Of The President*. The releasing label was the independent Mediarts. Mr. Welles was in top form in satirizing the diverse events surrounding the war and related issues. Among these were: (1) the discord within the Democratic Party over the pursuit of the war, (2) the Republican Party's taking advantage of the discord within the Democratic Party concerning the pursuit of the war, and (3) the riot which occurred at the Democratic National Convention in Chicago. With respect to (3), in most eloquent prose via the use of Biblical syntax, Mr. Welles quipped:

> "And the Democrats went unto Chicago that they might rejoice and take unto themselves a new king, and they came everyone from his own place. And foremost among them was Daley, Lord Of Hosts, and maker of kings. And the Hippites and the Yippites and the followers of Eugene came forth and jeered. Wherefore did Daley summon unto them his hosts and say unto them 'Let us welcome those children unto Chicago. Let us lay out a carpet of red. Let us silence this bleeding of the sheep, smite them and deliver them unto my hand.' And they smote the children. And there stood a watcher on the tower, and his name was Walter The Cronkite, and he cried out against this slaughter of the innocent. Wherefore did Hubert win the nomination."
> (Copyright © 1969, Myron Roberts, Lincoln Haynes and Sasha Gilien).

The Begatting Of The President was released on 8/22/70 and it rose to # 66 on Billboard's album chart.

b. Motion pictures
   1. *Klute*

Production began on location in New York City on the film *Klute*, which would star Jane Fonda. The film which would be released in 1971 had nothing to do with Vietnam. However, what is remarkable is that a producer was willing to devote resources to the production of a film which would star an actress whose anti-war stance was becoming increasingly known. To reiterate, prior to the instant war Hollywood had been quite reluctant to employ actors whose opposition to government policy might cause the public to shun films made by these persons. In this one can see another example of the transformation which the U. S. had undergone because of the war. One can therefore deduce that the reason why the producer of *Klute* decided to employ Ms. Fonda was because the war was becoming increasingly unpopular.

    Ms. Fonda stated in her autobiography that when filming of *Klute* was completed, she and her Hollywood connections feared that she would never work again. She further stated that she felt her life "spinning out of control" because of her anti-war activism and the resultant perception of harassment from the government (*My Life So Far*, p. 266). Consequently she seriously considered abandoning film making.

   2. *Patton*

The film *Patton* was released in February to both critical and public acclaim, in spite of the aforementioned studio opposition to the production of the film two years earlier. Polls taken at that time indicated that it was immaterial to the public that the film dramatized the Second World War. Most seemed to agree that the film was superb cinematic entertainment in spite of its subject matter. At the subsequent Academy Of Motion Picture Arts & Sciences "Oscar" ceremonies, the film would win seven awards including Best Picture and Best Actor.

   c. The White House Gala

The President's daughter Tricia held a gala at the White House to celebrate her coming out into society. Of course popular musicians were invited to perform. These included one of her favorites, the aforementioned rock band The Turtles. The band included the aforementioned "Howard

Kaylan" who had duped his draft board into rejecting him for military service in 1966. According to Gottlieb the attendees included members of the Students For A Democratic Society (S. D. S.) which opposed President Nixon's war policies. The S. D. S. also reportedly distributed anti-war literature at the gala. Substances which were reportedly consumed were French champagne and illegal narcotics. The President did not attend. (Gottlieb, *Hell No, We Won't Go!*, p. 48).

The Author's Situation, 1970

The author began his senior year in college in September. Having overcome some academic problems, he was in good academic standing. However, this information did not timely reach his draft board, #111. In November he received a "wake-up call." His draft board was informed by his university that he was not making satisfactory progress towards his academic goal. Accordingly, he received written notice from draft board #111 to report to the Armed Forces Examining And Entrance Station (AFEES) in St. Louis in order to be examined physically, morally and mentally for service in the Armed Forces Of The United States.

In December the author reported as ordered. While at the AFEES Examining Station the author encountered a former high school classmate. This person the author had not seen since before the aforementioned Tet Offensive of 1968. The individual was wearing the uniform of an Army corporal. He intimated that he recently had served "in-country." He further stated that he was seeking to return to Vietnam because "that's where the money is." It seems that there were significant financial benefits from serving "in-country."

After conversing with the former classmate, the author was then examined. As instructed during the physical examination, he turned his head and coughed while a physician fondled his genitalia. On the questionnaire to determine his moral suitability, he stated that he was not homosexual, and that he had never had sexual relations with another male (or even with a female for that matter, at that time). In addition he stated that he was not then, nor had he ever been a member of "un-American" organizations such as the Communist Party (U. S. A.) or the Ku Klux Klan. He further stated that he had no knowledge that any of his family members were so affiliated. In addition he stated that he had never used dangerous drugs such as marijuana (at that time). On the mental examination the author scored in the mid-eighties (out of a possible score of 100). Accordingly, the author was found to be suitable physically, morally and mentally for service in the Armed Forces Of The United States.

Reports From The Print Media, 1970

The print media continued to dutifully inform the public of its assessments on the war and on related issues. The following is a partial list of the articles which appeared in the print media this year:

1. *"Can Vietnam go it alone? Interview of President Nguyen Van Thieu" ed. By W. S. Merick and J. N. Wallace".*
   (U. S. News & World Report, 3/16/70, pp. 71 – 71)

2. *"Set a date in Vietnam. Stick to it. Get out".*
   (Life, 5/22/70, pp. 34 – 38)

3. *"Nixon's plan for Vietnam: the unfolding strategy".*
   (U. S. News & World Report, 6/15/70, pp. 20 – 21)

4. *"From the Vietnam War to the Indochina War" by J. Lacoutre*
   (Foreign Affairs, 7/28/70, pp. 617 – 628)

5. *"Cease fire: Hatfield-McGovern Amendment to end the war".*
   (Commonweal, 9/25/70, pp. 475 – 476)

6. *"Vietnamization is not peace: prospects".*
   (Newsweek, 11/23/70, p. 63)

7. *"Daring raids in Vietnam: purpose of Nixon's move".*
   (U. S. News & World Report, 12/7/70, pp. 22 – 23)

8. *"North targets hit: attempt to rescue U. S. prisoners".*
   (Senior Scholastic, 12/14/70, p. 4)

9. *"Nixon's new warning to Hanoi: bombing could be renewed" excerpts from news conference, R. M. Nixon.*
   (U. S. News & World Report, 12/21/70, p. 79)

CHAPTER ELEVEN: "VIETNAMIZATION" CONTINUES; ANTI-WAR PROTESTS ENTER A NEW FORUM, 1971

Despite the shifting of the burden for pursuing the war to the ally, domestic rancor over the war had likewise shifted to a new form of protester: those who had fought in Vietnam. The public was accordingly made more aware of the magnitude of the wedge driven into society because of the war.

The National Mood Over The War, 1971

This year one could observe a "thaw" in the discourse over the war. There were no violent clashes between the war's supporters and its detractors as there had been the previous year. This was possibly due to the fact that U. S. troop strength in Vietnam continued to decline. The Administration indeed appeared to be fulfilling its promise to phase out U. S. involvement in Indochina. The debate over the war moved to a different and unexpected arena, however. The use of this new forum to protest the war would set 1971 apart from every other year of the war.

a. The advent of military veteran war protesters
This year will be remembered as that in which criticism of U. S. involvement in Indochina came from quite an unlikely source: "in country" veterans. In apparent reaction to the atrocities which they had observed on the battlefield, and other things which they had seen in and out of battle, Indochina veterans organized to voice their opposition to the still-raging conflict. The group which became known as Vietnam Veterans Against The War gathered in Washington to speak truth to power.

b. Vietnam Veterans Against The War (VVAW)
The group Vietnam Veterans Against The War (VVAW) was begun primarily to call attention to what was actually occurring in Vietnam. As had been alleged by some for years including Halberstam, the government still was not telling the truth about our involvement in Indochina. Further, the rise of this group is possibly the most glaring example of how the reality of the war meshed with the popular culture. As discussed below, the gathering of the VVAW in Washington during the week of 18 – 23 April perfectly coincided with the public's embracing a popular song which did more than just decry the war. The song *What's Going On* which is discussed below was high on the national music charts at the time. It implored government leaders to listen to a part of the electorate who had an important message to impart. The VVAW likewise desperately sought to tell the public what was *really* going on (in Vietnam).

The actress-turned war protester Jane Fonda actively supported the VVAW and she was made the Honorary National Coordinator of the group. She attended a rally of the organization in Valley Forge, PA this year to protest the war. Ms. Fonda states in her memoirs that she was not introduced to one of the leaders of the group, one John Kerry, and that she was not photographed with him, as some who sought to discredit him subsequently alleged. She conceded however that she was quite in awe of him.

c. The VVAW agenda
The primary agenda of the VVAW was of course to make the public aware of what was actually happening in Indochina, including the futility and insanity of it all. At the top of its agenda was a demand that the government set a definite withdrawal date of our forces. Further, the group also wanted to promulgate the plight of veterans who had returned with drug addition, encountered unemployment, and who also suffered from the effects of chemicals such as the aforementioned Agent Orange. The group believed that their special problems were being ignored, especially by the Veterans Administration (VA).

A major part of the VVAW's agenda was to march and to demonstrate near the Capitol Building, then make speeches and also to return the medals which they had received for their combat service. Their original plan was to return these medals to government leaders when testifying before Congress. However, the group had to settle for making a public exhibition of discarding the medals. Pictures of the veterans discarding their medals on the steps of the Capitol Building is another image which will forever be seared into the minds of the public who will recall the war.

d. The VVAW Leadership
The VVAW was organized by numerous persons including one Jan Barry who was a former cadet at West Point, the U. S. Military Academy. However, the individual who would become possibly the most prominent member of the group was the aforementioned John Kerry. Possibly the most decorated member of the VVAW, his combat medals included three Purple Hearts from his having been thrice wounded in Vietnam. It would subsequently be revealed that his military commendations would be the subject of quite heated debate many years in the future. Further, Kerry would also be remembered as the most eloquent spokesperson

of the VVAW in his testimony before Congress. Indeed, President Nixon was known to have been impressed with his eloquence, if not agreeing with his sentiments. Kerry would further eventually figure quite prominently in U. S. society.

e. Sympathy for the VVAW

What is most noteworthy is that some prominent leaders in and out of government were in sympathy with the VVAW. One Congressman in particular lent the group the use of his office for the group to promulgate its message. At least two former senior military persons announced their support for the group. These included the former Commandant Of The Marine Corps and also Medal Of Honor winner General David Shoup. In addition, other prominent groups and celebrities gave financial support. This allowed members of the VVAW, which claimed a national membership of 12,000, to travel to Washington to make its sentiments known.

f. Allies of the VVAW agenda

Jane Fonda, along with another popular film actor who opposed the war, Donald Sutherland, launched an organization aimed at harnessing the film industry's potentially powerful anti-war voice. The organization was labeled the Entertainment Industry For Peace And Justice (EIPJ). It invited other Hollywood notables to help work toward its goals at a gala which was held in the grand ballroom of the Beverly Wilshire Hotel, Los Angeles. Ms. Fonda states in her autobiography that the response was tremendous and encouraging. The attendees were a virtual "Who's Who" of Hollywood, including the Titans of the entertainment world Barbra Streisand, Burt Lancaster, Tuesday Weld and Richard Widmark. The era of the "counter-culture celebrity" had indeed arrived. This is further testimony to the degree to which U. S. society had turned against the war. Further, the establishment of the EIPJ was testimony to the degree to which the government was losing its grip on its ability to control public opinion on the war.

The EIPJ was however not the only organization of celebrities which came out in opposition to the war. This year Ms. Fonda also started an organization known as the Free Theater Associates (F.T.A). It would produce a motion picture of the same name which would become known by another acronym: F--- The Army. It was begun as an alternative to the widely publicized live shows by another popular entertainer, one Lesley Townes Hope, a.k.a. Bob Hope. Mr. Hope and his shows for U. S. military personnel near the front lines of combat areas were, by the Vietnam War, an American institution. These shows which were begun during World War II in which Ms. Fonda's father served, were accordingly perceived by many as being pro-government and also pro - war. Ms. Fonda and her cohorts therefore were apparently set on countering Mr. Hope's efforts to "legitimize" the Vietnam War.

The F. T. A. traveled to military installations and put on shows near them. The themes of these shows of course centered around the war, military service and related issues. Ms. Fonda states in her autobiography that she and her associates were warmly received wherever they appeared.

g. Opponents of the VVAW agenda

What is also noteworthy is that the Administration began a campaign to inhibit the VVAW from informing the public of its agenda. The group caused much embarrassment for the Administration which promulgated that it was making significant contributions to alleviating the plight of returning veterans. The White House officially expressed its displeasure over the VVAW's message. What is further quite noteworthy is that Nixon stated in *RN* (p. 497) his belief that the VVAW and other "hard-core agitators" were "openly encouraged by the North Vietnamese." Further, White House officials lent its weight to pressure other government officials to deny the VVAW the use of public grounds to demonstrate and to domicile the visiting veterans.

h. Continuing government debate over military operations

Meanwhile the debate over continued U. S. presence in Indochina escalated within the government. The maneuvering by senior government officials is discussed below. The heightened rancor stemmed from the escalation of air strikes over North Vietnam. The U. S. had virtually stopped bombing the North in 1968. As discussed below however, U. S. air strikes increased this year because of continued reconnaissance missions over the North. These were carried out because U. S. forces had to monitor movements by the enemy. When the fighter planes which escorted the reconnaissance flights were fired upon, they were ordered to and indeed did return fire to protect all U. S. planes.

i. Continuing rancor within the civilian community over the war

Meanwhile certain segments of the public continued to be quite distressed over continuing U. S. involvement in Vietnam. There was accordingly a replay of the aforementioned incidents at Catonsville, MD in 1968. This time however, the number of protesters increased more than three-fold, to twenty-eight persons. On 22 August a group was apprehended inside the Federal Building at Camden, NJ burglarizing the Selective Service office. Their purpose was to destroy draft records. There were also indications that the group desired to show its outrage over the continuing hostilities. This group became etched in the nation's consciousness as The Camden Twenty-eight. As in the earlier incident at Catonsville, the group included a Catholic priest, an immigrant from Ireland. Each member of the group was indicted and prosecuted for burglary and conspiracy. As will be revealed later, the eventual resolution of the matter would not be forthcoming until after the first phase of the war had ended. However, the manner in which the case was eventually resolved and the reasons why a jury would rule as it eventually did, would reveal much about the nation's sentiments on the war at the time. The resolution of the case would also make a statement about the government's efforts to address anti-war protesters.

j. Problems of returning veterans

In one respect the national mood over the war soured in 1971. The public was made aware that many of our veterans were returning with "wounds" indirectly related to the war: heroin addiction. To reiterate, the VVAW was not satisfied that the government was aiding these addicted veterans to overcome substance abuse. The government did however acknowledge the problem when it announced its assessment of the numbers of veterans with such problems. The official rate at which returning veterans were assessed to be addicted was about 5%. Some Pentagon officials did concede however that the actual rate was somewhat higher. The rate of addiction of returning veterans was attributed to the wide availability of narcotics "in country", and also to the fact that morale was known to be low.

It bears mention that after the war would conclude a motion picture would be produced which would assert that an Army unit would engage in the extracurricular activity of conspiring to traffic heroin from Vietnam to the U. S. *The Boys In Company C* which would be released in 1978 would be the only U. S.-produced film which would assert such. The film suggested that the intent of one of the members of the unit was not to fulfill his military duties, but rather specifically to traffic in narcotics. The means by which the narcotic was trafficked to CONUS was in the body bags of slain comrades. It further bears mention that the trafficking in and use of heroin domestically would reach alarming levels at this time. Such societal concern could be seen in the release of two films concerning heroin trafficking and abuse which were released this year: *The French Connection* and *The Panic In Needle Park*.

Combat Operations In Indochina, 1971

a. Vietnamization continues
At the end of the previous year, there was a lull in the level of hostilities. This reduced level of combat operations would continue for most of the year because the Administration continued to fulfill its pledge to phase out the use of ground personnel. On 1 January there were approximately 340,000 troops "in country." This figure was well below the target number set by the Administration. "Vietnamization" was indeed becoming a reality.

b. The continuing Cambodian operation
However, the reason why combat operations were reduced in Vietnam is because much of the fighting had moved to Cambodia. To reiterate, efforts continued by the South Vietnamese, the U. S. and the new Cambodian government to destroy the enemy which was entrenched there. The brunt of the fighting was borne by the South Vietnamese. However, the U. S. did provide air support for its ally.

c. The Laotian incursion
There was also a grave situation in Laos which shares a long border with North Vietnam. To reiterate, the aforementioned Ho Chi Minh Trail was known to veer through Laos. In an effort to halt this movement by

the enemy, on or about 1 February the South Vietnamese mounted a major offensive into Laos. This effort was of course supported by U. S. air power, and it heartened the Administration. The code name for this effort was *Lam Son*, assigned by the Pentagon. *Lam Son* was in effect an expansion of the U. S.'s involvement in the war by proxy. No U. S. forces were officially involved in the Laos incursion on the ground. The ARVN troops who made the actual incursion were supported by U. S. air cover and also artillery. When the South Vietnamese originally encountered little resistance, the Pentagon believed for a while that the war could be won.

However, enemy troops rallied and then forced the ARVN to retreat while the latter sustained heavy casualties. Nixon conceded in his memoirs (p. 498) that the U. S.'s support of ARVN troops had not been adequate to support their ground effort. The offensive, which was first believed to help our "Vietnamization" Program, did not turn out to be the success which the allies had originally thought. On this subject Nixon opined:

> "The net result was a military success but a psychological defeat, both in S. Vietnam, where morale was shaken by media reports of the retreat (of the S. Vietnamese), and in America, where suspicions about the possibility of escalation had been aroused and where news pictures undercut confidence in the success of Vietnamization and the prospect of ending the war." (*RN*, p. 499).

However, despite the fact that within a short time the enemy supply lines had been reestablished, the U. S. hailed the South Vietnamese incursion a success because the level of enemy supplies being funneled into South Vietnam had been substantially reduced.

d. Continued air actions against North Vietnam

The U. S. increased air actions against North Vietnam. These operations were deemed necessary because the U. S. continued to fly reconnaissance missions over the North in order to track enemy movements. Reconnaissance planes which carried no armaments were accompanied by armed fighters which were ordered to return fire if fired upon. The reconnaissance planes were frequently fired upon. The fighters returned fire as ordered.

e. Administration plans for further troop withdrawals

Meanwhile, in view of the degree to which the South Vietnamese were shouldering their burden of fighting, in April President Nixon informed the public that more than 100,000 additional troops would be withdrawn by 1 December. As will be revealed later, Congressional leaders in addition to the VVAW were agitating for a complete pullout of U. S. forces by a definite date.

f. Allied plans for further troop withdrawals

Meanwhile, U. S. allies continued to withdraw. Both Australia and New Zealand stated their intentions to remove all of their forces by the end of the year.

Congressional Discourse On The War, 1971

The level of rancor in Congress over the war remained quite heated. Congressional leaders who had opposed the war for years introduced new legislation to both cut off war funding and also set a definite date for the total withdrawal of personnel. Congressional antiwar sentiments could mainly be seen in the Senate. Senators Mansfield of Montana, McGovern of South Dakota and Hatfield of Oregon were the most visible critics. The latter two were responsible for introducing possibly the most memorable legislative proposal to end the war: The McGovern-Hatfield Amendment. This was proposed to amend a bill which would have extended the military draft for another two years. The Amendment required that no funds be authorized, appropriated or expended under this or any other law in support of the deployment of U. S. forces in, or the conduct of, U. S. military operations in or over Indochina after 31 December.

Another Senator, Lawton Chiles of Florida proposed a substitute for that proposed by Senators McGovern and Hatfield. His amendment would have cut off war funding as of 1 June 1972, provided that all U. S. prisoners of war had been released or accounted for by 1 April 1972. This substitute was supported by Senators McGovern and Hatfield, but it was defeated.

Senator Mansfield then weighed in on the debate and offered another amendment to the proposed law which would have extended the draft for another two years. His amendment dictated that troops be withdrawn from Indochina within nine months after it had become law. This proposal was resoundingly adopted.

However, the Mansfield Amendment was opposed in the House, which adopted its own version of the law which would have extended the draft for another two years. The deadlock between the House and Senate caused the government's authority to conscript to expire. Accordingly, the U. S. was without legal authority to raise a military force by conscription for the first time in several decades. When the Mansfield Amendment was modified to appease the House however, the law which would extend the draft for another two years was finally passed. Accordingly, the government again began drafting men into the military. As will be revealed later, the passage of this law would have profound repercussions for many men including the author.

Presidential Action On War Funding, 1971

The President of course has the authority to expend funds for government operations, including the military. In November President Nixon signed a bill which authorized military procurement to the tune of $21.4 billion. The bill contained an amendment by Senator Mansfield which would have declared that it was government policy to cease all Indochina military operations as soon as was practicable, and also to withdraw all forces by a definite date, subject to the release of the POWs. President Nixon stated his intention to ignore the Mansfield Amendment.

The Civilian Judicial Perspective, 1971

a. The law on conscientious objection to the war settled

This year will also be remembered as that in which the judiciary rendered possibly its strongest statement on the war and related issues. Further, the Supreme Court decision in the case of *Clay v. United States* (403 U. S. 698) is a glaring example of the continuing "thaw" in the discourse over the war. The Court overturned the conviction of Muhammad Ali (a.k.a. Cassius Clay) in a unanimous decision on 28 June.

Recall that Mr. Ali had been convicted of violation of The Universal Military Training And Service Act in June, 1967. This conviction had come after Mr. Ali's draft board had rejected his application for conscientious objector status. The basis for the board's denial of the application was that he failed to meet any of the three tests required for the granting of such status. When he appealed the decision, the appeal board denied his claim without stating its reasons for doing so. To reiterate, Mr. Ali subsequently refused to be inducted into the military. As a result, he was convicted and was appropriately sentenced.

This case is unusual for two reasons. First, the government conceded after the case arrived in the Supreme Court, that two of the grounds on which Mr. Ali's original petition for conscientious objector status was rejected, were invalid. It is quite rare for the Government to admit impropriety in any case, especially in a petition before the highest Court.

Second, the fact that the case wound up in the Supreme Court at all was unusual. As in any case on which the Court renders a decision, the nine Justices give explicit reasons for their so ruling. It is worth noting that the Court invoked the aforementioned case of *Welsh v. United States* (398 U. S. 333) as a legal precedent for its decision in favor of the petitioner in this case. However, as anyone who is familiar with the legal system and of the functioning of the Supreme Court can attest, most of the petitions which arrive in the Court for review are rejected. The Court has no legal liability to consider every petition which comes before it.

Further, one should understand that the Court is only obligated to intervene in a dispute if such arises between or among any of the three branches of government, or among the states, or between or among any of the Federal appellate courts. In these cases the Court must intervene in accordance with its Constitutional mandate. Any other issue which comes before the Court is only considered at the Court's option. Accordingly, the Court must perceive something unusual about a case before it decides to place the case on its docket.

There was nothing unusual about the instant case. The petitioner's conviction had been rendered by a Federal judge and then sustained by the U. S. Court Of Appeals For The Fifth Circuit (New Orleans). Further, the law was well settled on the issues in question. Accordingly, there must have been a compelling reason for which the Court accepted the case. The likely reason was that the individuals who sit on the Court are human like the rest of us. They have opinions on the burning issues of the day which they want to have heard. The war was of course <u>the</u> most burning national issue at that time. Accordingly, the case merely offered a golden opportunity for the nine human beings who sat on the Court to voice an opinion on the war.

The Court also ruled during that session in two other similar cases. It ruled that the right to conscientious objection and therefore exemption from the provisions of the Universal Military Training And Service Act must be on the basis of objections to *all* wars, and not just to particular conflicts. The Court clarified this doctrine in *Gilette v. United States* and also in *Negre v. Larsen* (401 U. S. 437) which were decided together.

b. The Constitutionality of the war

As expected, the Court declined to debate Constitutional challenges to the war. It let stand a ruling of a U. S. Court Of Appeals which upheld the convictions of individuals who had sought exemption from military service on the grounds that the war was unconstitutional. The justices reasoned that the war was constitutional because, among other reasons, the government had decided to pay for it.

The Military Judicial Perspective On War Crimes, 1971

The final adjudication occurred concerning the issues of the aforementioned massacre at My Lai which had taken place in March, 1968. In March 1st Lt. William Calley was convicted via court-martial in the premeditated murder of at least twenty-two unarmed civilians there. He was sentenced to life imprisonment at hard labor. However, President Nixon ordered him released from confinement but held under house arrest pending further review of the case.

Captain Ernest Medina, Calley's immediate senior who was also court-martialed for complicity in the murders, was acquitted. He then announced that he was leaving the Army. These would not be the last judicial decisions on the matter, however. As will be revealed later, Calley's punishment would be altered considerably. The public would also be made more aware of the complexities of the matter in subsequent notices from the media.

Diplomatic Efforts To End The War, 1971

Meanwhile, efforts to resolve the hostilities by diplomatic means continued in Paris. Central to the debate was whether or not the release of POWs held by the enemy would come before or after the U. S. had withdrawn from Vietnam. This was part of a seven point proposed plan by the Provisional Revolutionary Government Of South Vietnam (one component of the enemy's ranks). The proposal was rejected by the Nixon Administration.

Also, one of the most significant but little known events at the Paris peace talks was that two members of the VVAW traveled there as an official delegation of the group to offer an apology to the North Vietnamese for the havoc that the U. S. had wreaked upon Vietnam. This was never reported in the U. S. press.

Further, the above apology was likely the only expression of remorse received by Vietnam. During the Administration of a future President who had actively opposed the war and who had avoided military service, he offered no apology after Vietnam had been unified. During the Administration of President William Jefferson Clinton (1993 -2001) he traveled to The Socialist Republic Of Vietnam on a diplomatic mission. Though he may have desired to apologize to the Vietnamese for U. S. intervention in their civil war, it was reported that he was advised to refrain from such an apology. To have done so, it was reported, would have been an insult to the Armed Forces.

The Literary Media Input, 1971

This year would see the publication of what was arguably the most inflammatory information published during the entire war concerning the conflict. It would also become, along with the aforementioned protesting veterans, the biggest news story of the year concerning the war. The *New York Times* began publication of a series of articles concerning the government's analysis of U. S. involvement in Indochina. The analysis had been commissioned in 1967 by then-Secretary Of

Defense Robert McNamara and was produced by The Pentagon. The study which was completed in 1968 was however classified Top Secret, the highest military classification. Accordingly, it was not supposed to have been released to the public.

a. Publication of The Pentagon Papers

When the Pentagon Papers were first published in serial format in *The New York Times* on 13 June, there was a firestorm of criticism from the government. As detailed below, the government did secure a restraining order from a court. The order halted for a while further publication of the series in that newspaper. However, other newspapers secured the Pentagon Papers and then began publication. The Papers confirmed what Halberstam and others had been saying for years: that the government repeatedly lied to the public concerning our involvement in Vietnam.

The publication of The Pentagon Papers, the formal title of which is "The History Of U. S. Decision-Making Process on Vietnam", is regarded as one of the "bombshells" of war era. As such, the Papers' publication is on the same level as the aforementioned Tet Offensive of March, 1968 because of the impact which the papers' publication had on the hearts and minds of the public. Indeed, Nixon conceded as much in his memoirs when he opined on the impact of the Papers' publication within the context of the times. Stated Nixon:

> "The Pentagon Papers leak came at a particularly sensitive time. At the secret Paris talks (National Security Advisor) Kissinger offered (to the N. Vietnamese) our most far-reaching proposal yet (to end the hostilities). On 13 June the Pentagon Papers were published, and on 22 June the Senate voted its first resolution establishing a pull-out timetable for Vietnam. Before long, the N. Vietnamese would slam the door on our new proposal and begin building up for a new military offense." (*RN*, p. 511).

Further on the subject of the impact of The Papers' publication, it would be an understatement to say that the Administration became paranoid upon their promulgation. The Papers had been labeled "Top

Secret-Sensitive" by the Pentagon. Further, it would subsequently be revealed that the two individuals' decision to promulgate the Papers was in part fueled by this security classification. It was a signal to them, they stated, that the government knew that The Papers contained data that it knew would cause embarrassment. Nixon stated that he saw conspiracy in several circles, within and without government (*RN*, pp. 512 – 13). He believed that numerous individuals were planning to sabotage his paramount foreign policy effort: the conduct of the war. He of course sought legal means to impede the efforts of those who he saw as enemies. His efforts in this regard included directing F.B.I. Director J. Edgar Hoover to blunt their activities. This effort to solicit Hoover's aid was to no avail however. The father-in-law of the one who would be exposed as the principal instigator of The Papers' leak, discussed below, was a personal friend of Hoover (*RN*, p. 513). There is also evidence in Nixon's memoirs which suggests that when such legal efforts to destroy his war critics began to fail, he then sought to use extralegal and also illegal means. (*RN*, p. 512).

Nixon stated in his memoirs that his paranoia over the Papers' publication was so great that those close to him were likely motivated by his demonstrated distress to commit the crimes for which some were eventually convicted. Nixon stated explicitly (p. 514) that an individual close to him, one Egil Krogh, had organized a burglary of the office of the psychiatrist of one Daniel Ellsberg, discussed below. This was done apparently in order to secure sensitive information about Ellsberg. Further, Nixon states that he did not recall whether or not he had been informed of the burglary beforehand. In addition, Nixon stated that:

> "Given the temper of those tense and bitter times and the peril I perceived, I cannot say that had I been informed of it beforehand, I would have automatically considered it unprecedented, unwarranted, or unthinkable." (*RN*, p. 514).

Nixon further suggests that the burglary was no worse than the behavior of the two individuals who had leaked the information which damaged his foreign policy.

b. Description and examination of the merits of The Pentagon Papers

Accordingly, in view of the impact of the Papers' publication, the subject of the documents therein deserves special discussion. Though the author is not a literary analyst, he is compelled to offer his perception of the information contained in the Papers. The document is an intricately detailed account of U. S. involvement in all of Indochina since the very beginning. The Papers detail U. S. intervention into the events of that region since the defeat and departure of Japan in 1945. Upon the departure of that defeated nation, the region controlled by France before the Japanese invasion and before the war of liberation began, started to agitate for independence. Of course France wanted to retain control of her colonies. In addition, the situation was complicated by the fact that France was allied ideologically and militarily with the U. S. in Europe and in Asia.

Possibly the most startling revelation of the Papers is that the government secretly admitted approximately ten years before the war began in earnest in 1965, that it had no right to intervene in Indochina. The U. S. apparently contrived the reasons for its stated mission there. In the late 1950s, as U. S. "advisers" were starting to be sent to the region, the official U. S. view was that South Vietnam was the victim of aggression from the North. This was justification, our policy analysts stated, for coming to the aid of that "country" in order to help it remain free. However, estimates by the Central Intelligence Agency (C.I.A.) as documented in the Papers, showed that the war began mainly as a rebellion within South Vietnam against a repressive and corrupt government. It was therefore perceived by the C. I. A. to be a civil war.

In addition, the Papers offer a revealing look at the decision making process at multiple levels within the government and in the military, which led to the decision to assume the greatest share of responsibility for pursuing the war. One of the most noteworthy documents in the Papers is Document #4, a 1954 report by the Special Committee on the Threat of Communism. This Committee was convened by President Eisenhower to assess the threat which the U. S. believed it faced in Indochina. Under "Conclusions" in the document dated 30 January 1954, the Report stated:

"Regardless of the outcome of military operations in Indochina (between the French and the indigenous forces), and without compromising in any way the overwhelming strategic importance of the Associated States (Vietnam, Laos and Cambodia) ... the U. S. should take all affirmative and practical steps ... to provide tangible evidence of western strength and determination to defeat Communism ... that for these purposes the Western position in Indochina must be maintained and improved by a military victory."

Accordingly, more than ten years before the aforementioned 1964 Gulf Of Tonkin Resolution, the U. S. had committed itself to using military force to further its interests.

c. Government efforts to inhibit dissemination of The Pentagon Papers

The government of course tried to stop further publication of the Papers. This effort by the government which was led by U. S. Attorney General John Mitchell, was muted however. A U. S. District Court did initially grant the government's request for a restraining order. This order inhibited further publication of the Papers until other courts could scrutinize the matter further. The issue eventually reached the Supreme Court which ruled against the government in *New York Times Company v. United States* (403 U. S. 719). The basis for the Court's allowing further dissemination of the Papers was that the government had failed to demonstrate that the previously granted restraining order continued to be justified. The Court also ignored the government's contention that the release of the Papers was damaging to national security. Here again one can observe the Court seizing upon a golden opportunity to voice its opinion on an issue related to the war.

d. The source of the leak of The Pentagon Papers

The government sought to determine the source of the leak of the Papers. This effort was initially to no avail. However, the principal individual who had leaked the Papers to the press eventually came forward. On 28 June one Daniel Ellsberg surrendered to the U. S. Attorney For The

District Of Massachusetts and admitted that he was responsible. His principal cohort was revealed to be one Anthony Russo.

Ellsberg and his cohort had been heavily involved with the government for years prior to their leaking the Papers. After having served as a Marine Corps officer, Ellsberg had worked as a civilian analyst on a study commissioned by the government to assess U. S. military capabilities. It was during his and his cohort's work on the study that they turned from "hawks" to "doves" on the war. The duo would eventually face harsh criticism from various circles, including from the government. Soon thereafter they were indicted in the U. S. District Court For The Southern District of California for having violated the Espionage Act Of 1917. The Act, enacted on 15 June 1917 shortly after U. S. entry into The First World War, prohibited any attempt to interfere with military operations, to support enemies of the U. S. during wartime, to promote military insubordination, or to interfere with military recruitment. The Act was subsequently upheld by the Supreme Court in the case of *Schenck v. United States* (249 U. S. 47). The Court held in that case that the Act does not violate rights of free speech under the First Amendment.

e. Illegalities engaged in by the government in response to the leak of The Pentagon Papers

On 17 June a close assistant to President Nixon, one John Ehrlichman, assigned a group of persons to determine the source of the leak of The Papers. The leader of the group was one Egil Krogh, a lawyer on the President's Domestic Council. The other members of the group were (1) David Young, also a lawyer, (2) Howard Hunt, a former agent of the C.I.A., and (3) one G. Gordon Liddy, a former agent of the F.B.I. In September some members of this group organized a break-in of the office of Daniel Ellsberg's psychiatrist in Los Angeles County, CA. The break-in was organized in an attempt to secure information concerning Ellsberg. In a startling coincidence, this break-in occurred precisely one year to the day prior to another break-in which would be orchestrated by persons close to the President at a place called The Watergate in Washington, D.C. Nixon conceded the circumstances of the break-in this year in his memoirs (*RN*, p. 514). Though Nixon failed to recall if he was informed of the prior break-in when it occurred, both of these illegal acts would have profound repercussions for him as the first phase of the war would conclude.

The Author's Situation, 1971

In January the author began his last semester in college. Expecting to receive a baccalaureate degree in business administration in June, he began a series of interviews with the various recruiters who visited his campus to seek professional employees. It was during one of these interview sessions that the author received another "wake-up call." The recruiter from a prominent local bank, after assessing the author's qualifications and interest in the banking field, asked the author about his draft status. When the author informed the official that he had a II-S Student Deferment, which was of course due to change to I-A upon his anticipated graduation, which would make him eligible for immediate call-up for military service, the official then appeared to be not interested in selecting the author.

One provision of the Universal Military Training And Service Act was that when an individual was employed by a firm, if the individual was selected for military service, then upon termination of the service under Honorable conditions, then the individual had the right to return to his job, with the same benefits which the person would have enjoyed if he had never left. This of course caused much distress for employers, for obvious reasons.

When the author perceived that a potential employer had expressed disinterest in employing him because of his draft status, he perceived this as a "wake-up call." As a result of his meeting with the aforementioned hiring official and with others, the author then understood that it would behoove him to satisfy his military obligation before he would be considered for a career. He then began making plans to enter the military upon his anticipated graduation from college in June.

The author then began weighing his options. The war was still on. From the news about the war it was not likely that the hostilities would end by his anticipated graduation. Consequently he understood that he would soon be subject to conscription. One option was to enlist in the Army as a private. The law allowed an individual to volunteer for the draft without waiting to be called. The individual's tour of duty would then be two years of active service, vice the normal four year tour of duty. It then dawned upon the author that he would soon be earning a college degree. Accordingly, he reasoned that the various military services should want an individual such as himself to be in a position of authority and responsibility. He therefore began a quest to enter a training program for officers. In February the author visited the Navy recruiter and applied for Navy Officer Candidate School (OCS). The author had indeed succumbed to the Navy recruiter's invitation to "Be our guest, you've got nothing to lose! Won't you let us take you on a sea cruise?"

On 10 June the author was awarded the degree Bachelor Of Science in Business Administration. Not later than 17 June, his draft board, #111, re-classified the author I-A, subject to immediate call-up for service in the Armed Forces. While the author waited for word from the Navy authorities, he worked at a variety of jobs including truck driver and file clerk.

Subsequently, on or about 14 October the author received the document provided in Figure 1, the aforementioned SSS Form 252, Order To Report For Induction, from President Nixon. As indicated on the document, he was ordered to report to the AFEES in St. Louis. Meanwhile, the author awaited word from the Navy Recruiter.

On or about 1 November the author received word from the Navy Recruiter that he had been accepted into Navy Officer Candidate School. Accordingly, he ignored the provisions of the aforementioned SSS Form 252. Note that the document excuses persons who had already committed themselves to another component of the military. The author did not report promptly on 18 November 1971 to the AFEES to be inducted, as he had been previously ordered. On 4 November he visited the office of the Navy Recruiter to sign a six year obligation for service in the U. S. Navy Reserve, due to expire on 4 November 1977. This obligation included three years of active duty, two years in the active Navy Reserve and one year inactive. The author thereby became a participant in one of the cornerstones of American democracy: the concept of the "citizen-sailor" who serves his nation when needed. He was then ordered to report to the Navy Officer Candidate School, Newport, RI on 3 January 1972 for training.

The rationale which the author used for joining the military were multi-fold. First, there was of course being associated with the U. S.

Navy in a supervisory capacity would look good on his resume'. Also, the author was keenly aware that organizations, especially agencies of the U. S. Government would view prior military service as a plus when considering an individual for employment. Indeed, it continues to be the policy of governments at all levels to afford veterans extra credit on employment examinations. As will be revealed later, these provisions would have profound repercussions for the author after the hostilities would cease.

Basically however the author's motivation for entering the military was that if the President requires his presence therein, then it must be the right thing to do.

Upon joining the Navy Reserve, the author was therefore in the company of one David Eisenhower, grandson of the former President and also son-in-law of the current President. A photograph of Eisenhower's induction and swearing-in into the Navy Reserve in the White House, with the President standing by, was widely promulgated in the media this year.

The Popular Culture, 1971

a. Phonograph recordings
1. *What's Going On*
Possibly the most memorable of the protest songs of the Vietnam Era was the aforementioned song *What's Going On* which was recorded by the soul singer Marvin Gaye. The song remains an enduring popular icon of the era, not only because it reflected the mood of the times, but also because it is generally recognized as a masterpiece of composition and arrangement. As the song went:

> War is not the answer
> For only love can conquer hate.
> Don't punish me with brutality.
> Talk to me, so you can see *What's Going On.*"
> (Copyright © 1971, Jobete Music Co., Inc.)

What's Going On was released by the entertainment conglomerate Motown Recording Corporation on 6 March. The very week when the Vietnam Veterans Against The War converged on Washington to protest the war, on 10 April the song peaked at #2 on the national music charts.

2. *Stop The War Now*
Also, as a follow-up to his mega-hit of the previous year, the soul singer Edwin Starr continued to capitalize on the alienation of the young by recording *Stop The War, Now!*, also released by the Motown Recording Corporation. As the song went:

> "*Stop the war, now!* Don't put it off another day!"
> (Copyright © 1970, Stone Agate Music)

As the year began, the song was #26 on the national music charts on 2 January.

3. *Bring The Boys Home*
Not to be outdone by the "boys", the soul singer Freda Payne recorded on the independent Invictus label *Bring The Boys Home*. It could go without saying what the song's message was. As the song went:

> "Send our sons back home.
> You marched them away on ships and planes,
> To a senseless war facing death in vain.
> *Bring The Boys Home*, bring them back alive!"
> (Copyright © 1971, Gold Forever Music, Inc.)

By the week of 5 June the song was #12 on the national music charts.

4. *Peace Train*
One song seemed to reflect the hope that many had that the war would end soon. The song *Peace Train* was recorded by the rock singer Cat Stevens and released on the independent but influential label A & M. The song also offered an expectation that the hostilities would cease soon. As the song went:

Come on now, *Peace Train!*
Yes, *Peace Train* holly roller!
Everyone jump on the *Peace Train!*
Come on now, *Peace Train!*"
(Copyright © 1970 Irving Music, Inc., & 1971 EMI
April Music, Inc.)

After its release on 9 October the public embraced the song to #7
on the national music charts during the week of 6 November.
And the beat continued…

b. Motion pictures
1. *Klute*
The film *Klute* starring actress and anti-war activist Jane Fonda was
released to generally good reviews. Ms. Fonda's performance in the
film was also widely praised by film critics. In addition, the film did
respectably at the box office.

Reports From The Print Media, 1971

Meanwhile, the print media continued to offer the public its assessment
of continued U. S. presence in Indochina and on related issues. The
following is a partial list of the articles which appeared in the print
media this year:

1. *"Operation Steel Tiger: U. S. sorties over the Ho Chi Minh
   Trail"*.
   (Newsweek, 1/18/71, p. 25)

2. *"The catch: continuance of the war"*.
   (The Nation, 1/25/71, p. 98)

3. *"New time of testing for the U. S. in Indochina"*.
   (U. S. News & World Report, 2/8/71, pp. 20 – 21)

4. *"Erosion of confidence: congressional opposition to the war"*.
   (The Nation, 3/15/71, pp. 323 – 324)

5. *"Lost crusade, America in Vietnam"*, review, C. Cooper
   (Bulletin Of The Atomic Scientists, 5/71, pp. 45 – 46)

6. *"Oil spill on troubled waters; question of why we are in Vietnam"*, G . W. Ball
(Newsweek, 5/3/71, p. 51)

7. *"Where peace is returning in Vietnam"*, interview, J. P. Vann.
(U. S. News & World Report, 5/31/71, pp. 29 – 31)

8. *"Gambling for one more year in Vietnam"*, H. Sidey
(Life, 10/8/71, p. 4)

9. *"Is ground war over for U. S. in Vietnam?"*, interview, R. Thompson
(U. S. News & World Report, 11/1/71, pp. 64 – 65)

CHAPTER TWELVE: THE WAR INTENSIFIES AND ENTERS A NEW PHASE; PEACE TALKS CONTINUE, 1972

The war remained at a stalemate. When no progress was being made at the peace talks the hostilities erupted anew. These would continue at a furious pace for the entire year and entail a tactic which had not before been used. International tensions would rise and then fall. Hope for peace would come, however.

The National Mood Concerning The War, 1972

By this year the public can best be described as exhausted by the war. This is the apparent reason why the mood was subdued. There were no memorable clashes between groups which supported the war and those which opposed it. Controversy over the war had significantly diminished from the previous year, and certainly from the prior election year of 1968.

President Nixon had not fulfilled his campaign pledge of four years prior to end the war. He had of course significantly reduced U. S. presence in Indochina. His Vietnamization program had been quite effective in relaxing the national mood. This change in mood apparently was because the news of troop casualty rates was virtually non-existent. However, the public wanted to believe that an end was in sight. By the end of the year, the nation seemed to be almost there.

a. The War's Progress

However, the collective American psyche would be on a roller coaster for almost the entire year. What would come to pass this year in news of the war was that it was indeed a futile effort. The U. S. had successfully transferred much of the burden of fighting the war to the South Vietnamese, but this was little consolation. The level of fighting continued furiously. It was proven that the ARVN could not shoulder the responsibility for fighting their war. The reasons for this are discussed below. The Vietnamization program therefore was only successful to the extent that it reduced U. S. participation, and therefore reduced the level of domestic rancor, but it did not cause the hostilities to diminish. This in turn made the public understand that the war was at a stalemate.

b. The War's Repercussions In The Political Arena

Nineteen seventy-two was obviously a Presidential election year. The President deemed himself vulnerable because the war was not being won. He would of course be challenged politically. As usual, soon after the year began, the political primary season was in the news. President Nixon's political opponents accordingly began jockeying for his job. He had no real opposition from members of his own party.

Most of the opposition to the President, and therefore to the war, was of course from the Democrats. Those who would seek the Presidency were of course those who had sought the job in 1968. These included the Vice Presidential candidate that year, Senator Muskie of Maine. However, the person who would eventually emerge as the standard-bearer for the Democratic Party, and who would therefore become the Administration's foremost critic on the war, was the senior Senator from South Dakota, George McGovern. Nixon's take on McGovern and his party's platform bears mention. Stated Nixon in his memoirs:

> "The Democrats were about to nominate a man who had called for immediate unilateral withdrawal from South Vietnam without any assurances concerning the return of our POWs; who favored unconditional amnesty for draft dodgers; who proposed a reduction in the defense budget." (*RN*, p. 622).

While McGovern opposed the war as he had in 1968, his message this year was not just that he opposed the hostilities. He primarily opposed continuing the war because he, as did many in and out of his party, saw the continued hostilities as draining resources that could be better used to solve domestic social ills. He accordingly campaigned on a pledge to end the war and use the savings to improve American life. There is more below on how the continuing hostilities continued to reverberate through the political arena.

c. Continuing protests over the ongoing hostilities

Ordinary citizens also continued their protests against the continuing involvement in Indochina. One of these was the aforementioned combat-wounded Vietnam Veteran Ron Kovic. He managed to execute quite a dramatic protest at the Republican National Convention where he first managed to invade the convention hall full of delegates. Then he drew much attention to himself, even to the national television network cameras which were positioned within the hall. When he began to disrupt the convention and an attempt was made to relegate him to the rear of the hall, he became even more loud and disruptive. This was after he managed to interrupt President Nixon's acceptance speech.

Extraordinary citizens also voiced their opposition to the continuing hostilities. The individual who had been President Johnson's Attorney General, one Ramsey Clark, began a collaboration with an anti-war group from Sweden by traveling to North Vietnam. He journeyed there with representatives of that group to inquire into "U. S. crimes in Indochina." His activities with that group were so characterized by Nixon in his memoirs (*RN*, p. 688). Mr. Clark's activities while in Hanoi included broadcasting over Radio Hanoi that U. S. bombing of that nation should immediately halt. He also visited a P. O. W. camp where U. S. prisoners were held, in order to assess the quality of their incarceration.

d. Continuing debate over the draft law

This year would bring a resurgence of an issue which had appeared shortly after the war had begun in earnest in 1965. This is an issue which, coincidentally, Ramsey Clark had been an integral part. As Attorney General he was charged with prosecution of men who had refused military service, or who had deserted the military. To reiterate, in 1966 there began an exodus of young men from the U. S. in order to avoid being conscripted. In addition, at that time military personnel also began to oppose the conflict by deserting and leaving for places both within and without of the U. S. As a matter of course these persons were much vilified and their actions were regarded a traitorous.

This year however, the rancor over these issues of draft dodging and desertion began to ease. This is another indication that the national mood over the war and related issues had relaxed. These persons of course were subjected to punishment under military and civilian law. However, it was reported that the sentences given to these persons were significantly less than the maximums prescribed by law. According to the official figures of sentences for draft avoidance for the fiscal year ended 30 June 1972, only 1,642 persons were convicted out of the 4,932 persons who were indicted under the applicable law. Of the 4,932 cases, 327 were acquitted, 2,963 cases were dismissed and of those dismissed, 70% accepted induction into the military in lieu of prosecution. These were the civilian cases. Of the military cases, it is quite noteworthy that 44% of those charged with desertion and who were convicted were not incarcerated in military prisons. It is also noteworthy that in January it was revealed that from 1966 when the Pentagon began monitoring the numbers of military personnel fleeing to foreign countries, and the present time, 3,731 military persons had left. Only 1,181 of these had returned.

e. The death of the Universal Military Training And Service Act
Lastly on the subject of military service in general, the last draft calls were announced by the Selective Service System in December. These would be the last draft calls made by the government, as of this writing. Accordingly, it appears that the Selective Service System had become undone by public opposition to the war.

A Domestic Attempt To Sabotage The War Effort, 1972

A most profound event occurred which is possibly unique to the Vietnam War in the annals of the U. S. military. A U. S. warship was the victim of sabotage, apparently by an individual stationed thereon. The *U.S.S. Ranger* (CVA-61) was apparently sabotaged when the vessel was docked at a pier within a U. S. military reservation in the continental U. S. (CONUS). The individual suspected of the crime was prosecuted under the provisions of the Uniform Code Of Military Justice. A seaman stationed aboard that vessel named Chenoweth faced a general court-martial (the highest order of military tribunal) and possible execution by firing squad for the act which is a capital offense in any military. From the reports which were released to the media, it seems that someone had managed to invade the apparatus which contains the ship's propulsion gears. The perpetrator had dropped a metal bolt into the gear which immobilized the ship. Seaman Chenoweth was tried but subsequently exonerated with the help of a legal defense fund collected by a civilian group which included Jane Fonda. Whatever motive the actual perpetrator had for committing such an act may never be revealed. He was never caught.

Combat Operations In Indochina, 1972

To reiterate, the reason why the mood in the U. S. over the war remained downcast was that the war was at a stalemate. Moreover, the hostilities this year would be characterized by the term to which the public had become accustomed: escalation. The war escalated in a number of respects: (1) the level of fighting among the combatants, (2) the number and type of weapons used, (3) the level of U. S. bombing in the North, (4) the disheartening of Allied troops, (5) the targets of the fighting, (6) the degree to which U. S. troops failed to comply with Pentagon orders, (7) awareness of the apparent failure of Vietnamization and (8) the resultant degree to which the civilian population of South Vietnam suffered. Further, one of the starkest messages which Nixon would impart in his memoirs was that this year he still believed that intensified bombing of the North would succeed in winning the war. He stated therein (*RN*, p. 606) that "I intend to stop at nothing to bring the enemy to its knees." The President uttered this statement at the approximate time that North Vietnam had launched an invasion of the South with regular troops in the early part of the year.

The situation could therefore be deemed critical this year. Another passage from President Nixon's memoirs is most apropos in this regard. As he was about to meet with the Soviet leaders, he detailed in *RN* (pp. 594-95) a meeting which he had in May with national security advisor Kissinger and his Chief Of Staff, Robert Haldeman. Kissinger entered the room where he encountered the others planning strategy. Kissinger thereupon informed the President of a message which had just been transmitted from the senior commander in Vietnam, General Creighton Abrams. The communiqué stated that in the wake of a major communist offensive, two areas of Vietnam of major strategic importance had "fallen" to the North Vietnamese. The evidence was therefore that Nixon's Vietnamization Policy was a failure. The ARVN had apparently lost the will to fight. Nixon then pondered the possibility that all of South Vietnam would "fall."

Increased U. S. combat action in Vietnam was a major point of contention between the U. S. and the Soviet Union for much of this year. In his memoirs Nixon repeatedly emphasized his apprehension that his efforts to reach détente with the Soviets, one of North Vietnam's ideological allies, would be impeded by the U. S.'s increased bombing campaign. Indeed, his decision to mine Haiphong Harbor, discussed below, caused much apprehension by the most powerful U. S. government leaders. These included those who repeatedly criticized Nixon's decisions on how the war was being pursued.

President Nixon was understandably pleased and also relieved that he was finally able to meet with Soviet leader Brezhnev in May. However, he detailed in *RN* that his meeting with Brezhnev was strained in their negotiations concerning the limiting of nuclear armaments. Nixon's take on the meeting with Brezhnev was thus:

> "Brezhnev's tone was cordial, but his words were blunt. He said that at the outset he had to tell me that it had not been easy for him (Brezhnev) to carry off this summit after our recent actions in Vietnam. Only the overriding importance of improving Soviet-American relations and reaching agreements on some of the serious issues between us had made it (the summit) possible." (*RN*, p. 610).

Nixon also went on to detail the Soviet leader's emotionally charged statements about continued U. S. presence in Indochina. These included Brezhnev's accusing Nixon of "… trying to use the Chinese as a means of bringing pressure on the Soviets to intervene in negotiations with the North Vietnamese." (*RN*, p. 613).

a. The offensive from the North

For the first few months of the year, the situation "in country" was relatively calm, or at least a continuation of the previous year. At the end of March however, the Pentagon became aware of a new phenomenon: that increasing numbers of North Vietnamese troops were engaged in the fighting. Recall that there were several groups which the U. S. regarded as the enemy, including the Viet Cong/Viet Minh. The numbers of North Vietnamese regular troops which the ARVN now encountered were in record numbers. This was observed when North Vietnamese regular troops launched a major offensive against South Vietnam on March 30. This new offensive was not a surprise to the Allies, however. Intelligence reports had indicated that the enemy would mount an offensive. What was surprising was its intensity. Indeed, this new offensive would prove to be the most ambitious by the enemy since the Tet Offensive of 1968.

Not only did many thousands of North Vietnamese regular troops trounce the ARVN forces nearly everywhere they clashed, the fighting also escalated to a degree which had previously been unheard of. Previously, the cities of the South were regarded as relatively safe. For example, during the Tet Offensive of four years prior, some cities were attacked by the enemy, but the Allies still managed to hold them. Few were captured. During this offensive however, the enemy managed to capture a number of cities, including a provincial capital. This is the equivalent of a state capital in the U. S. This was additional proof that the ARVN was not up to its job. Further, this was additional proof that U. S. bombing of enemy installations was not very effective in disrupting the enemy's activities. Indeed, this U. S. bombing effort was found to derive negative benefits. The provincial capital in question, Quangtri City, was the first provincial capital ever captured by the enemy. South Vietnamese forces did eventually retake the city. However, when the city had been retaken, it had been almost completely destroyed, with help from U. S. bombing. This in turn reignited the debate over the war. Some U. S. leaders suggested that the U. S. was destroying South Vietnam in order to save it from becoming communist.

b. New weapons introduced by North Vietnam

Further, the level of fighting took on additional characteristics, in that North Vietnamese forces were found in possession of weapons which they had previously not used. Here the Allies experienced what the French had discovered the hard way, in 1954. Recall that the French were defeated by the indigenous forces that year in a decisive battle at a place called Dien Bien Phu. That battle ended that war. The French did not believe that the indigenous forces had artillery, and they therefore were certain that the French would prevail. The indigenous forces did indeed have good artillery, and they knew how to use it. This is why the French lost and had to return to Europe. Accordingly, in 1972 the South therefore experienced a sense of "déjà vu."

This year the enemy began to use artillery effectively against the ARVN, together with tanks which they had also previously not used. The ARVN was therefore badly mauled. It was found however that the enemy was not adept at tank warfare. The ARVN eventually did manage to cope with the enemy tanks, but not before they had sustained heavy casualties. Morale in the ARVN also suffered because the enemy had won a psychological victory.

c. U. S. bombing support

South Vietnamese efforts were of course supported by heavy U. S. air attacks on the enemy. To give an indication of the level to which the U. S. escalated its air power against North Vietnam, an official Pentagon press release stated that in the first eight months of the year, the total amount of bombs which the U. S. dropped on the enemy exceeded the amount dropped on them during all of the previous year. To reiterate however, even this had limited effect on the enemy's war making capacity.

Further, the increased bombing campaign resurrected or intensified an issue which had arisen some years previously. In his memoirs Nixon detailed what he perceived as a "propaganda" campaign by North Vietnam to denigrate increased U. S. bombing of the North. This effort by Hanoi to promulgate the damage which the U. S. was supposedly causing to their irrigation system, which in turn was supposed to have caused many civilian casualties was, Nixon claimed, an effort by Hanoi to sway public opinion. (*RN*, p. 687). The massive U. S. bombing campaign did however have a significant effect on the U. S. military and on the level of rancor over the war, for another reason. This fact is detailed below.

1. The Lavelle Affair

Along with the aforementioned incident of sabotage, another event occurred which may also be unique in the annals of the U. S. military. A senior officer was alleged to have deliberately disobeyed orders from the Pentagon. The aforementioned air action significantly impacted U. S. morale because a senior commander, one Gen. John D. Lavelle, was found to have disobeyed orders. Recall that the U. S. had been bombing enemy targets heavily, but only in response to anti-aircraft attacks on the fighter planes which accompanied U. S. reconnaissance craft. Pilots had been ordered to take a defensive posture when on a bombing run. It was ruled by the Pentagon however that aircraft had been bombing North Vietnam without provocation even before the aforementioned North Vietnamese offensive. This was clearly not a

defensive posture. General Lavelle, as Commander of the U. S. Seventh
Air Force, was found to be responsible for such disobedience to Pentagon
orders. A Congressional investigation found that General Lavelle and
his subordinates had falsified intelligence reports in order to justify the
unprovoked attacks upon the North. He was demoted and then retired,
albeit at full retirement pay.

The demotion, disgrace and subsequent departure of Gen. Lavelle
was not the end of the matter, however. Many years after the war
would conclude, it would be revealed that the information used by the
Pentagon to adjudicate the matter was not as it appeared. The matter
would then be re-adjudicated by the Commander-In-Chief who would
assume that position in 2009.

2. Attacking U. S. allies

Another negative side effect of the bombing campaign over the North
was that the U. S. apparently inadvertently bombed allies. In October
a bomb which U. S. officials stated had misfired, severely damaged a
building of the French Diplomatic Mission in Hanoi. The resulting
explosion killed the chief of that mission.

3. Attacks upon the civilian population

Another phenomenon which caused an uproar was that the civilian
population was menaced by the heavy U. S. air assault upon North
Vietnam. The enemy charged that schools, hospitals and the dikes
needed for irrigation were being damaged by U. S. planes. Civilians
were also being killed. These charges received corroboration from
westerners who visited North Vietnam. The U. S. of course denied that
civilian areas were being deliberately targeted. The Pentagon conceded
however that civilian areas might have been bombed by accident, or
that bombing was justified if anti-aircraft guns were placed near these
areas.

d. The end of direct U. S. involvement in combat operations

This year would see the virtual end of direct U. S. participation in combat
operations. In other words, the war had been completely "Vietnamized"
by August. This fact was reflected in a ceremony at Da Nang where the
first U. S. combat troops arrived in 1965.

A corollary to the above is that President Nixon had "hedged his bet." That is, while significantly reducing and then eliminating U. S. direct involvement in combat operations, he simultaneously increased the number of personnel in the Indochina theater. To reiterate, heavy air operations against North Vietnam remained in effect throughout much of the year. Some of the raids were from U. S. air bases in Thailand, a close neighbor to Vietnam. The number of personnel there increased markedly during the year. Some of the raids were from aircraft carriers stationed in close proximity to South Vietnam in the South China Sea. These vessels likewise had their crews augmented. One of the ships in this Navy task force was the *U.S.S. Coral Sea* (CVA-43) which was "on the line" until July. As will be revealed later, this vessel would figure prominently in the author's military tenure.

e. The mining of Haiphong Harbor

The decision in early May by President Nixon to mine Haiphong Harbor deserves special mention. In the immediate aftermath of the aforementioned North Vietnamese offensive, that harbor was mined in retaliation for the increased level of fighting by the enemy. Nixon made this decision of course to inhibit the enemy's ability to wage war. This was a dangerous move because the harbor in question was visited by many ships of other nations, including those of the Soviet Union. Indeed, Nixon refers to the accidental death of a Soviet seaman killed when a bomb from a U. S. plane accidentally hit a Soviet ship in Haiphong Harbor (*RN*, p. 607). Accordingly, the mining operation dubbed Operation Pocket Money by the Pentagon, was viewed by some as escalating the war. They believed that the mining might cause other nations, especially the Soviet Union, to become more involved. This of course contributed to increased rancor within the government. Indeed, the Chairman of the Senate Foreign Relations Committee, Senator Fulbright, expressed dismay over the President's escalation.

An obvious reason for Senator Fulbright's dismay was that the increased air operations were exacting a heavy toll on the military. To reiterate, ever since the war had begun in earnest, large numbers of planes had been downed over North Vietnam. Many pilots had been injured, captured or killed. These figures accordingly escalated, especially with the increased bombing campaign of late December. The

Pentagon listed twenty-eight planes lost in this campaign and eighty-four personnel killed, captured or missing.

The Pentagon determined that the mining did negatively impact the enemy's ability to wage war. However, the mining did not completely disrupt the flow of supplies to North Vietnam. Its allies, mainly the Soviet Union and The People's Republic Of China did find other means to supply the North, including by rail.

The South Vietnamese Mood Concerning The War, 1972

a. Morale

Morale within the ARVN had always been abysmal, and it plummeted even further as a result of the offensive from North Vietnam. Moreover, the morale of the general population also declined considerably because of the onslaught. This could be seen in the number of refugees which fled from the hostilities, which reached into the hundreds of thousands. Among these was a girl who was photographed running naked along a road, her skin seared by the napalm dropped from U. S. planes. When the news of the refugees and this photograph reached the U. S., this caused quite a sensation. The public thereby was further made aware of the savagery of the hostilities, and of the devastation wreaked by continued U. S. presence there. The photograph of the girl in question is another image which was firmly etched in the minds of the public, and it in turn fueled the clamor for the war to end.

b. Disruption of South Vietnam's Pacification Program

The effect of the North Vietnamese offensive was multi-fold. First of all, the offensive disrupted the South Vietnamese "Government's" Pacification Program by which it tried to extend greater control over rural areas. This program became totally disarrayed because of the numbers of refugees which fled the fighting.

Further, the North Vietnamese offensive demonstrated that the North could likely never be defeated. This of course had a tremendous psychological effect on the allies, in that it strengthened the negotiating position of the enemy at the Paris peace talks. A passage from Nixon's memoirs concerning the psychological effect that North Vietnam's resilient military posture had on the leaders of South Vietnam is quite stark and revealing. The following excerpt also had the ring of prophecy. Stated Nixon in describing a meeting which National Security Advisor Kissinger had with the South Vietnamese on 18 October concerning the status of the ongoing peace negotiations:

> "Kissinger said that the South Vietnamese leaders had exhibited a surprising awe of Communist cunning and a disquieting lack of confidence in themselves. It was clear that they were having great psychological difficulty with the prospect of cutting the American umbilical cord." (*RN*, p. 696).

c. Economic repercussions on the South Vietnamese Economy

The combined effect of the North Vietnamese offensive and the rapidly departing U. S. military personnel had a devastating effect on the local economy. That economy had been mostly dependent upon U. S. expenditures since the allies arrived there in large numbers in 1965. This dependency stemmed not only from military operations, but also from money spent by individual military personnel. Each of these factors contributed significantly to the decline in morale in South Vietnam.

d. The need for ARVN retraining

Lastly, another indicator of the decline in the collective morale of the South Vietnamese was that most of its armed forces had to undergo retraining by the U. S. This is further indication that the "Vietnamization" program had at least been a partial failure.

Diplomatic Efforts To End The War, 1972

a. Peace efforts resonating in domestic politics

For most of the year, the talks which continued in Paris to resolve the hostilities remained at a stalemate. As with the hostilities, these efforts were on a roller coaster for nearly the entire year. President Nixon of course campaigned for reelection by emphasizing his continuing efforts to secure an honorable peace. This campaign apparently worked because he was reelected with the greatest electoral victory in U. S. history up to that time. He carried every state but Massachusetts and the District Of Columbia.

b. Details of Presidential peace efforts

Early in the Presidential campaign the President revealed that his close adviser Henry Kissinger had, for more than two years, been meeting secretly numerous times with a member of the North Vietnamese delegation in Paris to negotiate an end to the war. Also, the President revealed the particulars of his offer to the enemy to resolve the conflict. His offer included of course a cease fire and the immediate withdrawal of U. S. forces within six months of any signed agreement.

However, one particular point of the negotiations indicated that there was a mis-communication between the U. S. and South Vietnam. The President knew that the other side wanted the current South Vietnamese President Thieu to step down as a condition of any settlement. Indeed, the President wanted Thieu to leave because he believed that Thieu's departure would hasten the end of the war. He therefore offered Thieu's resignation as one of the points of a peace agreement. However, President Nixon failed to inform Thieu of such condition. Thieu had never indicated that he would step down as a pre-condition of a negotiated settlement. In any event, the other side rejected President Nixon's offer.

One particular point on which the negotiations hinged was the subject of prisoners-of-war (POWs). Recall that since the war had begun in earnest many U. S. planes had been shot down over North Vietnam. The result was that many pilots were still being held in North Vietnamese prison camps. It cannot be emphasized enough the pressure on President Nixon to end the hostilities in order to get these POWs released. News reports revealed that POWs were not being humanely treated. The sheer number of them dictated that the President give the matter his utmost attention. Further, the POWs remained a potent bargaining chip held by the North during the negotiations. It is therefore quite noteworthy that the first POWs to be released at any time during the first phase of the war were repatriated due to the efforts of a private peace group. This is discussed below.

There was an element of hope just before the presidential election that a negotiated settlement was near. In late October the parties seemed to have come closer to an accord on what it would take to end the war. The key point on which the outcome rested, remained what would be the role of South Vietnamese President Thieu. However, by the end of the year, with the election over, the two sides had not reached an accord.

Nixon's take on the complexity of the ongoing negotiations just before the elections is quite revealing. His perception of the mindset of Thieu indicates that the two allies were not in accord on how to end the war. Nixon's perception of Thieu reveals that Thieu was indeed "between a rock and a hard place" when he stated:

> "...he is terrified of the idea of the Americans being gone from South Vietnam. (U. S. Commander Creighton) Abrams, on the other hand, who is certainly no opponent of Thieu's, feels strongly that the time has come for us to get out and that we simply have to cut the umbilical cord and have this baby walk by itself."
> (*RN*, p. 706).

Nixon further opined that if the South Vietnamese could not stand on their own after all of the support which the U. S. and the other allies had provided since 1964, then they would never be able to do it. These sentiments would prove to be prophetic indeed.

c. Details of private peace efforts
1. The VVAW
Of course there were other efforts to end the hostilities in addition to those of the governments involved. Private interests, including the aforementioned Vietnam Veterans Against The War had sought a dialogue with the representatives of the other combatants.

2. Jane Fonda
Also this year Jane Fonda decided to act even more decisively in order to help bring an end to the seemingly endless hostilities. She traveled to North Vietnam alone, at the invitation of that government, to meet with the leadership there. She stated in her memoirs that she was not a representative of any group. Her primary purpose was to film the

destruction of earthen dikes which had been built for farming and irrigation. The Pentagon had a stated policy that these dikes were off-limits. The policy had been adopted because these dikes had no military or strategic value. Further, their damage would cause much suffering to the civilian population because it would inhibit the ability of North Vietnam to grow food. This would result in mass starvation. Accordingly, Ms. Fonda desired to demonstrate that U. S. officials had promulgated false information. Further, to reiterate, westerners had visited North Vietnam and had reported that the dikes were being bombed by U. S. planes.

When Ms. Fonda met with representatives of North Vietnam, she was welcomed by the Vietnam Committee For Solidarity With The American People. The Committee was well aware of the degree of anti-war sentiment in the U. S., hence its name. However, one of the most vivid remembrances Ms. Fonda had while visiting there was that she detected no hostility from her hosts or from anyone whom she met while there. The persons who she encountered did not know that she was a famous American movie actress. They knew only that she was an American and also a guest of their government. In addition, Ms. Fonda stated that she was quite moved by the fact that the North Vietnamese did not seem to regard the U. S. as their enemy. She further stated that she never observed any bitterness expressed toward Americans in general. The people of North Vietnam only seemed to regard U. S. leaders, especially President Nixon as their enemy, she stated.

Ms. Fonda did indeed film the destruction which U. S. planes had done and continued to wreak on the dikes in question. She stated that the "country" was subjected to almost continuous air assaults by U. S. planes, during which she was required to take cover in bomb shelters. She further noted in vivid detail the courage with which the people faced the seemingly constant bombardment, and the clever steps they had taken to counter such.

Ms. Fonda's visit to North Vietnam was of course noted by U. S. officials. The F.B.I. did make an official report of her activities there, it was subsequently revealed. However, the act for which Ms. Fonda will possibly be forever remembered is a photograph of her sitting on an anti-aircraft gun emplacement. The photograph of her at this weapon which was used to down many U. S. planes and enabled the capture or death of hundreds of U. S. pilots, caused much grief within the U. S. Many of her fellow citizens believed that she so acted to "thumb her nose" at the captured pilots. As of the publication of her autobiography in 2005, she stated, she was still vilified in some circles for having so acted.

However, Ms. Fonda also stated in her autobiography (p. 296) that she never meant to visit any military installations while in North Vietnam. Accordingly, her stated purpose was not to allow herself to be photographed sitting at an anti-aircraft gun. Indeed, she stated that she protested her hosts' having included the gun emplacement on her itinerary and then photographing her there. Her physical state and therefore her mental state apparently were impaired while she was there, however. It was documented in the press that she had suffered an accident prior to her arrival in North Vietnam while en route there. This caused her physical discomfort. Such may have been the cause of her impaired judgment, she stated.

In addition to photographing the bombardment of targets which the Pentagon had claimed were off-limits, Ms. Fonda went further and acted in another manner deemed un-patriotic. In this respect she emulated others in a previous war. Just as "Tokyo Rose" and "Axis Sally" had done during World War II, Ms. Fonda made radio broadcasts from Hanoi which exhorted U. S. troops to comprehend the insanity of the U. S. cause. She was of course further vilified in the U. S. for these efforts. Government authorities thereby sought to prosecute her for treason. The difference here is that she was never prosecuted as had been the aforementioned persons. Perhaps one can again observe here the degree to which the Vietnam War was unpopular. It also bears mention that one of the bureaucrats assigned to research whether Ms. Fonda had violated any laws by traveling to North Vietnam, seemed to be in sympathy with her. In her autobiography (p. 323) Ms. Fonda stated that the bureaucrat eventually revealed that the investigation of her possible wrongdoing had been undertaken simply because some senior government officials did not like her.

3. The Indochina Peace Campaign

This year would see a stronger link between the Hollywood film community and the anti-war movement. Recall that in 1968 a group of organizations had met in Chicago to protest the war. A leader of one of the groups was Tom Hayden of the aforementioned Chicago Seven. As a result of their separate but ideologically united activities to end the war, Jane Fonda began a close association with Mr. Hayden, both personally and otherwise. The two teamed to coordinate their efforts to end the war. This year they began the Indochina Peace Campaign (IPC) and embarked on a national speaking tour. Their stated goal was to expose the escalation of the war in the form of the aforementioned increased bombing campaign. A collateral purpose of the IPC was to re-energize the peace movement whose efforts had become muted in light of the reduced numbers of troops in Vietnam. Ms. Fonda stated in a subsequent interview that while on this tour she was subjected to physical assault for the first time in her anti-war campaign, by persons who objected to her anti-war efforts.

However unpopular the war was becoming, when Ms. Fonda returned home at least one politician called for a boycott of her films. As will be revealed later however, that call appears to have been unheeded by the film-going public.

4. The Committee Of Liaison

In addition to Ms. Fonda's activities to end the war, a little known group named The Committee Of Liaison, an anti-war group, was instrumental in inducing the North Vietnamese to release the only U. S. POWs to be released during the first phase of the conflict. In September three POWs were released: two Navy Lieutenants and one Air Force Major.

The Federal Judicial Perspective On Anti-war Protesters, 1972

On 21 November the Seventh U. S. Circuit Court Of Appeals (Chicago) reversed the convictions of all the original Chicago Seven defendants. These persons had been convicted in 1970 on charges stemming from the riot which had occurred in 1968 at the Democratic National Convention. The government had alleged that they had crossed state lines in order to violate civil rights. That Court cited errors by the trial judge in its decision to reverse the convictions. In addition, that Court found that the trail judge, Federal prosecutors and also the F. B. I. had engaged in illegal activities during the trial. With the knowledge of the judge and the prosecutors, the F. B. I. had wiretapped the offices of the defense attorneys.

Simultaneous with the aforementioned acquittals, all of the seven Chicago police officers who had been charged with violating the civil rights of the demonstrators by physically abusing them at the Democratic National Convention in 1968, were acquitted. Charges against an eighth officer were dismissed.

The Literary Input, 1972

The Best And The Brightest was published. That book is one of the primary resources for the information herein. It was deemed one of the most profound literary events which occurred during the war. The book is a penetrating examination of the decision-making process at the highest levels of government which led the U. S. into war. Halberstam's book was generally well received. Further, since its publication it has been used as a primary resource for anyone who has sought to comprehend how the U. S. could have become involved in an Asian civil war.

The Author's Situation, 1972

a. Orientation to military life

On 3 January the author reported as ordered at the Navy Officer Candidate School (OCS) at the U. S. Navy Base, Newport RI. Upon arrival, he was designated an Officer Candidate Under Instruction, Second Class (OCUI2). The slang term with which such persons designated themselves was "O. C." This was for pay purposes. Officer Candidates were paid at the same rate as enlisted personnel at the paygrade E-5. The author then embarked on a course of instruction to learn to become a Navy Officer.

The author was then assigned to one of the companies within the regiment, which company was in turn assigned to one of the barracks. The O.C.s were paired two to a room which was quite Spartan. The amenities included a bed, referred to as a "rack", two metal tables and accompanying metal chairs, and two lockers. The O.C.s were instructed to maintain a clean and orderly environment and were subjected to frequent inspections, both of the barracks and of the uniform.

b. The curriculum

The curriculum, in addition to being quite challenging physically and mentally, was quite diverse. The courses included ship handling, navigation, shipboard firefighting and engineering, tactics in warfare, training in the use of firearms and rudimentary instruction in the provisions of the Uniform Code Of Military Justice (UCMJ). It was clearly imparted the gravity of adherence to the rules therein. If an infraction of the UCMJ was of sufficient magnitude, then the perpetrator could face a firing squad.

The Officer Candidates were specifically instructed to ensure the quality of their military service upon completion of their contract with the government. The O. C.s were advised to pursue an Honorable Discharge. There are various types of military discharges, among them a General Discharge under Honorable conditions. (See Glossary). As will be revealed later, these two types of discharges would have special meaning for the author. The type of discharge to be particularly avoided was the Dishonorable Discharge such as that which the aforementioned former 1st Lt. William Calley received for violation of the UCMJ.

In addition, the O.C.s were taught how to be a leader of enlisted personnel. This course in Leadership included instruction on how to break up a fight between two sailors. The O.C.s were specifically instructed not to try to physically intervene when encountering such an altercation. It was warned that to do so would entail the officer becoming the "duty punching bag." Just the presence of an officer in close proximity to the altercation should be enough to cause the combatants to cease. The term "duty" is indicative of the new and exotic nomenclature with which the O.C.s were required to become familiar. (See Glossary). Becoming a "duty" punching bag means that the officer who would intervene in the altercation would in all likelihood, be "punched out." That is, he would be used as a punching bag. The author did indeed eventually encounter such a situation but he did not try to intervene. His mere presence induced the combatants to cease.

c. The military regimen

The daily regimen at OCS was therefore:

- rise at reveille, 0600 (6:00 A. M.);
- dress in the uniform of the day;
- assemble and march in formation to the "chow hall" for breakfast;
- "chow down";
- march in formation to classes;
- march in formation to "chow down"
- march in formation to afternoon classes;
- march in formation to "chow down";
- study in barracks;
- "hit the rack" (retire) at 2200 (10:00 P. M.)

  (repeat)

d. Special evolutions

Interspersed with the "normal" military academic regimen described above, were "special evolutions." These included visiting an actual ship and embarking on a cruise in order to observe life on board a vessel. Once during the course of instruction it was scheduled for the Commander-In-Chief himself, The "Honorable" Richard M. Nixon, to visit OCS, presumably to give the "boys in blue" a pep talk to motivate them to win the war. Extensive preparations were made for the honor of his visit. For some reason however, he failed to show.

e. Receipt of war news

One of the author's most vivid remembrances during basic training, or "boot camp", occurred in early May. It could go without saying that when a nation is at war, even an undeclared war, when important news of the war is released, then the reverberations within the military community are quick and strong. To reiterate, President Nixon had ordered the aforementioned Operation Pocket Money, the mining of Haiphong Harbor. This was the most important war news which the author and his classmates received during basic training. This mining in turn caused greatly heightened tensions between the U. S. and the nations which were allied ideologically with North Vietnam: the Soviet Union and The People's Republic Of China. Knowledgeable observers speculated that these two communist giants might directly enter the war because the mining of the harbor would put their ships and personnel at peril. This never came to pass. It was not reported that any ship of any nation was damaged or destroyed because of the mines. A little known fact of Operation Pocket Money is that it was timed to coincide precisely with the announcement by President Nixon in Washington that the operation had been ordered. Further, the mines were set with a seventy-two hour delay to become operational. This delay would permit ships to depart before the mines would become operational after having received timely warning.

The mining did inhibit shipping to and from the enemy. In this respect therefore, the decision by President Nixon to mine the harbor was a success. However, as a result of heightened tensions, it was strongly rumored that the author's class might be graduating sooner than expected because the O. C.s would be needed in the fleet. The war had indeed gotten hotter.

Moreover, one should understand that military actions such as the mining in question take on greatly enhanced meaning when one is in uniform than if one were among the civilian community. When one is in uniform, and especially when one is undergoing basic training, one is of course learning the technical aspects of waging war. Upon being informed of the military action in question, the question which the O. C.s immediately posed was: how could such have been accomplished? The mission to mine the harbor, which incidentally was accomplished by Navy planes from an aircraft carrier, the *U. S. S. Coral Sea* (CVA-43) which was then stationed in the South China Sea, was a successful one. It was not reported that any of the planes had been lost or damaged, or that any of the pilots therein had been captured. This was of course a worst case scenario. The most obvious questions which the O. C.s therefore had were (1) how could the planes have avoided detection and then drop the mines, and (2) how much resistance had the pilots encountered? It could go without saying that it was a dangerous mission in that the approaches to the harbor were well protected by the aforementioned SAMs. In consideration of national security, the author will not reveal how the mines were dropped. He was however, along with his classmates, impressed with the efficiency with which the mission in question was accomplished.

f. Graduation/technical training

On 30 June 1972 the author graduated from the Navy Officer Candidate School and was commissioned an Ensign (O-1), USNR with the designation 1105/Line Officer.

Upon receipt of his commission he was then ordered to first report to the Damage Control School, Naval Station, Treasure Island, CA in order to secure technical training in the specialty which he had requested. The author had also requested duty on an aircraft carrier which was home-ported on the west coast of the U. S. This would enable him to see what he had always wanted to observe: the other side of the Pacific Ocean. Upon graduation he was ordered to report to the United States Ship *(U.S.S.) Coral Sea* (CVA-43), whose home port was the Alameda, CA Naval Air Station.

g. First duty station

The *Coral Sea* was named after one of the most decisive battles of WWII: the Battle Of The Coral Sea. This encounter which was a naval battle between the U. S. and the forces of the Japanese Empire in the Pacific during May, 1942, established the reputation of the aircraft carrier as a formidable weapon. This weapon had not previously been tested in battle. The battle also further established the superiority of U. S. forces over their adversaries. Two aircraft carriers were involved: *U.S.S. Lexington* and *U.S.S. Yorktown*. At the height of that conflict, the keel of the *Coral Sea* was laid in 1944.

The *Coral Sea* was designated a conventionally-powered aircraft carrier, in order to distinguish it from other forms of U. S. aircraft carriers. The designation CVA means attack carrying vehicle for aircraft. This is opposed to a CVAN, which means nuclear-powered attack carrying vehicle. The vessel is the largest type of ship in the U. S. arsenal, although the *Coral Sea* was dwarfed by aircraft carriers which were subsequently commissioned. The ship displaced 66,000 tons with a full complement of approximately seventy-five jet aircraft.

The ship's personnel compliment also included 2,500 officers and enlisted men.

The mission of the aircraft carrier is of course to fly planes. For this purpose the ship was fitted with a steam-powered catapult. In order to launch a plane, the ship must first find the direction from which the wind is coming. An officer who stands watch on the bridge of a ship where the ship is controlled must constantly keep abreast of the direction of the wind. When preparing to launch planes, the ship then must maneuver into the wind in order to secure the most advantageous angle and the maximum amount of thrust needed to make the plane airborne. The plane must always fly into the wind. If the amount of wind available is insufficient however, then the ship must attain sufficient speed to take the place of the wind. Upon finding the wind, or generating sufficient speed to take the place thereof, the bow of the plane is then affixed to a hook. When sufficient pressure is built up in the catapult's mechanism, the device is then released with the plane affixed. The plane is then hopefully airborne, with help from the plane's powerful engines which are always at full throttle upon take-off. In this respect the catapult is merely an overgrown slingshot.

The return of the aircraft is quite another matter. The plane's return is aided by means of a tail hook which is affixed to the rear of the craft. The hook is supposed to catch on a wire which is strewn across the ship's flight deck. Sometimes it catches; at other times it does not. If the hook fails to catch, then the plane must make another attempt. This is the most dangerous part of conducting flight operations. If the seas are choppy, then the stern of the ship can reverberate violently and cause the tail hook to fail to take hold. As a matter of course carrier pilots are highly trained in this procedure. They are at great risk of injury and they sometimes must undertake dangerous maneuvers in order to avoid damage to the ship and to the plane. For these reasons all personnel associated with fight operations receive hazardous duty pay. It bears mention that two calamities did occur on aircraft carriers during the war. During flight operations aboard the *U. S. S. Oriskany* (CVA-34) in 1966 while on duty in the Pacific, a massive fire erupted. Forty-four sailors died.

Ironically, the *Oriskany* was the ship to which the aforementioned naval aviator LCDR John McCain had received orders one month before he was "killed" in October, 1967. In his memoirs he described in graphic detail the calamity of which he had partaken on board the *U.S.S. Forrestal* (CVA-59) approximately ninety days prior to his being "killed." On 29 July 1967 LCDR McCain was awaiting being catapulted from the *Forrestal* for a bombing mission. Just prior to take-off, ordnance on his plane was apparently ignited by an electrical charge from a nearby plane which also awaited launch. A stray missile struck his fuel tank which spilled jet fuel onto the flight deck. It then ignited. The explosion and fire killed his parachute rigger, an enlisted man. There then ensued a chain reaction of ordnance exploding. These explosions and fire lasted for at least twenty-four hours. Though heroism and quick thinking contained the damage, the conflagration cost the lives of one hundred thirty-four sailors. (*Faith Of My Fathers: A Family Memoir*, p. 178).

The *Forrestal* may have been "lucky" that the ordnance was conventional, i. e., not nuclear. LCDR McCain deemed himself "lucky" that he managed to survive with relatively minor wounds. He did manage to survive such an environment however until he was "killed" approximately ninety days later. This is the environment in which the author was about to serve for an extended period.

The author met the *Coral Sea* on 21 August when she was docked at the Hunter's Point Naval Shipyard, San Francisco, CA. She was there to undergo refurbishing after having returned to CONUS the previous month. Inasmuch as the war was still on, she was to be refit in order to return to duty in WESTPAC (see Glossary) and then resume her duty as a ship of war in Indochina.

Nearby the aforementioned *U. S. S. Ranger* was undergoing repairs from the sabotage which had incapacitated her. The author personally observed a huge gear which was being replaced in her hold.

h. Life aboard first duty station

The author was assigned as a Division Officer. All Navy ships are divided into various components, called departments. The departments are further sub-divided into divisions, which are the lowest sub-component. The author accordingly had various numbers of enlisted personnel under his authority. As such, he was required to ensure their well-being, direct their daily activities and also ensure that an individual was appropriately disciplined if he became in violation of the UCMJ.

While the *Coral Sea* was "standing down" from her position on the "line" in the South China Sea, the daily regimen of the ship's company was:

- reveille at 0600 (6:00 A. M.);
- "chow down" (mess deck for enlisted, wardroom for officers);
- muster in formation for inspection and review of the Plan Of The Day, 0730;
- set about daily chores, 0800 – 1200;
- "chow down", 1200;
- continue daily chores;
- liberty call, 1600 (for those with permission to depart);
- "chow down", 1700;
- "taps" (the end of the working day), 2200.

(repeat)

When not on duty the ship's crew enjoyed the sights and sounds of the nearby friendly ports of San Francisco, Berkeley and Oakland, CA.

i. Preparation for overseas movement (POM)

After the ship had returned to CONUS in July, the crew having taken desired leave, readjusted to surroundings, and the vessel had undergone shipyard repairs, *Coral Sea* then began preparation for overseas movement (POM). She was still a warship required to do her duty to help win the war. In November the ship began two evolutions to start such preparation: REFTRA (refresher training) and CARQUALS (carrier qualifications).

REFTRA pertains to the ship's company undergoing formal schooling in order to certify or increase competence in one's specialty. CARQUALS pertains to the ship demonstrating its maneuvering capability and fitness for sea duty. While undergoing this special evolution, the ship operated out of the Navy Base at San Diego, CA for the entire month. When not on duty the crew enjoyed the sights and sounds of San Diego. The nearby friendly port of Tijuana, Mexico also offered a diversion from the military regimen.

Upon completion of the aforementioned evolutions, *Coral Sea* steamed back to her home port of Alameda to prepare for deployment back to WESTPAC where she would again enter the war. Deployment was scheduled for 9 February 1973.

The Popular Culture, 1972

a. Phonograph recordings
1. *Why Can't We Live Together?*

No popular songs which protested the war were released this year. This is another indication of the thaw in the national discourse over the war. However, one song which reflected the exhaustion which much of the public felt over the continuing hostilities in Vietnam was *Why Can't We Live Together?* by the soul singer Timmy Thomas. The song was released by the independent label Alston. As the song went:

> "No more wars, no more wars! Just a little peace in this world. *Why can't we live together?*"
> (Copyright © 1972, Sherlyn Music Publishing).

And the beat continued…

The song was released on 23 December. The degree to which the song rose on the national music charts in early 1973, peaking at #3, is indeed indicative of the national sentiment when the hostilities were close to concluding.

b. Motion pictures
1. *American Graffiti*

By this year the war had become thoroughly ingrained into the American psyche, especially of those who had grown up with the war. Moreover, some had come to comprehend the degree to which U. S. society had been altered during the 1960s, especially since the advent of the conflict. This metamorphosis is likely due to a variety of causes, among them the modern civil rights and free speech movements, women's liberation, and the expanding economy. However, without question the leading factor in the country's "loss of innocence" during the prior decade was the ongoing war.

A glaring example of how the war impacted U. S. society and how this impact would reverberate far into the future could be observed on television in 2007. On 15 August 2007 the public was further reminded of the turmoil which characterized the decade in question and the changes which occurred. On that date the Public Broadcasting System (PBS) broadcast the documentary *The Sixties: the years that shaped a generation*. Stated the narrator: "The war would become the dark lens through which the entire decade would be viewed." The broadcast was a further reminder that the U. S. was a different country than it was before the war began. The 1960s will always be remembered as the decade of the twentieth century in which the U. S. came out of its age of innocence. Halberstam also recognized the changes which took place since the advent of the war. He stated that: "The country was undergoing vast economic and political changes which would be accelerated by the war itself." (Halberstam, p. 619).

Those persons not lucky or blessed enough to have observed the transformation which American society underwent during the 'sixties could never comprehend the magnitude of such transformation. The U. S. is fortunate however to benefit from the artistry of one of the generation who understood the societal upheaval and then had the foresight to commit his observations to film.

This year, the last full year of direct U. S. involvement in Indochina, the filmmaker George Lucas (b. 1944) began production on the film *American Graffiti*. Filming began on 26 June. The film would not be released until 1973. That year would be the last year of direct U. S. involvement in Indochina. However, inasmuch as production on the film began this year, the film merits mention within the context of the waning days of the war. The producers who included Mr. Lucas and Francis Ford Coppola certainly understood by this year what had taken place during the preceding decade. Perhaps this is why the film's logo asked the film-going public: "Where were you in '62?"

American Graffiti deserves special mention because it is one of three U. S. films produced during the war which referred to the conflict or to some facet thereof. The film neglects to explicitly mention the war or related topics, however. When the story begins in the late summer of 1962, most Americans had likely never heard of a place called Vietnam. Of course this would soon change. The audience only discerns the link between the war and the characters within the film after the story ends, when the viewer is provided with an epilogue. Then one understands the effect that the war eventually had on some of the film's characters, and indeed upon the fabric of American society. The cultural and societal effects that the war had wrought on the collective U. S. consciousness had indeed come home.

American Graffiti has no discernable plot. It is merely a portrait in the form of a series of vignettes of a group of persons within a certain segment of American society at a point in time. However, as the story unfolds, no one who had observed this segment of U. S. society or had been a part of it could miss the film's subtle but powerful message. The teen culture which was a thoroughly ingrained part of U. S. society in 1962 had "gone with the wind" just ten short years later. Indeed, it had completely disappeared by 1968 when the war was at its peak. Further, everyone who had observed the culture in question or who had been a part of it will likely be amazed at both its disappearance and also the speed with which it departed. The war had made the U. S. a different country indeed. In Navy jargon the U. S. appeared to be "180 out." Translated, the nation seemed to have embarked on a course directly opposite that which it had been on before.

The story told in *American Graffiti* concerns a group of teenagers who live in a small town in Northern California who, in the late summer of 1962 are on the verge of adulthood. All of them have recently graduated from high school or are on the verge of doing so. As a matter of course they are trying to "find" themselves, as all persons within this age group are wont to do. The story centers around two of these persons in particular. The character "Toad" is the most "nerdish" of the group. Much of this film's hilarity stems from the escapades which constantly plague his existence. One of his buddies, the character "Curt", is the opposite. He is the most serious of the group who is about to depart for college in some eastern city. However, the viewer soon perceives that he is looking for something in addition to himself. What it is, even he does not know, but he knows that it exists. He seems to want to grab onto something, apparently to give his life more meaning. Whatever it is, it is beautiful to him but elusive.

Curt began college in the fall of 1962. Accordingly, he presumably would graduate in 1966, shortly after the Vietnam War would begin in earnest, and just in time to help fuel the war effort. His graduation would also approximate the aforementioned departure of young men of draft age from the U. S. which would also begin in earnest in 1966. During the epilogue, the viewer is informed that Curt was now a resident of Canada. His opposite, the "nerd", had been reported missing-in-action (M.I.A. in Department Of Defense jargon) in South Vietnam in December, 1965 while serving in the Marine Corps. He obviously had been one of the "First To Fight" there. It therefore appears that both he and Curt had used the war to validate their lives.

As will be revealed later, *American Graffiti* would eventually figure prominently in U. S. society.

2. F. T. A.

The film *F. T. A.* was released by the organization which Jane Fonda and other anti-war celebrities had founded, Free Theater Associates. The film is a documentary account of the Associates' activities to bring their message to persons in the military. These were highlights of the skits and routines which the troupe had presented to active duty military personnel. The title of the film became known in the popular jargon as "F--- The Army."

3. *The Trial Of The Catonsville Nine*

Another motion picture released this year which examined an event which occurred during the war was *The Trial Of The Catonsville Nine*. The film, which was written from the play of the same name detailed the plight of the aforementioned individuals who took it upon themselves to disrupt the nation's military efforts in Vietnam.

4. *Klute*

To reiterate, the film *Klute* had nothing to do with Vietnam. However, by this year its star had become the most visible and vocal citizen to oppose the war. She however retained her position within the ranks of American-style "royalty." She was awarded the Academy Of Motion Picture Arts And Sciences ("Oscar") Award as Best Actress of 1971 for *Klute*. The fact that she was so honored by her peers may be further testimony to the continuing unpopularity of the war. The Hollywood Establishment obviously did not let Ms. Fonda's anti-war, and some say her unpatriotic views influence its recognition of her talent.

In accepting the aforementioned award in March, Ms. Fonda stated that she was of course elated by her win. She further stated subsequently that she did not perceive any hostility from the audience at the awards presentation. Lastly, she subsequently expressed relief that she was still in the business of making films.

Reports From The Print Media, 1972

During the year the media continued to print its observations on the war. The following is a truncated list of such articles:

1. *"Back to bombing."*
   (The New Republic, 1/1/72, pp. 9 – 10)

2. *"Air war resumes"*
   (Time, 1/3/72, p. 34)

3. *"Expanded air strike effort aimed at blunting communist capability"*
   (Aviation Week & Space Technology, 1/3/72, p. 18)

4. *"Something new in the sky: air war over Laos"*
   (Newsweek, 1/3/72, p. 19)

5. *"Suddenly a hot war in Indochina skies: Cambodia and Laos, new targets"*
   (U. S. News & World Report, 1/3/72, pp. 21 – 22)

6. *"Major North Vietnamese offensive seen"*
   (Aviation Week & Space Technology, 1/10/72, pp. 14 – 15)

7. *"New air war"*
   (The Nation, 1/10/72, pp. 34 – 35)

8. *"Vietnam: as war winds down, new worries spring up"*
   (U. S. News & World Report, 1/10/72, pp. 19 – 20)

9. *"And the war goes on: View from Hanoi: View from Moscow"*
   (Newsweek, 5/8/72, pp. 19 – 21)

CHAPTER THIRTEEN: THE FIRST AND SECOND PHASES END; DIRECT GROUND INVOLVEMENT CEASES; AIR ACTIONS CONTINUE; THE "PEACE" PROCESS BEGINS, 1973

The nightmare appeared to be over. Peace accords were ratified and all parties agreed to put machinery in place to enforce them. However, the two principal combatants were merely left to settle their differences, which were many. The U. S. by law became prohibited from intervening. The situation therefore reverted to that which existed in 1954 with the stronger of the two encroaching on the weaker.

The National Mood Concerning The War, 1973

For the first several weeks the national mood was one of anxious anticipation. Rumors abounded that the hostilities would cease soon. The optimistic mood was justified. Although the air war had recently escalated, U. S. troop strength was only a nominal 27,000, down from 171,000 the preceding January.

Though many leaders were optimistic about the expected end of the war, they still feared what the cessation of hostilities would bring. The reason for such fear was that they did not believe that the South Vietnamese could go it alone against the North or against neighboring states where communism was strong. The aforementioned Domino Theory was therefore still very plausible, they reasoned. Recall that this theory was that even if a country was not communist, if that country were in close proximity to a communist state, then the neighboring non-communist state would be threatened and would eventually succumb to an alien doctrine. The U. S. was aware that the communists were strong and indeed controlled large areas of Laos and Cambodia. Some U. S. officials therefore believed that if the U. S. withdrew from Vietnam, then this withdrawal would be perceived as a green light for the communist forces in those countries to begin pressuring South Vietnam. However, inasmuch as the U. S. expected the eventual end of the war, the government began to prepare for such by sending numbers of civilian officials to Vietnam to replace those of the military.

President Nixon of course was pressured early in January to end the war because his second inauguration was at hand. He had not ended U. S. involvement in Indochina as he had promised to do at the beginning of his administration. The situation was further complicated by the fact that January 20 was the date set to start the enactment of legislation in Congress to end the war. There was serious talk therein to simply cut off funds for further U. S. military operations in Indochina. In this regard, Senate Majority Leader Mike Mansfield stated:

> "There is no greater need than the termination ... of our involvement in Vietnam. It remains for the Congress to seek to bring about complete disinvolvement."

The President felt additional pressure from Congress to disinvolve the U. S. from Indochina. He understood that his overall legislative program would face tough going in Congress if he did not quickly end the war. Here one can see the classic battle between "guns vs. butter." Many believed, as had Senator George McGovern, that progress on domestic programs was being impeded because precious resources were being drained by the war.

In addition, the debate over military deserters continued. To reiterate, the Pentagon began keeping statistics on such personnel in 1966. Less than half of the approximately 3,300 persons who had deserted since that time up to January, 1972 had returned. The foreign destinations of these persons have already been detailed. Of those who chose to return from Canada, the reasons were:

> (1) Canada was experiencing a surge in nationalism and its attendant anti-Americanism because relations between the two began to sour at this time;

> (2) The rate of unemployment in Canada was rising markedly. Consequently, U. S. expatriates there found it more difficult to secure and to keep employment. It could go without saying that Canadians resented foreigners taking jobs away from native born Canadians;

> (3) At this time Canada began tightening immigration requirements for a myriad of reasons, which made it more difficult for foreigners to enter and to remain.

Canada was no longer the haven for opponents of the war which it had been when the war began. Lastly, this year the idea of leaving the U. S. in order to escape conscription became irrelevant. On 30 June the President's authority to draft men expired when Congress failed to renew it.

Diplomatic Efforts To End The War, 1973

The aforementioned bombing campaign did not "bring North Vietnam to its knees" as some had hoped and expected. Indeed, that campaign appeared to have little effect, if any, to induce the North Vietnamese to seriously talk at the peace table in Paris. However, one factor did apparently have significant effect on North Vietnam's leaders to negotiate. That "country's" major allies, the Soviet Union and The People's Republic Of China were known to be pressuring them to soften their demands on certain points of negotiation. The points on which there was substantial agreement among the negotiators were that:

- there would be a cease fire throughout South Vietnam;

- there would be a complete cessation of all bombing and mining of North Vietnam;

- all U. S. forces would be withdrawn within 60 days of the signing of any peace agreement;

- all U. S. P.O.W.s held by North Vietnam would be released within 60 days of the signing of any peace accords;

- an international commission would be appointed to oversee any proposed truce;

- a coalition to be called the National Council Of Reconciliation And Concord would be convened to arrange elections in South Vietnam;

- all foreign troops would leave Laos and Cambodia.

The points on which there was still contention at this time were:

- whether all of the 150,000 North Vietnamese troops still in South Vietnam would remain after a cease-fire, without an assurance from the North that these troops would eventually leave;

- whether freedom for U. S. P.O.W.s would be held up until South Vietnam released all of its political prisoners;

- whether Vietnam would be composed of two separate countries divided by a demilitarized zone (DMZ), or else be viewed as one country;

- whether the aforementioned proposed international commission should be an independent force composed of thousands of truce inspectors completely free to police the truce (U. S. contention), or if the commission should be composed of 250 persons severely restricted in their policing activities (North Vietnamese contention);

- whether any cease fire agreement should refer to the "Provisional Revolutionary Government", popularly known as the Viet Minh/Viet Cong;

- whether the aforementioned National Council Of Reconciliation And Concord would be a coalition government or only a temporary group formed only to supervise elections in South Vietnam;

- whether the North should be permitted to interpret the truce in the Vietnamese language version of the proposed agreement, and not in the English version.

"Peace" Realized, 1973

Two days before President Nixon was scheduled to be inaugurated, his adviser Henry Kissinger informed him that the deadlock at the peace talks in Paris had been broken. On 18 January all sides finally agreed on the terms which they believed would end the hostilities. Following is an outline of the finalized points which went into effect on 27 January:

- the U. S. contingent of approximately 27,000 troops would depart South Vietnam within 60 days;

- there would be an immediate cease-fire throughout Indochina;

- the U. S. would pledge 7.5 billion dollars to help all of the countries involved, including both Vietnams, Laos and Cambodia to recover;

- an international inspection team from Canada, Indonesia, Hungary and Poland would be chosen to supervise the peace;

- North Vietnam would be allowed to keep 150,000 troops in the South (this was the only major concession to North Vietnam);

- South Vietnamese President Nguyen Van Thieu would remain in authority in the South (this was the major concession by the North);

- a National Council Of Reconciliation And Concord would be formed with the Thieu Government;

- national elections were to be scheduled for the South;

- all of the 570 POWs which the North held would be repatriated to the U. S.

The above points met President Nixon's minimum criteria for "Peace With Honor", which were: (1) release of U. S. POWs, (2) an internationally supervised cease-fire and (3) lack of imposition of a communist government on South Vietnam.

It is worth noting that President Nixon calculated the length of the war at a mere twelve years. He stated in *RN* (p. 756) that after he officially announced cessation of the hostilities, "America was finally at peace for the first time in twelve years." That is, he had calculated that the war had begun in 1961, the first year of the Kennedy Administration. As will be revealed later, the government's calculation of the war's length would be modified considerably.

Further, Nixon's assessment of the quality of the "peace" agreement would compel him to state that "I had no illusions about the fragile nature of the agreement or about the Communists' true motives in signing it." (*RN*, p. 757). Accordingly, his apprehension about the negotiated truce did not bode well for the future of Indochina.

Assessment Of The Situation In Indochina, 1973

The war's first phase had ended. However, to reiterate, President Nixon had "hedged his bet." Nothing in the aforementioned peace accords referred to the disposition of U. S. forces in Thailand and also those stationed aboard ships in the South China Sea. Pentagon officials emphasized that a reduction in these personnel would only come when the peace of the region appeared to be secured. Indeed, the numbers of military personnel in the region outside of South Vietnam had increased markedly just before the peace terms were finalized. President Nixon was certainly aware that this force, which would soon include the author, was vital to the success of the negotiated peace. Further, he was prepared to engage in hostilities anew if circumstances would warrant such. He believed he had the backing of most of the public, and indeed he likely did. This would soon change, however.

Observers were quite apprehensive over the viability of the "peace" accords. Numerous assessments were made of the existing situation in Indochina, including the respective sizes and conditions of the forces of both North and South Vietnam, and also the attitudes of their respective populaces. Knowledgeable experts still worried that the South might not be in a position to repel any aggression from the North when the U. S. departed. One official of the Defense Department made the following statement:

> "North Vietnam cannot support another invasion of South Vietnam for at least two more years. By the same token, South Vietnam cannot invade North Vietnam without suffering heavy losses."

The first part of that assessment would indeed prove to be prophetic. The world was waiting to see what would happen within this two-year time frame.

The Level Of Civilian Carnage Quantified, 1973

As indicated in Figure 4, various observers tried to quantify the degree to which the civilian population in South Vietnam had suffered up to this point. This Herculean task was attempted by the U. S. Agency For International Development (AID), the Department Of Defense and also the body which bore the primary responsibility for the war, the U. S. Senate.

The figures from the three sources are difficult to compare. Observe that the three sources used different intervals to assess the degrees of civilian carnage. Further, the figures defy any rational explanation.

235

Any reasonable individual would be hard pressed to comprehend or to meaningfully examine the real impact of the carnage which these figures attempt to reveal. For instance, the same source of these figures also revealed that there had been mass imprisonment of persons who the ARVN had suspected of being NLF supporters. The interval given for the incarceration of such persons was from January, 1969 to April, 1971. This of course is a fraction of the interval of the war. The figure of 28, 978 persons who had been so subjected does not reveal the rate at which these persons were subjected to injury or death from torture which many likely experienced. Further, the Department Of Defense figures do not include the estimated 49,000 persons who had been abducted by the NLF between 1966 and 1972, according to the same source. These likewise likely suffered the same fate as their aforementioned counterparts. This information should be assessed in conjunction with the population data provided below in the section entitled *The Situation In Vietnam, 1975*.

Unresolved Issues Concerning The War, 1973 And Beyond

Although U. S. direct involvement in Indochina had terminated, serious issues needed to be resolved among the former combatants. By the end of March, all of the U. S. POWs who were known to have been held by the North would be repatriated. Upon being examined, it was found that most of the ex-POWs were in good physical condition considering what they had undergone, and generally in good spirits. However, 1,327 personnel were still listed as Missing-In-Action (M.I.A.). This would prove to be quite a point of contention between the U. S. and North Vietnam and its successor, The Socialist Republic Of Vietnam for many years into the future. For at least the next twenty five years U. S. officials would claim that North Vietnam and the succeeding unified nation had not been completely forthright in its accounting of the M.I.A.s. Perhaps this is because the numbers which both sides claimed were M.I.A. differed substantially. The U. S. claimed that 591 POWs were held at the war's end. The former enemy could only account for 555 such persons.

Further, the U. S. would persistently charge a lack of cooperation by the former enemy in efforts to locate the remains of persons who were known to have been lost in combat. However, history would prove that the American public's interest in the fate of the M.I.A.s would never dissipate. This could be seen in the bracelets which many U. S. citizens would wear as a sign of their concern for their lost countrymen. In addition, anytime the remains of an M.I.A. would be found, or the level of cooperation by the former enemy would increase, then this would become a major news story.

War's Aftermath?, 1973

a. Rebuilding efforts

As with all wars' aftermaths, the devastated lands began to rebuild. The 2.5 billion dollars promised by the U. S. in the peace accords was allocated not only to rebuild North Vietnam. There remained a major effort to locate and deactivate the many mines which had been laid in harbors and waterways. However, complications developed in the disbursing of the aid. These are discussed below.

As the situation developed, it appeared that North Vietnam was indifferent to its failure to secure the aforementioned aid, despite the continued danger from the mines. The halt of U. S. minesweeping efforts appeared not to deter foreign cargo vessels from entering North Vietnamese ports in increasing numbers. These vessels were of course laden with war materiel.

b. Monitoring activities

The U. S. of course had to closely monitor the situation all over Indochina in order to ensure that the former enemy lived up to the peace accords. As will be revealed later, the author was one of those designated to be part of a military force charged with such monitoring activities. Reconnaissance flights over North Vietnam were banned by the peace accords. However, the U. S. continued to monitor the situation from the air by means of special radar affixed to Navy and Air Force reconnaissance planes and also by means of other electronic inspection devices. These could observe activity in North Vietnam and Laos from the Gulf Of Tonkin without actually violating air space.

c. Relations among the former combatants

The hostilities had ended but the hostility between North and South Vietnam still was quite apparent. A most visible example of such hostility could be observed when the two sides were scheduled to meet at Saigon in order to confer and form an agreed upon Four Party Joint Military Commission. At Saigon's Tan Son Nhut Airport a delegation of North Vietnamese and the Viet Minh/Viet Cong had arrived but refused to deplane. They objected to completing customs and immigration forms which the South Vietnamese "Government" required. Consequently, U. S. officials were compelled to intervene in order to resolve the dispute. These officials persuaded airport personnel to waive the completion of the forms in question. U. S. Ambassador Ellsworth Bunker personally intervened.

Another most unusual phenomenon occurred which was a glaring example of how the U. S. presence was necessary in order to help peace to be realized. In some instances the South offered aid and equipment to their Northern brethren, only to be refused. Further, it was observed that the Northerners sometimes preferred U. S. assistance rather than from their Southern brethren. U. S. aircraft were also used to transport North Vietnamese officials to Saigon where they were housed in former U. S. military barracks. The U. S. accordingly expected to be the most influential member of the four parties to the Joint Military Commission. These included North and South Vietnam and the Viet Minh/Viet Cong.

d. Ongoing skirmishes

Minor skirmishes continued to erupt periodically in the rural areas of South Vietnam shortly after the peace agreement was ratified. These developed into major skirmishes as the two sides began to regroup, assess their respective resources and then maneuver to take advantage of the other. Casualties were as high as in any previous battlefield confrontations. The war was no longer guerilla-type, but conventional. On-site observers opined that these skirmishes were likely in preparation for the coming political struggle in which both sides would vie for control of South Vietnam. These observers also suspected that one side was preparing for further combat activities. When the North Vietnamese were caught attempting to bury a large cache of explosives, they left them behind. The North was also observed bringing anti-aircraft guns into rural areas.

e. Sentiments of the former military ally
Despite the U. S. promise of massive amounts of aid in the form of money and also technical assistance, some South Vietnamese feared that when all of the POWs had been repatriated, the U. S. would be so wearied by the hostilities that it would withdraw completely. This would of course leave them to sink or swim. Events which would develop within the next two years would reveal that South Vietnam had good reason for worry. (*U. S. News & World Report*, 2/26/73, "The New Role Of The U. S. In South Vietnam").

f. Ongoing efforts to ensure viability of the peace agreement
1. Continuing talks in Paris
It is noteworthy that the talks in Paris which resulted in the peace accords did not end when the truce was ratified in January. All of the concerned parties recognized their duty to create infrastructure to ensure that the peace would last. Accordingly, U. S. officials met in February with those of other concerned nations in Paris at an international conference aimed at doing just that. The conference had two tasks: to secure international endorsements of the aforementioned peace accords, and also to create an infrastructure to support the international commission's efforts to stabilize Indochina. The conference included five nations other than the U. S., the Soviet Union and the People's Republic Of China.

2. Reassessment of the situation
As the situation became more clear, all sides realized that the attendees at the peace conference other than the U. S. were somewhat disinterested in enforcing the truce. Their general attitude seemed to be one of "laissez-faire": let the former combatants work out their disputes between themselves. The reason why the attendees appeared to be less than interested is that the U. S. was not directly involved in implementing the peace accords. Further, knowledgeable observers believed that when the U. S. departed as scheduled at the end of March, then the peace talks would cease to have the leverage needed to ensure the viability of the truce. The U. S. and North Vietnam did indeed draft a nine-point

declaration which ratified the peace terms. However, the declaration failed to provide for the means to enforce the truce.

a. The "peace" placed in historical perspective

Here the situation must be put into historical perspective. This would be the second time in twenty years that a group of nations would meet to confer about the future of Indochina. Recall that the initial phase of the Indochina War which was begun by the French had ended immediately after that nation was defeated in 1954. This time these forces, among them the Viet Minh/Viet Cong, aided by North Vietnam, were not conferring from the position of strength which they had previously. They had won an outright military victory in 1954. Accordingly, this time these former combatants had to submit to compromises and accept terms which they did not want. This fact did not bode well for the future.

3. The U. S. position

In contrast with the position of the former enemy, the U. S. saw itself in a good position to confer on the future of Indochina. It deemed itself in a position of strength at the aforementioned conference because it believed that it had met its goal to keep South Vietnam independent. The strength of the U. S. position was perceived by outside observers.

The U. S.'s major ploy was to take advantage of the lack of complete trust among the three communist players: The Soviet Union, The People's Republic Of China and North Vietnam. The old suspicions among these three which kept the first two from intervening militarily in the war, remained. U. S. diplomats understood this and took advantage of the situation. The complexity of the situation was such that North Vietnam of course welcomed the 2.5 billion dollars which the U. S. had pledged to help them recover from the war. The "icing on the cake" from their perspective was that these monies would also allow them to become less dependent on their two ideological allies. This newfound greater independence apparently would therefore allow the North Vietnamese to play the two ideological giants against one another, if necessary.

4. Continuing diplomatic efforts

In June President Nixon labored for a new start in which he would reassess the entire situation in Indochina and also the position in which he found himself. His agenda was to:

(1) revitalize the White House
(2) damp down Watergate
(3) attack high prices
(4) accent the summit (among the U. S., the Soviet Union and China)
(5) save Vietnam truce

The drama of "Watergate" as examined below was detailed in "Nixon's fresh start", *U. S. News & World Report*, 26 June 1973, pp. 17 – 33.

With respect to (4), since the U. S. withdrawal from Vietnam and even before, the U. S. began to make diplomatic overtures to both the Soviet Union and to The People's Republic Of China in order to advocate greater cooperation among the three. The previous year when the war was still on and the U. S. was heavily bombarding North Vietnam, President Nixon had gone to the People's Republic Of China. His aim was to promote greater cooperation with them. At the present time, in the immediate aftermath of the U. S. withdrawal from Vietnam, President Nixon also met with Soviet Premier Brezhnev to do the same thing. The U. S. was accordingly reluctant to resort to any actions, military or otherwise, which might disturb this new diplomatic initiative. This in turn impacted the U. S. attitude towards the continuing hostilities in Indochina.

With respect to (5) above, the President sent his foreign policy adviser Henry Kissinger to meet with representatives of North Vietnam and its allies. In Paris on June 13 he induced them to sign a new agreement that the former enemy would abide by the peace accords of the previous January. In this agreement the U. S. agreed to (1) stop reconnaissance flights over North Vietnam which had resumed because of the continuing hostilities there, (2) resume minesweeping activities and (3) resume negotiations for promised aid to help the North Vietnamese to rebuild. The President did however resolve to continue the bombing campaign in Cambodia until he was satisfied that the insurgency there had abated, or until Congress cut off funds for such. The President did have cause for concern. The day after the agreement was signed, Congress began debate over whether all funding for combat operations throughout Indochina should be immediately terminated.

5. The return of the POWs

As during the first phase of the war, the POWs held by North Vietnam continued to be used as a pawn in negotiations between the U. S. and its former foe. These persons were not repatriated to the U. S. all at once. Rather, they were scheduled to be returned in groups at specified intervals. However, when North Vietnam perceived that all sides were not adhering to all of the peace accords, they halted the return of POWs until they were satisfied. U. S. officials were of course frustrated. In response to the disruption in the return of POWs, the U. S. in turn halted its agreed upon troop withdrawal and also stopped sweeping mines.

g. Continuing hostilities
1. In the rest of Indochina
a. In Cambodia

The "bottom line" of the entire affair is that the Indochina War had not ended when most thought that it had. In Cambodia in particular, U. S. air action continued throughout most of the year. Indeed, the U. S. press reported such, though the news of the bombing received little attention. This lack of concern by the public could be seen in the absence of the subject in the electronic media. Most Americans were likely glad that U. S. military efforts had apparently ended with the withdrawal of combat troops and the repatriation of most of the POWs. The government however had other ideas.

Although U. S. ground forces had been withdrawn by the end of March, the U. S. still had a sizeable force in the area, especially in Thailand. There 45, 000 troops were stationed at air bases, with 500 fighter-bombers and also B-52 bombers. This force flew 200 combat missions daily over Cambodia in the immediate aftermath of the signing of the peace accords in January. This bombardment had little effect on enemy ground activities, however. Despite the air support which the

Cambodian Government eagerly received, the situation there continued to deteriorate markedly. That country appeared to be helpless in the path of the domestic insurgency aided and abetted by North Vietnam.

What is most noteworthy is that some Cambodians welcomed U. S. intervention. Indeed, many Cambodians believed that their country could not survive without U. S. help. U. S. officials stated that the bombing was necessary in order to counter infiltration by North Vietnam and the Viet Minh/Viet Cong. Most observers agreed that the Cambodian Army was helpless. Accordingly, it appeared to be the new South Vietnam. However, to reiterate, the law was on the books which precluded the U. S. from sending ground combat troops or advisers. Congress had strictly stipulated that monies not be spent for that purpose.

b. In Laos

The situation in Laos was similar to that of its neighbor, Cambodia. This nation was likewise subjected to an insurgency which appeared to have been aided and abetted by the North Vietnamese and the Viet Minh/Viet Cong. As was the case with Cambodia, Laos was ideologically allied with the U. S. This is the obvious reason why the U. S. began an air bombardment against the Laos insurgency at the invitation of that government. The aforementioned Domino Theory accordingly appeared to gain new credibility. Some observers believed that Thailand, where a sizeable U. S. force was stationed, was next on the list of nations to be destabilized. The developments in the region are what prompted *U. S. News & World Report* to ask in its issue of May 7: "Can Indochina truce be saved?"

Congress responded to the aforementioned question, and the answer was "No!" Congress indicated that the truce could not be saved if the U. S. had to continue paying for it. The rancorous debate which continued U. S. participation in Indochina hostilities had generated, became increasingly heated. This debate was detailed in the July 16 issue of *U. S. News & World Report* in an article entitled "As the American fighting in Indo-china draws to a close" (pp. 52 – 53). Described therein is a compromise agreement between the President and Congress which stipulated that by 15 August all air strikes over Cambodia would be halted. In return for the President's agreement to halt all U. S. combat operations in Indochina in August and also to seek Congressional approval for any future U. S. military operations there, Congress forfeited its right to immediately cease funding for combat efforts in mid-July. Instead, Congress agreed to the aforementioned 15 August deadline. Accordingly, with this agreement the Indochina War's second phase thereby ended. It could go without saying that this compromise agreement between the President and Congress was noted by the Cambodian insurgents and by North Vietnam.

In the approximately five-week period between the date of the above agreement and the date on which it was to go into effect, the President used the only two weapons he had left: (1) more intense air actions in Cambodia and (2) greater diplomatic pressure by his foreign policy adviser Henry Kissinger.

Dr. Kissinger met with the Chinese Premier Chou En-Lai to enlist his help to persuade the Cambodian insurgents to cease hostilities. All observers knew however that U. S. air power was the only force standing in the way of a communist takeover of Cambodia.

In the aforementioned agreement between the President and Congress one can observe one of the most enduring legacies of the war. This agreement was hailed as a long-awaited victory for Congress in its efforts to exercise its Constitutional authority to curtail the President's war-making powers.

The situation in Cambodia remained even more heated than that in Vietnam. This was detailed in *"America's war ends, but Cambodia's ordeal goes on"*, an article in the August 27 issue of *U. S. News & World Report* (pp. 17 – 18). The U. S. bombing campaign of course had ended but that country remained in a crisis mode. The situation would continue to deteriorate even after the Vietnam War would eventually end, as will be revealed later. The world would then watch the country descend into mass genocide in 1975. However, inasmuch as that event is beyond the scope of this book, it will not be addressed here.

2. In Vietnam

The war never ended in Vietnam this year. It was documented that at least 50,000 persons died there from the date that the "truce" went into effect on 28 January and the end of the year. South Vietnam was subjected to massive infiltration from the North. The peace-keeping machinery which was supposed to have been put in place to police the truce had obviously broken down. The military buildup in South Vietnam by the North began shortly after the "truce." As of May 1 this buildup was estimated to be approximately 30,000 troops, 1,000 anti-aircraft guns and at least 8 SAM (Surface-to-air missile) sites. The situation prompted *U. S. News & World Report* in its issue of 23 April (p. 18) to paraphrase U. S. experts thusly:

> "Some U. S. experts argued that North Vietnam was only strengthening its forces to counter any attack that may be launched from Saigon. Others believed Hanoi was preparing for an offensive which might come in a matter of months but could be delayed while Hanoi first pushed a campaign to take over the South by political means."

One could thereby surmise that North Vietnam and its allies were definitely up to something. It was also revealed that North Vietnam was attacking aircraft belonging to the International Commission Of Control And Supervision (ICCS). The persons who flew these aircraft were the truce observers who came from neutral countries. Nine of these observers were killed, whereupon the ICCS suspended its air observing activities. The nations which comprised the ICCS also threatened to withdraw sooner than agreed. When it became apparent that its personnel were subjected to hostile fire, one of the nations involved, Canada stated its intention of doing just that. By 31 July this nation withdrew from the peace keeping force because North Vietnam and its allies repeatedly refused to work with the ICCS. Perhaps these facts are the reason why *U. S. News & World Report* published an article about the situation in its April 23 issue (pp. 17 – 19) entitled: "Indo-China: a war that won't go away."

"Now reds create a third Vietnam" was the title of the article in the July 23 issue of *U. S. News & World Report* (p. 29). As of mid-July, the North Vietnamese were observed creating what was essentially another "country" within South Vietnam proper. The apparent purpose was to carve out territory which they had seized since the "truce" went into effect. The conquered territory would then be turned over to its ally, the Viet Minh/Viet Cong Provisional Revolutionary Government. This organization was the political arm of North Vietnam in the South.

North Vietnam was able to essentially create a "country" within a "country" because it controlled approximately 25% of South Vietnam. Complicating the matter further was that the aforementioned Provisional Revolutionary Government of South Vietnam was recognized by over thirty other countries as the legitimate government, vice the "government" which the U. S. recognized. Of course the citizens of South Vietnam who were loyal to their "country" did observe this activity and how the North was building a political base. This of course caused them much grief. Many of them understood that the North could indeed use the captured territory as a base for a "winner-take-all" struggle to control all of South Vietnam. According to knowledgeable observers, this was indeed their goal.

To reiterate, U. S. combat activities in Indochina did not end with the aforementioned agreement in January. The actual date when U. S. activities finally ceased was on the aforementioned deadline of 15 August. Perhaps this is what prompted *U. S. News & World Report* to examine the situation in "With U. S. bombing over – the new era in Southeast Asia" in its issue of August 20 (pp. 20 – 22). To reiterate however, the actual date promulgated by the Department Of Defense as the date that the war eventually would end is 7 May 1975. One might therefore be prompted to ask: Then what happened between 15 August 1973 and that date?

A hint of what was to come could be seen in the opinion of knowledgeable observers who were quoted in the aforementioned article, opining that the Vietnam "truce" was "shaky." These same observers further opined that "Cambodia and Laos, and possibly South Vietnam are likely to become 'people's republics' (communist) within the next few years." The situation was such that *U. S. News & World Report* was compelled to ask in its issue of 5 November in an article entitled "Report from Vietnam – one place where a truce brings no end to woes: Is Hanoi preparing for another round of fighting?" As will be revealed later, this observation would indeed prove prophetic. Lastly, though his "country" was still showing significant will to resist, President Of South Vietnam

Thieu continuously warned of an impending offensive from the North. Apparently few were listening, or were able to do anything about it.

3. In Thailand

Besides South Vietnam, possibly the U. S.' staunchest ally in the region was Thailand. That nation had allowed the U. S. to launch air raids against North Vietnam and other places since the war had begun in earnest in 1965. After the U. S. withdrawal from Vietnam at the end of March, Thailand was still used as a base to launch air attacks against Laos and Cambodia. However, the U. S. position in the region and therefore its ability to participate in any future instability was complicated by a bloody upheaval in Thailand. In mid-October the military government was overthrown and replaced with a mostly civilian bureaucracy. At this time the U. S. still had six air bases there with 40,000 personnel. The bases were technically under control of the Government of Thailand.

An additional factor concerning the upheaval in Thailand was that even though the U. S. air assaults over Cambodia and Laos had ended by agreement between the President and Congress, this agreement still allowed the U. S. to provide supplies to allies. Accordingly, the U. S. was thereby still participating in the continuing war in Indochina. The Government Of Thailand still allowed the U. S. to use that nation as a supply route to funnel supplies to Cambodia and Laos.

The upheaval in Thailand of course affected the perception of the U. S.' ability to intervene in Vietnam also if the need should arise. There was a hint of anti-Americanism in the upheaval. However, the new government was deemed basically friendly to U. S. interests. A U. S. analyst gave his perception of the new situation, thusly:

> "If the North Vietnamese make another serious attempt to overrun the South by force, in violation of the cease-fire agreement, the aircraft in Thailand would be the first to respond. They are our insurance."

Was the U. S. able to call upon such "insurance" when and if the need arose? This question will soon be answered.

h. The U. S. reaction?/the changing domestic political landscape

The reaction in the U. S. to the deteriorating situation in Indochina was muted. A possible reason for the government's lack of response to the situation there, in addition to the aforementioned diplomatic initiatives to the Soviet Union and to The People's Republic Of China, is that the domestic political equation was also changing. A glaring indication of the changes occurring in the U. S. in the immediate aftermath of the end of U. S. direct involvement in Indochina, and what these would portend for the future, could be observed through the printed media. In its edition of May 7, *U. S. News & World Report* published two articles: (1) Can Indochina truce be saved?" and (2) Watergate: will Nixon be the big loser?" History has proven that these were the burning issues which would consume the rest of this year and a sizeable period thereafter. What occurred at this time was what some might call a "quirk of history." Two apparently unrelated events would coincide to not only radically alter history but would also reverberate for many years into the future. As will be revealed later, the fabric of American society would therefore be forever altered.

As of May the U. S. had labored long and hard to resolve a dispute between its ally and another "country." Through its considerable military might, it had not won an outright military victory, but it did succeed in inducing its enemies to sign a peace agreement. The U. S. thereby extricated itself from quite an unfortunate situation. However, this departure was coupled with a continuing military threat to its former enemy. The threat of the return of U. S. forces to Indochina apparently loomed large. But did it in actual fact? The hostilities there reignited at a furious pace after U. S. ground forces withdrew by the end of March. South Vietnam continued to be threatened. In retrospect one is compelled to therefore ask: Should the U. S. have returned to Vietnam in force to engage the former enemies in order to keep them from overrunning all of Indochina? A high-ranking U. S. Government official who was quoted in the May 7 issue of *U. S. News & World Report* summed up the dilemma with which President Nixon was faced, thusly:

> "One alternative would be to re-enter the war, at least
> in the air, and risk renewal of anti-war controversy in

the U. S. The other would be to stand idly by while the North Vietnamese built up their power to conquer the South by force of arms. If South Vietnam goes down that way, so does Mr. Nixon's 'peace with honor' and that would be unacceptable to the President."

It would soon be revealed what would become of the "peace with honor" for which President Nixon had labored so long and hard. The "bottom line" however is that the U. S. took no military action to help the former ally. The reason for this lack of follow-through on the threat of force to further U. S. interests will likely be debated into perpetuity. However, the situation in which the U. S. found itself at this time deserves close scrutiny.

In the ninety-day period after signing the agreement to end the war, North Vietnam and its allies clearly indicated that it would not adhere to the "truce." That "nation" was also apparently unconcerned with promised U. S. aid to rebuild itself. The U. S. however did nothing in response, although it continued its bombing campaign in Laos and Cambodia at least until 15 August. President Nixon stated that he favored a diplomatic course of action to resolve the ongoing hostilities. He did suspend the sweeping of mines from North Vietnamese waterways for a while. Further, he stopped the negotiations concerning the promised reconstruction aid. He did not however reintroduce ground forces into Indochina. The issue of whether the President could have mustered enough support from Congress for this purpose is of course another cause for debate. Be that as it may, President Nixon's threatened retaliatory measures against the former enemy never materialized. Perhaps the reason for this military inaction could be observed in the rapidly changing domestic political landscape.

i. The specter of Watergate

Previously, on 17 June 1972 when President Nixon was running for re-election, a group of individuals was apprehended burglarizing the Democratic National Headquarters at a place called the Watergate in Washington, DC. The police who apprehended them found evidence on the person of one of the burglars that he had connections to those close to the President. The news of this event of course soon appeared in the press. The story behind the burglary was initially small. However, as more facts were uncovered, the story of what had happened at the Watergate began to mushroom exponentially.

Here is where the aforementioned "quirk" becomes apparent. The likely reason why President Nixon failed to devote more attention to the deteriorating situation in Indochina is because he found it necessary to allot increasing amounts of his time to responding to charges that his Administration was involved in several crimes. Indeed, President Nixon conceded to these time-consuming activities in a televised address on 30 April at which he stated: "The (Watergate) affair has claimed too much of my time." Indeed, Nixon conceded in his memoirs (*RN*, p. 816) that the controversy over the Watergate affair caused a panic to come over many of those close to him "that was beyond anyone's control." The entire affair concerning what happened at the Watergate the previous June was spelled out in detail in the April 16 issue of *U. S. News & World Report*. Beginning with that issue, the public was inundated with information concerning the matter. Following is a partial listing of articles which were published in that periodical alone which give an indication of the magnitude of controversy to which the public was subjected:

(1) "Is Watergate Waterloo?" (5/14/74, pp. 70 – 72)
(2) "Watergate: Nixon's mood at a time of trouble" (5/21/73, p. 24)
(3) "Impeach? Unthinkable!" (5/21/73, p. 116)
(4) "Watergate upheaval – Is government at a standstill?" (5/28/73, pp. 17 – 19)
(5) "Watergate – Can Nixon still govern?" (5/21/73, pp. 20 – 21)

In (4) above one could see the first indications that the debate over the Watergate affair was leading to suggestions that the President should be impeached. The possibility of that happening is what a Senate Select Committee chaired by Senator Sam J. Ervin, Jr., of North Carolina would debate in televised hearings which commenced on 17 May. On 22 May the President was compelled to release a prepared statement concerning his side of the Watergate Case. Perhaps he was compelled to make this statement because he was becoming increasingly unpopular.

Despite President Nixon's increasing unpopularity, the Senate Select Committee deferred to the President in the area of foreign policy. On 18 June that Committee announced that it would postpone the testimony of an individual who had been the President's close adviser. The reason for the postponement was "to give President Nixon an opportunity to negotiate with Soviet leader Brezhnev without the distraction – and possible embarrassment – of the highly publicized hearings."

In one of the most detailed accounts of the possible link between the Watergate scandal and U. S. foreign policy, especially as it pertained to Indochina, in *Silent Coup* authors Colodny & Gettlin state explicitly that the scandal likely had a major impact on such policy. Stated the authors:

> "... foreign adversaries of the U. S. might make note of the potential turmoil going on in the U. S. over the Watergate issue, and might therefore use this fact to take advantage of the U. S." (Colodny & Gettlin, p. 353)

In addition to the aforementioned burglary, it was suggested that the Nixon White House had conspired to impede the investigation of the Watergate affair. A collateral issue was that certain individuals had perjured themselves in responding to inquiries by law enforcement officials. One individual, one G. Gordon Liddy, the alleged mastermind of the burglary, was convicted soon after the crime. He was sentenced to a prison term of from 6 years, 8 months to 20 years plus a fine of $40,000. Those penalties were in addition to another term of up to 18 months for refusal to cooperate with a Federal grand jury impaneled to investigate the Watergate affair. Another subsequent result of the controversy surrounding the affair was that President Nixon's nominee for Director of the Federal Bureau Of Investigation (F. B. I.), one L. Patrick Gray, abandoned his quest for that post. The F. B. I. was of course responsible for investigating the alleged crimes. As will be revealed later, the story would get even more bizarre.

The above details concerning the Watergate affair are provided to demonstrate the gravity of the situation which the President faced. The purpose here is to examine the possible link between the ongoing war in

Indochina and the U. S. reluctance to become further involved, coupled with the scandal which arose from the Watergate burglary. However, it is a safe bet that North Vietnam and its allies were watching political events in the U. S. with great interest.

In addition, one fact which must be noted is that the issue of the Watergate affair did not always deflect President Nixon from the issue of Vietnam after the scandal broke. This of course could go without saying. However, Nixon conceded in his memoirs that sometimes the opposite was the case. Nixon stated that in late December, 1972 after his reelection and when cessation of hostilities was imminent, the issue of the war deflected his attention from the Watergate affair when the latter threatened to become a major problem. In *RN* (p. 776) he stated that he was then "almost completely absorbed by the unfolding events concerning Vietnam" to the exclusion of the "knotty Watergate problem."

The above in turn prompts the question: Just how much did one issue (the war) suffer at the hands of the other (the political repercussions of the Watergate affair)? Another question which one might be prompted to ask is: Had the issue of Watergate not appeared at this point in time, then what would have been the U. S. reaction to the North Vietnamese flagrant violation of the peace agreement?

j. The specter of additional scandal

To the above controversy should be added that another person close to President Nixon was coming under increased scrutiny. On 10 April Vice President Spiro Agnew began consultation with Nixon's Chief Of Staff, Robert Haldeman. The Vice President sought help with a problem which had recently materialized. An individual with whom Agnew had been associated when he was an elected official in Maryland was being questioned by authorities there concerning allegations of corruption when Agnew had been a state official. Nixon stated in *RN* (p. 816) that Agnew had assured Haldeman that he was innocent of any wrongdoing. Nixon conceded in his memoirs that he was apprehensive that Agnew's troubles might rub off on his Administration. The allegations against Agnew concerned his alleged solicitation of campaign contributions and also "kickbacks" from those who had benefitted from Agnew's administration as County Executive in Baltimore County, MD and as Governor.

The Enactment Of Permanent Restrictions On The President's War-Making Capability, 1973

Since shortly after the conflict began in earnest, Congress was often wracked with heated debate concerning the President's Constitutional authority to wage war. The source of the debate was Article I, Sec. 8 of the Constitution which specifically grants Congress the authority to declare war. Accordingly, many within and without of government believed that the war was illegal because Congress had failed to declare war.

This year the debate on the issue of war-making authority was finally resolved. On 7 November Congress enacted the War Powers Resolution. This legislation permanently prescribes the conditions under which the President can use military force. Specifically, the law allows the President to commit U. S. forces to combat operations for a ninety day period without prior approval by Congress. However, the law reserves Congress' right to terminate any military action prior to that interval by a simple majority vote of both houses of Congress. After the legislation was passed by both houses, President Nixon of course vetoed the bill. His veto was overridden. As of this writing, the law is still in effect. Thus the war had served to clarify the Constitution.

The Atmosphere Within The Military Community, 1973

The Pentagon was of course up in arms at the developments in Indochina since the peace accords had been ratified in January. In spite of all of the resources which it had at its command, it could only sit and watch its past efforts falter. The most efficient military which the world had ever seen was indeed viewed as a pitiful, helpless giant. It was apparent that the turmoil in the White House over the rapidly changing political landscape was beginning to adversely affect the nation's defense posture. The media reported that the mood in Congress was causing erosion of confidence in the President's position as Commander-In Chief. Some of President Nixon's staunchest supporters who had been "hawks" on the war were deserting him. As stated previously, both houses of Congress moved to cut off funds for the continuing air war in Cambodia. These developments might be what prompted the highly respected Senator from Arizona, Barry Goldwater to state:

> "A visit to the Pentagon, the seat of our ability to maintain peace in the world leaves one with the impression that the (armed) services are suffering from a lack of civilian direction."

The Federal Judiciary's Perspective On War-Related Issues, 1973

a. The U. S. District Court For The Southern District Of California

One of the sources of the leak of the Pentagon Papers, Daniel Ellsberg, had all charges against him dismissed on 11 June. Recall that he had been indicted for having leaked the classified information to the press in 1971, thereby supposedly endangering national security. Judge Matt Byrne of the U. S. District Court For The Southern District Of California cited, in dismissing the charges, that the government had engaged in improper conduct. Among the improprieties was that it had improperly wiretapped Mr. Ellsberg's telephone conversations.

b. The U. S. District Court For The District Of New Jersey

Within one week after the peace accords had been signed on 28 January, the trial of the aforementioned Camden Twenty-eight began here. Recall that this group had been indicted for their anti-war activities in 1971. All of the members of the group were subsequently found not guilty by a jury in May.

The trial revealed that agents of the F. B. I. had essentially entrapped them. The jury thereby reasoned that the F. B. I. had been complicit in the burglary. The evidence presented at trail also revealed that an associate of the group had informed on them. The facts presented at trial would become quite bizarre, however.

Just prior to the aforementioned burglary, another Selective Service office in the immediate vicinity at Media, PA had also been broken into and entered and draft records destroyed. Evidence presented at the New Jersey trial suggested that the F. B. I. had set up this group for entrapment in order to link this group to the person(s) who had perpetrated the prior burglary. The evident aim of the F. B. I. was to prove a wider conspiracy, possibly to secure more severe punishments and also to net more anti-war protesters. The jury indicated that its rationale for releasing the defendants was, in addition to their apparent entrapment, that the jury also wanted to express its outrage over the war.

The case of the burglary at Media, PA was never solved.

The Anti-war Community's Reaction To The Government's Efforts To Silence It, 1973

Jane Fonda filed a civil action against the U. S. Government for alleged violation of her civil rights. The action was in response to information which she had received from the syndicated columnist Jack Anderson. He had obtained Ms. Fonda's F. B. I. dossier. She claimed in the action that the information had been illegally obtained.

Ms. Fonda held a press conference to announce the action. In a subsequent interview of Ms. Fonda, the interviewer stated that as a result of that press conference, no one in Hollywood was surprised by her action. Indeed, some in Hollywood seemed to encourage it. The film community's lack of surprise by her action is further testimony to the degree to which the U. S. changed during the war. Ms. Fonda's stature both within and without that community only seemed to have grown because of her anti-war efforts. According to the interviewer Ron Ridenour, if a major film star had taken such action only ten years previously, then the country would only have perceived the affair to be a publicity stunt. Ms. Fonda would likely therefore have been scorned by all segments of society, including Hollywood. As will be revealed later, more details of Ms. Fonda's legal action would be forthcoming.

Recognition By The International Community Of The "Progress" In Promoting "Peace" In Indochina, 1973

The Nobel Prize Committee is an internationally recognized organization which annually awards prizes to individuals who they believe have worked for the benefit of mankind. The awards are given at the Committee's headquarters in Oslo, Norway. This year the recipients of the Nobel Prize For Peace were Dr. Henry Kissinger who had been elevated to President Nixon's Secretary Of State, and Le Duc Tho, a powerful member of the North Vietnamese policymaking Politburo. Le Duc Tho rejected the award however, giving as his reason that there was no peace in his "country." As of this writing he is the only person ever to reject the award.

As *U. S. News & World Report* stated in its issue of 29 October (p. 84), the aforementioned two men "negotiated a cease-fire in South Vietnam that exists more in word than in deed." The article further concedes that the peace agreement was never fully implemented. Further, the awarding of the Prize on 16 October came amidst all sides trading charges that the others had violated the peace accords. Observers believed that the charges from North Vietnam and the Viet Minh/Viet Cong were in preparation for a future military offensive to take over South Vietnam. Some believed this offensive to be inevitable.

There was further speculation that in awarding the Prize, the Nobel Committee was aware that the hostilities were ongoing, and that no peace had been achieved. However, there were indications that the Committee had so acted because it believed the selection of the two men in question would eventually bring a final end to the war.

Lastly, it bears mention that two of the other nominees for the Prize this year were President Nixon and the individual who had co - leaked the Pentagon Papers, one Daniel Ellsberg.

The Author's Situation, 1973

Within forty-eight hours after the "peace" agreement had been ratified in January, all of the officers on board *Coral Sea* were ordered to report to the wardroom where the officers dine. Everyone knew what the meeting was about. Since the hostilities had officially ceased, everyone wondered how the ship's mission would be changed. *Coral Sea* had initially been scheduled to deploy from CONUS for duty in the Gulf Of Tonkin and the South China Sea on 9 February.

Mid-winter is the midst of the dry season in Southeast Asia. The weather would be, until June, perfect for conducting flight operations. At the wardroom meeting however, the Commanding Officer announced that the ship's orders had changed. Deployment would be delayed for precisely thirty days, until 9 March. The ship's evolutions were accordingly modified to adhere to the revised orders from the Pentagon. *Coral Sea* deployed for WESTPAC from the Alameda, CA Naval Air Station on the specified date, with the ship's company lining the entire perimeter of the ship's massive flight deck. Amidst brilliant sunshine, decked out in immaculate service dress blues, the ship and her full company of officers and men and aircraft bid adieu to the city which was her sponsor. It was sad for the city to see San Francisco's Own on her way to the other side of this planet. She would not be back for many a day. Waving good-bye to the beautiful city, *Coral Sea* passed through San Francisco's Golden Gate and into the ice blue waters of the Pacific, with the course set for the U. S. Navy Base at Pearl Harbor, HI. The purpose of the visit was to take on stores including nuclear ordnance. This was the "muscle" which President Nixon apparently decided was necessary to enforce the negotiated peace. After a forty-eight hour stay at Pearl Harbor to *carefully* load the aforementioned ordnance into her hold, *Coral Sea* again set her course for her ultimate destination.

After about three weeks at sea, having been entertained by schools of flying fish in the middle of the Pacific, with the attendant changes in heat and humidity, and having wound her way through the narrow straits and picturesque islands of the Republic Of The Philippines, *Coral Sea* docked at the U. S. Naval Base at Subic Bay, on the western coast of that Republic. This was to be the port from which the ship would operate while in the region. It would soon become apparent to the ship's company that its mission would be primarily to "show the flag." There would be no more lengthy "line" periods as there were during *Coral Sea's* previous deployment from November, 1971 to July, 1972. During that interval the vessel was a major force in the barrage against North Vietnam.

It must be emphasized here that the *Coral Sea* did not participate in the aforementioned air war over Laos and Cambodia this year. As an officer on board that vessel, the author can state unequivocally that in the seven months during which the *Coral Sea* patrolled the waters adjacent to Vietnam, he did not observe any plane launched with ordnance with the intention of unloading such. His regular duty was to stand watches on the bridge from where the ship is controlled.

From this vantage point he would indeed have observed if ordnance was affixed to the planes catapulted from her deck. He never observed such. Accordingly, the aforementioned bombardment of Cambodia and Laos from January through August originated from U. S. air bases in Thailand.

As the only aircraft carrier assigned to the Indochina Theater at this time, *Coral Sea's* only mission was to maintain U. S. presence in the Far East. The itinerary of the ship during its scheduled deployment from 9 March to 8 November was:

- patrol the narrow straights of the Gulf Of Tonkin during April to ensure that the former enemy adhered to the provisions of the peace accords. The ship was purposely visible in order to demonstrate U. S. military strength. During the first two months of the deployment from April to May, the Gulf Of Tonkin was still officially designated a hostile fire zone by The Pentagon. That is, there was still a possibility that the ship would be required to engage in hostile actions, be fired upon and therefore have to return fire. Accordingly, the crew received several benefits from serving in such a zone. The most beneficial of these was that the first $500 earned monthly was not taxable. When the potential threat eventually dissipated, the money dried up;

- continuously engage in flight operations whenever practicable in order to keep the pilots trained and the crew occupied. This type of operation is dangerous even when an aircraft carrier is not engaged in hostile actions. Two jet aircraft were lost at sea when the planes malfunctioned while airborne. The author was the officer-in-charge of the duty motor whaleboat and crew sent to search for one of the pilots and his plane. No trace of either was found;

- steam to Manila in early May to partake of the sights and sounds of the capital city of the Philippines, Quezon City;

- engage in more flight operations and training exercises for the rest of May in The South China Sea;

- steam to the U. S. Naval Base at Sasebo, Japan to partake of the sights and sounds there for ten days in early June. *Coral Sea* was originally scheduled to remain in Sasebo for two weeks. However, the crew's presence there was so disruptive to the civilian population that the ship was asked to depart early. During this port call, there was continuous strife in the streets among the crew. This was possibly due to the fact that everything which the crew desired was much more expensive in Japan than it had been in the Philippines, including "female companionship";

- steam to the British Crown Colony (B.C.C.) of Hong Kong the first week in August (mid-deployment) for R&R (rest and recuperation).

The rest of the deployment was spent engaging in flight operations whenever practicable in the South China Sea, then re-visiting Manila in early September. Much time was spent eluding hurricanes which plague the southwestern Pacific from July through November. One port call at Subic Bay was abruptly truncated when the ship had to depart early to evade an approaching hurricane. Some of the crew had to be left on the pier.

During October after having departed WESTPAC to return to CONUS, the ship was at a heightened state of alert because of the Yom Kippur War in the Middle East in September. *Coral Sea* returned to CONUS and tied up to the pier at the Alameda, CA Naval Air Station on schedule on 8 November. As will be revealed later, this would be the last incursion of the author and the next to last incursion of the *Coral Sea* into Indochina during the war.

The Popular Culture, 1973

There were no wild celebrations of the end of the war, either in Times Square as there had been at the conclusion of World War II, or in celebrations elsewhere. No popular songs were released which reflected the relief which the American public felt. The public seemed to simply be relieved that the nightmare of the Vietnam War was believed to be over. History would prove however that the conflict had not been completely resolved. However, as with all conflicts in which the United States had been engaged, the film industry began to produce films which offered its perception of the war.

a. Motion pictures
1. *Hearts And Minds*

The first of the films undertaken at the end of the first phase of the war to explain what had occurred was *Hearts And Minds*. Production began shortly after the first phase had ended, but with U. S. military personnel still stationed in Vietnam. The film was completed this year. It holds the additional distinction of being the only filmed documentary of the Vietnam War produced for commercial release.

The phrase "hearts and minds" which became one of the most enduring phrases of the war, was apparently coined by President Johnson at the outset of the conflict. The film shows him uttering the following famous phrase which apparently inspired the film's title: "Victory (in Vietnam) will depend on the *hearts and minds* of the people who actually live out there."

Another utterance from one of the major players in the Vietnamese drama came from General William Westmoreland, the Commander of U. S. forces at the outset of the conflict. In the film he is shown making his infamous statement that "the Oriental doesn't put the same high price on life as the Westerner." The General's quote may have been indicative of the degree to which race permeates U. S. society. It may also have been indicative of the perception by many in the U. S., both white and non-white, that the war had been waged by racist Americans. The film shows General Westmoreland uttering the statement after a Vietnamese boy was shown crying over the death of his father who was killed by U. S. bombs.

The film also shows the aforementioned footage of a young girl running naked down a highway, her skin on fire from having been napalmed in an attack by U. S. planes. The film additionally shows the aforementioned footage of a Viet Minh/Viet Cong prisoner being summarily executed on a street by the Saigon Police Chief with a bullet fired into his brain.

Other unforgettable scenes in the film take place in, of all places, a Vietnamese brothel where some of the employees are indeed nude. Apparently U. S. military personnel who were there until the end of March were concerned not only with Vietnamese *hearts and minds*, but also with certain other of their body parts.

Hearts And Minds justifiably won critical acclaim upon its initial release. Leonard Maltin, the world-renowned movie critic was "right on" when he labeled the film:

> "..documentary about our misguided involvement in Vietnam was a political hot potato for a while, but may rate more frequent showings now that the country has caught up with it. Packs a wallop, regardless of one's political persuasion."

Mr. Maltin made that statement because the film generated much controversy and angered many. The film was withheld from release for a year after it was completed. The original distributor of the film justifiably feared legal problems. It did not go into release until late 1974 when the war would heat up again, as will be examined below.

2. *Introduction To The Enemy*

This year would see the strongest and most visible link between the popular culture and the anti-war movement. Approximately one week prior to the ratification of the aforementioned peace accords, Jane Fonda and Tom Hayden were married.

This year the newlyweds also returned to North Vietnam to produce a film entitled *Introduction To The Enemy*. The purpose of the film was to document life there in the wake of the apparent cessation of the hostilities. A collateral purpose was to describe the manner in which the place had been devastated.

Reports From The Print Media, 1973

During the waning days of the first phase of the conflict, the print media continued to promulgate information concerning the merits of the war. The following is a truncated list of articles which were published as U. S. direct involvement in Indochina terminated:

1. *"More bombs than ever."*
   (Time, 1/1/73, pp. 10 – 12)

2. *"Why Vietnam War drags on."*
   (U. S. News & World Report, 1/1/73, pp. 9 – 12)

3. *"As the war hit a peak."*
   (U. S. News & World Report, 1/8/73, p. 17)

4. *"Diplomacy by terror: what the bombing did."*
   (Newsweek, 1/8/73, pp. 10 – 12)

5. *"Nixon's blitz leads back to the table."*
   (Time, 1/8/73, pp. 9 – 14)

6. *"Peace! Peace! And there is no peace."*
   (America, 1/13/73, p. 9)

7. *"Worse than silence: destruction of Bach Mai Hospital."*
   (The Nation, 1/15/73, pp. 68 – 69)

8. *"Bombing and morality."*
   (National Review, 1/19/73, p. 74)

9. *"End of Vietnamization."*
   (National Review, 1/19/73, pp. 110 – 111)

10. *"After Truce – next turn in Vietnam; final touches on a cease-fire document were all that were needed to free U. S. from a seemingly endless war in Indochina."*
    (U. S. News & World Report, 1/29/73, pp. 11 – 16)

11. *"Why many runaway Americans find Canada no longer is home"*
    (U. S. News & World Report, 1/15/73, p. 27)

12. *"The POWs Came Home: unbounded joy, but – "*
    (U. S. News & World Report, 2/26/73, p. 25)

13. *"The Most The U. S. Can Really Hope For In Vietnam"*
    (U. S. News & World Report, 3/12/73, p. 25)

14. *"Cambodia: still in agony"*
    (U. S. News & World Report, 3/12/73, p. 25)

15. *"Was Vietnam Worth It?"*
    (U. S. News & World Report, 4/2/73, pp. 23 – 25)

16. *"Back Of U. S. Decision To Keep On Bombing In Cambodia"*
    (U. S. News & World Report, 4/16/73, pp. 37 – 38)

CHAPTER FOURTEEN: PERCEIVED INTERLUDE WHILE HOSTILITIES CONTINUE; THE WORLD WATCHES WHILE THE DRAMA CONTINUES TO BUILD, 1974

Despite complete removal of the U. S. from the never-ending hostilities, domestic controversy over the Indochina situation continued. Cambodia continued to be threatened by a communist insurgency. The U. S. continued to support the South financially. Some citizens favored a clean break. Others favored increased intervention because the enemy failed to honor the provisions of the truce. The Commander-In-Chief was however paralyzed politically.

The Situation In South Vietnam, 1974

In January the total number of U. S. military personnel in Vietnam stood at 225. The other 5,700 U. S. personnel there were civilians. The situation had indeed changed in the approximately one year since the peace accords were signed. However, the war was officially still on. An assessment of the new situation was detailed in the January 14, 1974 issue of *U. S. News & World Report* in an article entitled "After turmoil a new Asia emerges." Pentagon officials who monitored the situation were quite concerned about the capability of North Vietnam to make inroads into the South even further than what they had already accomplished. The article stated:

> "Responsibility for assessing communist (North Vietnamese) capabilities and intentions – is still very much an American function. It is easy enough to assess North Vietnam's capabilities. It is something else to assess Hanoi's intentions."

Among those U. S. military personnel "in country" was the aforementioned Col. Harry Summers. He was sent there in July to act as chief of the Negotiations Division of the Four Party Joint Military Team (FPJMT). The task of that body was to determine the status of U. S. personnel who were still listed as Missing In Action (M. I. A.).

a. The current state of South Vietnam's military capacity

As previously stated, the hostilities continued unabated in Vietnam throughout 1973. All observers knew that something would happen sooner or later, but the questions were: What? and When? As this year began, fighting among all sides was quite intense and observers believed that all sides were preparing for heightened ground action. South Vietnam's capability to weather any ground offensive by the North was not where their attention was focused, however. In an article entitled "Biggest test ahead for South Vietnam's Air Force" from the January 28 issue of *U. S. News & World Report*, knowledgeable persons examined their capability to defend against any offensive which could conceivably materialize.

As the year began, North Vietnam stepped up its attacks on the South. The ARVN would of course bear the brunt of any such ground offensive. The primary responsibility however to repel such an offensive would go to the Air Force. This Force had large amounts of U. S.-supplied planes with competent U. S.-trained pilots. However, it was not certain that even this capability would suffice to blunt an offensive from the North. In an assessment of the situation, a U. S. observer quoted in the aforementioned issue of *U. S. News & World Report* stated:

> "An offensive the size of the communist invasion in the spring of 1972 would be more than the South Vietnamese Air Force could handle."

b. Assessments by Pentagon officials

The situation in South Vietnam was such that the U. S. Secretary Of Defense James Schlesinger stated that President Nixon might ask Congress for the authority to aid South Vietnam with air power if North Vietnam began a major offensive.

The individual most likely knowledgeable concerning the Indochina situation was one Graham A. Martin, the U. S. Ambassador to South Vietnam. In an article entitled "Envoy to South Vietnam answers his critics" (interview), published in the April 29 issue of *U. S. News & World Report* (pp. 72 – 74), the envoy's assessment of the situation was basically upbeat. He apparently was compelled to submit to the interview because some observers were confused about the continuing U. S. role in the region. This is the possible reason why the sub-caption of the interview was "Are Americans getting a 'distorted' view of the realities in Vietnam?" It bears mention that the interview came in the wake of a pronounced lull in the hostilities. Stated Ambassador Graham:

> "… we should end it (U. S. involvement in South Vietnam) quickly, and I believe that this can be done. I have said our objective should be to end it leaving Vietnam economically viable, militarily capable of defending itself with its own manpower, and free to choose its own government and its own leaders. I believe this can be done within the next three years."

Though the hostilities were continuing, the Thieu Regime seemed to be weathering the situation during the early part of the year. That regime was however still in the throes of much political discord. Observers knew that because of such discord, the North had the capability to take advantage and mount an effective offensive anytime the situation seemed right. One of such observers stated that if that should happen, "then the U. S. would face a critical decision – how far would it go to support a non-communist government in South Vietnam against an unremitting communist campaign to drive it into the sea?" That question would soon be answered.

c. General assessments of the relationship between North and South Vietnam

In its issue of 26 August, *U. S. News & World Report* published an article by its "in-house" observer who had just ended an eleven year assignment to observe all of Indochina. His opinion was that Hanoi and its ideological allies had made serious tactical errors in pursuing its campaign against the South. He further opined that Hanoi had erred by failing to perceive weaknesses in its opponent. This was the apparent reason why it had failed to control or dominate the region.

The observer further stated that the lack of perception by Hanoi was obvious because it had ample opportunity in the first six months of the year to mount an effective military campaign. Such a campaign might have achieved its goals, he opined. However, it failed to avail itself of this opportunity. The observer further opined that if Hanoi had done so, then they would likely not have encountered any resistance from the United States. He further stated that the most glaring example of Hanoi's missteps could be seen in an offensive during the spring of this year when its troops were supposed to have been within twenty miles of Saigon. In addition, the ARVN troops which stood between them and Saigon were known not to be competent. Yet for some reason the North abandoned this offensive which might have allowed it to overrun Saigon and therefore all of South Vietnam. This was of course its overriding goal. Instead, the North diverted its efforts to another area further north from Saigon.

An indication of South Vietnam's perceived lack of ability to withstand an offensive could be seen in the amount of aid requested by the White House. The amount requested for South Vietnam was a mere 1.5 billion dollars for the Fiscal Year ending 30 June 1975. Half of this was supposed to be economic aid. The final amount decided upon in military aid was 700 million dollars, a decrease of 30% from the previous fiscal year. The result was that the Thieu Regime planned to cut its troop strength by 10%.

"Is the U. S. sending Saigon to its death?" was the title of the article in the September 30 issue of *U. S. News & World Report.* In this article Army Maj. General John Murray (Ret.) observed that South Vietnam appeared to be helpless against the military campaign from the North. The fighting definitely heated up during the latter part of the year. One reason the general gave for his pessimistic assessment was that the North was known to be better supplied than the South in numbers of tanks supplied by the Soviet Union. Gen. Murray also stated that "today, without question Hanoi has by far the strongest, best-positioned and best-supported military machine it has ever fielded in South Vietnam. When the time is ripe, Hanoi will strike." Lastly, Gen. Murray also opined that these known military capabilities were being ignored by the U. S. The question of course was: What will these phenomena bode for the near future? The next year would tell the tale.

Meanwhile, other knowledgeable persons continued to assess the situation. These assessments were detailed in the November 4 issue of *U. S. News & World Report* in which another "in-house" observer for this periodical questioned whether the three remaining non-communist states in the region, Cambodia, Laos and South Vietnam, could be kept out of North Vietnam's hands. The consensus of other observers in this regard was that:

1. If the U. S. cut all military aid to South Vietnam, this would not necessarily mean that the "country" would be overrun by the North; and

2. If all of Indochina fell to North Vietnam, then this would not be a disaster for the U. S.

The second of the above assessments would prove to be partially prophetic.

The Situation In North Vietnam, 1974

North Vietnam appeared to emphasize rebuilding efforts to repair the damage which had occurred during the war. It still looked forward to the 2.5 billion dollars which the U. S. had pledged for such efforts. However, U. S. officials stated that no more aid would be forthcoming until the North strictly adhered to the peace accords of January, 1973. The aid was desperately needed because the North was known to be in dire economic straights, apparently because of mismanagement by its leadership.

Some observers suggested that the situation in North Vietnam was influenced by the diplomatic overtures President Nixon had made and would continue to make to both the People's Republic Of China and to the Soviet Union. The President did travel to Moscow in July. The same observers suggested that the leaders of the two communist giants had asked North Vietnam to "cool it" while the high level summit meetings occurred.

The North's campaign against the South was observed to have abated markedly early in the year. Some believed that another reason in addition to that above for such abatement was that the North simply did not have the resources to make further territorial inroads into the South, as it had during much of the previous year. It is a safe bet however that North Vietnam was observing the political situation in the U. S. and also the relationship between the U. S. and the two communist giants with great interest. One could also properly speculate that North Vietnam's leaders read the aforementioned "expert" opinion that it was incapable of proper planning to achieve its goal of national unification. North Vietnam's leaders also probably read the August 26 issue of *U. S. News & World Report* and likely took issue with that "expert's" statement that "North Vietnam is so used to winning military battles but losing political wars that it doesn't know how to achieve total victory." Events which would soon develop would dispute the validity of that assessment.

The Continuing Preoccupation Of The Commander-In-Chief With Concerns Other Than Indochina, 1974

Meanwhile, the U. S. domestic political climate continued to be wracked with rancor. It could go without saying that any issue, domestic or foreign, which might deflect the attention of the Commander-In-Chief from directing the Armed Forces deserves to be scrutinized. Accordingly, the rancor over the aforementioned Watergate affair bears mention within the context of the increasingly critical situation in Indochina. President Nixon seemed to be perpetually on the defensive on the Watergate issue. Perhaps this is the reason why the January 28 issue of *U. S. News & World Report* had on the cover: "Mystery Deepens On The Watergate Tapes."

The dual issues of Vietnam vs. Watergate demand in retrospect to be placed in historical perspective. Upon the occasion of Nixon's death in 1994, the issue of the possible link between the aforementioned scandal and also Nixon's inability to govern and to pursue the war more aggressively this year, such was still an issue of controversy after his death. In examining Nixon's legacy, a political observer summed up such legacy within this context, thusly:

> "And Vietnam led in a roundabout way to Watergate. The connection between the war and the scandal that destroyed a president is ultimately a state of mind: Nixon's deep hostility toward prominent antiwar activists like Daniel Ellsberg, and the "bunker mentality" that pervaded the White House after the invasion of Cambodia and the shootings at Kent State. Nixon in 1970 was a man besieged." ("The Rise And Fall And Rise And Fall And Rise Of Nixon", *Newsweek*, 2 May 1994).

President Nixon continued to be besieged after 1970. This year the investigation of the aforementioned burglary of the Watergate Hotel on 17 June 1972 was continuing. Federal investigators were still trying to assess the President's possible complicity in the matter. By this date, the investigators had uncovered the fact that President Nixon had, since the burglary, tape recorded conversations which he had with others in the Oval Office of the White House. Some of these conversations were with persons who had already been convicted of crimes concerning the affair. Accordingly, some in Congress were seriously considering the issue of impeaching the President. This is the likely reason why the February 4 issue of *U. S. News & World Report* had on its cover: "If Nixon is impeached, what then?" In the next issue of that magazine, in an article entitled "Barry Goldwater speaks his mind on Richard Nixon", (p. 39) the "Grand Old Man" of the Grand Old Party stated that "A large, large number of Republicans (President Nixon's political party) want Nixon to resign."

To demonstrate the degree of rancor which materialized over the Watergate affair and President Nixon's possible complicity in it, the following is a listing of all of the articles, in addition to those already referenced, which were published in the aforementioned periodical this year which pertained to the matter:

1. **"Charges against the White House"** (3/11/74) which discussed more than a dozen of the President's former associates who had been sentenced to prison or were awaiting sentencing because of their complicity in the Watergate affair.

2. **"Can Nixon stand new shocks?"** (3/18/74) which examined the President's relationship with one Charles Colson who was the President's Special Counsel, and who had been indicted for his possible complicity in the Watergate affair. On 3 June Colson would plead guilty to complicity in the burglary of the office of the psychiatrist of Daniel Ellsberg, the person who had leaked the Pentagon Papers three years previously. He further pleaded guilty to obstruction of justice. He was accordingly sentenced to a prison term of from one to three years and a $5,000 fine.

3. **"Odds on impeachment now"** (5/20/74, cover) examined the continuing debate concerning whether the President should be impeached because of his possible

complicity in the Watergate affair. The subtitle of the accompanying article was: "In view of Congressional leaders: those transcripts Nixon made public have hurt the President, make his future more uncertain." Previously, the President had been compelled to turn over tape recordings which he had made in the Oval Office which prosecutors believed might reveal the degree to which he may have been complicit in any one of a number of crimes.

4. "**The Nixon crisis: where will it lead?**" (5/27/74, cover) examined the continuing efforts of prosecutors to determine the degree to which the President may have been complicit in a number of crimes.

5. "**Is Watergate strangling the U. S. Government?**" (6/3/74, cover) examined the paralysis to which the Government appeared to have to endure because of its preoccupation with whether President Nixon was fit to continue to serve.

6. "**Watergate: three more shocks for the President**" (6/17/74) examined the indictment against a person close to the President who was involved in the Watergate affair. The article also examined the fact that the President was named in the indictment as an unindicted co-conspirator in the known cover-up of the Watergate burglary.

7. "**Furor over Watergate leaks**" (7/1/74, cover). The accompanying article (pp. 22- 25) detailed the process in which information damaging to the President had been exposed to the public. This issue also ran a story about the President's aforementioned diplomatic overtures to the Soviet Union and his journey there for a summit meeting with Soviet leader Leonid Brezhnev. Accordingly, in light of the above it is safe to say that the continuing hostilities in Indochina were not foremost on the President's mind.

8. "**Where impeachment stands now**" (7/15/74, cover and article, pp. 18 – 20) examined the continuing debate in Congress over what charges should be brought against the President.

9. "**Impeachment crisis – key decisions at hand**", (7/22/74, cover and article, pp. 15 – 17) examined the continuing Congressional debate over how that body should exercise its Constitutional authority to bring impeachment charges against the President.

10. "**Impeachment: down to the real issues**", (7/29/74, cover and Article, pp. 16 – 18) further discussed the specific articles of impeachment with which Congress intended to bring charges against the President.

11. "**Nixon: the case for and against**" (8/5/74), cover and article, pp. 11 – 15) examined the specific articles of impeachment which Congress had decided on to formally charge the President. The article also detailed the ruling from the Supreme Court which compelled the President to surrender tape recordings which he had made in the Oval Office. These could shed light on his possible complicity in several crimes growing from the Watergate affair. These recordings had been subpoenaed by the Special Prosecutor assigned to scrutinize the matter of possible White House complicity in the Watergate affair. The White House had refused to surrender them. The ruling from the Supreme Court was unanimous.

12. "**Impeachment: the formal charges**. Outlook in the House, Nixon's defense strategy, what the people say" (8/12/74, cover and article, pp. 15 – 22) detailed the specific articles of impeachment with which the President was formally charged in the House Of Representatives. In an accompanying article, this issue also detailed the scope of the Watergate affair and to what degree the affair had permeated the White House. The second article entitled "Watergate casualties: the list

grows longer" (p. 23) detailed the numerous individuals associated with the President who were known to have engaged in illegal activities, the indictments which they faced and also the sentences which some had already faced in various courts.

To comprehend the degree to which the Watergate affair deflected Nixon's attention from Indochina, as well as from other pressing matters, one need only examine his memoirs. Nixon concedes therein that from April, 1973 until the ultimate end of his tenure, he was more preoccupied with his political survival than with any other matter. The following passage from his memoirs is indicative of the distress which Nixon suffered during his last year as President. In October, 1973 when the controversy over the Watergate affair was blazing and becoming even more heated, and his popularity according to opinion polls was dwindling markedly, he stated:

> "The situation was intolerable. Week by week, month by month, we were being worn down, trapped, paralyzed." (*RN*, p. 928).

The degree of detail in his memoirs to which he allocated the Watergate crisis would lead one to believe that after 1973 he could not have cared less about the deteriorating situation in Indochina.

The Watergate affair culminated in the resignation of Richard M. Nixon as the thirty-seventh President Of The United States on August 8. Gerald R. Ford was immediately sworn into the Office. President Ford of course set his sights on the various crises which the nation faced, including the continuing situation in Indochina.

The National Mood Concerning Citizens Who Had Avoided Participation In The War, 1974

U. S. direct involvement in Vietnam from 5 August 1964 to 28 January 1973 had of course caused public division on a number of issues. One of the issues which continued to cause much rancor concerned those who had evaded military service. The discourse over military deserters and those who had not served therein but who had left to escape military service or had otherwise evaded such, continued to be the subject of quite heated debate.

As soon as he entered office, the new Commander-In-Chief took up the issue of what to do with the aforementioned individuals. Approximately one month after assuming office, President Ford promulgated his plan to address the issue. Such was detailed in the September 16 issue of *U. S. News & World Report* in an article entitled "Ford's "amnesty plan – will it satisfy anybody?" Public opinion was mostly against granting amnesty to those who had shunned military service during the war. The President presented a five-point plan based on recommendations from the Secretary Of Defense and the Attorney General. These points were:

> **1.** Each individual subject to the proposed plan would have to apply for a position of alternative civilian service in lieu of serving in the military;
>
> **2.** Amnesty for these individuals would not be considered. The infraction which each individual had committed would only be forgiven if and when the individual had completed the alternative civilian service which they had requested. Organizations mentioned where these individuals would serve were such as the Peace Corps;
>
> **3.** No person who had deserted the military would be eligible for an Honorable Discharge even after completing the alternative service which they had selected;
>
> **4.** Those draft dodgers and deserters who declined to participate in the program of alternative civilian service would still have to serve a prison term if such was adjudicated by a competent court;
>
> **5.** Persons already charged with desertion or draft evasion who chose to enter this program would have to report to a designated place for processing. After their choice of alternative service was completed, the individual would have to swear an oath of allegiance to the United States.

The above plan which was labeled "earned amnesty" or "clemency" was decided by the President and required no Congressional action. President Ford's plan was by and large rejected out of hand by the consensus of persons who had evaded or dodged the draft. Many of these were still living in Canada and Sweden.

Many of the individuals in question did however avail themselves of the President's plan. The degree to which military deserters came forward and accepted the government's offer of a "clemency" discharge was detailed in the November 11 issue of *U. S. News & World Report*, the publication of which coincided, incidentally, with Veterans Day. The article entitled "Now that deserters are coming home – some surprises" (pp. 30 – 32) revealed just that. Administrators of the program were surprised that nearly all of the persons who volunteered for the program gave reasons other than opposition to the war for having deserted. Most of them merely had personal problems which caused them to desert.

Continuing Private Efforts To Extricate The U. S. From Indochina, 1974

Though the U. S. had withdrawn from Indochina, in addition to maintaining a large presence in Thailand the U. S. continued to financially support the Thieu Regime. This fact appeared to be lost on the public at large. However, certain circles were aware that the South Vietnamese "government" was being propped up by the U. S. This was wrong and unnecessary, they believed. The Thieu Regime was widely known to be corrupt and also to violate human rights. Two individuals who continued to lobby for the complete extrication of the U. S. from Indochina were Jane Fonda and her new husband, Tom Hayden. In an April interview they expressed the details of their activities to further their beliefs. Stated Mr. Hayden:

> "We cannot conclude that peace with honor has been achieved, that the war is over, when the greatest bombing offensive in history has ended, only to be replaced by the biggest police state in the world, funded ninety percent by American tax dollars. South Vietnam isn't

even a country or a government; it's a war machine and it's still an American responsibility." (*Playboy* interview, April, 1974).

The pair stated that their efforts to expose and oppose the U. S.'s continuing support of the Thieu Regime had continued throughout much of 1973 after the U. S. had withdrawn combat troops. These activities continued to early this year. In the interview Ms. Fonda further stated that she had not perceived that anyone had boycotted her films because of her anti-war stance.

In addition the pair expressed their theories on the cause of other major events which had occurred during the first phase of the war. Recall that the Rev. Dr. Martin Luther King, Jr. had been killed in April, 1968 when the hostilities were at their peak. Opined Ms. Fonda:

> "King was beginning to talk about the relationship between the black movement and the (Vietnam) war. He was starting to make links – between racism in this country and racism as acted out by our white leaders sending blacks to kill yellow people – that hadn't been made before." (*Playboy* interview, April, 1974).

Ms. Fonda theorized that Dr. King had been therefore targeted for assassination because he spoke out so eloquently against the war. Other prominent individuals also embraced this theory.

The Final Adjudication Of War Crimes Committed During The War, 1974

The only member of the Armed Forces who had been convicted of war crimes during the war, former 1st Lt. William Calley, was paroled by the Secretary Of The Army. Previously, after he had been convicted of such crimes in 1971, his original sentence of life in prison at hard labor was reduced to ten years. However, as will be examined later the matter of Calley's war crimes would receive media notoriety long after the war would conclude.

The Author's Situation, 1974

As indicated in Figure 2, Report Of Separation/Form DD214N, the author was Honorably Discharged and released from active duty in the U. S. Navy Reserve from the *Coral Sea* with the rank of Lieutenant (j. g.) (O-2) on 10 August. He was of course happy that he had satisfied the first part of his contractual military obligation with his government. Upon his discharge he made the Bay Area of San Francisco his primary domicile. His domicile was partially funded with a guarantee of six months of unemployment benefits by the government. He was accordingly in a position to observe the last deployment of the *Coral Sea* from the Alameda, CA Naval Air Station on 5 December for deployment to WESTPAC and for duty in Indochina. That vessel would participate in the third and final phase of U. S. participation in the war and in other crises in the region.

CHAPTER FIFTEEN: THE "GOVERNMENT" OF SOUTH VIETNAM CAPITULATES; TIES TO U.S. SEVERED; *LE COMÉDIE VIETNAMIEN C'EST FINI,* 1975

The worst fears were realized. South Vietnam, left to its own devices could not withstand the juggernaut from the North. The only option for the U. S. was to help persons who had aided the allied cause. Token aid was given at the last moment in this regard. The U. S. finally understood the prior warnings and the sentiments of a former President that the war would be an exercise in futility, and that the Indochinese had a right of self-determination. They had earned it.

Domestic Sentiments Concerning Vietnam, 1975

At the beginning of the year Vietnam was quite far off the radar scope of American consciousness. This year would see however the U. S. again be involved in the ongoing hostilities, but for the last time. Of course during this third and final phase of the war, the name would have to change. It was no longer an Indochina War. The name would have to revert to its original name and that by which the war would forever be known: the Vietnam War. The reason for this distinction is because after 1974, by law U. S. aid would be targeted only at South Vietnam. That "country's" neighbors who were in dire need of U. S. help would receive none whatsoever. The law in question specifically prohibited distributing aid of any kind to the nations involved, including that which desperately needed help: Cambodia. This law which prohibited the distribution of aid had gone into effect on 15 August 1973. Accordingly, when emergency aid eventually reached the ally, such monies would only be spent for South Vietnam. The prohibition of U. S. funds at the beginning of this year, and the paucity of aid which eventually did arrive, would be that "nation's" undoing. In a nutshell, all of the U. S. allies in the region would be left to sink or swim on their own. They sank, one into communist-inspired genocide this year. That subject however is beyond the scope of this book.

The Situation In Vietnam, 1975

Refer to the above section entitled *The Level Of Civilian Carnage Quantified, 1973*. In spite of the carnage which had wracked all of Vietnam, the populations of North and South Vietnam had increased markedly since the war began in earnest. The same source which provided the level of carnage above also detailed the estimated respective populations of North and South Vietnam this year as 23.8 million and 19.7 million. (Collier's Year Book, 1976/Covering The Year 1975). These of course should be compared with the population figures when the foreigner intervened in 1965. Recall in the above section entitled *The Political Situation In Vietnam, 1964-65* that the respective populations of the two "countries" at that time were 18 million and 15.5 million.

At the beginning of the year the hostilities were in a lull. However, the world would soon watch the situation develop into what many had long feared. The beginning of the end for the "government" of South Vietnam was detailed in the January 27 issue of *U. S. News & World Report* in an article entitled "Reds' big drive in Vietnam: will America rush to rescue?" (pp. 26 – 27). The article detailed a renewed North Vietnamese push against the rebellious southern provinces. The major battlefield successes by the North prompted President Thieu to request emergency aid from the U. S. President Ford of course wanted to provide aid for the ally. Congress however tied his hands when it invoked the aforementioned law which prohibited funding for any form of direct U. S. combat involvement in Indochina.

The Pentagon's initial perspective was that it doubted that the latest offensive by the North was the beginning of Hanoi's push to control the South. U. S. military observers did however recommend that the requested aid be provided. The Pentagon analysts further believed that the latest offensive from the North was not of great magnitude, and that neither would it lead to the ultimate demise of South Vietnam. The reason for such an assessment was that they believed Hanoi was afraid of U. S. retaliation.

Further, U. S. analysts knew that Hanoi had the capability to deliver a "knockout" punch to Saigon and then overrun the entire South anytime that it wished. They also believed however that Hanoi was moving cautiously in order to control the South by more subtle means until it could further consolidate its military position.

The Renewed Debate Over Additional Funding For The Continuing Conflict, 1975

President Ford of course was cognizant of South Vietnam's deteriorating position in mid-February. The situation there was detailed in the February 17 issue of *U. S. News & World Report* (pp. 37 – 38) in an article entitled "The flow of arms to Saigon – why Congress balks at more." The President asked Congress for an additional 300 million dollars to aid South Vietnam. Congress refused, giving as its reason that too much had already been spent to prop up the Thieu Regime which was notoriously inefficient and wasteful.

Possibly the most influential Member Of Congress offered what might be a summary of Congress' sentiment and also of the national sentiment over the issue of additional aid for South Vietnam. The Senate Majority Leader Mike Mansfield led the fight to restrict any more money from being spent on what was believed to be a futile effort. Moreover, he invoked the reasoning which some senior government leaders had uttered one quarter century earlier, in 1949. At that time some persons had advocated U. S. intervention in China to keep it from being taken over by the communists. Recall that these interventionists also wanted the U. S. to intervene in Vietnam at that time to aid the French effort to retain its Vietnamese colony. Stated Senator Mansfield:

> "People were saying we 'lost' China when we never had it to lose. South Vietnam has never been ours to lose, either."

Presidential Sentiments On The Rapidly Changing Situation In Indochina, 1975

Though President Ford was concerned about South Vietnam, what is remarkable is that he first directed his attention to the rapidly deteriorating situation in Cambodia. Observers believed that this nation was about to be overrun by the communist insurgency there. That insurgency of course was aided and abetted by the North Vietnamese. The situation in Vietnam, adjacent to Cambodia, had not yet reached a crisis mode. In a televised address on March 6, the President spelled out his new policy which became known as the Ford Doctrine. This was hailed as the beginning of a new era in U. S. foreign policy. The President stated that the U. S. would support its friends abroad. The new policy was basically a plea to Congress for emergency military and humanitarian aid to save Cambodia. In his address the President stated:

> "If we abandon our allies, we will be saying to the world that war pays. Aggression will not stop, rather it will increase."

The response from Congress to President Ford's request for emergency aid for Cambodia was: "No!" The vote in the House was 189 – 49. The subsequent vote in the Senate was 38 – 5.

Further on the subject of emergency aid for Indochina in general, the President stated prior to the vote in Congress:

> "This is not a question of involvement or re-involvement in Indochina. We have ended our involvement. All American forces have come home. They will not go back."

The leaders of North Vietnam likely took note of that statement.

Finale For *Le Comédie Vietnamien*, March – April, 1975

The pursuit of a military campaign normally entails much planning and coordination. However, one should consider the following events with the understanding that at this time North Vietnam already had much of the necessary infrastructure in place long before the following events occurred. To reiterate, the war which many thought had ended in January, 1973 never had actually done so. Accordingly, it is safe to conclude that the military offensive which would end the war was in preparation long before the final campaign began. Accordingly, it appears that the final campaign by North Vietnam to annex the rebellious provinces known as South Vietnam was in the planning stages before Richard Nixon left office. Therefore, his departure likely only fueled, rather than caused, the will of North Vietnam to complete the task of unifying Vietnam which had begun in 1945.

North Vietnam's last offensive began in mid-March. Just prior to this effort, the U. S. accused Hanoi of again flagrantly violating the "peace" accords of January, 1973. Specifically, Hanoi was accused of (1) seizing numerous towns in the South, (2) sending another 160,000 troops into the area and also (3) flooding South Vietnam with massive military hardware. Pentagon analysts knew that Hanoi was well supplied with everything that it needed. The U. S. however did nothing. Though Cambodia was receiving most of the attention from the U. S. at this time, an article in the March 24 issue of *U. S. News & World Report* was entitled "Hanoi's No. 1 target: still South Vietnam."

On the other side, South Vietnam had regular military forces estimated at 370,000, which did not include 800,000 paramilitary and support troops. Saigon's forces were woefully short of supplies, however. These forces were reduced to rationing fuel and ammunition.

The end of the Thieu Regime and the final end of U. S. involvement in Indochina would come very soon, and swiftly. The chronology of events which would lead to the unification of Vietnam is as follows:

a. March

In mid-March, virtually simultaneous with the rapidly deteriorating situation in and expected "fall" of Cambodia to the communist faction there, North Vietnam also broke a lull in the hostilities. It launched a major assault against the South. This offensive took the form of a huge number of tanks, troops and artillery which was spread over a large portion of South Vietnam.

Meanwhile in mid-March Congress was still considering President Ford's request for an additional 300 million dollars in emergency aid for the Thieu regime. At the same time that Regime did not appear to be overly concerned with the latest developments. They reportedly opined that the latest offensive by the North was merely an effort to lay the groundwork for a "go-for-broke" offensive which they expected to materialize in 1976.

"South Vietnam is by no means a 'basket case'" was the title of an article published in the March 31 issue of *U. S. News & World Report* (pp. 12 – 14). Pentagon observers and others were therefore still optimistic that South Vietnam could rally its forces to thwart any intensified action by the North. This was also apparently the sentiment of South Vietnam's leaders. The Thieu Regime's policy was simply to trade territory for time. They believed that they could allow the North to swallow large amounts of territory while still consolidating their own strength in the southern areas. Then after they had so strengthened their defenses, they anticipated having the capability to repel any offensive which might materialize.

Possibly the most detailed account of the situation which South Vietnam faced at this time was documented by a high-ranking official of that "government." The aforementioned Bui Diem who had held several responsible positions in South Vietnam since the 1954 truce, was quite eloquent in his detail and assessment of conditions there as the "government" was fast disintegrating. As the Ambassador-At-Large at this time, he was in a position to know. For anyone interested in the excruciating details of conditions there as the enemy was approaching, his book *In The Jaws Of History* demands to be read. Diem specifically pegged March 11 as date of the beginning of the end of the twenty year effort of South Vietnam to be free from domination by the North. On that date he stated that Banmethout, a provincial capital in the Central Highlands, had been overrun by a surprise attack from three North Vietnam divisions. (Diem, p. 4).

Though the aforementioned observer opined that South Vietnam was not a "basket case", the C. I. A. Station Chief for East Asia labeled the President as such. One Ted Shackley conveyed to Bui Diem that President Diem was essentially a "basket case" at this time. He stated that as North Vietnam was daily conquering vast amounts of territory, Thieu was "overwhelmed" and "numbed." (Diem, p. 4).

By late March South Vietnam proved that it was incapable of thwarting any offensive. The forces of Hanoi were rapidly advancing towards Saigon. These latest setbacks for South Vietnam were, some observers stated, "the most crushing defeat suffered by either side in the long history of the war."

What is most noteworthy is that in the midst of the latest surge in fighting, the official journal of the North Vietnamese Communist Party, the *Hoc Tap*, offered its take on its military campaign. That journal stated that Hanoi perceived it had a free reign to do whatever it wanted because they knew that the U. S. was unwilling to provide additional aid to South Vietnam. This fact was also reported in the aforementioned issue of *U. S. News & World Report*.

b. April

"Fortress Saigon – bracing for a last ditch stand" was the title of the article in the April 7 issue of *U. S. News & World Report* (pp. 18 – 21). South Vietnam was accordingly testing its strategy of consolidating its position in anticipation of meeting the enemy on the battlefield via the traditional mode of warfare. The guerilla tactics with which the war had begun were now obsolete. At the end of March half of the "country" had fallen into enemy hands by means of conventional war tactics. The previously expressed optimism of South Vietnam's leaders accordingly began to fade. Much of the erosion of such optimism and therefore the ARVN's morale was of course due to indications that the much needed and anticipated aid from the U. S. would not materialize.

One of the biggest problems South Vietnam faced was the flood of refugees streaming south in ever increasing numbers to escape the onslaught from the North. The "country" simply did not have the infrastructure to address this problem. This was of course due to its incompetent leadership. Such assessment was recognized by the Ambassador-At-Large Diem who opined:

> "...Thieu's Cabinet was made up almost entirely of passive incompetents, many of them corrupt and none of them willing to do more than acquiesce to the President's wishes." (Diem, p. 5).

However, becoming aware of the refugee problem the U. S. did send token emergency assistance in the form of chartered planes to evacuate the refugees.

With the situation rapidly deteriorating, talk began to appear of a coup in South Vietnam by disgruntled military personnel and by senior politicians. Indeed, a number of these politicians were arrested by the Thieu Government, then incarcerated and charged with plotting its overthrow. In the midst of the coup rumors and the general disorganization within the "country", rumors began to circulate that South Vietnam's cause was lost.

All of the above factors started a general panic in the urban areas which knew that they were in the path of the military offensive. Civilians thereupon began to hoard food, which of course caused prices of basic staples to skyrocket by as much as 50%. The general morale accordingly plummeted to new lows.

The consensus in mid-April in South Vietnam and around the world was that the end was soon and inevitable. This perception was reflected in the article "Where U. S. stands after Vietnam debacle", published in the April 14 issue of *U. S. News & World Report* (pp. 27 –

31). President Ford was of course on top of the situation. In a televised address on April 3, he stated:

> "I must say with all the certainly of which I am capable: No adversaries or potential enemies of the U. S. should imagine that America can be safely challenged, and no allies or time-tested friends of the U. S. should worry or fear that our commitments to them will not be honored because of the current confusion and changing situation in Southeast Asia."

President Ford's statement came on the heels of the latest bad news of the war. This was the first indication that the government realized that the war was all but lost. Here again some knowledgeable observers put the situation in historical perspective. They compared the impending "loss" of South Vietnam with the situation which existed twenty-six years previously when China was "lost" to communism. The 151 U. S. military personnel who were still "in country" were simply waiting on the sidelines. They were of course forbidden by law from participating in combat operations. A U. S. official was quoted as saying "This ain't our war no more." The U. S. personnel still there feared that the population would turn against them and that they would be targets of violence.

The aforementioned Col. Harry Summers was one of those ordered to remain. Before his evacuation from the roof of the U. S. Embassy in Saigon on a helicopter, his female civilian secretary had been killed in the crash of one of the craft designated to evacuate other civilians. His departure was on the last Marine helicopter to leave the Embassy at 5:30 A. M. on 30 April. He was reputed to have sincerely regretted leaving the 420 Vietnamese slated for evacuation that day. They were forced to remain. Col. Summers would become a prominent author of books about the Vietnam Experience. Some of these will be detailed below.

Also included in the aforementioned issue of *U. S. News & World Report* was an article entitled "In the end, not even Saigon will hold" (pp. 30 – 31). The article stated that in just three short weeks since the advent of the offensive from the North, the situation deteriorated from worry to apprehension to complete disaster. Everyone there who had been observing the situation, which apparently included anyone over the age of five, understood that it was only a matter of a short time until the forces of Hanoi would prevail.

In the rush to avoid possible death or incarceration by the Hanoi forces, airline ticket offices were jammed with people trying to book passage on any next available plane to depart. The funds for the departures were purchased with the last piaster (the South Vietnamese currency) which had been withdrawn from banks. Every bank in the "country" which was still open was experiencing a run on deposits. Passports which were of course needed to enter foreign countries were reportedly fetching $11,000 (U. S.), under the table.

The U. S. relented somewhat from its previous position not to aid its ally. The government chartered planes to evacuate orphans which the government hoped would be adopted by U. S. families. The first group of these orphans totaled 2,000. The images of those children on U. S. television screens being hurriedly herded onto the planes are additional images which will forever be etched into the nation's consciousness. As indicated below, this mass evacuation would find its way into the popular culture this year shortly after the war would conclude.

Many Vietnamese of course blamed the U. S. for the "country's" impending demise because the U. S. failed to follow through on its promise of aid. However, in interviews some placed most of the blame for the "nation's" woes on their own leaders, some of whom had already departed. Such persons were known to be incompetent.

The April 21 issue of *U. S. News & World Report* commented on the gravity of the situation. In an article entitled "How Hanoi will treat its enemies", one Douglas Pike of the State Department's Policy And Planning Staff, responded to the primary question of what would likely happen to those who had helped the U. S. He responded that a degree of "bloodletting" would certainly occur. He could not however begin to assess such degree. He did opine that there would likely be a modicum of restraint by the North in taking anticipated reprisals against those who it regarded as traitors. Hanoi obviously knew that it had a big job in pacifying the South. The population was quite on edge because many were hungry due to a shortage of food in a land regarded as among the most fertile on the planet.

The aforementioned issue of *U. S. News & World Report* also offered a companion article to that above. The article entitled "Is it too late for U. S. aid to save Vietnam?" described the hostilities which were knocking at the gates of Saigon. Intelligence reports speculated that the North was preparing for its last siege against the capital. The South had deteriorated to a terminal state because of poor leadership, by most assessments. President Thieu was still nominally in charge. However, the ARVN was rapidly disintegrating and abandoning the military hardware which had been provided by the U. S. It was obviously no match for the six advancing infantry divisions, their tanks, artillery and anti-aircraft guns.

The rapidly advancing force was known to be so strong that it had the capability to close Saigon's airport anytime that it wished. This in turn would impede the evacuation of those who desired to leave. The threatened closure of the airport is what caused the U. S. military personnel who eventually arrived to resort to the use of a limited number of helicopters to aid in the evacuations. From the roofs of buildings hastily scrounged, the massive evacuations began in a seemingly unending stream to U. S. aircraft carriers waiting in the South China Sea. This task force included the *Coral Sea* which was ordered on 19 April to respond to the rapidly changing situation. Ten days later she would be a part of the last U. S. military operation of the war, dubbed Operation Frequent Wind. This was the name of the aforementioned evacuation.

Amidst the confusion, rumors of a coup against President Thieu abounded. These rumors were heightened when a South Vietnamese Air Force pilot bombed the Presidential Palace while the President was still there. He escaped injury but numerous others were killed.

Meanwhile, the flood of refugees streaming south to escape the carnage numbered in the hundreds of thousands. This attempt to escape the fighting fueled the refugees' anger. This anger was apparent despite the perception by the enemy force that they were the refugees' liberators.

The title of the article in the April 28 issue of *U. S. News & World Report* posed the question which was on the minds of all: "Saigon's fate: quick kill, slow death – or a deal?" Many wondered if Hanoi would opt for (1) dictating peace terms to the last remaining authority in Saigon, in order to see if its citizens would submit to their new masters, (2) stop at the gates of the capital, encircle it and then starve it into submission by impeding the flow of food and supplies, thereby fomenting disorder and the overthrow of the Thieu Regime, or (3) lay siege to Saigon and take a quick military victory. Option (1) was of course possible and was indeed hoped for because it would save lives and effort.

Hanoi's perspective seemed to be understood by a senior U. S. military official who was still "in-country." He stated: "If I were running the communist show, I'd strike now for the heart of South Vietnam and not take any chances." Hanoi's leaders appeared to be on the same wavelength. In the end they chose (3), above. A possible reason for Hanoi's decision is that the date May 1ˢᵗ is the most important holiday on the communist calendar. One could logically assume that they had a deadline to meet.

1. Final U. S. Efforts To Aid South Vietnam

President Ford was closely monitoring the rapidly deteriorating situation. His immediate reaction to the latest war news was to seek $700,000,000 for the embattled ally. Such aid was of course regarded by Congress as useless in view of the hopelessness of the situation. Most assessments regarded the situation as terminal. Of course military intervention was out of the question because Congress would never agree to such.

However, in the face of the inevitable triumph by Hanoi, Secretary Of State Kissinger ordered the number of U. S. personnel in South Vietnam reduced from 4,000 to fewer than 1,000. Further, the State Department announced a waiver of immigration restrictions in order to allow for 132,000 South Vietnamese and also Cambodians to enter the U. S. As will be revealed later, this proposed resettlement of vast numbers of Indochinese to the U. S. would be the object of humor in the popular culture after the hostilities would cease.

2. Disintegration Of The U. S. - led Military Alliance
a. Exit Thailand

Meanwhile, in related developments while the hostilities were flourishing, it became increasingly apparent that a new order was coming in Indochina. This was detailed in an article entitled "Why U. S. is losing in the world", published in the aforementioned issue of *U. S. News & World Report*. The Government Of Thailand, one of the U. S.'s staunchest allies since the inception of the war, had suddenly decided to distance itself from the U. S. Thailand ordered the withdrawal of all U. S. service personnel within a year. This decision by the Thai Government was apparently in response to the news of the aforementioned battlefield successes by North Vietnam.

b. Exit The Republic Of The Philippines

In another development related to that above, the Government Of The Philippines announced that it was re-evaluating its relations with the U. S. This re-evaluation included whether the two U. S. military bases, Clark Air Field and the Navy Base at Subic Bay, would remain. Recall that this government had been one of the U. S.'s most loyal allies in the war. It had also been an active participant in combat operations since the war began. News reports surfaced that the Philippines' leader, Ferdinand Marcos, apparently made his decision because he recognized that there was a new reality coming in the Indochina political situation. As with his counterpart in Thailand, Marcos had made his decision even before the anticipated triumph of North Vietnam. Both could indeed read the "writing on the wall." Accordingly, the U. S.-led alliance among several nations which had vowed twenty years previously to halt the spread of communism in the region, the Southeast Asia Treaty Organization (S. E. A. T. O.), was as dead as the "government" of South Vietnam.

The Final End Of U. S. Involvement In Indochina, 7 May 1975

The situation in South Vietnam became so hopeless that President Thieu resigned and then left the "country" on 21 April. Many followed, or at least wanted to. The refugee situation had indeed reached crisis proportions. In a desperate attempt to either leave or allow their close relations to depart, it was reported that some wealthy Vietnamese offered U. S. personnel large amounts of money to marry or adopt their children. This would of course ensure their safe evacuation to sanctuary in the U. S. It was further reported that some men were offering their wives.

In the midst of the capitulation of the "government" of South Vietnam and the general disorder, the U. S. was indeed true to its word.

It did not abandon its ally completely. On 23 April the Senate voted to give President Ford limited authority to use military personnel to aid in the aforementioned evacuations. The House Of Representatives concurred the next day. The U. S. then hastily organized a helicopter airlift to first evacuate its last remaining personnel. Then military personnel began to do the same for those Vietnamese who were known to be likely targets of retribution. The U. S. began evacuations at the rate of 5,000 to 10,000 per day by use of the aforementioned helicopters.

All of the above culminated in the final end of U. S. involvement in all of Indochina. Nearly eleven years after the formal decision was made by Congress at the request of President Johnson in the form of the Gulf Of Tonkin Resolution on 5 August 1964, the allies' cause was finally lost. The name of the article in the May 5 issue of *U. S. News & World Report* (pp. 16 – 19) summed up the situation and described the end of the war. It stated "The end in Vietnam: the finish came with a shocking suddenness, Americans in full flight. The long struggle is over, but the scars – here and abroad – are deep and painful."

a. The war's finale and the popular culture are forever entwined
Those who followed the popular culture during the war and also observed the conflict would likely recall what was arguably the most memorable line spoken in a motion picture during the war. Here is another example of how the sentiments of the war were reflected in the popular culture. Long after the war would conclude, it would be revealed that at the time the motion picture *Patton* was in production in 1968, some persons associated with the studio which would eventually release the picture, had opposed its production. Recall that 1968 was the height of the war and also the year in which public sentiments became firmly entrenched against the conflict. The Twentieth Century-Fox motion picture studio executives reportedly opposed the production because they believed that the film was too pro-war. The film was however produced and released to good reviews and it did respectably at the box office. The noted film critic Leonard Maltin's assessment of the film is that it is a "milestone in screen biographies" and "an intelligently written, finely wrought biographical war drama."

In the opening scenes of *Patton*, the late actor George C. Scott in the title role of General Of The Army George S. Patton, Jr., was motivating his troops to defeat the enemies of the United States. These included the Empires Of Germany, Italy and the last which would capitulate, Japan. At that time, in 1942 the U. S. was preparing to unleash the fullest fury of its already considerable and rapidly growing military might against its enemies. One by one these all would eventually capitulate in the path of the formidable U. S. war machine. That conflict of course culminated in the use of a nuclear weapon. The following line which General Patton was alleged to have spoken would return to haunt the leader of the Free World. Stated Mr. Scott in the role of General Patton (paraphrased):

> "This nation of course will win this war, because America has never lost and will never lose a war, because the very <u>thought</u> of losing is *hateful* to Americans."

b. The media's take on the grim finale to the conflict
In light of the above movie line, the following statement in the aforementioned article in *U. S. News & World Report* therefore caused much grief in the U. S.: "America's first defeat in war." This news was all the more profound considering that only thirty-two months prior, the majority of the public appeared to believe that the war was winnable. Further, the bulk of the electorate seemed to continue to support Nixon's handling of the war at that time. This is apparent from the information which Nixon imparted in his memoirs. He stated therein that (detailing the figures from a recent poll):

> "A Harris poll found in early September (1972) that 55 percent supported continued heavy bombing of North Vietnam ... and 74 percent thought it was important that South Vietnam not fall into the hands of the Communists." (*RN*, p. 689).

The images broadcast worldwide accordingly spoke volumes. They are therefore firmly etched into the national lexicon and consciousness. These images included America's finest, "The First To Fight", U. S. Marines in a frantic frenzy to escape onto helicopters from the roof of the U. S. Embassy in Saigon. They were fleeing from a military which was, before this war, regarded as quite inferior to that of the U. S., by anybody's standard. The North Vietnamese Army and its allies in the southern part of the now-unified country had no nuclear weapons. Further, it was never reported during the course of the entire war that the North fielded any jet aircraft south of the Demilitarized Zone (DMZ). Its primary opponent was of course the nation which has the most formidable Air Force the world has ever seen.

Again the aforementioned article clearly summed up the situation, thusly:

> "A clear lesson. Forces of the U. S., strongest and richest nation on earth, has been driven away by an impoverished country that in its 30 years of existence has barely moved into the industrialized twentieth century in anything but military capability."

The article further detailed the total estimated U. S. losses: 57,000 lives and $150,000,000,000. The article further placed the total number of persons who had escaped the North Vietnamese offensive just before the war was lost, at 100,000. These persons who were labeled "high risk" because of their past association with the allies, had left both with and without U. S. help. The "liberators" labeled them "social negatives." It was estimated that tens of thousands of such persons were left behind to face certain murder, deprivation or at least capture, to be incarcerated in "re-education camps."

The New York Times headline on the April 30 edition also explained the profound impact of the events unfolding in Vietnam. Writing of the latest President, one Duong Van Minh, it stated: "Minh surrenders, Viet Cong in Saigon; 1,000 Americans and 5,500 Vietnamese evacuated by helicopter to U. S. Carriers." The photograph coupling the headline depicted a helicopter crew leading a large group of persons awaiting evacuation to U. S. ships from the roof of a building. Sub-heading the headline was the caption "Ford Unity Plea: President says that departure 'closes a chapter' for U. S.'" It should be noted that President Minh was one of the leaders of the coup which had occurred some twelve years earlier, in which the President Of South Vietnam was assassinated.

Eighty-one helicopters were initially assigned to the evacuation mission. The 1,000 combat U. S. Marines sent to protect and aid in the evacuation received air cover from U. S. Navy and Air Force F-4 fighter-bombers, some of which had flown from aircraft carriers. The helicopter evacuation took more than nineteen hours – far longer than the four hours which the Pentagon had originally estimated. The destination of the helicopters was primarily to the *U. S. S. Blue Ridge* (L.C.C. – 19). That vessel was designated the command and communications vessel of the task force of the U. S. Seventh Fleet, which totaled forty ships. Four Marines were lost during the evacuation. Two of these were presumed dead after their helicopter crashed into the South China Sea. Two others were killed in a rocket attack at Saigon's Tan Son Nhut Airport while they were standing guard. These last two deaths were what initially prompted President Ford to order the evacuations. The U. S. Ambassador To South Vietnam, Graham Martin and his closest aides were on the last helicopter to leave the U. S. Embassy.

In the midst of the evacuations, U. S. Secretary Of Defense James Schlesinger stated:

"Americans will recall that their Armed Forces served them well. Under circumstances more difficult than ever before faced by our military services, you accomplished the mission assigned to you by higher authority. In combat you were victorious and you left the field with honor."

Sub-heading two of the above headline was "Defense ends: general tells his troops to turn in their weapons." President Minh announced the unconditional surrender of his "government" and his troops to the Provisional Revolutionary Government Of South Vietnam. President Minh declined to mention North Vietnam in his address to his troops. President Ford had no comment on the decision to surrender.

Sub-heading three of the April 30 edition of *The New York Times* stated: "74 Saigon planes fly 2,000 to Thailand." As the "government" of South Vietnam was capitulating and its newest President was ordering all military personnel to surrender, some units willfully disobeyed that order. The seventy-four planes in question flew to a military base in Thailand. Recall that the Government Of Thailand had already disassociated itself from the war and from the United States. The planes landed without permission. They were not however challenged by that government's military when they entered Thailand's air space. All of the personnel on the planes requested asylum. This request was flatly denied.

The planes in which the aforementioned passengers had flown included 30 F5 jet fighters. The rest were C–47 transports and C–130 cargo planes supplied by the U. S. American officials there were asked to turn over the aircraft to the Government Of Thailand but this request was ignored. However, that government ordered all of the personnel on the planes to leave that country. The ultimate disposition of the aircraft in question was uncertain.

Meanwhile, there were many South Vietnamese still stranded. Another image which is seared into the minds of all who were paying attention is the hoards of Vietnamese trying to scale the fence of the U. S. Embassy compound in Saigon in order to secure some means of leaving. These were met with the rifle butts of Marine guards who were ordered to repel them. Still, some did manage to scale the fence by climbing on top of others.

Meanwhile, at least one important U. S. official remained as the forces of the North were laying siege to Saigon. The U. S. Counsel at a city near Saigon tried to leave per the orders of Secretary Of State Kissinger. However, his party was fired upon by South Vietnamese military units. U. S. officials thereupon ordered Navy fighter planes to give the Counsel air cover in order to allow him and his party to escape.

Seven days after the triumph of North Vietnam and its allies, the conflict finally came to a screeching halt. The date 7 May 1975 is now officially promulgated as the date that the Vietnam/Indochina Conflict ended.

Such an end could have been predicted. Indeed, some had predicted that the above scenario would occur. Indicators of such had materialized in November, 1972 when the aforementioned negotiations to end the war were taking place. Immediately after the reelection of Richard Nixon, as he has provided in his memoirs on the details of such negotiations, the fate of the national mission had already been determined. Perhaps the major point of contention to which President Thieu objected was the continued presence of North Vietnamese troops. Over Thieu's strong objections, Nixon decided to allow these troops to remain. Stated Nixon concerning the message which his emissary delivered to Thieu:

> "I also urged Haig to remind Thieu that although I had won the White House by a landslide, he must remember that the Senate was now even more dovish than it had been before the election. There was no question that if we did not have a settlement completed before Congress returned in January (1973) … the Senate would cut off the funds that South Vietnam needed to survive." (*RN*, p. 718).

It therefore appears that the aforementioned agreement which supposedly ended the war and which allowed North Vietnam to keep its troops in the South after January, 1973 was indicative of a disaster waiting to happen.

The cover of the May 12 issue of *Time* Magazine also spoke volumes on the gravity of the situation. Against a blood-red silhouette of the now unified nation of Vietnam was the effigy of the father of his *country*, Ho Chi Minh. The capital Saigon had been renamed Ho Chi Minh City. The words on the cover said it all: The Victor.

c. North Vietnamese prophecies realized/Presidential sentiments neutralized

Accordingly, the words which had been broadcast by North Vietnam to the opponents of the war in the U. S. on 14 October 1969 had by now fulfilled a prophecy. Recall that previously, 15 October 1969 had been designated as Moratorium Day in the U. S. The leaders of the U. S. antiwar activists had designated this day to demonstrate for the hostilities to cease. That planned moratorium is the apparent reason why the leader of North Vietnam at that time, Premier Pham Van Dong, broadcast on 14 October from Radio Hanoi a message to the war's opponents in the U. S. Stated the Premier (paraphrased):

> "This fall large sectors of the U. S. people, encouraged and supported by many peace and justice-loving personages, are launching a … powerful offensive

throughout the U. S. to demand that ... Nixon ... put an end to the Vietnam aggressive war. We are firmly confident that ... the struggle of the Vietnamese people and U. S. progressive people against U. S. aggression will certainly be crowned with total victory."

Those were prophetic words indeed. Further, this complete military victory by North Vietnam and its allies completely neutralized the assertion by former President Nixon that North Vietnam had abandoned its quest for national unification in 1972. Nixon stated in his memoirs concerning the events just prior to the withdrawal of U. S. forces in 1973 that (speaking of the negotiations by National Security Advisor Kissinger):

"...they (the North Vietnamese leaders) dropped their demand that Thieu resign. These provisions alone amounted to a complete capitulation by the enemy: they were accepting a settlement on our terms." (*RN*, p. 692).

War's Summation/Presidential sentiments realized

Accordingly, for thirty years since the Japanese had been ejected, through the French attempt to re-colonize all of Indochina, through the truce of 1954 after the indigenous forces prevailed decisively against their former master, through the efforts of alien governments to help a portion of Vietnam to remain "free", through the efforts of those alien governments to assume the fight for a "country" which had only token desire to fight for itself, through an armistice which was never viable and indeed never took root, and lastly through force of arms, on 30 April 1975 a majority of Vietnamese finally achieved what, precisely thirty years previously to the month, a President Of The United States had deemed them entitled.

That therefore, *is* a "popular" war that won't go away.

The Popular Culture, 1975

Only one recording was released during this final year of the war which recalled the war or related events. The very month that the war concluded, on 26 May the late comedian Richard Pryor recorded "live" in concert *Is It Something I Said?* This recording revealed Mr. Pryor in top form, doing that for which he will forever be remembered: demonstrating his mastery of making light of cultural or societal events. Recall that the U. S. was instrumental in the evacuation of Vietnamese orphans and others who faced certain deprivation and possible death if left to live in a war-ravaged Vietnam this year.

In April in a televised plea to the public to adopt the orphans, a well-known actress was quite emotional in her tearful request to U. S. families to adopt and to help resettle the children. In making light of this actress's televised plea in his recording, Mr. Pryor opined in the track on the album entitled *New N------* (paraphrased):

> "Oh, my goodness! The little orphans!
> We've got to do something!
> B---- (woman) almost had me going to get an orphan!"

Further on the subject of the orphans, Mr. Pryor also injects levity into the likely fate of those orphans who would be settled in certain sections of the United States.

In another segment of the recording, Mr. Pryor further ruminated on the prospects of a flood of adult Indochinese refugees who were being resettled in the U. S. These would of course need to assume a means of livelihood. It bears mention that the U. S. was in the throes of a severe recession which began at the approximate time that the author was released from active duty in the military. Opined the comedian concerning the U. S. Government's efforts on behalf of these people:

> "Bring 'em over, bring <u>all</u> of 'em over!
> N------ (black Americans) won't mind!
> They didn't ask us s---! (solid excrement)
> We're the m----- f------ (people) that
> will have to give the jobs up for them!"

Is It Something I Said was released on the major label Reprise/Warner Brothers on 25 July and it peaked at #12 on the national album charts this year. The recording accordingly holds the distinction of being one of the most popular comedy albums ever released, and certainly one of the top five. Further, it was awarded the National Academy Of Recording Arts & Sciences ("Grammy") award for Best Comedy Album this year. The recording also holds the distinction of being the final U. S. recorded reference to the Vietnam/Indochina Conflict.

It bears mention that Mr. Pryor was a veteran of the U. S. Army, having served therein at the time that the U. S. began to send "advisors" to South Vietnam. He would die in 2006.

Epilogue

The Vietnam/Indochina War of course had a most profound impact on the lives of the persons involved. These could of course be found at all levels of U. S. and Vietnamese society. Further, the repercussions of that conflict continue to reverberate through U. S. society and upon the lives of the war's participants, as of this writing. Following is an account of either the fate of these persons after the war ended, or of the transformation which the lives of some of the major and minor characters therein underwent because of their appearance in the cast of "*Le Comédie Vietnamien.*"

Spiro Agnew

The individual who was President Nixon's "Hatchet Man" on the war, who would level a vicious attack on anyone or any organization which criticized the Administration's war policies, savored his electoral victory with the President in 1972. While on the campaign trail he continuously asserted his belief in the value of hard work, discipline, patriotism and morality. He then announced his intention to seek the highest elected office when Nixon was scheduled to leave that post in January, 1977. However, Agnew resigned the Office of Vice President on 10 October 1973.

Agnew's resignation was the culmination of an investigation of his tenure as an elected official in Maryland before he assumed the Office Of Vice President. This investigation by the U. S. Attorney For The District Of Maryland uncovered the allegation that while he was a state official in Maryland he had been soliciting and accepting bribes.

Subsequently Agnew pleaded *nolo contendere* (no contest) to income tax evasion. He had failed to report $29, 500 in income which he received in 1967 while he was Governor, on which he was supposed to have paid $13, 500 in Federal taxes. The income upon which the taxes were supposed to have been paid was from firms which sought public works projects with the state. Further, it was revealed that Agnew had continued to receive the monies in question after he had assumed the Office Of Vice President on January 20, 1969.

Judge Walter E. Hoffman, U. S. District Judge For The District Of Maryland, sentenced Agnew to a $10, 000 fine. Agnew was also placed on three years' probation. Other criminal charges against him concerning alleged solicitation of bribes in return for the awarding of public works contracts while he was County Executive Of Baltimore County, MD from 1962 – 66 and after he was elected Governor in 1966, were dropped.

Agnew never returned to politics. However, he was subsequently interviewed in the airport in Riyadh, Saudi Arabia. He was employed as a lobbyist for a firm which did business with the House Of Saud, the Royal Family of Saudi Arabia. Except for the television crew which interviewed him, he passed virtually unnoticed. He died in 1996.

Muhammad Ali

The man who became the most visible symbol of national opposition to the war from 1966 to 1971 went on to even greater heights in his usual occupation, both during the war and after the conflict ended. On 30 September 1974 in Kinshasa, Zaire in the famous "Rumble In The Jungle", he regained the Heavyweight Boxing Title from then-champion George Forman. He had been regarded as the underdog.

In a well-publicized 1975 photograph, Mr. Ali was shown with President Gerald Ford in the Oval Office of the White House. He then appeared onstage at the 1976 Academy Of Motion Picture Arts & Sciences awards ceremony with a cinematic icon. On 15 September 1978 he became the only pugilist in history to regain the Heavyweight Boxing Title for the third time when he prevailed against then-champion Leon Spinks. That pugilist had taken the title from him precisely six months previously. Mr. Ali of course went on to have mixed success in his usual occupation until he retired from the ring. After his last retirement he became a goodwill ambassador, of sorts, spreading the message of his adopted faith, Islam.

In the 1980s Mr. Ali retired from the ring. In November, 2005 he was awarded the Presidential Medal Of Freedom by the President Of The U. S., George W. Bush. This Medal is the United States' highest civilian award. It is presented for meritorious achievement in public service, in science, the arts, education, athletics, business and in other fields of endeavor. In his remarks concerning Mr. Ali, the President stated that he has "a beautiful soul. He was a fierce fighter and a man of peace. Across the world, billions of people know Muhammad Ali as a brave, compassionate and charming man, and the American people are proud to call Muhammad Ali one of our own." The rancor over his stated disinterest in the war in 1966 had subsided.

Suffering from the effects of Parkinson's Disease, Mr. Ali lives in seclusion with his family at his farm in Michigan.

The Film *American Graffiti*

The film which is arguably the most profound cinematic representation of the transformation which U. S. society underwent because of the war, went on to gain a cult following. Upon its successful release it was praised by critics and it did well at the box office. The film which made Americans conscious of the domestic changes which had taken place during and largely because of the war, was ultimately recognized for its cultural merit. The film was one of those first selected in 1995 for inclusion in The National Film Registry. The honor which is announced annually by the Librarian Of Congress and is sponsored by both the Librarian and the National Film Preservation Board, is limited to U. S. films that are at least ten years old and also deemed culturally, historically or aesthetically significant. The film remains a cultural icon of the Vietnam War era.

Dwight Armstrong

The individual who drove the getaway vehicle for the four-person team which bombed an Army research laboratory at the University Of Wisconsin to protest the war in 1970 was the last to be caught. He was found living in Toronto, Canada, in April, 1977. Having pleaded no contest to second degree murder and to conspiracy, he was sentenced to concurrent terms of seven years on both charges. Having served part of his Federal sentence, he was paroled in 1980. He was however arrested again in Indiana in 1987 for his participation in operating a methamphetamine lab there. For this crime he was sentenced to ten years. He was released in 1991 when he returned to his hometown of Madison, WI. He then drove a cab and cared for his mother. Armstrong died in Madison on 20 June 2010, aged 58. (*New York Times* obituary, June 26, 2010).

Karleton Armstrong

The individual who lit the fuse of the bomb which damaged an Army research laboratory at the University Of Wisconsin to protest the war in 1970 served part of his Federal sentence of twenty-three years. He was paroled in 1980 when he returned to his hometown of Madison. His usual occupation as of this writing is taxi driver. Part time he is the owner and manager of a juice cart near the University Of Wisconsin.

The Rev. Daniel Berrigan

One of The Catonsville Nine who defied the government's war policies by destroying Selective Service records, Rev. Berrigan went underground after his sentencing. He was subsequently captured by the F. B. I. and then served his sentence in a Federal prison.

Rev. Berrigan was further investigated after having served his sentence for the aforementioned crime. He then became a member of The Harrisburg (PA) Seven when the F. B. I. accused him and several others of, among other things, plotting to kidnap presidential advisor Henry Kissinger. This and other charges against him and the others were dropped, except for the crime of smuggling letters out of prison. Rev. Berrigan was paroled in 1972, one month prior to the end of the first phase of the war.

After his release from prison, Rev. Berrigan continued to work for causes in which he believed, including an end to the nuclear arms race. In 2000 Rev. Berrigan was sentenced to thirty months in prison for having vandalized planes at an Air National Guard base in Maryland.

Rev. Berrigan died of cancer on 6 December 2002.

The Rev. Philip Berrigan

Another of the Catonsville Nine who, along with his older brother, defied the government's war policies by destroying Selective Service records, likewise went underground with his brother after having been sentenced to three years in prison. He was subsequently captured in 1970 and then he served eighteen months of a reduced sentence in a Federal prison.

Rev. Berrigan then became a prolific writer of plays and especially poetry. However, he continued to work for causes in which he believed, especially in the area of nuclear arms. In 1980 he was again arrested with several others for protesting the manufacture of nuclear weapons. He was further convicted of damaging nuclear warheads which were under construction at a General Electric plant. He was sentenced to from three to ten years for this infraction, but he appealed. In 1991 the original sentence was reduced to time served.

Rev. Berrigan continues to participate in causes which he believes further the Gospel.

Julian Bond

The individual who was one of the first African-American civil rights leaders to speak out against the war went on to achieve much notoriety during and after the conflict, though not in the anti-war movement. Mr. Bond served his Atlanta district in the Georgia House from 1965 to 1975. He then went on to serve in the Georgia Senate from 1975 to 1986. During the 1968 Presidential campaign he became the first African-American by a major party to be nominated for the Office Of Vice President. He was compelled to decline this honor however, in that he was, at 28, too young.

After serving in the Georgia Legislature, Mr. Bond ran for a Congressional seat from Georgia in 1976. He lost that hotly contested race, albeit to a more popular Democrat. He did however go on to teach at several major universities including American, Drexel, Harvard and the University Of Virginia.

As a result of all of the above undertakings, Mr. Bond went on to become an elder statesman in the arenas of civil and human rights. As of this writing he is Chairman of the National Board Of Directors of the National Association For The Advancement Of Colored People (N. A. A. C. P.).

Marlon Brando

The actor who had starred in *The Ugly American*, the first motion picture which caused the public to question U. S. involvement in Indochina, did not subsequently make any other films which addressed such involvement. He did however continue to make motion pictures, with mixed success, including a second win as Best Actor from the Academy Of Motion Picture Arts And Sciences for the film *The Godfather*, in 1972. Further, it has never been reported that he was as outspoken a critic of U. S. intervention in Vietnam as was his contemporary and co-star in another film of the Vietnam era, Jane Fonda.

Mr. Brando did however offer his take on one of the most profound events of the war, an event possibly related to the conflict. This was the assassination of the Rev. Dr. Martin Luther King, Jr. on 4 April 1968. In a *Playboy* Magazine interview in January, 1979 Mr. Brando (speaking of political assassination in general and those prominent citizens who he believed were targeted for death) stated:

> "... they (government authorities) ... don't care what you say ... as long as you don't *do* anything. If you start to do something and your shuffling raises too much dust, they will disestablish you. That's what happened to Martin Luther King. (F.B.I. Director) J. Edgar Hoover ... hated Martin Luther King. If he (King) stayed in the civil rights area, fine ... but when he got on the issue of the Vietnam War ... that was too heavy."

Mr. Brando died in 2004.

McGeorge Bundy

The individual who was Presidents Kennedy and Johnson's national security advisor was arguably the government's fourth most ardent advocate of the war. Those in front of him were of course the President, Secretary Of Defense Robert McNamara and then Secretary Of State Dean Rusk. He deserves the appellation given to him by Halberstam, "the best and the brightest." As of this writing he still enjoys, even posthumously, a well-deserved reputation as an anti-communist ideologue.

In resurrecting the details of the war in 2008, another principal player during the conflict, Dr. Henry Kissinger detailed Bundy's flawed brilliance as he advocated continued U. S. involvement in Indochina. In his review of a book about Bundy, *Lessons In Disaster: McGeorge Bundy And The Path To War In Vietnam*, discussed below, Dr. Kissinger labeled Bundy a "co-manager" of the war, to a certain degree. The book was begun by Bundy with a research associate. The manuscript was never finished. *Lessons In Disaster* represents a culmination of the research which was begun by both and then completed by the researcher, one Gordon M. Goldstein. For anyone who desires to be enlightened concerning the complexities of the conflict, the work deserves to be read.

Bundy left government service in early 1966, shortly after the war began in earnest. A likely reason for his departure was his differences with the Commander-In-Chief, Lyndon Johnson. Bundy did however remain a "player" during much of the rest of the conflict, providing advice to Johnson until his departure in January, 1969.

It has been revealed that Bundy was a primary proponent, if not the initial proponent of the policy of "Vietnamization" which was eventually adopted in 1968 by Johnson and by Johnson's successor. In spite of this, Bundy was forever dogged by his association with the Johnson Administration and his reputation of having been an architect of the government's flawed policy on Vietnam.

After leaving government, Mr. Bundy headed the Ford Foundation until 1979. He then taught at New York University for ten tears. He died in his native Massachusetts in 1996.

George Walker Bush

The son of a U. S. Congressman during the war and also the son of a future President, never served on active duty in the Armed Forces. He was however a member of the Texas Air National Guard during much of the conflict, flying F-102 aircraft from 1968 – 73.

After having run unsuccessfully for a Congressional seat in Texas, he became an oil company executive. In 1989 he purchased the Texas Rangers baseball team. In 1994 he was elected Governor of Texas, defeating the incumbent Democrat. In 2000, running against one who had voluntarily joined the Army and who had served in Vietnam, he won election in the electoral college, though not in the popular vote, as the forty-third President Of The U. S. He was succeeded by one who was born the year that the U. S. first significantly augmented the ranks of its "advisors" in Vietnam. The winner of the 2008 Presidential race defeated one who served "in country" and who was "killed" there.

William Calley

The only person convicted of war crimes in the Indochina Theater went into the insurance business after having returned to his native Georgia. During the war he would receive the harshest criticism from one who emerged as the foremost authority on U. S. involvement in Vietnam, Col. Harry Summers.

In further testimony to the lingering repercussions of the war, in 2009 the ugly incident of civilians being murdered by U. S. forces would be resurrected. In a press release published in domestic periodicals on 22 August entitled "Calley apologizes for My Lai", the public was further made aware of the brutal aspects of the war. The article concerned a news conference held in Columbus, GA before the Kiwanis Club Of Greater Columbus. At the news conference Calley apologized for his acts in 1968. He stated that he daily feels remorse for having murdered innocent civilians. These were Calley's first public utterances on the matter since his dishonorable discharge from the Army in 1971. He did not deny what had happened at My Lai at the height of the war. However, as he stated at his General Court-martial, he continued to insist that his acts had been directed by those senior to him.

Stokely Carmichael

The civil rights activist and "Black Power" advocate who advised blacks not to participate in a "white man's war", was true to his word that "Hell no, *I* won't go!" He never served in the Armed Forces. He may possibly have been rejected for military service because of his prior arrests for defying laws permitting segregation. During the war he traveled around the country and also to foreign countries including North Vietnam in 1967 to show the solidarity of some American blacks with the causes of other people of color.

In 1969 he moved to Guinea, West Africa where he died of cancer in 1998, an ex patriate, having changed his name to Kwame Toure.

Richard Cheney

The individual who received a series of deferments exempting him from military service during the war, never served in the military. Cheney instead became active in politics. From 1970 to 1971 he held a series of key administrative posts in the Nixon White House. After Nixon's resignation in 1974 he joined the White House team and became a Deputy Assistant to President Gerald Ford from 1974 to 1975, and then again as Assistant to the President from 1975 to 1977 when Ford left office.

In 1978 Cheney was elected to a seat in the U. S. House Of Representatives, representing a district in Wyoming. He served six terms there.

In 1989 Cheney was selected as President George Herbert Walker Bush's Secretary Of Defense, serving until 1994 under Bush and Bush's successor, William Jefferson Clinton.

In 2000 after having served as President and Chief Executive Officer of the industrial giant Halliburton, he ran successfully for the Office Of Vice President with George Walker Bush as his running mate. In 2004 he was reelected. Cheney's activities during the Vietnam War again became an issue when he ran for reelection. In an article in *The New York Times* dated 1 May 2004, reporter Katharine Q. Seelye resurrected information about his non-participation in the war. She noted that after he had registered for the draft in 1959, he requested and was granted five deferments from military service until January, 1967 when he became too old.

In a break with U. S. political tradition he declined to run for President in 2008.

Eldridge Cleaver

The individual who ran for President on the Peace And Freedom Party ticket in 1968 which entailed vocal criticism of the war, had a most volatile life before and after that election. In 1968 after publishing his popular and controversial memoirs, *Soul On Ice*, he was involved in a gun battle with the police of Oakland, CA. Shortly thereafter he fled the U. S. and lived in a variety of places including Cuba and Algeria. After seven years abroad, in 1975 he returned to the U. S. and more legal battles. Eventually he renounced violent revolution and radical philosophy and became an arch conservative, even seeking endorsement from the Republican Party. He was also reputed to have embraced the Mormon faith.

After embracing and espousing a variety of causes and philosophies, including promoting a line of clothing, he died on 1 May 1998, aged 62, from a heart attack.

William Jefferson Clinton

The individual who had requested a deferment to pursue studies as a Rhodes Scholar at Oxford University in England during the war, and also participated in anti-war protests there, had a colorful and successful career in government. His apparent disdain for military service and his attendant protests against the war did not seem to have harmed his political persona in the eyes of the electorate. After completing his studies in England he returned home and earned a law degree from Yale University in 1973. He then joined the faculty of The University Of Arkansas School Of Law. He had an appetite for bigger things however, both within government and outside of that realm.

Mr. Clinton's first successful bid for public office came in 1978 when he was elected the youngest governor in the U. S. in forty years. While his first bid for reelection was unsuccessful, he was subsequently returned to the same office in 1982. This earned him the appellation used to describe him for the rest of his political career: The Comeback Kid.

In 1992 Mr. Clinton successfully challenged the incumbent President George Herbert Walker Bush, winning a plurality. He went on to have a generally successful Presidency until he left office in 2001. As detailed below, he seized the opportunity to voice his last sentiments on one aspect of the war, in the case of *Mister* Preston King.

In 2004 Mr. Clinton published his memoirs, *My Life*, which set a one-day sales record for a non-fiction book. The work was generally well received, earning the Biography Of The Year Award at the British Book Awards ceremony in London.

Mr. Clinton then went on to work for disaster relief. For this he received the 2006 Liberty Medal from the National Constitution Center Of Philadelphia.

During the 2008 Presidential race Mr. Clinton labored unsuccessfully for the election of his wife for the office of President. As of this writing he maintains a high visibility in national and international affairs.

Lawrence Colburn and Hugh Thompson

In 1998 almost thirty years to the day after the aforementioned My Lai Massacre in Vietnam, the two individuals who stopped the bloodshed were appropriately honored as heroes. Helicopter pilot Thompson and Door Gunner Colburn, upon recognizing that a war crime was occurring, landed their craft between the U. S. troops who were committing the crime, or not intervening to prevent it as required by the Uniform Code Of Military Justice. Recall that these two individuals halted the bloodshed by threatening to fire upon Lt. William Calley and his company if they did not cease firing upon innocent, unarmed civilians.

The official Army statement at the award ceremony said that Mr. Thompson was being honored "for heroism above and beyond the call of duty while saving the lives of at least ten Vietnamese civilians during the unlawful massacre of non-combatants by American forces at My Lai." Both Mr. Thompson and Mr. Colburn were awarded the Soldier's Medal, which is the highest award the Army can bestow for bravery not involving direct contact with an enemy. The pair received their medals in the shadow of the Vietnam Veterans Memorial in Washington. The individual who emerged as the foremost authority on U. S. involvement in Vietnam, Col. Harry Summers, would praise the actions of this pair.

Coral Sea

The floating fortress on which the author had served in the waning days of the war indeed did its duty during the final days of the conflict, and beyond. As stated previously, the ship was one of a task force sent in mid-April, 1975 to aid in the evacuation of those who had helped the allied cause. The ship received on her flat decks the refugees from helicopters which had flown from the roofs of buildings in Saigon. *Coral Sea* then aided in the transport of these refugees to Clark Air Base in the Philippines. From this duty she returned to her Far East operational port of Subic Bay, R. P.

Immediately after the war ended, a major operation in which *Coral Sea* participated was the rescue of the U. S. merchant ship *Mayaguez* in May, 1975. That ship had been seized by pirates in international waters off the Cambodian coast on 12 May. The Mayaguez was rescued, but not without U. S. forces sustaining numerous casualties. For this effort *Coral Sea* was awarded the Meritorious Unit Commendation on 6 July 1976.

From the last combat mission in Indochina, *Coral Sea* steamed to her home port at the Alameda Naval Air Station, CA in July, 1975. This was after she had been designated CV-43 on 30 June. She was no longer a vehicle used for attack. She was however useful to further national interests.

In February, 1980 *Coral Sea* was part of a task force sent to the Arabian Sea to help alleviate the Iran hostage crisis which began in November, 1979.

In October, 1980 *Coral Sea* was ordered to the Mediterranean to become part of the U. S. Sixth Fleet. This was her first duty in this area since 1957. On 24 March 1986 while still assigned to the Sixth Fleet, she was attacked by the military forces of Libya. She responded by launching planes in order to protect U. S. ships in the task force from Libyan aircraft. On 15 April 1986 she was part of Operation El Dorado Canyon in which she launched aircraft for strikes against the Libyan shore installations which had been harassing U. S. ships. No planes were lost in the Operation.

On 26 April 1990 *Coral Sea* was decommissioned and then stricken from the Naval Vessel Register. She was then sold to Seawitch Salvage of Baltimore, MD in 1993 for scrapping.

Walter Cronkite

The individual who originated the term "Credibility Gap" and was at the forefront of the broadcast media effort to inform the public of the gap between what the government was telling the public, as opposed to what was actually occurring in Vietnam, emerged from the war unscathed. His many detractors were unsuccessful in destroying his credibility. Indeed, after the war he emerged a bigger man than he was prior to his questioning U. S. involvement in Vietnam in 1968.

In 1971 he was honored by the International Radio And Television Society as the Broadcaster Of The Year. He went on to reign as the Dean of U. S. broadcast journalists for the duration of his career. While still at the top of his game, he worked to promote peace in the Middle East. Mr. Cronkite retired in 1981. He died in 2009.

Rennie Davis

One of the Chicago Seven which had been prosecuted for crossing state lines to protest the war, left the counterculture in 1972. He eventually was reputed to have had a religious conversion. He then moved to India to become a follower of Eastern religions.

The Domino Theory

One cornerstone of U. S. justification for intervening in Vietnam was that a stand had to be made there. Either the U. S. would stand and fight in Vietnam, government leaders reasoned, or eventually all of the other countries in the region would fall to communism. However, even before the hostilities ceased in 1975, this Theory would be marked for oblivion. The November 4, 1974 issue of *U. S. News & World Report* stated the consensus of most of the nations in Indochina or in close proximity thereto, that is, Indonesia, Malaysia, the Philippines, Singapore and Thailand. The consensus was that the Theory was of diminishing relevance. Indeed, as of this writing all of the listed nations show no signs of being subverted by communism. They are all in close proximity to The Socialist Republic Of Vietnam. Further, the conventional wisdom after the collapse of The Soviet Union in 1989, which ended the Cold War, was uttered by Gottlieb, author of *Hell No, We Won't Go!* She stated therein that "In spite of these dire predictions (of every nation in danger of falling to communism like the proverbial stack of dominoes if U. S. efforts fail in Vietnam), as I write these words in 1990, Communism is dead nearly everywhere."

Daniel Ellsberg

The Pentagon analyst who first worked on The Pentagon Papers and then released them to the public, thereby incurring the government's wrath, continued to work for change after the war. He stayed active in the anti-war movement after he was exonerated in 1973 for allegedly having leaked The Papers.

In 2002 Dr. Ellsberg published his memoirs, *Secrets: A Memoir Of Vietnam And The Pentagon Papers*. On 1 Oct 2010 he appeared on the PBS television broadcast *Need To Know*, discussing in retrospect his involvement with promulgating The Papers. On the program he was steadfast in his insistence that he had a duty to bring the truth to the public concerning the deception which the government had perpetrated concerning U. S. involvement in Indochina. The broadcast of *Need To Know* was virtually simultaneous with the broadcast of the film *Daniel Ellsberg: The Most Dangerous Man In America*, which was released in theaters and in a DVD format in 2010. The film provides the utmost penetrating look at the controversy surrounding the war when public sentiment had become firmly entrenched against it. The film further revealed that the odious appellation had been bestowed upon him by National Security Advisor Henry Kissinger. Dr. Ellsberg continues to labor for causes which he deems worthwhile.

David Fine

The individual who was part of the four-person team which bombed a building at the University Of Wisconsin to protest the war in 1970 paid for his crime. He eluded capture until 1976 when he was apprehended in California. As did two of his cohorts he likewise pleaded guilty to the multiple charges he faced. He was sentenced to seven years in a Federal prison. In 1979 he was paroled.

Henry Fonda

The "American Royal" who was one of the "Silent Majority" to whom Richard Nixon appealed, remains a cultural icon. The name of the actor who portrayed the President in the 1964 film *Fail Safe* is firmly etched in the pantheon of Great Americans. The Silent Majority was that which seldom if ever spoke out against the war, but apparently trusted government leaders to do what was in the nation's best interests. It was never documented that Mr. Fonda ever spoke out against the war or opposed it in any manner.

Mr. Fonda went on to practice his craft, quite successfully, until shortly before his death. He ultimately earned the Academy Of Motion Picture Arts & Sciences ("Oscar") Award as Best Actor Of 1981 for the film *On Golden Pond*. The film incidentally co-starred his daughter. The differences which the two had over the conduct of the war were ultimately resolved. He died in 1982.

Jane Fonda

The "American Royal" who emerged as the most visible anti-war activist settled her lawsuit against the government in 1979. She declined to reveal the details of that litigation in her autobiography. From there she returned to practice her usual occupation, and successfully. In 1979 she received her second award from the Academy Of Motion Picture Arts & Sciences as Best Actress for the film *Coming Home*. The film detailed the lives of a Marine Corps officer who served in Vietnam, and his wife (played by Ms. Fonda) who attempt to adjust to the effects of the war on their union. Her co-star in the film, Jon Voight, also won the comparable award for Best Actor for his portrayal of a paraplegic Vietnam veteran.

By most accounts, Ms. Fonda emerged from the war she had so long opposed, a bigger woman than when the war began and certainly when she began to actively oppose the conflict. In the 1980s she became an icon of fitness and a successful businesswoman through the marketing of her exercise books and videos.

Also in the 1980s Ms. Fonda's life diverged from that of her husband, Tom Hayden. They were divorced in 1989. In 1991 she did what should forever dispel the allegation that she was sympathetic to communist ideology, as some had alleged during her anti-war activism. That year she married a Titan Of Capitalism, one Ted Turner, the President and Chairman Of The Board of Turner Broadcasting. After her divorce from Mr. Turner, Ms. Fonda took occasional film roles and also devoted herself to causes which she deemed worthy. She lives today in Atlanta, GA.

Gerald R. Ford

The President who was Commander-In-Chief when Vietnam was "lost" was never blamed for having allowed South Vietnam to come under the communist sphere. He was however praised for being instrumental in easing the nation into peaceful endeavors after the war ended. He ran for election in 1976 but was defeated by one who had promised during the Presidential campaign that he would order a general amnesty to those who had opposed the war. After leaving office in 1977 Mr. Ford stayed active in politics. He was a major contributor to the Republican Party platform in the 1980 Presidential race. He sought to be on that party's ticket as Vice President to the individual who he had beaten in the 1976 primaries. After unsuccessfully lobbying to appear on the ticket, he campaigned for the victor in that race. Mr. Ford died in 2007. The accolades and eulogies he received did not fault him for having "lost" Vietnam.

"G"

The author's cousin who was a part of the early U. S. buildup in Vietnam, had a satisfying tenure in the Air Force. To reiterate, in 1966 he was sent with his unit to South Vietnam. In his capacity as a Combat Engineer, in addition to continuously being subjected to small arms fire from the Viet Minh/Viet Cong, he also came into regular contact with the aforementioned chemical defoliant, Agent Orange. His tour of duty in Vietnam ended in September, 1967. In 1969 he was Honorably Discharged from the Air Force and he returned to what he believed would be a "normal" civilian life.

However, sometime during the period 1980 – 85 "G" began to notice abnormalities in his physical condition. One of the first of these was slight hearing impairment. Then he began experiencing kidney problems and high blood pressure. Eventually he developed prostate cancer, from which he suffers as of this writing. All of these ailments culminated in his being awarded a 100% disability rating by the Veterans Administration because of his prostate cancer and also what has come to be known as Post Traumatic Stress Syndrome (P.T.S.S.). This is a common ailment reported by persons who had experienced combat "in country" during the war.

"G" today leads a productive life in his hometown of St. Louis, MO.

Barry Goldwater

The Senator who was the most "hawkish" of the candidates for President in 1964 because of his views on the conduct of the war, lost his bid for that Office. He was however re-elected to a Senate seat from Arizona in 1968. For all of the time he served in the Senate, he was regarded as the elder statesman of the conservative cause. During the tenure of one of his successors as leader of the Republican Party, Ronald Reagan, it was stated by a political observer that "Goldwater moved the Republican Party to the far right, and Reagan nailed it there." He served in the Senate until 1989 when he retired from politics. Mr. Goldwater died in 1998.

Senator Albert Gore, Sr.

One of the foremost critics of the war in the Senate retired from politics after he lost his bid for reelection to that body in 1970. The same year he published his semi-autobiographical *The Eye Of The Storm* in which he examined at length his efforts to end the war.

After leaving the Senate Mr. Gore continued to be active in academia and on the boards of major corporations. He also served as a member of the General Assembly of the United Nations.

Senator Gore died in 1998.

Albert Gore, Jr.

The son of a Senator who never protested the war and who volunteered for the Army at the war's peak, successfully completed his military obligation. After having been Honorably Discharged, Mr. Gore began a career in journalism in his native Tennessee. He then was elected to the U. S. House Of Representatives and he served there from 1977 to 1985, representing a Tennessee district. He then was elected to the Senate, again representing his native state from 1985 to 1993. He then was elected to the Office Of Vice President Of The U. S. with his running mate, William Jefferson Clinton. In 2000 he ran for the highest elected office but was defeated. This election was one of the most unusual in U. S. history, in that Mr. Gore won in the popular vote, but he was defeated in the Electoral College. The final outcome of the election was decided by the Supreme Court. His opponent, one George Walker Bush, to reiterate, had never served on active duty in the military.

After leaving public office, Mr. Gore found success in several fields of endeavor. His first positions outside of government were in academia. He accepted visiting professorships at Columbia University, Middle Tennessee State University, the University Of California-Los Angeles and at Fisk University.

In 2006 he starred in the documentary film *An Inconvenient Truth* which alerted the public to the environmental dangers of global warming. The film won the Academy Of Motion Picture Arts & Sciences "Oscar" Award for Best Documentary.

In 2007 Mr. Gore was awarded the Nobel Peace Prize for his efforts to alert the public to the issue of global warming. As of this writing he is regarded as an elder statesman of the Democratic Party.

Dick Gregory

The individual who made the first spoken word recorded reference to Vietnam released in the U. S. and who ran for President in 1968 to protest the war, went on to success in a variety of fields. After having lost his bid for the Presidency he returned to the entertainment field until 1973. In a "live" night club recording that year, his last, entitled *Caught In The Act*, he made light of the political troubles of President

Nixon concerning the Watergate Affair. On the recording he informed his audience that while the first phase of the war was still on, he was told by a reporter that he had made the President's "Enemies List." When asked by the reporter for his comment, he stated: "Yes, call him and tell him I accept before he changes his mind!" He then became a writer and lecturer concerning a variety of issues.

Mr. Gregory found arguably his greatest success in the field of nutrition and the field of business. After becoming an advocate for improved nutrition, he started his own business, which is the manufacturing, marketing and sale of a successful nutrition product. He lives today with his family in Massachusetts.

Tom Hayden

One of the Chicago Seven which was prosecuted for crossing state lines to protest the war, continued to work with his wife, Jane Fonda, to advocate leftist causes. He unsuccessfully ran for a Senate seat from California in 1975. He did however win a hotly contested race for a seat in the California State Assembly in 1982.

After securing a place in government, Mr. Hayden's life with that of his wife began to diverge. By 1989 they were divorced.

Abbie Hoffman

One of the Chicago Seven who was prosecuted for crossing state lines to protest the war, continued to pursue leftist causes. In the 1980s he became a link between causes that the leftist movement had abandoned and the additional causes which that movement chose to pursue. He mobilized student forces to agitate for the end of apartheid in South Africa and also for restrictions on recruiting by the Central Intelligence Agency on college campuses.

After the war ended Hoffman was subsequently arrested for possession of cocaine. He then fled to avoid prosecution for such. After nearly seven years as a fugitive, Hoffman resurfaced and continued to agitate for leftist causes. These included restricting Central Intelligence Agency recruiting on college campuses.

Mr. Hoffman died in 1989 under mysterious circumstances.

Joseph Robert Kerrey

The Navy officer who led a raid on a suspected Viet Minh/Viet Cong hideout in 1969 on a mission to kill an enemy official, went on to capitalize on his military record. After having been severely wounded in combat in Vietnam and having lost a leg as a result, Mr. Kerrey then began an illustrious political career. He was however haunted by the aforementioned episode in Vietnam for many years after the war ended.

Mr. Kerrey would continue to have surgery on the leg which was partially amputated, until 1978. He did however achieve remarkable success in a variety of endeavors, especially in politics. After having been discharged from the Navy in 1969 and having been awarded the Congressional Medal Of Honor by President Nixon in 1970, he became a successful businessman. He married and had two children. In 1982 he was elected Governor Of Nebraska, serving one term. He then was elected to a Senate seat from Nebraska and served two terms from 1989 to 2001. His challenge to fellow Democrat William Jefferson Clinton for the nomination for President in 1992, was unsuccessful.

However, possibly the most remarkable attribute of Mr. Kerrey is the controversy which has reverberated through the media concerning his service in Vietnam. Other than the aforementioned William Calley, no other individual who served there in a combat role has been plagued by more controversy than him. On the twenty-sixth anniversary of the end of the war, the cover of the May 7, 2001 issue of *Time* magazine portrayed Mr. Kerrey in two images. In the foreground is an effigy of him as he was on that date. In the background one can see him in his combat uniform as he was on the approximate date of the aforementioned atrocity in Vietnam in which he participated. The caption on the cover read: "Ghosts Of Vietnam: Decorated hero Bob Kerrey's admission that he killed women and children in a raid 32 years ago turns a private agony into a public controversy."

The aforementioned issue of *Time* magazine devoted a nine page essay entitled "The Fog Of War" to examining the role of Mr. Kerry in the incident in question. What prompted the story was that an individual who had served with him in Vietnam and had participated in the killings, had come forward to a reporter from another magazine.

That individual was plagued with remorse for having participated in the incident at Tranh Phong on 25 February 1969.

After the aforementioned reporter had researched the military records of the incident, he then sought and was granted an interview with Mr. Kerrey. During the interview he told the reporter that all of the six individuals who had accompanied him on the mission in question had met shortly before the interview. They then discussed what had happened. All agreed that nothing improper had occurred on the mission. The group then jointly released a statement indicating that "We took fire and we returned fire." Mr. Kerrey conceded that a mistake had been made when all of the casualties turned out to be women and children. This is contrary to what the individual who had met with the reporter had stated.

It must be noted that the Congressional Medal Of Honor which Mr. Kerry received was for another raid which Mr. Kerry led, subsequent to the aforementioned tragedy.

The controversy concerning the raid at Tranh Phong in 1969 has never been resolved. After leaving the Senate in 2001, Mr. Kerry assumed a prominent place in academia.

John Kerry

The much-decorated Navy officer left active duty in 1970. He then went on to protest the war as a leader of the Vietnam Veterans Against The War (VVAW). The three Purple Hearts he had received for being thrice wounded, in addition to the Bronze Star and Silver Star awarded to him for bravery, did not hurt his image in the eyes of the electorate. Quite the contrary, in keeping with the traditions of every society he was rewarded with numerous honors for his military service and for his dedication to public service.

Mr. Kerry established a political base in Massachusetts. After his aborted initial run for public office for a Congressional seat there, he was elected Lieutenant Governor in 1982. He then was elected to the Senate in 1984.

What is most remarkable about Mr. Kerry's military service however, is that in one respect it appeared to be a detriment to his seeking higher office. In 2004 he challenged the incumbent President George Bush.

What occurred after he secured his party's nomination was nothing less than astounding. Some of his compatriots in the war questioned his war record. The point which a group known as the Swift Boat Veterans For Justice tried to make to the electorate, apparently with some success, was that Mr. Kerry lied about his war record. The apparent fabrication made him less than desirable for the Office Of President in the eyes of some. Mr. Kerry had been the commander of a swift boat when he served in Vietnam. The fact that Mr. Kerry had also led the VVAW was also a point of contention which the aforementioned group used to keep Mr. Kerry from becoming Commander-In-Chief.

It will likely be long debated the effect that the Swift Boat Veterans For Justice had on the outcome of the 2004 Presidential race. After that group made its accusations, the press generally did not heed them. The press mostly stated that the group's advertisements and accusations against Mr. Kerry were misleading. However, Mr. Kerry did lose a close race. The President won, 51% to Mr. Kerry's 48%. The electoral outcome was 286 to 252 in favor of the President who had never served on active duty in the military. Shortly after the election, it was revealed that a shift of 30,000 votes in one state would have given Mr. Kerry the electoral victory. He remains however a strong voice in the Senate, as of this writing.

Preston King

The individual who was prosecuted and convicted in 1961 for violation of the draft law, thereby exposing the inconsistencies in the way that the law was administered during the war, sat out the war by pursuing his studies in England. He eventually earned a doctorate there from a British university. He then became a professor at the University Of Lancaster there.

In February, 2000 he received a pardon from his conviction by President William Jefferson Clinton. President Clinton intimated that the decision-making process was expedited in his case because of humanitarian concerns. At that time *Mister* King desired to return to the U. S. in order to attend the funeral of his brother. In 2000 he returned home for the first time in thirty-nine years. *Mister* King was also apparently forgiven by the Federal judge who had sentenced him in 1961. U. S. District Judge William A. Bootle of the U. S. District Court For The District Of Georgia stated in a letter to the President to advocate the granting of the pardon, that *Mister* King had "followed his conscience just as Rosa Parks had followed hers." Lastly, a new Federal courthouse in Albany GA was subsequently named for one of *Mister* King's brothers. These facts were detailed in the February 22, 2000 edition of *The New York Times* in an article entitled "Pardon lets black exile come home."

Henry Kissinger

President Nixon's advisor on affairs of national security during the war was awarded the Nobel Peace Prize for 1973 for negotiating an end to the conflict. He then went on to greater heights in the area of international relations. He was elevated to Secretary Of State the same year, a position which he held through the administration of Richard Nixon's successor. While in this capacity his name became synonymous with the term "shuttle diplomacy", through his efforts to secure peace in the Middle East. After leaving government, he became a consultant in the field of international relations. He also became a consultant and a commentator on a variety of issues. One of these issues is detailed below.

Eartha Kitt

The only individual who dared to confront President Johnson's family on the war inside his home at the height of the war, suffered as a result. Shortly after the aforementioned confrontation in The White House in 1968 she was effectively banished from pursuing her usual occupation in her native land for ten years. However, in 1978 she returned to the U. S. after performing abroad. She then regained the stature which she formerly enjoyed within the U. S. entertainment community. After enjoying her regained status as an entertainer including successes on the stage and in film, she died on Christmas Day, 2008, aged 81.

Ron Kovic

The individual who joined the military in order to do something positive for his country, and was left a paraplegic as a result, maintained a high visibility on the anti-war front and on other fronts after the war ended. Among the things he protested were nuclear development and U. S. involvement in civil wars in Central America. These were in addition to his continuing protests of the way that this nation treats its war veterans.

In 1976 Mr. Kovic was invited to speak at the Democratic National Convention. The same year he also published his memoirs, *Born On The Fourth Of July*. The book was generally well-received by the critics and by the public. In a review of the book by *New York Times* critic C. B. D. Bryan, the book was labeled "the most personal and honest testament published thus far by any young man who fought in the Vietnam War." In 1989 the book was made into a motion picture of the same name. This was Mr. Kovic's goal and it was the result of a close collaboration between him and the director of the film, Oliver Stone.

Since *Born On The Fourth Of July* was released, Mr. Kovic has led a life of semi-seclusion in Redondo Beach, CA.

Nguyen Cao Ky

The Prime Minister of the "government" of South Vietnam at the war's peak, left during the evacuation of April, 1975. Just prior to his departure, he had been in retirement from Vietnamese politics and from the military for about four years. However, he returned to his military duties as a commander in 1975 as the forces of North Vietnam were beginning to directly threaten the South. When he realized that the South's efforts to resist were futile however, he left. It was promulgated in the U. S. news media the year that the war was lost, he had immigrated to the U. S. and managed a liquor store in Huntington Beach, CA.

In 1976 Ky published his memoirs, *Twenty Years And Twenty Days: How The U. S. Lost The First War With China And The Soviet Union*. Whatever are the book's overall merits, the book did reveal facts pertaining to U. S. involvement in Vietnam which had not previously been promulgated. He admitted for instance his complicity in the coup and subsequent assassination of President Ngo Dinh Diem in 1963. In addition, possibly the most profound statements he made in the book were his perception of the failure of U. S. officials to comprehend the Vietnamese mentality. Stated Ky: "They (the U. S.) never understood that it is impossible to impose a Western mask on an Eastern face." What is further remarkable about the book is that it also revealed the intricacies of the plot against Diem. These revelations included the personal relationships among the South Vietnamese military officers who conspired to overthrow him. For this reason alone it deserves to be read. Ky further revealed that he was rewarded for his complicity in the plot against Diem with a promotion to Air Marshal Of South Vietnam. He used this position to eventually become the head of state. There is more below concerning the 1963 assassination plot. It has never been revealed the ultimate disposition of his liquor business.

Gen. John D. Lavelle

The Air Force General who in 1972 was alleged to have disobeyed Pentagon orders in conducting air operations in Vietnam and then forced to retire in disgrace was subsequently exonerated. In *The Washington Post* edition of 5 August 2010 appeared an article entitled "Honor restored for general blamed after Nixon denied authorizing Vietnam bombing." This and other periodicals published reports that the current Commander-In-Chief had taken action to restore Gen. Lavelle's rank the previous day. Gen. Lavelle was exonerated of charges that he violated Presidential restrictions on aerial bombing during the Vietnam War, or that he had ordered records falsified to conceal the illegal bombing missions. Gen. Lavelle died in 1979, still maintaining his innocence, as he had in Congressional hearings in 1972, of the illegalities in question. It bears mention that Gen. Lavelle was forced to retire at the rank of Major General. This was two steps below that which he had previously held.

The restoration of Gen. Lavelle's rank and character resulted from the research by another retired Air Force General, one Aloysius Casey and his son. Their efforts to clear Gen. Lavelle's name began in 2007. The two examined declassified documents and transcripts of recordings made by Richard Nixon in the Oval Office in 1971.

These documents and recordings proved that Nixon had personally authorized more aggressive bombing of targets in North Vietnam, while claiming otherwise in February, 1972. The bombing campaign was not justified because U. S. planes had not been subjected to hostile fire from North Vietnamese anti-aircraft batteries, which supposedly justified the more intensive bombing. The research found that the falsification of intelligence reports which supposedly justified the more aggressive bombing resulted from collusion among (1) Nixon, (2) the senior Navy Commander in Vietnam, (3) Adm. Thomas H. Moorer, Chairman Of The Joint Chiefs Of Staff and also (4) the Commander of all U. S. forces in Vietnam, Army Gen. Creighton Abrams. No other individual had faced discipline over the matter in 1972.

The above research results were then forwarded to the Air Force Board For The Correction Of Military Records. In 2008 that Board found no evidence that Gen. Lavelle had disobeyed Pentagon orders in 1972, or that he had falsified documents to conceal illegal bombing missions. The Air Force further found that the decision to relieve Gen. Lavelle was based on incomplete information. It further found that White House officials in collusion with others had withheld facts in the adjudication of the original matter. Further, the aforementioned research and Air Force examination of the facts found that Gen. Lavelle had ordered a halt to the falsification of reports about hostile fire from North Vietnam which supposedly justified the illegal bombing in question.

The facts determined by the Air Force Board then were forwarded to the Secretary Of The Air Force with a petition to correct the military record of Gen. Lavelle and also to restore his four star rank of General. The petition alleged that the general had been used as a scapegoat.

After review by the Secretary Of Defense, he concurred with the recommendation by the Air Force Secretary and forwarded the matter to the President & Commander-In-Chief. President Obama then asked the Senate to re-confirm Gen. Lavelle to the rank of General. As of this writing the recommendation before the Senate is pending. Gen. Lavelle's widow thanked all parties to the matter. (Department Of Defense News Release No. 695-10, 4 August 2010; *New York Times* editorial 7 August 2010).

Norman Mailer

The most eloquent chronicler of the activities of the anti-war movement, the so-called New Left, remained a highly respected member of the literary community. He continued to write fiction and non-fiction works which were highly praised. In a testimony to the reverberating effects of the war, in 2003 he finally made his personal opinions of the war public, in his book *Why Are We At War?* When Mr. Mailer died on 10 November 2007, he was remembered and lauded as an icon of the Vietnam War era and of his profession.

John McCain

The Navy carrier pilot who had been "killed" in air action over North Vietnam in 1967, remained in a North Vietnamese prison camp until after the first phase of the war ended. After his release from five and one-half years of confinement in 1973, this officer returned to active duty as a Captain (O-6), from which rank he retired in 1981.

Mr. McCain then embarked upon a political career which first elevated him to the House Of Representatives in 1983, representing a district in Arizona. From there he moved to the Senate, assuming the seat vacated by Barry Goldwater in 1989. Ever since that victory, he has pursued the Office Of The President several times. In the 2000 campaign for that office, his opponents smeared him viciously by asserting that he was mentally unstable because of the conditions which he endured in captivity in North Vietnam. Those opponents made such assertions despite the fact that McCain had been examined numerous times by military psychiatrists when he was in uniform and been found completely "normal." During the 2004 and 2008 campaigns for the same office, the same questions arose about his fitness, both physically and mentally. Such was detailed in the February 11, 2008 issue of *Newsweek* magazine in an article entitled "What These Eyes Have Seen: He's endured the unendurable and survived. Inside the mind and heart of John McCain." The cover of that issue of *Newsweek* portrayed Mr. McCain in two effigies: (1) a photo of him in uniform and apparently prior to his captivity and (2) as he appeared when the essay was published. No basis in fact was found in any of the assertions alleging his unfitness for the Office Of President. Despite a spirited campaign, he was however defeated decisively. He has since returned to his duties in the Senate where he remains a respected voice.

Robert S. McNamara

The person who was the principal architect of the war as Secretary Of Defense from 1961 to 1968, and who was characterized by most of those who he sought to help as a "cold and arrogant man" (Bui Diem, p. 213), stayed in the public arena after he left that post. After leaving that post in February, 1968 he went on to head the World Bank. In his memoirs which he published in 1995 entitled *In Retrospect: The Tragedy And Lessons Of Vietnam*, he stated that he was never sure if he was fired or if he resigned from his position as Secretary Of Defense.

Also in his memoirs Mr. McNamara conceded that he and other officials had been "terribly wrong" on their assessments of the Indochina situation. Inasmuch as he was also characterized by Diem as the one who conceived the "Vietnamization" of the war in early 1967, he obviously realized his miscalculation sooner than others. These sentiments he reiterated in the documentary in which he "starred" in the aforementioned award-winning film *The Fog Of War* in 2003. He further conceded therein that the U. S. should have withdrawn its forces from Vietnam approximately in 1963. The aforementioned book further explains in great detail how U. S. leaders erred in assessing the odds of winning the conflict by military means. He accepted the blame for such miscalculations. Mr. McNamara died in 2009.

John Mitchell

President Nixon's chief law enforcement officer during the war suffered for his efforts to exact retribution against Nixon Administration war critics. His efforts to stifle those critics almost universally failed. In March, 1974 during the interlude between the second and third phases of the war he was indicted along with several others. The charges concerned their alleged complicity in a cover-up of the crimes arising from the Watergate scandal. On 1 January 1975 after having pleaded not guilty, he was convicted of conspiracy, obstruction of justice and of lying under oath. He was disbarred. A judge of the U. S. District Court For The District Of Columbia sentenced him to from thirty months to eight years for these crimes. After losing two appeals, Mitchell who was the only U. S. Attorney General to serve prison time, served his sentence until he was paroled in January, 1979, after having served nineteen months.

Mitchell died in 1988, aged seventy-five.

Madame Nhu

The sister-in-law of the leader of South Vietnam who was assassinated in 1963, left shortly thereafter. She never returned to her native land. In an article entitled "Dragon Lady" in the June 5, 1978 issue of *Newsweek*, she was described as living a life of leisure in a villa in Rome. Her only child, a daughter, had been killed in an automobile accident in Europe. She was reputed to busy herself with gardening, attending a daily Roman Catholic mass, and also upgrading her property. Further, she was reputed to have stated that she believed the communist regime which had unified and still ruled Vietnam at that time, was transitory. Lastly, she was reported as labeling the U. S. "heartless."

Richard M. Nixon

The Commander-In-Chief when the first and second phases of the war ended, who was eventually exposed in the aforementioned film *Daniel Ellsberg: The Most Dangerous Man In America* as an advocate of (1) using nuclear weapons against North Vietnam and also (2) bombing the irrigation dikes there, began a life of semi-seclusion after his resignation. He was never again active in politics, although he traveled widely and appeared at political meetings on behalf of select causes. In 1978 he published his memoirs, *RN: The Memoirs Of Richard Nixon*. The book did not apologize for his actions in pursuit of the war, or for any other activity while in office. Nixon also published several other works in which he opined on the global political situation. These received predictably mixed reviews, although they sold well.

Nixon died in 1994.

James Danforth (Dan) Quayle

The individual who avoided active service in the war reaped benefits far beyond what one would expect of a person who appeared to shun such service. While in the National Guard he completed law school at Indiana University. He then began a political career which has been described by some as a political marvel. In 1976 at the urging of Indiana Republican leaders he competed for a Congressional seat against a far more experienced and senior Democrat. Even his Republican backers were surprised at his win.

During Quayle's second term in Congress which had been described as "undistinguished" by some observers, in 1980 he challenged another far more experienced and senior Democrat for a Senate seat. He won. Some suggested that his win was on the "coattails" of Ronald Reagan, the Republican candidate and victor for the Presidency. Mr. Quayle was reelected in 1986 however, a year characterized as one in which other Republicans who apparently had ridden on Reagan's coattails in 1980, lost their bids for reelection.

Quayle had been characterized as "hawkish" and a "hard line" conservative in the Senate. Though he had also been described as a "dumb blond" by his detractors, he attained a reputation as an effective legislator prior to his election to the Vice Presidency. His apparent victory on the "coattails" of George H. W. Bush in 1988 did not translate into reelection however. In 1992 both were defeated by two men, one of whom likewise had been characterized as a "draft-dodger." The victor's running mate was one who volunteered for the Army the same year that Mr. Quayle joined the National Guard. In the final analysis Mr. Quayle's defeat and that of his running mate may have been due to his inability to spell.

Mr. Quayle left politics shortly after his electoral defeat. He lives today in semi-retirement with his family in Paradise Valley, AZ, pursuing his avocation, golf.

Charles Robb

The Marine Corps officer who survived two tours of duty in Vietnam and then married the daughter of the Commander-In-Chief apparently used his wartime service to achieve bigger things. His military service was likely a factor in his election as Governor Of Virginia in 1982. Having served one term there, he then was elected to the Senate in 1988 from his native Virginia. Having served two terms there, he then was still visible in the public arena. In 2004 he chaired a commission which was convened to inquire into Iraq intelligence, the Iraq Intelligence Commission. In 2006 he was appointed to the President's Intelligence Advisory Board. He resides with his family in McLean, VA.

Jerry Rubin

One of The Chicago Seven who with his compatriots was prosecuted for crossing state lines to protest the war, eventually abandoned the "counterculture movement." He then devoted his life to activities more in the mainstream. Ultimately he moved to New York City and became a businessman, facilitating "networking" for business executives.

Dean Rusk

One of the principal architects of the war as Secretary Of State under Presidents Kennedy and Johnson, never wavered in his insistence that the U. S. was obligated to continue to support the "government" of South Vietnam. His rationale was that the U. S. was bound to honor its treaty commitments.

After leaving his position as Secretary Of State at the end of the Johnson Administration in 1969, Mr. Rusk returned to academia, assuming a post as a Professor of International Law at the University Of Georgia.

Mr. Rusk died in his native Georgia in 1994.

Anthony J. Russo

Information on the principal cohort of Daniel Ellsberg in the leaking of The Pentagon Papers in 1971, which in turn exposed the deception the government had perpetrated upon the public concerning the war, is quite sketchy. Mr. Russo was of course exonerated as was Mr. Ellsberg in 1973. However, it has not been reported that he regained the position of prominence in the Federal Government which originally allowed him and Mr. Ellsberg access to classified information. Indeed, it has never been reported that either individual ever again worked within the Federal Government. However, it is known that Mr. Russo remained in the civil service at the state level. He worked for the Los Angeles (CA) County Probation Department for many years. He died in 2008, aged 71. (*New York Times* obituary, 9 August 2008). That obituary further revealed how the war was instrumental in bridging the racial gap in the U. S. Russo was, as was Ellsberg, an integral part of "The Establishment." Both were Pentagon analysts assigned to work on the study commissioned by Secretary Of Defense Robert McNamara which spawned the Papers. Russo informed the *New York Times* at the time the Papers were initially promulgated in 1971, when both he and Ellsberg were indicted for violation of the Espionage Act Of 1917, that "He always credited the Black Panthers with being his strongest supporters."

SSgt Barry Sadler

The individual who co-wrote and sang the only patriotic song recorded and released during the war, left the Army after having been seriously wounded by a booby trap while in combat in Vietnam. He then briefly pursued an acting career. In 1978 he was charged with the murder of a songwriter, but acquitted. In 1981 he was charged but eventually found not guilty of shooting a former business partner. His obituary in *The New York Times* edition of 7 November 1989 stated that he had suffered brain damage and was partially paralyzed from wounds he received from having been shot during an apparent robbery at his home in Guatemala in 1988. He died on 8 September 1989, aged 49.

The Socialist Republic Of Vietnam

The country which was unified in 1975 despite opposition from the U. S., among others, took its seat as a member of The United Nations in 1977. The nation which purportedly had the capacity to exert control over Vietnam, The People's Republic Of China, invaded that country in 1979, but was repulsed. Foreign observers attributed this success in repulsing the invader to the fact that its military was battle-hardened and quite disciplined.

Further, it has never been documented that The Socialist Republic Of Vietnam has ever been subjected to domination by a foreign power. It has also never been revealed that another nation has dictated to it how it must behave. This of course was the fear that U. S. leaders had which prompted intervention in Vietnam's civil war.

"Ron Stone"

The individual who was close to those in power in the Senate and who subsequently began to agitate against the war and then leave the U. S., successfully evaded military service. He spent seven years in Canada. While there in 1975 he became aware of an attorney in Chicago where his case for draft evasion was still active in F.B.I. files. The attorney was randomly examining cases such as "Ron's" in order to determine if some of such cases might be dismissed for legal technicalities. There was such a technicality in "Ron's" case. For the interval during which "Ron" was in Canada, the F.B.I. knew he was there, but they had no precise address. They sent an induction notice to him at his address of record in Toronto. "Ron" however had moved to Vancouver, B.C. He could therefore prove that he never received the induction notice, inasmuch as it was returned to the U. S. unopened. Accordingly, the attorney in question agreed to take "Ron's" case and argue for dismissal for a fee of $1,200. "Ron" subsequently was notified by the F.B.I. that his case of draft evasion had been dismissed.

"Ron" then returned to the U. S. and became active in politics in Southern California until his death in 1988, aged forty, from Acquired Immune Deficiency Syndrome (A.I.D.S.).

Col. Harry G. Summers, Jr.

The twice-wounded career soldier who was part of the early build-up in Vietnam would figure prominently in society. He would become known as the most knowledgeable and eloquent author of books about the entire Vietnam Experience, as it pertained to military matters. The aforementioned *Vietnam War Almanac* is one of his numerous writings on the war.

After occupying the prestigious Douglas MacArthur Chair Of

Military Research at the Army War College, Col. Summers retired from the Army in 1985. However, he remained on the scene in matters of national defense. During the Gulf War of 1990-91, he was a military analyst for the news division of The National Broadcasting Company (NBC). Based on his observations of that war, he was prompted to write *On Strategy II: A Critical Analysis Of The Gulf War.*

Other prominent positions which Col. Summers occupied after his retirement were syndicated columnist for *The Los Angeles Times.* He also lectured at The White House, the State Department and the Central Intelligence Agency. It was said of Col. Summers by Richard Holmes of the British Royal Military College Of Science that "He was very well regarded by many British historians as an example of the soldier-scholar who combined sword and pen, and did so much for the revival of military thought in the West."

Col. Summers died at the Walter Reed Medical Center, Washington, on 14 November 1999. He is buried in Arlington National Cemetery. There is more about Col. Summers below.

Nguyen Van Thieu

The head of state of South Vietnam for most of the time that she was propped up by the U. S., departed his native land in 1975. His departure occurred as South Vietnam was being united with the northern part of the country. After departing, Thieu began traveling around the world to bolster the morale of his countrymen who had left with him. He encouraged them to help improve the situation there, and he also stated that he wished to return. He further stated that if and when he would return, he did not desire to occupy any position of leadership because he was too old. It has never been documented that he ever returned to his native land.

The United States Of America

The nation which inherited the war from an ally and likewise failed to keep all of Vietnam from falling under the communist sphere, was of course profoundly affected by the war. Whether the U. S., in Navy jargon was "one hundred-eighty out" after the war ended, or on a completely different course than that which it pursued before the war, is of course debatable. The degree to which the U. S. was transformed by the war has indeed already been examined in substantial depth. Perhaps also more published scrutiny about the degree to which it was transformed by the war may be forthcoming. All concerned can only hope so. However, the author will leave that task to those cultural anthropologists more qualified than he. In any event, the author hereby conveys the results of his research and of his personal observations:

a. The healing process

Of course the U. S. began a period of healing after the war ended. In light of the experience of Senator John Kerry who may have lost his bid to become President in 2004 because some persons raised issues about his service in the war, one might say that the healing process had not been completed even in the first decade of the twenty-first century. However, within two years after the war finally terminated in 1975, there began a healing process, of sorts. The individual who became President in January, 1977 understood that the war had been so divisive that an act of healing was needed. In order to foment the sorely needed healing process, President Jimmy Carter in accordance with the promise which he made while campaigning for President, granted a blanket pardon to all persons who had evaded the draft during the war. The pardon was full, complete and unconditional. Of course there was an expected, vehement protest from some circles, not the least of which was from those who had served in the military during the conflict.

President Carter's blanket amnesty accordingly went further than did his predecessor's program of clemency. Recall that President Ford's clemency through earned amnesty program required a period of alternative service in lieu of the military service which some had evaded or avoided. President Carter's pardon therefore pleased those who had evaded or avoided military service by leaving the U. S. Many of these were still living abroad. Their pleasure stemmed from the fact that the pardon went further than did the alternative service program of President Ford. Some stated that they shunned that program because to have embraced it would imply that they would have to admit to having acted illegally. Many of those who had evaded military service and were still living abroad felt that they had done nothing wrong. Some still believed that the war was illegal. Accordingly, some of these persons were pleased that the Carter pardon relieved them of having to admit that they had so acted.

The President's pardon did have its limitations. It did not include those who had deserted the military. The pardon further did not apply to those who otherwise opposed the war by illegal means. These were still liable for prosecution. There were still unresolved issues that were not addressed by the pardon, however. One of these was the question of how many had evaded the draft, and who these persons were. The government still did not know the identities of all who evaded the draft by refusing to register with the Selective Service System, for instance. Recall that the cornerstone of that system was registration of anyone who might come under the system's jurisdiction. The government of course knew that many who had been subject to the law had failed to register as required. To complicate the matter further, the government knew that it had no means of determining who these non-registrants were. Gottlieb estimates that one-quarter million persons never registered for the draft. (Gottlieb, p. 211).

Possibly the most succinct and eloquent statement from one who welcomed the President's act of pardoning came from the individual who had led the effort to end the war in 1972. George McGovern, the Democratic candidate for President that year and still a Senator in 1977, stated:

"The pardon of Vietnam draft resisters is a compassionate and courageous first step consistent with President Carter's campaign pledge to put the painful Vietnam era behind us."

1. Remedial actions

The aforementioned controversy over the use of the chemical defoliant Agent Orange did not end with the war. Information concerning the lingering effects of the chemical on personnel who had served in Vietnam would receive notoriety for at least a quarter century after the conflict ended. Government and private efforts to extend treatment to those who had been subjected to the chemical would be fruitful. The best indication of such efforts which are in turn indicative of the magnitude of the problem would be the placing of a poster in Veterans Administration (VA) hospitals worldwide in 2000. The poster states:

"VA CARES ABOUT VIETNAM VETERANS EXPOSED TO AGENT ORANGE

For information and assistance, contact the nearest VA Medical Center, Vet Center or Regional Office

- Register Health Examination
- Special Eligibility Medical Care
- Disability Compensation
- Outreach and Education
- Research"

(VA Poster 10-71, Feb. 2000)

b. Elements of transformation
1. Greater aversion to war

One phenomenon which could readily be observed concerning the national transformation is that the U. S. certainly has a greater aversion to war than when the conflict began. Whenever the subject would arise concerning the U. S.' involvement in a foreign military campaign, voices will immediately arise to examine the wisdom of such. Witness the cries which arose during the Persian Gulf War of 1990 – 91 where the protesters screamed "No blood for oil!" Witness also the debate which is occurring as of this writing concerning the U. S.' continued presence in Afghanistan and in Iraq. The debate over U. S. presence there indeed is quite fierce, as it has been since those military campaigns began.

However, possibly the most profound legacy of the conflict concerning the national aversion to war concerns the statutory relationship between the two most active branches of government. Throughout much of the war there was fierce debate over how the U. S. became embroiled in another nation's civil war. When it became obvious that the war could never be won militarily, Congress vowed to never again let a President lead the nation into another futile military venture. This is the reason why, less than two weeks after the first phase of the conflict ended in January, 1973 Congress asserted its Constitutional authority and enacted legislation which severely limited the President's war-making powers. This indeed was one of the most profound transformations which this nation underwent because of the war.

2. Greater aversion to military service in general

A myriad of attitudes on a variety of national issues also changed because of the war. For example, national attitudes concerning military service in general were profoundly affected. As the war was ending, the Armed Forces experienced a marked drop in enlistments, to the extent that one branch of the service fell short of recruiting goals.

3. Increased scrutiny of politicians' backgrounds

Another area in which the U. S. was transformed by the conflict can be seen in attitudes towards persons who appeared to have shunned military service during the war. As of this writing it has become an axiom of U. S. politics that any individual who seeks elective office and was subject to military service during the war will have his behavior during the war closely scrutinized. William Jefferson Clinton and John Kerry, referenced above, are possibly the most glaring examples.

The degree to which the electorate seems to have altered its perception of such persons since 1975 was detailed in tabloid form during the 1988 Presidential campaign. The cover of the August 29, 1988 edition of *Time* Magazine portrayed the aforementioned James Danforth (Dan) Quayle with his running mate, George H. W. Bush. The caption thereon was "The Quayle Factor." The attendant article (pp. 16 – 22) entitled "The Quayle Quagmire" is an excellent example of how the U. S. had altered or acquired perceptions of such persons since the conflict ended. The article was also likely the first in-depth discussion of the military record of any politician since the war ended. This edition of *Time* was a landmark in that it revealed and examined for the first time the nation's obsession with the military records of politicians who were subjected to military service during the war. Further, this edition of *Time* is likely the first instance in which the military record, or lack thereof, of such a person was scrutinized in order to determine the individual's fitness for higher elective office.

In the aforementioned article, Mr. Quayle is shown in a 1971 photograph in his National Guard uniform, quite nonchalantly leaning against a vehicle. The impression one should immediately feel is that he indeed had it "made in the shade." Translated, he had not been compelled to actively engage in the conflict. By 1988 he had been elected and reelected to the Senate. He conceded during the Presidential campaign that his assumption of a National Guard billet which effectively barred him from any form of combat duty while the war still raged, resulted from his wealthy family's connections. This concession is what led some to believe that the Republican standard-bearer in 1988, George H. W. Bush, had made a grave mistake by adding Mr. Quayle to his ticket.

The aforementioned article examined the dilemma which Mr. Bush faced quite succinctly:

> "..by anointing Quayle, Bush also stepped into deep boo-boo. During an awkward press conference and five erratic television interviews, Quayle was constantly unhinged by the question that torments many of his generation: "What did you do during the Vietnam War?"

During one of the aforementioned interviews Mr. Quayle further intimated that he may have joined the National Guard in 1969 because he did not know then that he would be seeking the second-highest elective office in 1988. This apparent admission did not seem to hurt the ticket's chances in the general election, however. The ticket won decisively.

Quite interestingly, the aforementioned article compared Mr. Quayle with his running-mate, George H. W. Bush. It was noted therein that Mr. Bush had interrupted his studies in 1944 to join the military. He sought combat duty and he received it in direct conflict against the Japanese. As a Navy aviator he was shot down over the Pacific, then was rescued. No one has ever questioned that Mr. Bush did so out of anything but pure, unvarnished patriotism. Yet he chose a running mate who conceded that his wealthy family pulled strings to help him avoid active military service. Here one can see another glaring example of how national attitudes were transformed by the war. The article in question crystallized such transformation in attitudes by stating:

"Attitudes and behavior that were commonplace in (up to and including) the late 1960s are now viewed with post-factum moralism through the prism of two decades of cultural revisionism."

As of this writing such revisionism is a permanent part of the U. S. political landscape.

4. Increased political discord

The Commander-In-Chief during the bulk of the conflict demonstrated his mastery of perception of political and societal changes because of the war. Richard Nixon in his memoirs was "right on" when he offered his take on how political discourse had changed during and because of the ended conflict. Demonstrating his mastery of the revised political landscape, he opined:

"Vietnam had precipitated perhaps the most serious and significant change of all: the passing of the tradition of bipartisan support for a President's foreign policy. The long years of war and the national confusion over Vietnam had eroded this concept and further divided Congress against the President, and the two houses against themselves." (*RN*, p. 771).

a. National and international reflection
1. The print media

To reiterate, one of the primary themes explored herein is how the issues of the war have continued to reverberate within this society since the war ended. The war and peripheral issues are indeed stories that won't go away. Strong evidence of this continued reverberation is the aforementioned article dated 10 October 1983 in *U. S. News & World Report*, "Untold Story Of The Road To War In Vietnam." The article purported to shed new light on the war and related issues. The authors apparently believed that such information had never before been revealed. From the author's examination of that article, this does not appear to have been the case. It does not appear that the article uncovered any information which had not before been discussed. The article appears to merely rehash information which had already been examined in depth. Accordingly, the only thing that the article seems to have demonstrated is (1) the public's fascination with the war, (2) how deeply ingrained the war is to the national consciousness, and (3) how many still wanted to know why the war occurred.

A quote from the article is most apropos:

> "In the ten years after the (1963) coup (against President Of South Vietnam Diem), U. S. servicemen – both living and the 58,000 dead – came back to a homeland adrift in anger, pessimism and determination to forget the tragedy of the most bitterly divisive conflict, save for The Civil War, that Americans have ever fought. Even today the Vietnam imprint cuts across American politics, economy and ideals. And it will not soon disappear."

However, even though the article in question failed to provide much new, relevant information, it does provide minor new information concerning the war. Specifically, it details in greater depth than had been reported previously, even in The Pentagon Papers, how the President Of South Vietnam and his brother were killed in 1963. To reiterate, upon learning of the death of the two, President Kennedy was purportedly quite stunned. The article in question further stated that both had been shot, and that Diem was also stabbed. Kennedy's reaction therefore indicates that he did not advocate their assassination, but rather their ouster. Further concerning the assassinations, it was revealed the year after the war ended that persons close to President Nixon had manufactured false documents to discredit Kennedy's legacy. These were in the form of phony State Department documents which were prepared in 1971 which purportedly offered proof that Kennedy had ordered the assassinations. A scheme had allegedly been concocted by persons close to Nixon to leak such information to *Life* Magazine. Such was the claim of one John Dean who had been President Nixon's counsel from 1971 to 1973 (Dean, *Blind Ambition*, p. 115).

Other indications that the conflict is still within the national consciousness as of this writing can be seen in an article published in the December 8, 2008 edition of *The New York Times*. That article detailed events during the 1968 presidential campaign. Recall that the conflict was borne to some degree of the traditional rivalry between the Democratic and Republican parties. The article in question describes in greater detail than was previously available how such rivalry likely affected the course of the war. President Johnson accused close associates of Richard Nixon of "treason" because of their purported efforts to sabotage his efforts to end the war. The purported aim of these individuals was to disrupt the peace-making process in order to gain political capital with the electorate. Apparently they saw an opportunity to delay the end of the war, and then allow Nixon to assume office and then resolve the conflict, thereby allowing him to assume the credit. These facts came to light forty years after the fact because of recordings recently declassified and released by the government. Here again one can see that the controversy over the war is still in the national consciousness in the first decade of the third millennium.

The wisdom of U. S. involvement in Indochina has further recently been examined by another principal player in the conflict, one Dr. Henry Kissinger. Virtually simultaneous with the publication of the above article, Dr. Kissinger wrote an article which resurrected the burning issues of the conflict. One can clearly observe therein that Richard Nixon's foreign policy advisor and then his Secretary Of State had not lost his memory, eloquence and also his grasp of the complexity of the issues of the war. Stated Dr. Kissinger:

> "For America, the Vietnam War was the traumatic event of the second half of the last century. Entered into with a brash self-confidence … our engagement ended with America as divided as it had not been since the Civil War." (Dr. Henry Kissinger, "What Vietnam Teaches Us" *Newsweek*, 3 November 2008, pp. 44 – 46).

The catalyst for Dr. Kissinger's resurrection of the war's complexity was the posthumous publication of a book in 2008 about another principal player during the conflict, one McGeorge Bundy. To reiterate, Bundy was a prominent foreign policy advisor to Presidents Kennedy and Johnson until his departure from public service in 1966. The book entitled *Lessons In Disaster* is, as so eloquently and aptly put by Dr. Kissinger, "further evidence of the inability of America to transcend the debates that tore it apart two generations ago." For this reason alone it deserves the utmost scrutiny.

2. The broadcast media
a. *Vietnam: A Television History*

Possibly the most detailed examination of the war since its termination was in the form of a thirteen part PBS documentary which aired in 1983 entitled *Vietnam: A Television History*. Quite coincidentally, or most appropriately, the series was a tri-production of the local PBS station in Boston, WGBH, also the British Central Independent Television and lastly France's Antennae-2. The multiple broadcast program meticulously examined the complete history of the origins of the conflict as it was borne of western intervention from the end of the Second World War to its termination. Though the series was not well received by all, it did receive praise and garner awards from certain circles.

b. *The Fog Of War*

One of the principal "players" in the war, former Secretary Of Defense Robert McNamara was the subject of the documentary *The Fog Of War: Eleven Lessons From The Life Of Robert McNamara*. The superb documentary primarily details the rationales for entering every war in which the U. S. was engaged in the twentieth century. Also detailed are the strategies for fighting such conflicts. What set the Vietnam War apart from the others was of course that the rationale and the strategy for fighting the war were based on faulty reasoning. McNamara concedes this in the film. Further detailed in the documentary were the explicit details of the rationale in pursuing the war which had not previously been made public. The fact that *The Fog Of War* was produced in 2003 is of course further testimony to the nation's continuing obsession with the ended conflict. The noted film critic Leonard Maltin describes the film as:

"An emotional powerhouse for anyone who lived through the era depicted here so vividly."

The Academy Of Motion Picture Arts And Sciences agreed with Mr. Maltin's assessment. That is why the documentary was awarded the "Oscar" for Best Documentary Feature of 2003.

5. Recriminations
1. Via the broadcast media

The first recriminations over the departed tragedy that was Vietnam occurred in 1982, less than seven years after the war ended. In January, 1982 the Columbia Broadcasting System (CBS) broadcast a documentary entitled *The Uncounted Enemy: A Vietnam Deception.* The program was produced by that network's news division, CBS News. It has never been made clear why that network decided to air the program at that time. However, there must have been compelling reasons why CBS would dredge up information which helped to fuel the debate over the war while it still raged, but which appeared to be no longer relevant. Recall that one of the major points of contention between the government and the public during the war was the aforementioned Credibility Gap. This was the gap between what the government promulgated concerning the war, as opposed to what was actually occurring "in country." Recall also that the individual who first caused that term to come into common use was Walter Cronkite, one of the titans of the CBS television network. His name was not associated with the production, however.

The documentary's major premise was to question the credibility of the U. S. Commander in Vietnam, General William C. Westmoreland. The program's producers suggested that in May, 1967 during the last year of his tenure, Gen. Westmoreland deliberately falsified data concerning enemy troop strength. As required by Pentagon standard procedure, planners there deemed it vital that it be furnished accurate information concerning the enemy's resources. CBS suggested in the documentary that General Westmoreland was personally responsible for submitting false or misleading information to his seniors concerning enemy troop strength. The documentary further suggested that General Westmoreland discounted even the information which was furnished to him by those close to him in the field. The result of course was that the war was being mismanaged and that the public was being misled, CBS News asserted.

Consequently, upon learning of the information promulgated

by CBS News, General Westmoreland filed a civil action against that organization in September, 1982. That action which sought $120,000,000 in damages for libel, was filed in the U. S. District Court For The Southern District Of New York.

The jury trial of *Westmoreland* v. *CBS News* commenced in September, 1984. Testimony rendered at the trial revealed that the defendant's allegations against General Westmoreland in the aforementioned documentary were substantially credible. From the testimony rendered at trial it did appear that the plaintiff had indeed falsified information to his seniors concerning enemy troop strength and therefore impeded progress on the war. Among those witnesses subpoenaed were two persons who had served with General Westmoreland in the field in 1967. They testified for the defense that the general had ignored their assessments of enemy troop strength and then he willfully provided false data to The Pentagon. General Westmoreland had apparently mismanaged the war.

However, the trial came to a screeching halt in February, 1985 after five months, and just one week before it was scheduled to go to the jury. General Westmoreland's attorney moved the judge to dismiss the case, "with prejudice." In legal jargon this means that the plaintiff's allegations could not again be raised in any court. The judge granted the motion.

Several factors came into play which compelled the plaintiff to move for a dismissal. In addition to the fact that General Westmoreland's own trusted lieutenants testified against him, public sentiment appeared to be in favor of the defendant. The highlights of the trial were of course promulgated via the news media, which provided feedback concerning public sentiment. Further, after the dismissal it was also promulgated in the media that most of the jurors favored the defendant. It was revealed that seven of the twelve jurors were leaning towards CBS. Lastly, it was revealed that General Westmoreland had inadequate legal representation.

The cost of the trial was assessed by knowledgeable observers at $7,000,000 for the plaintiff and $10,000,000 for the defendant.

a. The author's assessment of the issue of contention

Here the author is compelled to provide his assessment of one of the aforementioned issues of contention. With respect to allegations that during the war the government had not disseminated truthful, accurate information concerning the war's progress, the author must concur. His research has revealed that there is some substance to such allegations. The author cannot address the original point of contention that responsible individuals "in country" violated established procedures for reporting accurate information to The Pentagon. That issue is beyond the scope of his research.

However, information which the author uncovered during his research has revealed that information which the Department Of Defense released to the media in one year, 1967, differed substantially with the data which the government recorded for its own archives. Recall that in 1967 the war was becoming an embarrassment for the government because (1) it could not claim that progress was being made in defeating the enemy, and (2) casualties on both sides were rising at an alarming rate. Recall also that this was the year in which persons within and without government were beginning to question the strategy used to pursue the war. These persons also were beginning to question the wisdom of pursuing the war further. Recall further that 1967 was the year about which CBS News subsequently broadcast the aforementioned report which suggested that military officials deliberately fabricated information concerning enemy troop strength.

As in any military campaign the government is obligated to provide the media with information concerning the progress, if any, the military achieves in securing its objectives. Statistics are always provided to the media in order that the media can inform the public that the nation's resources are utilized efficiently. With respect to the year in question, the author has uncovered that the information which the government promulgated to the media differed substantially from that which it recorded in its own archives. Refer to Figure 3. The author compared these government figures with those which it promulgated to the media for two consecutive years: 1966 and 1967, which is the year of contention. Specifically, the author compared the government statistics with the data published by Crowell Collier And Macmillan, Inc. in the form of Year Books. The information published by that firm did not differ substantially from the government's figures for 1966. That publisher stated explicitly that "U. S. losses throughout 1966 averaged about 100 dead and 600 wounded a week." (Collier's Year Book 1967,

Covering The Year 1966, p. 592). These figures substantially concur with those released by the government for that year. Observe in Figure 3 that deaths were reported that year as 5,008. The figure for wounded was reported as 30,093. The figures from the two different sources substantially match.

However, the information published by Crowell Collier And Macmillan differed substantially from the figures promulgated by the government in 1967. That publisher stated that "U. S. losses rose to an average of 140 killed per week, up from the previous year's average of under 100." (Collier's Year Book 1968, Covering The Year 1967, p. 613). This computes to 7,280 U. S. deaths annually. Observe however in Figure 3 that deaths for 1967 were reported by the government as 9,378. The numerical difference between its own figures and that which it released to the media is therefore 2,098. The statistical difference between that which it released to the media and that which it recorded in its archives is therefore 28.8%. Accordingly, CBS News' basic contention that the government was not completely honest in the information it released concerning the war's progress, was substantially credible.

Accordingly, the above information augments the aforementioned episode concerning Air Force General John D. Lavelle which confirmed that government officials including Richard Nixon engaged in deceptive practices to justify pursuing the war.

2. Via the print media

Another profound revelation concerning how the war was pursued and how the issues have continued to reverberate through U. S. society occurred in 1995. That year former Secretary Of Defense Robert McNamara published his memoirs. To reiterate, in the aforementioned book entitled *In Retrospect: The Tragedy And Lessons Of Vietnam*, Mr. McNamara admitted that the U. S. should have withdrawn from Vietnam approximately ten years before it actually did. This admission by the former Secretary set off the proverbial firestorm of criticism from numerous circles including the current President. One of the most startling reactions to McNamara's admission however was the legal action taken by four brothers who had served in Vietnam. The Bolanos brothers of Texas tried to sue Mr. McNamara over his revelation that the war had been a mistake. The lawsuit which never came to fruition sought $100 million and an injunction which would have precluded McNamara from profiting from the book.

However, the controversy surrounding McNamara's conduct of the war and his subsequent revelations about its merits, still did not end in 1995. To reiterate, in 2003 the aforementioned documentary *The Fog Of War* was produced which examined the decision-making process at the highest levels of government concerning the war. It was revealed therein that McNamara conveyed to President Johnson that the war could not be won militarily. Then the U. S. earnestly tried to win it through force of arms. The conversation between the Commander-In-Chief and his Secretary Of Defense had taken place shortly after the Gulf Of Tonkin Resolution of 5 August 1964.

6. Memorialization

Perhaps the war's most enduring legacy in addition to engendering perpetual controversy, is the Vietnam Veterans' Memorial. The Memorial was the result of the Vietnam Veterans' Memorial Fund which began in 1979. After a nationwide competition to find the design which would most symbolize the war, the design of Yale University student Maya Lin was selected. When interviewed and asked why she chose the design, Ms. Lin stated that "form follows function." The Memorial is a black granite sculpture which is below ground. On observing the Memorial, one cannot help but readily comprehend Ms. Lin's rationale for the design. One end of the Memorial reveals the names, etched in the stone, of the few who were sacrificed as the war began. Then as the Memorial extends, the sculpture symbolizes this nation's deepening involvement by revealing more and more names of those killed in action as the war dragged on. The bottom of the memorial is of course the year in which U. S. involvement was deepest, 1968. Then as the nation began to extricate itself from the quagmire, the number of names becomes fewer until the final end of the conflict in 1975. As of this writing the number of names etched on the Memorial is 58, 249.

The Memorial was completed in 1982. However, it was modified three times as of this writing, to include first a statue of three servicemen in 1984, and then of servicewomen in 1993. A plaque was dedicated in 2004 which honors those who died after the war from injuries incurred during the conflict.

Here the author is compelled to point out the inconsistency between the number of names on the Memorial and the number promulgated by the government in official statistics. Refer to Figure 3 which was compiled from the Statistical Abstract Of The U. S. This chart entitled Vietnam Conflict – U. S. Military Forces In Vietnam And Casualties Incurred: 1961 – 1974 reveals a total figure different from that indicated on the Vietnam Veterans' Memorial. The reason for this discrepancy is that the number of persons indicated on the Memorial includes those which are still missing and are presumed dead, and also those who eventually succumbed to their war wounds. Also, the dates used to compile the casualties are different for the Statistical Abstract, compared with those of the officials who planned the Memorial. The beginning date of the war from the perspective of such officials was 1956.

7. Analytical Introspection

As any nation which has borne the burden of war, the U. S. began the process of analyzing the various aspects of the conflict. When the war ended, many still could not believe how the U. S. could have so blundered by intervening in the civil war of a nation whose culture and values were so alien. The aforementioned motion pictures and literature are lasting testimony to the continuing fascination with the war. Also, as any nation which has engaged in armed conflict, the U. S. began the task of examining the past conflict to determine how the war could have been better pursued. These tasks were borne by the aforementioned Col. Harry Summers, both by choice and by profession. Col. Summers returned from the war to be elevated to the Office of Army Chief Of Staff. As such, he had the ear of those close to the President. In 1979 he was assigned to the faculty of the Army War College. It is the stated mission of that body to examine how past wars were pursued. The U. S., as does any nation, desires to learn from its past mistakes in wartime. Col. Summers would be at the forefront of this effort.

In 1982 Col. Summers wrote and published what would become the seminal work on U. S. military activities in Vietnam. *On Strategy: The Vietnam War In Context* provides in great detail why the U. S. likely lost the war. The basic premise therein is that the U. S. lost because it had no coherent strategy. One of his most startling revelations was that the Viet Cong/Viet Minh which had traditionally been regarded as the primary enemy, did not participate in the final siege. He revealed that the Viet Minh/Viet Cong had been substantially annihilated during the aforementioned Tet Offensive of 1968. The final, successful siege of Saigon was accomplished primarily by units of the Regular Army Of North Vietnam.

In 1988 Col. Summers founded *Vietnam* Magazine. Its stated purpose was to unlock the enigma of Vietnam.

c. Change in national attitudes?

The above is further indication that the issues concerning the war have continued to reverberate through society long after the war ended. However, the above facts also indicate that the collective national attitude toward veterans of the conflict has modified considerably since the war terminated.

Further on the subject of attitudes which materialized after the war, as opposed to those which prevailed before the war began, one might examine the issue of race. To reiterate, the U. S. has always had a problem with this issue. Recall that at least one prominent individual theorized during the war that if ethnic minorities would demonstrate support for the nation's war effort at the inception of the conflict, then they postulated that this might lead to greater acceptance of them in society. For a validation of that theory, the experience of the author, below, is most revealing.

d. Reverberations in the popular culture

With respect to the popular culture, repercussions of the war's controversies still reverberated through society as of 2000. That year the studio which originally produced and released the film *Patton* in 1970 re-released the film in the DVD format. To the original footage the studio added a documentary which described the film's production. This documentary revealed what had been little known at the time of its initial release: some influential persons at the studio initially objected to the film's production. The documentary further revealed that the film's star, George C. Scott, had opposed its production. The documentary also revealed that some studio executives believed that the film would not be well-received because of its subject matter. This was of course at the height of the war. However, since its initial release the film has earned a well-deserved reputation as a masterpiece of cinematic story-telling and also a cinematic icon of that era.

Lastly on the subject of cultural metamorphosis, one apparent phenomenon which may already have been noted is that the public's fascination with the war appears to have dissipated. Again this can be observed in film output. Recall that in the 1970s there began an effort by the U. S. motion picture industry to examine the war. Other than the aforementioned documentary *Hearts And Minds*, the effort began in 1978 with the release of two films: *The Boys In Company C* and the aforementioned *Coming Home*. The effort was quite prolific, in that numerous excellent films were produced by the U. S. film industry which examined the subject in myriad ways. However, no motion picture has been produced by that industry on the war since 1996.

Sgt. Perry Watkins

The most notorious homosexual who was drafted into the Army in 1968 despite his being "out", and after having informed Army officials of this fact before his induction, liked the Army. Further, he reenlisted after his initial tour ended. The government apparently needed his services because of the needs of the war. He eventually attained the rank of Staff Sergeant (SSgt./E-6), a highly respected pay grade in any military. In 1979 he applied to re-enlist but he was told that he could not because he was homosexual. He then fought to stay in the Army.

SSgt. Watkins eventually sued the Army in a U. S. District Court. In October, 1982 a judge ruled that he was eligible to re-enlist for six years. The court held that the Army could not discharge him for homosexuality because he had previously informed the Army of his sexual preference before he was conscripted.

The Army of course appealed the district court ruling. In 1988 the Ninth U. S. Circuit Court Of Appeals (San Francisco) ruled that the government's attempt to discharge SSgt. Watkins because of his sexual preference was improper, and that he should be allowed to re-enlist. The Army appealed to the Supreme Court.

In 1990 the Supreme Court refused to entertain the petition to overturn the lower court ruling. The previous ruling of the appellate court was therefore allowed to stand. Under a settlement agreement,

SSgt. Watkins was allowed to retire with a promotion to Sergeant First Class under honorable conditions and also to receive appropriate back pay. (*New York Times*, 3/21/96).

That same year Mr. Watkins died of Acquired Immune Deficiency Syndrome (A. I. D. S.).

Gen. William C. Westmoreland

The first commander of U. S. forces in Vietnam after its official start was involved in controversy for many years after he was relieved by President Johnson in 1968. He was subjected to much scorn because of the battlefield losses that year, plus the fact that he had failed to make progress in the war.

After having been relieved, he was recalled to Washington and made Army Chief Of Staff. However, he was rarely thereafter consulted on war matters by any President. In 1972 just prior to the end of the first phase of the war, he retired from the Army and then returned to his native South Carolina.

General Westmoreland then embarked on a speaking tour of the U. S., including stops on college campuses where he was met by angry protesters. After forsaking his lecturing, he unsuccessfully launched a political career, running for Governor of his native state.

In 1976 General Westmoreland published his memoirs entitled *A Soldier Reports* in which he defended his actions in Vietnam. Therein he continued to insist that the U. S. had not lost in Vietnam. Rather, he claimed that the South Vietnamese lost the war because the U. S. had abandoned its ally. Whatever are the merits of his book, one can observe therein much intelligence, insightfulness and candor. General Westmoreland stated succinctly that the war had not been pursued as well as it might have been. What is remarkable however is his analysis of how the war could have been avoided. He had closely observed the situation in South Vietnam during the two year period prior to the buildup in 1965. This is obviously what prompted him to assess the situation he observed, thusly:

"Between 1963 and 1965, for example, when political chaos gripped South Vietnam and the lack of cohesiveness in the nation's heterogeneous society became clearly evident, the U. S. could have severed its commitment with justification and honor ..." (*A Soldier Reports*, p. 409).

General Westmoreland clearly understood the folly of intervening in such a situation as what existed in South Vietnam at that time. Further, he seemed to be in accord with President Kennedy and Secretary Of Defense McNamara on the issue of intervening further in an Asian civil war.

In 1982 General Westmoreland was again drawn into controversy when the Columbia Broadcasting System (CBS) produced and broadcast a documentary which resurrected some of the issues which had wracked the U. S. during the war. The program entitled *The Uncounted Enemy: A Vietnam Deception*, claimed that General Westmoreland had personally changed and repressed intelligence concerning enemy troop strength during the last two years that he was Commander. Further, the documentary claimed that the General had intentionally tried to deceive his seniors and the public into believing that the war could be won. He sued CBS for $120 million. To reiterate, for the aforementioned reasons the civil action was dismissed. General Westmoreland was satisfied at that time that he had received a concession from the defendant that he did not willfully distort intelligence. CBS has never conceded that it erred in producing the program.

General Westmoreland died in Charleston, SC on 18 July 2005.

The Author

A member of Richard Nixon's "Silent Majority" who never protested the war except to don a black arm band in 1969 and who complied with his Order to report for military service, and having Honorably completed such, went on to have a productive life after the military. Immediately upon his release from active duty the author found professional employment, albeit temporary, with a municipal government in California and also subsequently with the State Of California. The state employment was on the basis of his examination score which included ten additional points by virtue of the author being an Honorably Discharged veteran.

While employed with the municipal government and scouting businesses as part of his regular duties, the author reviewed a news article published in the Daly City, CA *Epoch Times*. The article detailed the situation of an ex-three star General Of The Army Of The Republic Of Vietnam. He had just immigrated to the U. S. in the spring of 1975. He was unemployed and living with his family over a Vietnamese restaurant in downtown Daly City. That municipality experienced an influx of Vietnamese refugees.

After returning to his hometown in 1976 the author entered graduate school at his *alma mater*, with his education funded by the government under the "G. I. Bill." He therefore began to accrue the benefits which had been guaranteed him by the government because of his military service. The same year he was promoted to the rank of Lieutenant (O-3) in the U. S. Navy Reserve, although he did not attend any meetings therein. Such was not required in his contract. Also the same year he was examined for employment with the U. S. Government by taking the Professional And Administrative Career (P. A. C. E.) Examination. His earned score was (85). To this was added five additional points because he was an Honorably Discharged veteran. His final score on the examination was therefore (90) in three of the six categories.

In January, 1979 the author was graduated again from his *alma mater* with the degree of Master Of Public Policy Administration.

In March, 1979 the author was offered employment as a Management Analyst with the U. S. Dept. Of Health, Education & Welfare (HEW), now Health & Human Services (HHS), Washington, DC, by virtue of his score on the P. A. C. E. Examination. He was informed that the lowest score his personnel office had reached to fill the multiple slots in the agency was (89). Accordingly, in view of the intense competition for Federal professional employment, the author would likely not have been hired for such had he not been a veteran. It also bears mention that the author's assumption of Federal employment via the P. A. C. E. Examination occurred one year before the U. S. District Court For The District Of Columbia ordered that examination invalidated because it was deemed discriminatory against blacks.

In 1982 the author was honored, along with his compatriots who had served during the war, with the aforementioned Vietnam Veterans' Memorial which had just been completed. The dedication of this

Memorial was virtually simultaneous with the author's application for employment as a Management Analyst with the U. S. Department Of The Navy (DON), Washington.

On 30 May 1986 the author filed civil action (CA) 86 – 1582, _Brown v. Department Of The Navy_, in the U. S. District Court For The District Of Columbia, proceeding _pro se_. The basis for the action was alleged violation by the defendant of Title 42 U.S.C.: employment discrimination/race/black. As stated previously, in 1982 while employed with the Government the author had applied for more lucrative employment with the DON. He was invited to interview for the position. However, the selecting official, a European-American, stated that he did not believe that the author had written his job application himself. That official stated explicitly that someone had written the author's application for him. The author responded to the contrary. The official was aware of the author's educational accomplishments and the details of his military tenure. Also, at the time the author applied for the position in question, he was employed by the U. S. Dept. Of The Treasury as a Personnel Staffing Specialist (Recruitment). His regular duties were therefore to examine applications for Federal employment.

The selecting official chose a white female. Having been informed that he had not been selected for the position, and believing that he had been denied the job because of a non-merit factor, he filed an Equal Employment Opportunity (EEO) complaint, as was his right as a Federal employee. The basis for the complaint was race: black. The matter was investigated by a DON investigator who found in favor of the author. The DON was accordingly required by the then-existing regulation to resolve the matter by offering the author the job, or a similar position, with tenure retroactive to the date on which the selectee had begun the job. DON refused, giving as its reason that it disagreed with its investigator. The DON did not have the option to disagree with its "in-house" investigator. The author's plea personally to the Secretary Of The Navy to resolve the matter as required by DON regulations, was ignored. Accordingly, the author began to pursue the matter administratively as required by regulations. Failure of the administrative process on 1 May 1986 resulted in the aforementioned litigation.

The same month that the author filed his civil action, he was invited to remain in the U. S. Navy Reserve at the rank which he currently held, O-3/Lieutenant. The invitation was in the form of a certified letter from DON dated 16 May 1986. However, the contract into which the author had previously entered with the government had expired on 4 November 1977. The author had not been discharged at that time however. He was retained in the Navy Reserve until 1986, apparently because of the needs of the government.

Inasmuch as the United States was not then engaged in hostilities with any foreign power, the author declined the government's invitation to remain in the Navy Reserve. He was however Honorably Discharged therefrom in August, 1986 while his lawsuit was being pursued in the aforementioned Court.

The case of _Brown v. Department Of The Navy_ was heard on 21 – 22 April 1987. During the trial it was revealed from the aforementioned investigation that the white female selectee possessed qualifications inferior to those of the author in every respect. She had never served in the Armed Forces. She possessed only a baccalaureate degree which was not related to the position in question. Indeed, the DON personnel office which had screened the applications had awarded her a score markedly inferior to that of the author. Further, the author was rated numerically the best qualified of all of the other applicants.

Under the author's direct examination at trial, the selecting official who appeared under subpoena stated that: (1) there had not been a black Management Analyst in his work center for at least a twenty year period prior to the author's having applied for employment there, (2) that he had nothing against blacks in general, and (3) that he had previously employed blacks in his work center. He volunteered that these were only in temporary, clerical positions. When asked if he had ever served in the military, the official volunteered that he was an Army veteran of World War II, having attained the rank of Master Sergeant. When questioned who he believed had written the author's application, the official conceded that the author had written the application himself.

At the conclusion of the trial of _Brown v. Department Of The Navy_, during closing argument, the author's plea to the judge was that, in view of his Honorable military service to the Government, he deemed himself entitled to fair consideration for employment by said government. The judge agreed. On 30 September 1987 he ruled in favor of the plaintiff. DON was accordingly ordered to hire the author for the position which he originally sought. DON was further ordered to pay him back pay retroactive to 27 December 1982, the date that the selectee had assumed the job.

The author began actual employment with the DON by court order on 1 February 1988. His personnel office informed him that the original selectee for the position had been asked to leave the job shortly after the conclusion of the aforementioned trial. She was so asked because she could not perform the duties therein. She resigned.

Subsequent to his tenure with the Federal Government, the author found an avocation in casino gaming. During his practice of the game of casino roulette, the author searched for an authoritative and comprehensive publication concerning the game. When his exhaustive search failed to find such a source, he wrote it. In 2009 he self-published *The System Is The Key At Roulette: A Practical Guide To Interpreting Occult Patterns And Winning At Casino Gaming*. (See section entitled Other Books By The Author). This publication was released under the author's own imprint, Blessed Bet Publications, in partnership with iUniverse.

Subsequent to his tenure with the Federal Government the author also found an avocation in writing. In 1998 in a search for information concerning the series of laws pertaining to government hiring preferences for Honorably Discharged veterans, he failed to find a central reference for all of such laws. So he wrote it. The resulting work entitled *Veteran Preference Employment Statutes: A state-by-state and Federal government handbook* was published in 2001. (See section entitled Other Books By The Author). The work revealed, among other things, that there is a lack of uniformity among all of the fifty-two government entities which have the laws in question on their books. These are all of the fifty states, the Federal Government and the District Of Columbia. Such lack of uniformity stems from the different interpretations by the various government entities over the quality of military discharges which must be verified prior to the granting of the preference.

As indicated in the work in question (pp. 16 – 17), only a few states explicitly require that a veteran have an Honorable Discharge in order to receive preference in hiring. Recall that upon entering the military in January, 1972, the author was informed that one should set his sights only on an Honorable Discharge. This is purportedly the only type acceptable by U. S. society. In his research, the author found this not always to be the case. Most states and the Federal Government merely require that in order to receive hiring preference, one must only have received a discharge under Honorable conditions. Accordingly, these states and the Federal Government regard a General Discharge under Honorable conditions as being equal to an Honorable Discharge for the purpose of granting employment preference under the applicable law. Lastly in this regard, the author has been employed by a state government as well as by the U. S. Department Of The Treasury in a professional personnel capacity. He was informed while so employed that the general policy of these organizations was not to distinguish between the two types of discharges in question.

Chronology Of The Vietnam Conflict

1945: The Second World War ends with the defeat of Japan; President Roosevelt uses leverage to induce France to release her Indochinese colonies and allow them to form a government of their choosing; France vows use of military force to quell rebellion of Cambodia, Laos and Vietnam; Roosevelt dies on 12 April;

1954: France loses its war to retain Indochinese colonies; the U. S. pledges support to allow the southern part of Vietnam to acquire a democratic government;

1955: Hostilities are settled in internationally accepted accords; the U. S. pledges not to disrupt the implementation of and the ideals of the accords which allow Vietnam to choose its own form of government;

1957: Elections which are scheduled to allow the Vietnamese to choose their own form of government are cancelled with the help of the U. S., when the communist faction appears on the verge of victory; civil war erupts;

1958: The U. S. sends military personnel to Vietnam in an "advisory" capacity to help its allies in southern Vietnam to become independent;

1959: The first U. S. military personage is killed in Vietnam;

1961: U. S. military presence in Vietnam increases to 12,000 "advisors";

1962: Journalists, among them David Halberstam begin to expose the government's deception of the U. S.'s role in Vietnam;

1963: the ranks of the Army Of The Republic Of Vietnam (ARVN) are augmented by 16,600 "advisors" from the U. S. Military Assistance Command (M.A.C.); South Vietnam is perpetually wracked with strife between the Buddhist majority and the Catholic government in authority; President Diem is assassinated in a coup encouraged by the U. S.; prior to President Kennedy's assassination three weeks later, plans were being laid for a phased withdrawal of U. S. forces by the end of 1965;

1964: The Gulf Of Tonkin Resolution is ratified by Congress on 7 August; the ranks of the Army Of The Republic Of Vietnam (ARVN) are augmented by 22,000 "advisors" from the U. S. Military Assistance Command (M.A.C.); the Army Of The Republic Of Vietnam (ARVN) is perpetually trounced by the Viet Minh/Viet Cong and by North Vietnam;

1965: the U. S. recognizes an emergency when North Vietnam and its allies are poised to overrun all of Vietnam; by December the ranks of the Army Of The Republic Of Vietnam (ARVN) are augmented by 200,000 combat troops from the U. S. Military Assistance Command (M.A.C.);

1966: the ranks of the Army Of The Republic Of Vietnam (ARVN) are augmented by 400,000 combat troops from the U. S. Military Assistance Command (M.A.C.); the total of U. S. "in-country" ground forces exceeds for the first time the numbers of "in-country" forces which the U. S. had fielded in Korea when that war was at its peak; domestic protests against the war begin;

1967: the ranks of the Army Of The Republic Of Vietnam (ARVN) are augmented by 475,000 combat troops from the U. S. Military Assistance Command (M.A.C.); protests against the war in the U. S. escalate markedly;

1968: First Bombshell is dropped; the Tet Offensive in which U. S. forces are caught by surprise and enemy strength rebounds is a pivotal point which causes the majority of the public to be swayed against the war; the ranks of the Army Of The Republic Of Vietnam (ARVN) are augmented by 550,000 combat troops from the U. S. Military Assistance Command (M.A.C.), the peak number of U. S. forces "in-country" during the entire war; for the first time the concept of "Vietnamization" is promulgated by the government;

1969: Second Bombshell is dropped; the My Lai Massacre of the preceding year is the first wide exposure of war crimes whereby innocent civilian Vietnamese were revealed to have been murdered and brutalized by U. S. forces; the ranks of the Army Of The Republic Of Vietnam (ARVN) are augmented by 472,500 combat troops from the U. S. Military Assistance Command (M.A.C.) as "Vietnamization" is implemented;

1970: Third Bombshell is dropped; President Nixon's foray of U. S. troops into Cambodia sets off a firestorm of protest and also results in the first and only deaths in the U. S. of war protesters; the ranks of the Army Of The Republic Of Vietnam (ARVN) are augmented by 434,000 combat troops from the U. S. Military Assistance Command (M.A.C.);

1971: Fourth Bombshell is dropped; the Pentagon Papers reveal the deception which the government had perpetrated to justify U. S. intervention in Vietnam; original war protesters are joined by Vietnam veterans who protest the war at home; on 1 January the ranks of the Army Of The Republic Of Vietnam (ARVN) are augmented by 340,000 combat troops from the U. S. Military Assistance Command (M.A.C.); by 31 December the troop level had declined to 171,000;

1972: Hostilities intensify with a major offensive from North Vietnam, which was opposed by the U. S.' mining of Haiphong Harbor, coupled with a resurgence in U. S. air assaults; on Aug. 12 the U. S.'s direct combat role is formally ended with the lowering of the Flag at Da Nang; on 31 December the Army Of The Republic Of Vietnam (ARVN) is augmented by a token 27,000 combat troops from the U. S. Military Assistance Command (M.A.C.); at year's end this force was augmented by 39,000 personnel stationed on ships in the South China Sea and also 45,000 personnel still stationed in Thailand;

1973: The first phase of the war ends on 27 January with the effective date of the agreement ending the hostilities; by 31 March all of the P.O.W.s are finally repatriated to the U. S.; the hostilities continue without U. S. participation but the air war over Cambodia continues until 15 August; the Nixon Administration's attention is continually deflected from Indochina by the Watergate scandal;

1974: the hostilities between the original combatants continue and flourish at a furious pace while the U. S. is barred by law from intervening;

1975: the hostilities between the original combatants flare with the North trouncing the South while the U. S. is first barred by law from intervening; in April Congress relents and grants token aid to evacuate friends of the U. S. and also thousands of orphans; on 30 April North Vietnam emerges victorious in its eighteen year effort to discipline its rebellious southern provinces; the flag of the Socialist Republic Of Vietnam is symbolically planted atop the former Presidential Palace of South Vietnam; the southern provinces known as South Vietnam surrender unconditionally; the thirty year effort to unify Vietnam is complete; by 7 May all U.S. military personnel have been evacuated; the U. S. Department Of Defense designates 7 May 1975 as the date of the official conclusion of the Vietnam Conflict.

St. Louis — 70   SELECTIVE SERVICE SYSTEM   Approval Not Required.

ORDER TO REPORT FOR INDUCTION

The President of the United States,

To V~~████~~ I~~██~~ Brown
~~████ ████████~~
University City, Missouri 63130

Selective Service Board No. 111
Federal (Clerk) B~~████~~
4~~██~~ S. 12~~██~~ St., ~~████~~ ~~████~~
St. Louis, Missouri 63102
(LOCAL BOARD STAMP)

..........October 12, 1971..........
(Date of mailing)

SELECTIVE SERVICE NO.			
23	111	49	469

GREETING:

You are hereby ordered for induction into the Armed Forces of the United States, and to report

ARMED FORCES EXAMINING & ENTRANCE STATION

at ....12th & Spruce Streets, St. Louis, Mo. 63102........
(Place of reporting)

on ....18 November 1971.... at ....6:30 A. M. Promptly....
(Date)   (Hour)

for forwarding to an Armed Forces Induction Station.

....
(Member, Executive Secretary, or clerk of Local Board)

IMPORTANT NOTICE
(Read Each Paragraph Carefully)

If you are so far from your own local board that reporting in compliance with this Order will be a serious hardship, go immediately to any local board and make written request for transfer of your delivery for induction, taking this Order with you.

IF YOU HAVE HAD PREVIOUS MILITARY SERVICE, OR ARE NOW A MEMBER OF THE NATIONAL GUARD OR A RESERVE COMPONENT OF THE ARMED FORCES, BRING EVIDENCE WITH YOU. IF YOU WEAR GLASSES, BRING THEM. IF MARRIED, BRING PROOF OF YOUR MARRIAGE. IF YOU HAVE ANY PHYSICAL OR MENTAL CONDITION WHICH, IN YOUR OPINION, MAY DISQUALIFY YOU FOR SERVICE IN THE ARMED FORCES, BRING A PHYSICIAN'S CERTIFICATE DESCRIBING THAT CONDITION, IF NOT ALREADY FURNISHED TO YOUR LOCAL BOARD.

Valid documents are required to substantiate dependency claims in order to receive basic allowance for quarters. Be sure to take the following with you when reporting to the induction station. The documents will be returned to you. (a) FOR LAWFUL WIFE OR LEGITIMATE CHILD UNDER 21 YEARS OF AGE—original, certified copy or photostat of a certified copy of marriage certificate, child's birth certificate, or a public or church record of marriage issued over the signature and seal of the custodian of the church or public records; (b) FOR LEGALLY ADOPTED CHILD—certified court order of adoption; (c) FOR CHILD OF DIVORCED SERVICE MEMBER (Child in custody of person other than claimant)—(1) Certified or photostatic copies of receipts from custodian of child evidencing serviceman's contributions for support, and (2) Divorce decree, court support order or separation order; (d) FOR DEPENDENT PARENT—affidavits establishing that dependency.

Bring your Social Security Account Number Card. If you do not have one, apply at nearest Social Security Administration Office. If you have life insurance, bring a record of the insurance company's address and your policy number. Bring enough clean clothes for 3 days. Bring enough money to last 1 month for personal purchases.

This Local Board will furnish transportation, and meals and lodging when necessary, from the place of reporting to the induction station where you will be examined. If found qualified, you will be inducted into the Armed Forces. If found not qualified, return transportation and meals and lodging when necessary, will be furnished to the place of reporting.

You may be found not qualified for induction. Keep this in mind in arranging your affairs, to prevent any undue hardship if you are not inducted. If employed, inform your employer of this possibility. Your employer can then be prepared to continue your employment if you are not inducted. To protect your right to return to your job if you are not inducted, you must report for work as soon as possible after the completion of your induction examination. You may jeopardize your reemployment rights if you do not report for work at the beginning of your next regularly scheduled working period after you have returned to your place of employment.

Willful failure to report at the place and hour of the day named in this Order subjects the violator to fine and imprisonment. Bring this Order with you when you report.

SSS Form 252 (Revised 4-25-65)   (Previous printings may be used until exhausted.)

Figure 1

BROWN, V̶̶̶̶̶̶̶̶̶ I̶̶̶			M	500			DATE OF BIRTH	49	10	31

5. DEPARTMENT, COMPONENT AND BRANCH OR CLASS	6a. GRADE, RATE OR RANK	b. PAY GRADE	7. DATE OF RANK	YEAR	MONTH	DAY
NAVY — USNR	LTJG	O-2		74	06	30

8a. SELECTIVE SERVICE NUMBER				b. SELECTIVE SERVICE LOCAL BOARD NUMBER, CITY, STATE AND ZIP CODE	c. HOME OF RECORD AT TIME OF ENTRY INTO ACTIVE SERVICE (Street, RFD, City, State and ZIP Code)
23	111	49	469	111 ST. LOUIS, MO 63103	▓▓▓ ▓▓▓▓▓ DRIVE UNIVERSITY CITY, MO 63130

9a. TYPE OF SEPARATION	b. STATION OR INSTALLATION AT WHICH EFFECTED			
RELEASE FROM ACTIVE DUTY	USS CORAL SEA (CVA 43), ALAMEDA, CA			
c. AUTHORITY AND REASON		EFFECTIVE DATE	YEAR 74	MONTH 08	DAY 10

d. CHARACTER OF SERVICE	e. TYPE OF CERTIFICATE ISSUED	10. REENLISTMENT CODE
HONORABLE	NA	NA

11. LAST DUTY ASSIGNMENT AND MAJOR COMMAND	12. COMMAND TO WHICH TRANSFERRED
USS CORAL SEA (CVA 43)	NAVAL RESERVE MANPOWER CENTER BAINBRIDGE, MARYLAND 21905

13. TERMINAL DATE OF RESERVE/ MSS OBLIGATION	14. PLACE OF ENTRY INTO CURRENT ACTIVE SERVICE (City, State and ZIP Code)	15. DATE ENTERED ACTIVE DUTY THIS PERIOD
YEAR 77	MONTH 11	DAY 04	▓▓▓ ▓▓▓▓▓▓▓▓ DRIVE UNIVERSITY CITY, MO 63130	YEAR 72	MONTH 06	DAY 30

16a. PRIMARY SPECIALTY NUMBER AND TITLE	b. RELATED CIVILIAN OCCUPATION AND D.O.T. NUMBER	18. RECORD OF SERVICE	YEARS	MONTHS	DAYS
3421 – PERS PERF OFFICER	166 – PERSONNEL ADMINISTRATOR	(a) NET ACTIVE SERVICE THIS PERIOD	02	01	11
		(b) PRIOR ACTIVE SERVICE	00	05	28
		(c) TOTAL ACTIVE SERVICE (a+b)	02	07	09
17a. SECONDARY SPECIALTY NUMBER AND TITLE	b. RELATED CIVILIAN OCCUPATION AND D.O.T. NUMBER	(d) PRIOR INACTIVE SERVICE	00	01	29
9278 – SHIP BOSN	197 – SHIP OFFICER	(e) TOTAL SERVICE FOR PAY (c+d)	02	09	08
		(f) FOREIGN AND/OR SEA SERVICE THIS PERIOD	01	11	20

19. INDOCHINA OR KOREA SERVICE SINCE AUGUST 5, 1964	20. HIGHEST EDUCATION LEVEL SUCCESSFULLY COMPLETED (In Years)
☒ YES ☐ NO	SECONDARY/HIGH SCHOOL ___ YRS (1-12 grades) COLLEGE 4 YRS

21. TIME LOST (Preceding Two Yrs)	22. DAYS ACCRUED LEAVE PAID	23. SERVICEMEN'S GROUP LIFE INSURANCE COVERAGE	24. DISABILITY SEVERANCE PAY	25. PERSONNEL SECURITY INVESTIGATION	
NONE	42	☐ $15,000 ☐ $5,000 ☒ $20,000 ☐ $10,000 ☐ NONE	☒ NO ☐ YES AMOUNT	a. TYPE NAC	b. DATE COMPLETED 26APR72

26. DECORATIONS, MEDALS, BADGES, COMMENDATIONS, CITATIONS AND CAMPAIGN RIBBONS AWARDED OR AUTHORIZED
NATIONAL DEFENSE SERVICE MEDAL

27. REMARKS
LAST DATE OF ACTIVE DUTY: 2 AUGUST 1974.   SEVEN (7) DAYS TRAVEL TIME.

28. MAILING ADDRESS AFTER SEPARATION (Street, RFD, City, County, State and ZIP Code)	29. SIGNATURE OF PERSON BEING SEPARATED
▓▓▓ ▓▓▓▓▓▓▓▓▓ DRIVE UNIVERSITY CITY, MO 63130	Lt jg _Vincter Brown_

30. TYPED NAME, GRADE AND TITLE OF AUTHORIZING OFFICER	31. SIGNATURE OF OFFICER AUTHORIZED TO SIGN
A. CRUZ, JR., WO-1, USN SHIP'S SECRETARY, BY DIR OF THE CO	_G. Cruz Jr._

DD FORM 214N
1 NOV 72

PREVIOUS EDITIONS OF THIS FORM ARE OBSOLETE.
S/N 0102-002-0202

THIS IS AN IMPORTANT RECORD
SAFEGUARD IT.

REPORT OF SEPARATION FROM ACTIVE DUTY

1

Figure 2

STATISTICAL ABSTRACT OF THE UNITED STATES
VIETNAM CONFLICT - U.S. MILITARY FORCES IN VIETNAM
CASUALTIES INCURRED: 1961 - 74

FIGURE 3

DEATHS:	1961-64	267	
	1965	1369	
	1966	5008	
	1967	9378	
	1968	14592	
	1969	9414	
	1970	4221	
	1971	1380	
	1972	300	
	1973-74	444	**46373**
			TOTAL DEATHS

WOUNDED,			
NON-	1961-64	783	
FATAL:		748	**1531**
	1965	3308	
		2806	**6114**
	1966	16526	
		13567	**30093**
	1967	32371	
		29654	**62025**
	1968	46799	
		46021	**92820**
	1969	32940	
		37276	**70216**
	1970	15211	
		15432	**30643**
	1971	4817	
		4180	**8997**
	1972	587	
		634	**1221**
	1973-74	24	
		36	**60**

303720 *TOTAL WOUNDED, NON-FATAL*

Note: The first of the figures for Wounded, non-fatal represents casualties requiring hospital care. The second figure is for casualties not requiring such care.

VIETNAM CONFLICT
CIVILIAN CASUALTIES

	A	B	C
SOURCES:	U. S. SENATE COMMITTEE ON THE JUDICIARY Subcommittee On Refugees And Escapees	DEPARTMENT OF DEFENSE	AGENCY FOR INTERNATIONAL DEVELOPMENT
TYPE OF CASUALTY:	Killed/Wounded	Killed	Killed
VICTIMS:	(S. Vietnamese)	(S. Vietnamese)	(S. Vietnamese)
PERPETRATOR:	N/A	National Liberation Front (NLF)	Army Of The Republic Of Vietnam (ARVN)
INTERVAL:	Jan. 1966 - Oct. 1972	Jan. 1967 - Dec. 1971	Jan. 1969 - April 1971
TOTAL: CASUALTIES:	415,000 / 935,000	31,463	20,587

NOTES: Department Of Defense figures exclude the numbers of abductees.

Figures for the numbers of N. Vietnamese civilian casualties have never been revealed.

SOURCE: Collier's Year Book For 1974, Covering The Year 1973

FIGURE 4

368

About the Author

This work is an expression of the author's fascination with history. He has no formal education in this field, however. Having been born and bred in the middle of the Twentieth Century, there is a lot for him to be fascinated with. He is a native of St. Louis, MO where he was educated in the public schools there. Subsequently he furthered his education in public universities in both Missouri and in Maryland from which he earned multiple undergraduate and graduate degrees in Business Administration, Paralegal Studies and in Public Policy. His graduate education was funded completely by resources secured from the "G. I. Bill."

All of the author's previous works were also works of fact. His first effort, *Veterans Employment Preference Statutes: a state-by-state and Federal Government handbook*, published originally by McFarland & Co., Jefferson, NC, in 2001 was a reference text. To reiterate, that book details all of the laws of the fifty-two government entities in the U. S. which require that hiring preference be given to Honorably discharged military veterans. It is the only work of its kind available.

The author's second and most recent effort was *The System Is The Key At Roulette: A Practical Guide To Interpreting Occult Patterns And Winning At Casino Gaming*. That work was published in 2009 by the author's publishing firm, Blessed Bet Publications, in partnership with iUniverse. That work details to the fullest extent the casino game of roulette. It expresses the author's fascination with numbers as they are manifested in gaming.

The author is retired and living in metropolitan St. Louis, enjoying the casino game of roulette whenever practicable.

Glossary

CONUS – the Continental United States. This area includes the Hawaiian Islands because Hawaii is the home of U. S. military installations.

Duty - an item of equipment which is assigned to a military installation such as a ship, or a space therein. It is placed there for anyone to use, if necessary. An example of a "duty" piece of equipment is a machine gun which is affixed to the bow of a ship. If any member of the crew thereon should detect enemy planes approaching, then they would man the "duty" machine gun to down the planes.

"G. I. Bill" or "G. I. Bill Of Rights" – the law formally entitled The Servicemen's Readjustment Act Of 1944 (as amended). With the expected termination of the Second World War, the law was enacted and signed into law by President Franklin D. Roosevelt on 22 June 1944. The purpose of the law was to help released servicemen and women to readjust to civilian life. The statute remained in effect substantially as it was first enacted, throughout the Vietnam War.

Line - refers to any officer or ship being designated for use on the front line of any conflict. Observe on the enclosed DD 214 N (Figure 2) that the author was designated a "line" officer (1105) upon having been commissioned. His primary duty was therefore to serve on the front "line." This is opposed to the designations of officers in support activities.

Ordnance – any device which is engineered to explode, thereby inflicting harm to an enemy. The smallest example is a round placed in the chamber of a pistol. The most extreme example is an Intercontinental ballistic missile (I. C. B. M.) with a nuclear warhead.

WESTPAC – the Western Pacific. This globe is delineated by the Department Of Defense by distinct regions. Each region comes under the authority of a specific military Commander. In this instance WESTPAC comes under the authority of the Commander-In-Chief, U. S. Pacific Fleet (Seventh Fleet).

MILITARY OFFICER PAY GRADES

The senior officer hierarchy begins at O-4. Every inferior pay grade is a junior officer.

Navy	Army/Marine Corps/Air Force
O-1 Ensign	Second Lieutenant
O-2 Lieutenant, Junior Grade (j. g.)	First Lieutenant
O-3 Lieutenant	Captain
O-4 Lieutenant Commander	Major
O-5 Commander	Lieutenant Colonel
O-6 Captain	Colonel
O-7 Commodore	Brigadier General
O-8 Rear Admiral	Major General
O-9 Vice Admiral	Lieutenant General
O-10 Admiral	General

MILITARY SECURITY CLASSIFICATIONS

The Armed Forces have several levels of security classifications. They are, in ascending order of secrecy: (1) Confidential, (2) Secret and (3) Top Secret. The classifications are based on an individual's need to know information. The author who was not deemed a security risk, was granted the second of these classifications upon entering basic training in the Navy. The reason for his having been granted such is that it enabled him to perform his military duties. The author had a need to know the codes which are transmitted to other ships for instance, to evade enemy submarines. Such codes are indeed vital to the nation's security.

The classification of the Pentagon Papers was unusual in that they were labeled Top Secret-Sensitive by the Pentagon. The Papers were accordingly deemed of the utmost importance. However, the nature of the Papers was such that they were not vital to the security of the U. S. None of the information therein could have made the U. S. less safe if it were disseminated to persons who did not have a need to know the information. Accordingly, the promulgation of the Papers by the *New York Times* and other periodicals in 1971 did not in fact compromise the security of the U. S. Their dissemination merely caused embarrassment for the government. This is likely one of the arguments used by Daniel Ellsberg's and Anthony Russo's attorneys to have them acquitted of violation of the Espionage Act Of 1917.

MILITARY DISCHARGES

The various types of discharges from the Armed Forces are (in descending order of merit/desirability):

Honorable – given for meritorious service or for having earned awards for gallantry in action or heroism; also given for disability incurred in the line of duty

General – given under Honorable conditions for not having engaged in service sufficiently meritorious to receive an Honorable discharge

Other Than Honorable – given for having engaged in misconduct or for security reasons

Bad Conduct – given for having engaged in conduct sufficiently unsavory to have been court-martialed and having received a sentence by a general or special court-martial

Dishonorable – given for having engaged in conduct sufficiently unsavory to have been court-martialed and having received a sentence by a general court-martial and as appropriate for serious offenses calling for dishonorable separation as part of the punishment

Bibliography

The Reader's Guide To Periodical Literature, The H. W. Wilson Company, New York, NY

Department Of State Bulletin, 24 August 1964

Ali, Muhammad, *The Greatest: My Own Story*, Random House, New York, NY, 1975

Brinkley, Douglas, *Tour Of Duty: John Kerry And The Vietnam War*, William Morrow/HarperCollins, New York, NY, 2004

Brooks, Tim and Marsh, Earle, *The Complete Directory To Prime Time Network And Cable T. V. Shows, 1946 – Present*, Ballantine Publishing Group, 1979

Butterfield, Fox, Kenworthy, E. W., Sheehan, Neil, and Smith, Kendrick, *The Pentagon Papers: The Secret History Of The Vietnam War*, The New York Times Company, New York, New York, 1971

CBS REPORTS: A VIETNAM DECEPTION/The Uncounted Enemy (video recording), The Columbia Broadcasting System (CBS) News, 1982

Collier's Year Book, 1965/Covering The Year 1964, Crowell-Collier Educational Corporation, Great Britain, 1965

Collier's Year Book, 1966/Covering The Year 1965, Crowell-Collier Educational Corporation, Great Britain, 1966

Collier's Year Book, 1967/Covering The Year 1966, Crowell-Collier Educational Corporation, Great Britain, 1967

Collier's Year Book, 1968/Covering The Year 1967, Crowell-Collier Educational Corporation, Great Britain, 1968

Collier's Year Book, 1969/Covering The Year 1968, Crowell-Collier Educational Corporation, Great Britain, 1969

Collier's Year Book, 1970/Covering The Year 1969, Crowell-Collier Educational Corporation, Great Britain, 1970

Collier's Year Book, 1971/Covering The Year 1970, Crowell-Collier Educational Corporation, Great Britain, 1971

Collier's Year Book, 1972/Covering The Year 1971, Crowell-Collier Educational Corporation, Great Britain, 1972

Collier's Year Book, 1973/Covering The Year 1972, Crowell-Collier Educational Corporation, Great Britain, 1973

Collier's Year Book, 1974/Covering The Year 1973, Crowell-Collier Educational Corporation, Great Britain, 1974

Collier's Year Book, 1975/Covering The Year 1974, Crowell-Collier Educational Corporation, Great Britain, 1975

Collier's Year Book, 1976/Covering The Year 1975, Crowell-Collier Educational Corporation, Great Britain, 1976

Colodny, Len & Gettlin, Robert, *Silent Coup: The Removal Of A President*, St. Martin's Press, New York, New York, 1991

Dean, John, *Blind Ambition*, Simon & Schuster, New York, New York, 1976

Diem, Bui, *In The Jaws Of History*, The Houghton Mifflin Company, Boston MA, 1987

Dunnigan, James F. & Nofi, Albert A., *Dirty Little Secrets Of The Vietnam War*, St. Martin's Press, New York, New York, 1999

Ellsberg, Daniel, *Secrets: A Memoir Of Vietnam And The Pentagon Papers*, Viking Press, New York, New York, 2002

The Fog Of War, (DVD video recording), Sony Pictures Classics, 2003

Foley, Michael S. *Confronting The War Machine: Draft Resistance During The Vietnam War*, The University Of North Carolina Press, Chapel Hill, NC, 2003

Fonda, Jane, *My Life So Far*, Random House, New York, New York, 2005

Fonda, Peter, *Don't Tell Dad: a memoir*, Hyperion Books, New York, New York, 1998

MacLachlan, Suzanne and Siems, Shelby, *Four Vietnam Veteran Brothers*, Christian Science Monitor, p. 2, 5/17/95

Goldwater, Barry M., *Goldwater*, Doubleday Books, New York, New York, 1998

Gorman, Robert F., *Great Debates At The U. N.: an encyclopedia of fifty key issues, 1945 – 2000*, Greenwood Press, 88 Post Road West, Westport, CT, 2002

Gottlieb, Sherry Gershon, *Hell No, We Won't Go!*, Viking Penguin, New York, New York, 1991

Graham, Don, *No Name On The Bullet: A Biography Of Audie Murphy*, Viking Press, New York, New York, 1989

The Guinness Encyclopedia Of Popular Music, Ed. By Colin Larkin, Guinness Publishing, Ltd., Middlesex, England, U. K., 1992

Halberstadt, Hans, *Green Berets: Unconventional Warriors*, Presidio Press, Novato, CA, 1988

Halberstam, David, *The Best And The Brightest*, Random House, New York, New York, 1972

Jacobs, Clyde Edward, *The Selective Service Act: A Case Study Of The Governmental Process* (1967)

Kerrey, Joseph Robert, *When I Was A Young Man: A Memoir*, Harcourt, Inc, New York, New York, 2002

King, Rev. Dr. Martin Luther, *Why I Oppose The War In Vietnam* (sound recording), Black Forum Records, 1970

Kovic, Ron, *Born On The Fourth Of July*, The McGraw-Hill Book Company, New York, New York, 1976

Kuban, Bob, *My Side Of The Bandstand*, Epic Publishing, St. Louis, MO, 2005

Ky, Nguyen Cao, *Twenty Years And Twenty Days: How The U. S. Lost The First War With China And The Soviet Union*, Stein And Day, Publishers, Scarborough House, Briarcliff Manor, New York. 1976

Mailer, Norman, *Armies Of The Night*, Random House, New York, New York, 1968

Mailer, Norman, *Why Are We At War?*, Random House Trade Paperbacks, New York, New York, 2003

Maltin, Leonard, *Leonard Maltin's Movie Guide, 2009 ed.*, Penguin Books, Ltd., London, England, 2008

McCain, John, *Faith Of My Fathers: a family memoir*, Random House, New York, New York, 1999

Miller, Donald L., *The Story Of World War II*, Simon & Schuster, New York, New York, 2001

The New York Times: Great Stories Of The Century/Major Events Of The 20th Century As reported in the pages of The New York Times, Galahad Books, New York, New York, 1999

Nicosia, Gerald, *Home To War: A History Of The Vietnam Veterans' Movement*, Crown Publishers, New York, New York, 2001

Nixon, Richard Milhous, *RN: The Memoirs Of Richard Nixon*, Grosset, 1978

Nixon, DVD video recording, Cinergi Pictures Entertainment, Inc. 2008

Office Of The White House Press Secretary, 9 November 2005

Order of the U. S. District Court For The District Of Columbia, *Brown v. Department Of The Navy*, CA 86 – 1582 (LFO), 30 September 1987

The Playboy Interviews: larger than life, edited by Stephen Randall and the Editors of Playboy Magazine, Milwaukie Press, Milwaukie OR, 2006

Pollock, Dale, *The Life And Films Of George Lucas*, Harmony Books, New York, New York, 1985

Sanders, Jacquin, *The Draft And The Vietnam War*, Walker and Company, New York, NY, 1966

Statistical Abstract Of The United States, U. S. Department Of Commerce

Summers, Col. Harry G., *The Vietnam War Almanac*, Facts On File Publications, New York, New York, 1985

Talalay, Kathryn M., *Composition In Black And White*, Oxford University Press, New York, New York, 1995

Vietnam: A Television History (video recording), WGBH Boston Video, 2004

Westmoreland, William C., *A Soldier Reports*, Doubleday, Garden City, New York, 1976

Whitburn, Joel, The Billboard Book Of Top 40 Hits, Billboard Publications, Inc. New York, NY, 1992

Whitburn, Joel, The Billboard Book Of Top Pop Albums 1955-1992, Billboard Publications, Inc., New York, NY, 1995

Index